WAR IN THE MODERN WORLD
SINCE 1815

Conflict is central to human history. It is often the cause, course and conse-quence of social, cultural and political change. Military history therefore has to be more than a technical analysis of armed conflict. *War in the Modern World since 1815* addresses war as a cultural phenomenon, discusses its meaning in different societies and explores the various contexts of military action.

This collection brings together ten new essays on military world history by leading scholars in the field. Areas and subjects range from Japan and China to Latin America and sub-Saharan Africa, breaking away from a Western focus on war history. The result is a unique study of war across the world in the last 200 years, showing connections, similarities and contrasts.

Contributors: Jeremy Black, John Buckley, Miguel Angel Centeno, Edward Drea, Jan Glete, John Lamphear, Douglas Peers, Spencer Tucker, Hans van de Ven and Peter Wilson.

Jeremy Black is Professor of History at the University of Exeter. His numerous publications include *War and the World 1450–2000* (1998), *Why Wars Happen* (1998) and *The World in the Twentieth Century* (2002).

D1059765

Warfare and History
General Editor
Jeremy Black
Professor of History, University of Exeter

WAR IN THE MODERN WORLD SINCE 1815

Edited by Jeremy Black

Routledge
Taylor & Francis Group

LONDON AND NEW YORK

First published 2003
by Routledge
11 New Fetter Lane, London EC4P 4EE

Simultaneously published in the USA and Canada
by Routledge
29 West 35th Street, New York, NY 10001
Routledge is an imprint of the Taylor & Francis Group

Typeset in Bembo by Steven Gardiner Ltd, Cambridge
Printed and bound in Great Britain by MPG Books Ltd, Bodmin

British Library Cataloguing in Publication Data
A catalogue record for this book is available from the British Library

Library of Congress Cataloging in Publication Data
War in the modern world, 1815–2000 / [edited by] Jeremy Black.
p. cm.
Includes bibliographical references and index.
1. Military history, modern – 19th century.
2. Military history, Modern – 20th century. I. Black, Jeremy.
D361.W37 2003
355'.009 – dc21   2002156183

ISBN 0-415-25139-7 (hbk)
ISBN 0-415-25140-0 (pbk)

FOR ROGER BURT

CONTENTS

CONTRIBUTORS

Jeremy Black is Professor of History at the University of Exeter. His publications include *War and the World 1450–2000* (1998), *Why Wars Happen* (1998), *War. Past, Present and Future* (2000), *Western Warfare 1775–1882* (2001), *War in the New Century* (2001), *The Politics of James Bond* (2001), *America as a Military Power. From the American Revolution to the Civil War* (2002), *Warfare in the Western World 1882–1975* (2002), *The World in the Twentieth Century* (2002), and *War. An Illustrated World History* (2003).

John Buckley is Lecturer in History and War Studies at the University of Wolverhampton. His publications include *The RAF and Trade Defence 1919–1945* (1995) and *Air Power in the Age of Total War* (1999).

Miguel Angel Centeno is Professor of Sociology, Master of Wilson College and Director of the International Networks Archive at Princeton University. His publications include *Mexico in the 1990s* (1991), *Democracy within Reason: Technocratic Revolution in Mexico* (second edition 1997) and *Blood and Debt: War and Statemaking in Latin America* (2002).

Edward Drea is a graduate of Canisius College, Buffalo, New York. After military service in Japan and Vietnam, he received his MA from Sophia University, Tokyo, Japan and his PhD in History from the University of Kansas. He taught at the US Army Command and Staff College and the US Army War College and served as Chief, Research and Analysis Division, US Army Center for Military History. He is the author of *MacArthur's Ultra: Codebreaking and the War against Japan, 1942–1945* (1992) and *In the Service of the Emperor: Essays on the Imperial Japanese Army*.

Jan Glete is Professor of History at Stockholm University, Sweden. He has published several studies of Swedish industrial and financial history of the nineteenth and twentieth centuries, as well as studies of Swedish naval and military history from the sixteenth to the twentieth century. In English he has published *Navies and Nations: Warships, Navies and State Building in Europe and America, 1500–1860* (1993), *Warfare at Sea, 1500–1650: Maritime Conflicts and the Transformation of Europe* (2000), and *War and the State in Early Modern*

Europe: Spain, the Dutch Republic and Sweden as Fiscal-military States, 1500–1660 (2002).

John Lamphear is Professor of History at the University of Texas at Austin, where he teaches African and military history. He has lived and conducted research for over six years in East Africa, working especially with Nilotic-speaking pastoral communities. Currently he is working on *A Military History of East Africa in the 19th Century*, together with several shorter projects, including a study of the early East African firearms trade. He has also been advising the Ugandan Ministry of Northern Reconciliation on strategies to curtail on-going conflict in that region.

Douglas Peers is Professor of History at the University of Calgary. He has written *Between Mars and Mammon: Colonial Armies and the Garrison State in India, 1819–1835* (1995) and edited *Warfare and Empires. Contact and Conflict between European and non-European Military and Maritime Forces and Cultures* (1997).

Spencer Tucker is the holder of the John Biggs Chair in Military History at the Virginia Military Institute, and the author or editor of numerous books on military and naval history, including studies of World War One and Vietnam.

Hans van de Ven is Reader in Modern Chinese History at Cambridge University. His most recent works include *War and Nationalism in China, 1925–1945* (2003) and he has edited *Warfare in Chinese History* (2000).

Peter Wilson is Professor of Early Modern History at the University of Sunderland and has published widely on the history of warfare in early modern and modern Europe, as well as on German social, political and military history.

PREFACE

Conflict is central to human history. It is frequently the cause, course and consequence of change, and plays a major role in determining the character of society. Yet the study of war is increasingly marginalized within academic circles, while most of the attention devoted to war focuses on Europe and North America. When the rest of the world is considered, it is generally with reference to the impact of Western military power. Thus, for example, Somalia appears only in order to provide a cautionary tale about the limitations of American strength, or at least resolve, in 1993–4.

This book seeks to redress this imbalance. Europe is deliberately allocated only one chapter, and that is not placed first. A team of distinguished international scholars offer accounts designed to limit the Western-centric perspective and, in the Introduction, an attempt is made to contextualize the 'rise' and role of the West in the light of the volume's emphasis on the importance, often vitality, of non-Western military systems. This is designed to contribute to the book's importance for work on the nature of military history. Because of limitations on length, it has been necessary to omit consideration of systems in several parts of the world. It is hoped that they will be covered in subsequent volumes.

This collection is a contribution to the project of expanding the reach and relevance of military history. Our efforts go beyond an attempt to expand the geographical focus of military history. Rather, this is a call to reconceptualize military history in a more complex manner. A focus on hardware misses far too much. It is important to draw attention to other factors, such as organization, strategic culture and the eliciting of consent to the consequences of military capabilities.

The attempt to expand our approaches to, and accounts of, military history is important and finds analogies in the world history literature. Conceptual schemes oriented around developmental models that presume the West (really only certain subsets of the West) offers the normative experience are under assault. The difficulty comes when we try to construct new conceptual schemes. This collection offers a contribution to this project. Others will object, and they may raise some points that need to be heeded. But in the dialectic of debate and reconsideration, a more satisfactory account should emerge.

I am most grateful to the contributors for producing such first-rate pieces and to time. Regrettably one other scholar failed to fulfil his promise to participate. I have benefited greatly from the comments of Ed Drea, Jan Glete, John Lamphear, Hans van de Ven, Peter Wilson, and Donald Yerxa on earlier drafts of the Introduction, and from the opportunity to develop themes outlined there in papers delivered at the Near East/South Asia Forum of the Department of Defence, the National Defence University, the Naval Strategy School at Monterey, the Universities of Delaware and Tennessee, at Adelphi, Anderson, Hawaii Pacific, and Rutgers Universities, the College of William and Mary, and Radley and Wabash Colleges, to conferences organized by the Service Historique de l'Armée de Terre, the University of Tsukuba, and the Oxford University Department of Continuing Education, and to military meetings at Baltimore, Hawaii, Naples, and Norfolk, Virginia.

It is a great pleasure to dedicate this collection to a friend and colleague who is not only a fine scholar and good companion in pubs and on country walks but also one of the all too few of us not swept aside by the tide of political correctness.

1

INTRODUCTION

Jeremy Black

Writing toward the close of 2002, it is readily apparent that the general neglect of military history in academic circles is singularly unfortunate. The role, on the airwaves, of conflict, the preparation for war and its possible consequences, is important for a range of its cultural and psychological impacts. In addition, all three are clearly central to political and economic events, plans and fears around the world.

Yet if the general neglect among academics is troubling[1] so too is the treatment of war in much of the literature. There are two interrelated problems: first the tendency to consider the subject from the perspective of Western powers and attitudes[2] and, second, the habit of discussing military capability and change in terms of the material culture of war, specifically technological prowess and the resources that can be brought to the production of weaponry. As far as the first problem is concerned, an emphasis on Western powers and perspectives leads not only to an unbalanced account but also to one that is unduly limited in analytical concepts. There are, of course, many aspects of the military history of the West that remain obscure and repay attention.[3] Even familiar episodes, such as pre-1914 German war planning[4] and the Japanese attack on Pearl Harbor in 1941,[5] appear to be more problematic than was once assumed. In addition, scholarship over the last two decades has led to fundamental re-evaluations, for example of First World War conflict on the Western Front (and, more particularly, a positive assessment of the British development of artillery–infantry co-operation[6]), and also of that on the Eastern Front in World War Two.[7] Yet, compared to the scholarship devoted to the military history of the West, most of the rest of the world has been neglected, especially when it has not clashed with Western powers.[8]

As far as the second problem is concerned, clearly it would be naïve to neglect the value of military *matériel*, both in quality and in quantity. Providing troops with better arms than their opponents not only enhances their effectiveness, but also their morale. Furthermore, technology, force structure, doctrine, and tasking are in a dynamic relationship. The greater capability provided by advances in weaponry makes it possible to envisage and carry out missions that had not, hitherto, been practical. In 2001, the Americans were able to use helicopters to lift troops into combat from ships in the Arabian Sea to Kandahar in Afghanistan, a distance of 450 miles. In addition, American planes, refuelling in the air, could bomb Afghanistan from a base in the USA.

Both these capabilities helped 'collapse' geography and were of particular value to the Americans because their ability to strike at a distance lessened their vulnerability to counter-attack or, at least, to a direct counter-attack: this has always been one of the prime advantages of a capability gap. Similarly, the spread, in the 1990s, of long-range missile technology, as well as of knowledge, machinery and raw materials, gave a number of states in an arc from Israel to North Korea, including Iraq, Iran, Pakistan, and India, the ability to use or threaten to use nuclear, chemical or bacteriological warheads against targets several hundred miles away.[9]

Yet, it is mistaken to study military history in terms of a weapons-driven approach. To do so neglects, or at least underrates, the degree to which war, and responses to it, are culturally constructed, both in terms of societies as a whole and with regard to particular militaries, or, indeed, even, units.[10] For example the meanings of victory, defeat, loss, and suffering vary considerably and so, with that, does the willingness to accept casualties. This is true not only of non-Western societies, but also of the West.[11] There has been a major shift from the willingness to take heavy casualties seen in the two World Wars, to the far greater sensitivity to casualties seen over the last three decades.

Again, this is an issue that requires careful consideration. Sensitivity to casualties in the 1980s and 1990s has not prevented offensive operations. Although in 1982 the British War Cabinet believed that domestic public opinion would not accept a thousand fatalities, that did not prevent them from launching the successful reconquest of the Falkland Islands from the Argentinian invaders. Similarly, in 1991 an American-led coalition drove Iraqi invaders from Kuwait. To go further back, the strength of pacifist and anti-war sentiment in Europe after World War One (1914–18) did not prevent a willingness to fight other European powers again from 1939. This was true both on the part of aggressive regimes, particularly Germany but also Italy, and also of people whose countries were attacked or that felt threatened by German aggression. However, this pacifist sentiment, which was strongly revived from the 1960s, has made it difficult to understand World War One, not least the British army's learning curve during it and its eventual success in 1918.[12] Briefly returning to the 1930s, it is worth pointing out the need also to consider the Italian conquest of Ethiopia, while outside Europe there was a major war between Bolivia and Paraguay, as well as the Japanese invasion of, first, Manchuria and then the rest of China.

In response to the claim that there has been a major shift in Western culture towards a reluctance to fight and, even more, suffer, has come the rejoinder, especially in the USA after the terrorist attacks of September 2001, that people will respond to a crisis. This turns our attention to the respective role of author and reader, for there is no point my going in for the usual authorial device when faced by a difficult issue: argument by assertion with apparent Olympian detachment or Delphic omniscience. Instead, it is important for the reader to be aware that what is treated and how it is written about, in this case the current international crisis, reflects a process of choice. Differences in the way in which the past is discussed should lead us to more searching questions about what is being discussed and about the process of writing history. This is most apparent and valuable when discussing the recent past, and indeed the present as the cusp between past and future. Then, considering any work of history necessarily throws light on both subject and process.

Rather than arguing that civic militarism can (or cannot) revive, it is more appropriate to say that the evidence for civil militarism is limited and, even more, that the military effectiveness of such militarism is likely to be problematic. The notion of fighting to the end in defence of home and hearth, as brilliantly portrayed by Winston Churchill in response to the threat of German invasion in 1940, is not one that is helpful in light of the likely character of modern attacks on the West. Furthermore, Western states rely on a professionalized military whose characteristics include not only an ability to use complex weaponry but also a willingness to take orders (and remain physically fit) that separates them from the bulk of civilian society.

Thus, for the close of the period under consideration (1815 to the present), it is possible to point to the social, political and cultural contexts that frame military capability and expectations about its use, and to make the point that they vary greatly across the world. It is also possible to reverse the standard approach by arguing that, instead of weapons dictating tactics, strategy, doctrine, and tasking, it is the assigned tasks that determine doctrine and force structure. This is even more the case now than earlier, as the range (and cost) of procurement options in weaponry are greater than hitherto. Furthermore, the institutional nature of military systems and the particular interests and political weight of military–industrial complexes[13] ensure that there are lobby groups able to press for each option, which returns attention to the role of choice in policy-formation.

Strategic cultures

Choices are guided by strategic cultures,[14] although these are not immutable and, instead, are framed by political debates in which military developments play a role, although within geopolitical constructs.[15] These constructs have been transformed not only by alliance politics and domestic political transformations but also by geographical changes. For example, the opening of the Panama Canal in 1914 transformed the strategic place of the Caribbean in naval plans.[16]

Strategic cultures are shown in the broadest extent by the contrast in force projection. The ability to fight wars far from their own territory has been limited to a small number of states, primarily Britain and the USA, but, to a lesser extent, also France, Germany and Japan. More than technology, geography and security interests are involved. What may be called culture or mentality also play a role. For example, the USA behaved for much of the twentieth century much as Britain had done in the nineteenth, although it had the option of isolating itself on the American continent (which indeed a section of American public opinion usually wishes to do). Several decades after the end of empire, Britain continues to put much emphasis on 'out-of-area' operations. In contrast, China has for more than half a millennium developed little capability to fight wars far from its own territory. Using missiles or other means, several states, and even terrorist groups, now have the ability to bring explosives and other dangerous warheads or bombs to large parts of the world, but only a few states are able, or seek, to deploy operational forces as instruments of a more sophisticated policy far from their own borders or coasts.

It is important to note variety in strategic cultures and in the way they develop, both subjects that require more study. For example, concern about domestic challenges to authority, rather than external threats to power, are more present in some states than others. In part, this is a matter of political systems. Democratic societies are willing to accept demands for changes in government that threaten authoritarian counterparts, and the nature of the latter is such that these demands are likely to be violent.[17]

Yet, particular contingencies are also important. Democratic societies can still face violent insurrectionary or terrorist movements, generally in part of their country. In the event of the failure of the police or para-military forces to end or contain the problem, this situation has important consequences for military tasking. Indeed, much of the military history of the last quarter century focuses on the suppression of such movements, both by democratic governments, as in Britain, Colombia, India, and Sri Lanka, and by authoritarian counterparts, as in Syria and Iraq. Control over areas against the wish of the local population, as with the Israelis on the West Bank and the Turks in Kurdish-populated regions, complicates any simple dichotomy of democracy and authoritarianism.[18]

Militaries confronted with such problems are obliged to operate in a very different fashion to those that specialize in preparing for war with other militaries. Concentration of effort in order to produce an overwhelming application of force is frequently seen as particularly valuable in the latter,[19] but is inappropriate in combating guerrillas and terrorists. The emphasis there is instead on a much more protracted process and one where it is necessary to bring political and military strategies into line in order to lessen support for opponents. Technology is useful, not least aerial surveillance and the mobility provided by airborne forces, as with the French in Algeria in 1954–62;[20] but state-of-the-art weaponry alone can only achieve so much, both against guerrillas[21] and against terrorists.

Having mentioned Afghanistan at the outset as an instance of the effectiveness of modern Western military technology, it is also important to draw attention to the failed Soviet intervention in Afghanistan in 1979–89. The

Soviets failed to understand both their opponents and the nature of Afghan politics and society. Relations with the (allied) Afghan army were poor, and the strategy followed from 1983 – driving the population off land that could not be controlled – did not win support. Furthermore, the Soviets deployed insufficient troops, in large part for political and logistical reasons, and therefore lacked the numbers required for the consecutive operations that Soviet warfighting envisaged. Furthermore, total dependence on supplies from the Soviet Union ensured that much of the army was committed to convoy escort. The Soviets were unable to force large-scale battle on their opponents, although the airborne and special forces were able to carry the fight to their opponents. However, sweeps and operations, such as the relief of Khost in 1987, were followed by a return to base that brought no permanent relief. The limitations of an advanced military in conflict with motivated irregular forces were readily apparent.[22] This, again, was scarcely novel, as the failure of the American expedition of 1916–17 to find the Mexican guerrilla Pancho Villa illustrates.[23]

In the case of opposition from a domestic terrorist force, it is not very helpful to resort to the politics of high explosives. Domestic terrorism poses in a particularly acute form the problem that faces all militaries. War involves obliging others to heed one's will, but victory in engagements is only so useful in this process. Like superior weaponry, it is far better than the alternative; but victory does not ensure that the defeated accepts the verdict. Instead, the victor can find itself in an unresolved situation, unable to obtain closure, but denied a clear target whose defeat will ensure it. This has been the fate of the Israeli military since the Intifada, a rebellion in occupied Arab territories, began in 1987. A force developed to win quick victories over Arab states has found an adjustment of doctrine and force structure difficult, not least because it has to implement policies in the face of constraints posed by domestic and international opinion.[24]

More generally, there is the problem of timespan and the duration of control. States find it difficult to impose their timetables on opponents. The American historian Victor Hanson told me on 17 May 2002 that America had the power to 'take out' fourteen other states, by using air strikes and missiles to wreck their infrastructures; but my response was to wonder 'what then?'

Complexities of capability

Consideration of the current situation, indeed, invites a shift of attention from the habit of treating the world as an isotropic (uniform) plane, under the sway of the pyrotechnics of modern weaponry, and, instead, to a consideration of the complexities of military capability and warfare, and the problems this poses for all states and militaries, both Western and non-Western.

It is important to consider these perspectives when looking back at the military history of the last two centuries, for there is a tendency to provide a narrative and analysis whose clarity would arouse more scepticism were they applied to current developments. In particular there is an interlinked account of the 'rise' of the West and the triumphs of advanced-industrial technology. This account, however, appears more problematic as the age of Western colonial empire recedes and its brevity appears more apparent. Western territorial control of many colonies and Russian/Soviet control of much of the Caucasus and Central Asia both lasted for less than 150 years, and in much of Africa and South-East Asia, for less than seventy years. In part, the loss of imperial control reflected defeats at the hands of other imperial powers with cutting-edge militaries. Such defeats led to the collapse of the German, Italian and Japanese empires, each of which proved particularly short-lived as a consequence.

Yet, although badly defeated by Japan in Malaya, Singapore and Burma in 1941–2, there was no such defeat in the case of Britain, the Western state with the largest and most populous colonial empire, while France, the Netherlands and the USA, each of which had lost colonies to Japanese occupation or conquest in 1940–2, were able to regain them as the Japanese empire was destroyed in 1945 (although the Dutch did not regain control of the East Indies, now Indonesia, to any meaningful extent). Instead, it was to be disaffection and active opposition on the part of native populations, combined, eventually, with a lack of determination to persist with imperialism, that led to the demise of imperial territorial colony in the three decades from 1945 to the end of the Portuguese empire in Africa in 1975.

The extent to which this was a major shift in global military power was disguised by the fact that the US, the dominant world power, did not seek to exercise its influence by formal empire – by spreading territorial control – and thus did not use its military power to that end. This can be seen in two ways. First it can be suggested, not least in light of the experience of the Vietnam War, that the Americans would not have been able to overcome the same problems had they chosen to match the Western powers clinging on to control, for example by seeking to retain the Philippines or, indeed, to maintain their post-war occupation of Japan, which ended in 1952. To take this approach would be to argue that a fundamental shift had occurred, rather than a transition within the global power system that made the European colonial powers less able to maintain their position.

Conversely, American hegemony across much of the world after 1945 can be seen to demonstrate the ability of the leading world power to turn to its advantage (or, at the least, to be able to respond to) shifts in the political culture of particular regions. China and Vietnam represent important question marks. In both the Chinese Civil War (1946–9)[25] and the Vietnam War, American client regimes proved unable to prevail against less well-armed domestic rivals; in the second case despite a large-scale American military commitment.[26] Both conflicts also demonstrated that superiority at sea and in the air could not be translated into victory on land.

The case of China

This offers a way to approach the history of what was, throughout the period, the most populous country in the world: China. Like most other states and areas outside Europe and North America, with the conspicuous exception of Japan, China appears as both failure and victim in general histories of war. The two are closely linked: it is China's failure to match the achievements of European states and the USA, as Japan successfully set out to do, that doomed it to victim status. Failure and victimization thus apparently provides the military history of China (and, indeed, most of the world) until the mid-twentieth century when Japan's defeat in World War Two led to a new political and military order in East Asia.

Like most dominant interpretations, there is a basis to this approach. China in the eighteenth century had been the most powerful state in the world on land and the Qing (Manchu) dynasty's defeat of the Dzunghars in the 1690s and, conclusively, in the 1750s had overcome the traditional Chinese weakness towards the peoples of the steppe. Yet, in 1860 British and French forces seized Beijing, and from 1937 until 1945 it was to be occupied by the Japanese army.

China's failure might appear to justify a Western-centric approach to military capability and warfare, but the limits of Western pressure are also worth considering. In essence, the Chinese suffered from the weakness at sea they had displayed since they abandoned long-range naval expeditions in the late 1430s; from the degree to which coastal areas in the nineteenth century were vulnerable to amphibious forces; and from the defeat in 1894 of the new navy that was created. Furthermore, the potential of amphibious forces was increased in the nineteenth century, when steam engines and metal bottoms enabled warships to sail up the major rivers of the world, such as the Irrawaddy, the Nile and the Mississippi. China suffered defeat at the hands of Britain in the Opium War of 1839–42, as amphibious forces seized Amoy, Guangzhou (Canton), Shanghai, and other coastal positions. The British made effective use of paddle-wheel iron gunships that were able to sail up the Yangtze river. Advancing to the walls of Nanjing and cutting off the Grand Canal, its supply line to the north, the British forced the Chinese to negotiate and to cede Hong Kong. In 1884–5, China failed to block French ambitions in Vietnam. At Foochow in 1884, the French made the first recorded successful day attack using torpedoes.

A decade later, the better-commanded Japanese fleet won the battle of Yalu over the less speedy and manoeuvrable Chinese, while, in the war of 1894–5, Japanese forces advanced speedily through Korea, driving the Chinese before them, and then advanced into Manchuria. Port Arthur, the port of Weihaiwei, and the Pescadores Islands all fell to Japanese forces. In 1900, when the anti-Christian Boxer movement besieged the foreign legations in Beijing, an international relief expedition fought its way through to Beijing, breached its walls and rescued the legations. The alliance of Western and Japanese troops paraded through the Forbidden City, a powerful sign of Chinese loss of face. The subsequent treaty with China, signed in 1901, decreed very large reparations, as well as twelve foreign garrisons between the coast and Beijing, and the prohibition of imports of foreign-made weapons for two years.

Thereafter, Russia and Japan were the foreign powers that intervened most vigorously, for long in competition with each other, most obviously in the Russo–Japanese wars of 1904–5 and 1945 and in clashes in 1938 and 1939. The Chinese found it difficult to defend their most exposed region, Manchuria. In 1928, the Soviet Union sent forces into Manchuria. Using modern artillery, tanks and, in particular, airplanes, they defeated Zhang Xueliang, the local warlord, and inflicted heavy casualties. In turn, helped by the Soviet willingness not to contest their advance, the Japanese overran Manchuria in 1931–2, and, thereafter, made further gains in China, before, in 1937, beginning what became a full-scale war. Beijing, Shanghai and Nanjing were captured that year, Wuhan in 1938 and, by the end of 1944, a continuous corridor under Japanese control had been created from Manchuria to Vietnam.[27]

These campaigns would seem to demonstrate both failure and victim status, but, as Hans van de Ven shows, the situation is more complex. Assailants found it harder to achieve success than these examples might suggest; it proved difficult to translate success into a desired outcome unless goals were limited; and civil wars in China were as important in determining outcomes as were conflicts with foreign powers, although it is difficult to separate them given that they were often connected.

Anglo-French success in 1860 followed a less successful campaign in 1859. The Chinese could fight well: the British found Chinese fire as accurate as their own at the mouth of the Peiho in 1859 and British warships were badly damaged by the Chinese artillery, while the earthen Chinese fortifications absorbed British shot. The British landing at Taku was defeated, although the port fell the following year. The Chinese army certainly lagged behind Western forces in technology, but this gap was not large enough to explain the eventual British victory. Chinese disunity was more serious: this was the period of the large-scale civil war due to the Taiping rising. In 1900, the first international relief expedition for Beijing was blocked by the Chinese and forced to retreat to Tianjin. Furthermore, eventual Allied success was related in part to the Qing withdrawal of their forces from the North China plain. During the harsh winter, hopes for territorial aggrandisement cooled rapidly: the north was poor and difficult to supply without Chinese assistance.

Although successful in Manchuria in 1931–2, and thereafter in nearby parts of China, the Japanese, from 1937, sought large territorial gains in China, but found themselves unable to subjugate opposition. The Chinese military was badly affected by successive defeats in the late 1930s, losing well-trained units and equipment. Most of what was left was indifferently trained and badly led, and, also, lacked equipment, especially adequate artillery, let alone motorized transport and air support. However, within occupied areas, Japanese control outside the cities was limited and episodic. Japanese military leaders were surprised, and frustrated, by their failure to impose victory. In rural areas, the ratio of strength and space told against the Japanese. Neither attempts to win Chinese support nor a resort to brutality won, and Japanese conquests in China indicated a lesson that Hitler would have done well to consider before attacking the Soviet Union in 1941: that high-visibility gains did not necessarily lead to overall victory.

Although the Japanese attacks on China from 1931 were more serious than Western or Japanese attacks in the nineteenth century, it is important, as in the nineteenth century, not to underrate the extent and severity of civil conflict. Conflict in the 1920s and 1930s involved the Chinese Nationalist government, independent warlords and Communists. As commander of the Guomindang (Chinese Nationalist) forces, Jiang Jieshi (Chiang Kai-shek), who had been trained in Japan, commanded the Northern Expedition: a drive north from Canton against warlords that began in 1926 and benefited from Soviet military advisers, money and equipment. Jiang reached the Yangzi that year, defeating Wu Peifu in Hunan and Sun Chuanfang in Jiangsu. In 1927 he captured Nanjing and Shanghai. Jiang's forces occupied Beijing in 1928, agreed terms in Manchuria, and was joined by two powerful warlords, Yan Xishan of Shanxi and Feng Yuxiang of Shaanxi, in 1929–30. However, this success depended on the co-operation of other warlords. Like the Russian Civil War (1917–21), warfare in China in this period indicated that mobility had not been lost due to increases in firepower. Purchasing modern weapons from Europe, especially France and Italy, the warlords had plenty of artillery and other arms, including aircraft, plus large armies: that of Wu Peifu was 170,000 strong in 1924, while in 1928 the Manchurian warlord and his allies deployed 400,000 men against the Nationalists' 700,000.[28]

China also witnessed the ideological conflict that was so important to the nature of war during the century. In 1927, the Communists formed the Red Army. Initially, it suffered from a policy of trying to capture and hold towns, which only provided the Nationalists with easy targets. The Red Army was more successful in resisting attack in rural areas. There it could trade space for time and harry its slower-moving opponent, especially as the Nationalists lacked peasant support. The Nationalist responses were major operations. In his campaign in March 1933, Jiang Jieshi deployed 250,000 men.

The conflict between Nationalists and Communists resumed in intensity after 1945. In the Chinese Civil War (1946–9), which ranks as the largest in number of combatants since World War Two, the Communists under Mao Zedong made the successful transfer to large-scale conventional warfare. In 1946 the Nationalists occupied the major cities in Manchuria, but most of the rest of the region was held by the Communists, who benefited from Soviet support, especially in the provision of captured Japanese *matériel*. The following year Communist guerrilla tactics had an increasing impact in the north. In 1948, as the Communists switched to conventional, but mobile, operations, the Nationalist forces in Manchuria were isolated and then destroyed, and the

Communists conquered most of central China. Much of the rest of China, including Beijing, Nanjing and Shanghai, was overrun the following year. Beijing fell in January at the close of a campaign in which about 890,000 Communist troops had successfully advanced out of Manchuria against an enemy force of about 600,000 Nationalist troops. In the same period, forces 600,000 strong on both sides fought over the route to Nanjing, a struggle won by the Communists, who crossed the Yangzi in April 1949. The rapid over-running of much of southern China over the following six months testified not only to the potential speed of operations but also to the impact of success in winning over support. In 1950 Tibet was conquered by the Communists. The Nationalists were left only with Taiwan, where they were protected by American naval power and by the limited aerial and naval capability of their opponents.[29]

It is unclear why Chinese military history should not be a chronology that commands attention and analysis as much as more familiar military narratives. The case of China serves to underline the importance of civil wars over the last two centuries. Despite the massive attention devoted to the American Civil War, these have received insufficient attention, in large part because thereafter the US (as well as Britain and Germany) did not experience civil wars, and it was therefore apparently possible to focus on war as a struggle between sovereign states.

Civil conflict and strategic cultures

This is a less than complete account, which underplays dramatically the significance of civil conflict, not least for military tasking, in Latin America and Africa once European imperial control had ceased. Thus the Nigerian Civil War (1967–70) was one of the largest conflicts in Africa over the past half century,[30] while the war in the Congo from the late 1990s involved civil conflict as well as foreign intervention. It is frequently not helpful to separate the two, and this indicates the problems with searching for a precise definition of war. This issue indeed touched on the problem of how far it is also appropriate to disregard large-scale uses of force, such as massacres, and high levels of societal violence.[31] To distinguish these too readily from 'war' is very much to adopt a definition that has only limited value across much of the world.

As far as Africa and Asia are concerned, it is important to remember that on those continents military history over the last two centuries did not begin with Western conquest, let alone with independence. It is also important to consider conflict prior to Western conquest or intervention. This underlines the extent to which a more pluralistic approach to the study of war has to embody not only more of the non-Western experience but also its variety. John Lamphear's chapter on sub-Saharan Africa is particularly valuable in this respect, as his emphasis on raiding war contrasts with the situation in China described by Hans van de Ven.

The nature of conflict within Europe might seem very different to that in the 'Third World'. The standard narrative moves from the final defeat of Napoleon in 1815 to the Wars of German and (to a lesser extent) Italian Unification, and then to the two World Wars and the Cold War. In practice this neglects the role of rebellion and its suppression, most particularly in the 1820s–50s but also thereafter, for example the major uprising against Russian rule in Poland in 1863–4, or the Spanish Civil War of 1936–9.

Rather than treating both these types of conflict and the wars of imperialism – expeditions, conquest and counter-insurrection – as in some ways lesser forms of warfare that, at most, represented adaptations of existing methods, it is worth asking whether a more pluralistic account of warfare would be useful. Indeed, the small wars/constabulary tradition has been important not only for the European imperial powers, but also for the USA.[32]

An emphasis on the diversity of warfare would entail moving away from the notion that, at any one moment, there was a clear ranking of capability and prowess, and moving towards the view that it is necessary to integrate different rankings. Linked to this is a measure of scepticism about the notion of a 'paradigm' power that others sought to emulate. This situation was true to a certain extent within particular military systems, as when Vichy France sought to digest lessons from the German victory of 1940,[33] but less so at a global level.

In part this was a matter of the applicability of the diffusion of whatever might be supposed to be best practice. Here, again, it is necessary to move away from the dominance of weaponry. The spread of particular weapons is not the same as their use in a similar fashion. Thus, in 1925 the British noted the use of modern weapons in conflict between tribes on the North West Frontier of India – 'Alamzeb is reported to have used two machine guns (in all probability Lewis guns) in the fighting, manning one himself, and it is said that they played a great part in the victory'[34] – but their use was different to that in conflict between Western powers. Such differences should not be understood in terms of a failure to use them appropriately, but rather as a product of the variety of particular military circumstances.[35]

This was not simply a matter of differences between cultures. In addition, within individual military cultures, such as nineteenth-century Europe, there were major contrasts in tasking, organization, doctrine, and strategy between powers that had access to similar weaponry. This can be seen not only in land warfare, where, for example, the recourse to conscription varied greatly, but also at sea and in the air. Thus, Britain had to protect maritime routes that provided her with food and raw materials, while challengers, particularly France in the late nineteenth century and Germany in both world wars, sought a doctrine, force structure, strategy, and operational practice that could contest these routes. This encouraged interest in warships that could counteract British numerical superiority: torpedo boats in the late nineteenth century and submarines in the two world wars.[36]

Strategic cultures, and the resulting military taskings, took precedence over weaponry. For example, the impact of air power on warships was clear from the Norway campaign of 1940. Dudley Pound, the British First Sea Lord, wrote: 'The one lesson we have learnt here is that it is essential to have fighter protection over the Fleet whenever they are within reach of the enemy bombers'. The recipient of his letter, Andrew Cunningham, the Commander-in-Chief in the Mediterranean, in turn wrote in May 1941 that it was clear that 'you cannot conduct military operations in modern warfare without air forces which will allow you at least to establish temporary air superiority'.[37] Yet the British still felt obliged to risk warships where they lacked such superiority, sometimes, as against the Japanese off Malaya in December 1941 and Ceylon (Sri Lanka) the following April, with disastrous results.

Strategic cultures were also important in the air. As John Buckley shows, different states put an emphasis on strategic bombing or ground support. As on land and at sea, there was also a varying emphasis on 'anti-' weaponry, tactics, strategy, and doctrine, in the case of air warfare, interceptor fighters, and anti-aircraft guns and control systems. This contrast between strategic bombing and ground support, which became, if anything, even stronger when aircraft were the sole weapons system that could be used to deliver atomic warheads,[38] remains pertinent today. Furthermore, what is 'out of date' in one country and one region remains utility to another country in a different region.

War and society

War and Society has been one of the major themes of work on military history over the last forty years, but it has essentially been a theme pursued in relation to the West, for example in the fashionable field of gender and war.[39] There is a need in War and Society studies for far more work on other parts of the world, but it is unclear whether the topic's analytical concepts pursued hitherto in relation to the West are appropriate. 'Modernization', an ambiguous concept, however, is one that can be employed for military, society and state-formation. The role of war and force in leading to change, and across a wide range from racial desegregation in the military[40] to encouraging a meritocratic ethos, is readily apparent – although war, force and the military are not co-terminous. In many states, it has been bodies other than the regular military that have been primarily responsible for maintaining governmental power and for enforcing policies.

Furthermore, in a 'Darwinian' sense, the relationship of war with change is not necessarily beneficial. Military preparedness and conflict can be seen as leading to positive developments, but they can also restrict them, not least by creating or exacerbating burdens that are too great for political and governmental structures. The number of countries referred to as 'failed states' in the 1990s, for example Afghanistan, Liberia and Sierra Leone, invites consideration of how far this process had an earlier genesis. In each case in the 1990s, conflict led to an accentuation of the influence of regional strongmen and a rise in 'predatory warlordism'.[41] This can be seen as a parallel to the state-development frequently traced to military factors, albeit at a different scale.

Indeed, there is the general question of the relationship between force and new states. Much of the world in this period has been governed by political systems that are less than fifty years old and, in a large number of cases, within states whose boundaries were also less than fifty years old. This, for example, was a problem in Latin America in the nineteenth century and in sub-Saharan Africa after the end of European colonial rule in the late twentieth century. This situation creates problems for both legitimacy and for dealing with differences over policy. Force played a major role in the creation of many new states, especially where earlier imperial systems were challenged by violence. In turn, it was not always easy to contain this violence once independence had been achieved. For example, the major upsurge of piracy and privateering that accompanied the Latin American Wars of Independence created problems not only for the Spaniards but also for neutrals and for the newly-independent states.

Across much of the world after independence had been achieved, force continued to play, or began to play, a major role in politics and government, while the military has frequently been the prime representative of the state. The role of force was particularly apparent in the creation of military regimes, for example Chile in 1973 and Pakistan in 1958, 1969, 1977, and 1999, but also played a role in changes in civilian government, such as those in Peru and Colombia in the 1980s and 1990s. In 1992, President Alberto Fujimori used the army to shut down Peru's Congress and courts. Dictators generally appealed to a desire for order, stability and competence, rather than to a continuity based on legitimism – although in some states, for example Turkey in 1960 and 1980, the military staged coups in order to maintain what they saw as the constitution.

Some military regimes were long-lasting, for example in Brazil from 1964 until 1985. In the short term, however, authoritarian regimes, whether military or civilian dictatorships, were far less powerful or rigid in practice than they appeared, and could only operate by accepting the circumvention of their nostrums and structures by their own members, as well as by vested interests and by the public itself. In the long term, these regimes found it difficult to contain political problems and to satisfy popular demands. Thus, in Thailand the military lost power in 1992. In Indonesia, General Suharto, the Chief of the Army Staff who had taken over power in 1966 and became President in 1968, was forced to surrender power in 1998.

The relationship between the domestic use of force and external war varied. Some authoritarian regimes supported expansionism, or otherwise embarked on foreign conflict, in part in order to define and sustain their domestic position. This was true of the brutal expansionism attempted in the former Yugoslavia by Croatia and Serbia in the 1990s. The Croatian Democratic Union was typical in the authoritarianism of its leader, Franjo Tudjman, President of

Croatia between 1991 and 1999, and in its use of nationalism to provide both identity and rationale. The same was true of Serbia under Slobodan Milošević. He, however, found that an attempt to pursue 'ethnic cleansing' (brutalization and expulsion of an ethnic group) in Kosovo led to a hostile response from Western attacks, culminating, in 1999, in an air attack on Serbia and in support of the ethnic Albanians resisting the Serbs in Kosovo. Thereafter, the continuing isolation of Serbia in a form of economic and financial warfare helped cause an erosion of support for Milošević and his fall in 2000. Some dictators, such as Idi Amin of Uganda (1971–9) and Mobutu Sese Soko of Zaire/Congo (1965–97), only fell as a result of foreign invasions, while another invasion of Congo was launched in 1998 in an unsuccessful attempt to overthrow Mobutu's replacement, Laurent Kabila. Unsuccessful wars led to the fall of other military regimes. Defeat by India in 1971 and by Britain in 1982 led to the fall of military governments in Pakistan and Argentine.

Domestic coups and violence put paid to more dictators, including Kabila in 2001, although others, such as Colonel Qaddafi of Libya (President 1969–), who had seized power in a coup, proved more durable. The same was true of the military dictatorship in Myanmar (Burma), which crushed the 1988 democracy movement.

The case of Myanmar is an instance of the habitual use of force by authoritarian regimes in order to ensure their power. This was underlined the following year, when troops were employed by China's Communist government to crush a democratic movement. There was a particularly pronounced tendency to use force to suppress regional separatism. In Iraq, force was used in the 1990s to suppress the Kurds and the Marsh Arabs. Southern secessionism in the Yemen was crushed in 1994, the Chinese suppressed Muslim separatism in Xinjiang in 1990 and 1997, while in 1998 the Tajik army suppressed a rebellion in the Khojand region of Tajikistan where many Uzbek-speakers lived.

Force was also employed to push through policies of social and economic transformation, most obviously in Communist countries such as the Soviet Union in the 1920s. In China, the Agrarian Reform Law of 1950 was enforced at the cost (estimates vary) of 200,000–2,000,000 landlords' lives, and in other campaigns of the early 1950s against alleged counter-revolutionaries, capitalists and corrupt cadres, maybe 500,000–800,000 were killed. The Communist Khmer Rouge movement led by Pol Pot that controlled Cambodia from 1976 until 1979 was responsible for the death or imprisonment of millions of people there.

These and other policies were presented in terms of war: wars with the enemies of the state and the people. Civil war was thus seen in some countries as a continuous state. Violence, indeed atrocities, at the expense of real or supposed domestic opponents was particularly, but not only, characteristic of what objectively may be seen as civil wars, as with anti-semitic massacres by White Russian forces in Ukraine in 1919.[42]

Non-military forces

Such violence serves as a reminder not only of the limited value of seeing wars only as conflicts between states, but also of the need to consider forces other than those of the regular military. It was no accident that secret police forces, such as the German Gestapo, Soviet NKVD and KGB, the Hungarian AVO, and the Iranian Sarak, became important props of authoritarian regimes and also helped mould their ethos. Authoritarian regimes also developed large-scale forces that were not part of their regular military structure. Thus, Saddam Hussein of Iraq developed the Revolutionary Guards and Robert Mugabe of Zimbabwe the less-well-armed and less-numerous Veterans. Such forces could be used for external conflict, as with Nazi Germany's Waffen SS and Iraq's Revolutionary Guard, but most were not thus employed. Relations with the regular military were frequently poor.

More generally, surveillance came to be a major way in which states operated against both domestic and foreign opponents. State intelligence bodies, such as the American Central Intelligence Agency (CIA), created under the National Security Act of 1947, and the British MI6, were established and became larger and more sophisticated. By the end of the century the USA, Britain, Australia, Canada, and New Zealand were joined in Echelon, an electronic eavesdropping service, while France and Germany also co-operated in such covert monitoring.

It might appear surprising to see such topics covered in a book on war, but intelligence was fundamental to developments in military capability, as well as in planning.[43] This is an aspect of the degree to which war should be seen as an aspect of general political history. Thus, in World War Two the intellectual resources of the competing sides were mobilized in order to enhance and apply technological advances, such as radar, and to take part in an intelligence war focused on trying to establish opposing moves, primarily by the interception and deciphering of messages, a field in which the Western Allies came to have a powerful advantage.[44]

For the major powers, this macro-level of intelligence was accentuated in the post-war world and was supplemented by other developments, not least that of satellite surveillance capable of providing 'real time' information. At the same time, intelligence was increasingly devolved to, and developed at, 'micro'-levels: individual units, weapons such as pieces of artillery and, eventually, soldiers. For each, there was more information and it was both up-to-date and, therefore, constantly changing. This underlined the need to integrate information and activity systems effectively and, more generally, the extent to which command and control was under great strain at every level.

Conclusion

This offers one of the central themes of the period on which to conclude this introduction. The availability and role of information in warfare were of potential importance throughout the period, but their use varied. For example, in the nineteenth century, the development of telegraphy offered a means of rapid communications and became important to geopolitics and strategic capability,[45] while British warships charted the oceans of the world and then used these charts and the related knowledge of currents and winds to act against others who sought to use the sea, such as slavers as well as those considered pirates in East and South Asian waters.[46] As the ability to measure and record contours, and the large-scale mapping of topography developed in the same period, again among Western powers, so it was possible to plan to operate in hilly terrain and to align artillery effectively. Such developments were part of a continuum that linked to the present and future.

The alignment and aiming of artillery to shell mountain fastnesses that had hitherto been largely invulnerable was employed by expanding Western powers in the nineteenth century, for example the Russians in the Caucasus and the British on the North West Frontier of India (i.e. the western frontier of modern Pakistan). Such activity provides the second theme for this conclusion, that the crucial military relationship has been between the West and the non-West, although it is important to allow for the variety of both, especially the latter. Furthermore, this relationship has to be seen not only in terms of battle but also of wider processes of eliciting and coercing consent, and of losing such support. The limits of modern offensive warfare, specifically the ability of advanced weaponry to facilitate coercive diplomacy, depends on the political context, both their national and the domestic situation in the states involved. Again, military history becomes an aspect of total history; not in order to 'demilitarize' it, but because the operational aspect of war is best studied in terms of the multiple political contexts that gave, and give, it meaning.

Lastly, this book has deliberately been left without a closing date because there was no abrupt shift at 2000, the original date chosen, nor is there a marked discontinuity at the moment of writing. The ongoing 'Revolution in Military Affairs' that is discerned in American prowess in air power and advances in information warfare and precision weaponry[47] is partly at issue here, but so also are less spectacular developments elsewhere in the world, such as the continued inability of 'advanced' militaries to end violent opposition, whether in Colombia or Kashmir, the West Bank of the Jordan or northern Sri Lanka. A related aspect of continuity is the efforts by would-be local hegemons, such as, now, Brazil, India, South Africa, and Nigeria, and in the nineteenth century, Egypt, Japan and Ethiopia, to develop military forces to give effect to their regional aspirations. Furthermore, to return to the present, the instability of regions such as the Caucasus, Congo, Central Asia, and Afghanistan will encourage intervention in order both to cement and to overthrow particular situations. The interaction of hegemony and neighbouring weakness will continue, will help to sustain instability and will spread. As in Congo, Rwanda and Burundi, the resulting chaos will not observe state frontiers and the export of violence will encourage intervention.

Partly as a result of such conflict, it is likely that one of the most important developments will not be the use of new military technologies (which tend to dominate the futurology of war), but the spread of established technologies to states that hitherto had not possessed them. This will include nuclear weaponry, which is likely to create a series of deterrence relationships around the world.[48] Whatever the technology, the problem of eliciting consent to the consequences of military capability will remain a central issue.

Notes

The place of publication is London, unless indicated otherwise.

1 J. Lynn, 'The Embattled Future of Academic Military History', *Journal of Military History*, 61 (1977), pp. 777–89; V. Hanson, 'The Dilemma of the Contemporary Military Historian', in E. Fox-Genovese and E. Lasch-Quinn, *Reconstructing History* (1999), pp. 189–201, esp. p. 190, 196–7. See, for example, the neglect of the subject in two recent surveys, *What is History Now?* (2002), edited by David Cannadine and *History and Historians in the Twentieth Century* (2002), edited by Peter Burke.

2 For a recent example of a good collection that is weakened by this general approach, M. Knox and W. Murray (eds), *The Dynamics of Military Revolution, 1300–2050* (Cambridge, 2001). For the neglect of China, H. van de Ven, 'Introduction' in his (ed.) *Warfare in Chinese History* (Leiden, 2000), pp. 1–11.

3 E. Greenhalgh, 'The Archival Sources for a study of Franco–British Relations during the First World War', *Archives*, 27 (2002), p. 171.

4 See the contrasting approaches in A. Mombauer, *Helmuth von Moltke and the Origins of the First World War* (Cambridge, 2001) and T. Zuber, *Inventing the Schlieffen Plan. German War Planning 1871–1914* (Oxford, 2002).

5 H.P. Willmott, *Pearl Harbor* (2001), for example pp. 142–57.

6 See, for example, P. Griffith, *Battle Tactics of the Western Front: The British Army's Art of Attack, 1916–1918* (New Haven, 1994) and J. Bailey, *The First World War and the Birth of the Modern Style of Warfare* (Camberley, 1996).

7 For example D.M. Glantz, *Barbarossa. Hitler's Invasion of Russia 1941* (Stroud, 2001).

8 Even when alien environments are considered, they are done so as problems for Western forces, for example H.A. Winters, *Battling the Elements. Weather and Terrain in the Conduct of War* (Baltimore, 1998).

9 J.M. Black, *War in the New Century* (2001).

10 For a controversial approach, C.M. Cameron, *American Samurai: Myth, Imagination, and the Conduct of Battle in the First Marine Division, 1941–1951* (1994). See also T. Farrell, 'Culture and Military Power', *Review of International Studies*, 24 (1998), pp. 405–14.

11 J.M. Black, *War. Past, Present and Future* (Stroud, 2000).

12 B. Bond, *The Unquiet Western Front. Britain's Role in Literature and History* (Cambridge, 2002).

13 P.J. Dombrowski, E. Cholz and A.L. Ross, 'Selling Military Transformation: The Defense Industry and Innovation', *Orbis*, 46 (2002), pp. 526–36.

14 R. Jervis, *Perception and Misperception in International Politics* (Princeton, 1976); C.G. Reynolds, 'Reconsidering American Strategic History and Doctrines', in his *History of the Sea: Essays on Maritime Strategies* (Columbia, South Carolina, 1989); A.I. Johnston, *Cultural Realism: Strategic Culture and Grand Strategy in Chinese History* (Princeton, 1995); L. Sondhaus, 'The Strategic Culture of the Habsburg Army',

Austrian History Yearbook, 32 (2001), pp. 225–34; W. Murray, 'Does Military Culture Matter?' in J.F. Lehman and H. Sicherman (eds), *America the Vulnerable. Our Military Problems and How To Fix Them* (Philadelphia, 2002), pp. 134–51.

15 I.C.Y. Hsu, 'The Great Policy Debate in China, 1874: Maritime Defence v. Frontier Defence', *Harvard Journal of Asiatic Studies*, 25 (1965), pp. 212–28; A.J. Bacevich, *American Empire. The Realities and Consequences of U.S. Diplomacy* (Cambridge, Mass., 2002).

16 D.A.Yerxa, *Admirals and Empire. The United States Navy and the Caribbean, 1898–1945* (Columbia, South Carolina, 1991), p. 53.

17 S.E. Finer, *The Man on Horseback: The Role of the Military in Politics* (1962); S.P. Cohen, *The Pakistan Army* (Berkeley, California, 1984); H. Crouch, *The Army and Politics in Indonesia* (2nd edn, Ithaca, New York, 1988); A.H. Young and D.E. Phillips (eds), *Militarization in the Non-Hispanic Caribbean* (Boulder, Colorado, 1986).

18 I.F.W. Beckett, *Modern Insurgencies and Counter-Insurgencies* (2001).

19 For example, Field Marshal Haig, 'Memorandum on operations on the Western Front 1916–1918', London, British Library, Department of Manuscripts, Additional Manuscripts (hereafter BL. Add.) 52460 pp. 2, 4, 51.

20 C.R. Shrader, *The First Helicopter War: Logistics and Mobility in Algeria, 1954–1962* (Westport, Connecticut, 1999).

21 D.M. Drew, 'U.S. Airpower Theory and the Insurgent Challenge: A Short Journey to Confusion', *Journal of Military History*, 62 (1998), pp. 809–32, esp. pp. 824, 829–30; C. Malkasian, *A History of Modern Wars of Attrition* (Westport, 2002), p. 205.

22 The Russian General Staff, *The Soviet–Afghan War. How a Superpower Fought and Lost*, L.W. Grau and M.A. Gress (eds) (Lawrence, Kansas, 2000).

23 J.A. Stout, *Border Conflict: Villistas, Carrancistas and the Punitive Expedition, 1919–1920* (Fort Worth, 1999).

24 A. Bregman, *Israel's Wars, 1947–93* (2000), and *A History of Israel* (2002).

25 T. Tsou, *America's Failure in China, 1941–1950* (Chicago, 1963).

26 Among the numerous works on the war, D.R. Palmer, *The Summons of the Trumpet: A History of the Vietnam War from a Military Man's Viewpoint* (New York, 1984); W.D. Duiker, *Secret War: Nationalism and Revolution in a Divided Vietnam* (New York, 1995); S. Tucker, *Vietnam* (1999).

27 F. Dorn, *The Sino–Japanese War, 1937–41: From Marco Polo Bridge to Pearl Harbor* (New York, 1974).

28 D.A. Jordan, *The Northern Expedition: China's National Revolution of 1926–1928* (Honolulu, 1976).

29 E.R. Hooton, *The Greatest Tumult: The Chinese Civil War, 1936–1949* (1991); E.L. Dreyer, *China at War, 1901–1949* (1995).

30 J. de St Jorre, *The Nigerian Civil War* (1972); A. Clayton, *Frontiersmen: Warfare in Africa Since 1950* (1998), pp. 92–8.

31 M. Levene and P. Roberts (eds), *The Massacre in History* (Oxford, 1989); M. Bellesiles (ed.), *Lethal Imagination. Violence and Brutality in American History* (New York, 1989).

32 M. Boot, *The Savage Wars of Peace. Small Wars and the Rise of American Power* (New York, 2002), p. xiv.

33 J.M. Vernet, 'The Army of the Armistice 1940–1942: A Small Army for a Great Revenge?' in C.R. Shrader (ed.), *Proceedings of the 1982 International Military History Symposium. The Impact of Unsuccessful Military Campaigns on Military Institutions, 1860–1980* (Washington, 1984), pp. 245–7.

34 Public Record Office, War Office 33/1135 p. 2.

35 Re Turkey, Egypt, China, and Japan, see D. Ralston, *Importing the European Army. The Introduction of European Military Techniques and Institutions into the Extra-European World, 1600–1914* (Chicago, 1990).

36 L. Sondhaus, *Naval Warfare 1815–1914* (2001) and *Navies of Europe 1815–2002* (2002).
37 Pound to Cunningham, 20 May 1940, Cunningham to Pound, 28 May 1941, BL. Add. vol. 52560 fol. 120, 52567 fol. 118.
38 H.R. Borowski, *A Hollow Threat: Strategic Air Power and Containment Before Korea* (Westport, Connecticut, 1982).
39 L.G. De Pauw, *Battle Cries and Lullabies: Women in War from Prehistory to the Present* (Norman, Oklahoma, 1998).
40 S. Mershon and S. Schlossman, *Foxholes and Color Lines: Desegregating the U.S. Armed Forces* (Baltimore, Maryland, 1998).
41 W. Maley, *The Afghanistan Wars* (Basingstoke, 2002), p. 207.
42 P. Robinson, *The White Russian Army in Exile 1920–1941* (Oxford, 2002), pp. 6, 11.
43 M.I. Handel, *War, Strategy and Intelligence* (1989); M. Herman, *Intelligence Power in Peace and War* (Cambridge, 1996).
44 R. Bennett, *Behind the Battle: Intelligence in the War with Germany, 1939–45* (1994).
45 P.J. Hugill, *Global Communications Since 1844; Geopolitics and Technology* (Baltimore, 1999), pp. 27–48.
46 M. Rodman and M. Caper (eds), *The Pacification of Melanesia* (Ann Arbor, 1979); B.M. Gough, *Gunboat Frontier: British Maritime Authority and North-West Coast Indians, 1846–1890* (Vancouver, 1984); R. Howell, *The Royal Navy and the Slave Trade* (1987).
47 B.R. Schneider and L.E. Grinter (eds), *Battlefields of the Future: 21st Century Warfare Issues* (Maxwell Air Force Base, Alabama, 1998); B.S. Lambeth, *The Transformation of American Air Power* (Ithaca, 2000); C. Coker, *Waging War Without Warriors? The Changing Culture of Military Conflict* (Boulder, 2002), pp. 182–95. For criticism, with particular reference to the 1991 Gulf War, H.P. Willmott, *When Men Lost Faith in Reason, Reflections on War and Society in the Twentieth Century* (Westport, 2002), e.g. pp. 218–20, 229–52, 259.
48 P. Bobbitt, *The Shield of Achilles. War, Peace and the Course of History* (2002), pp. 759–60.

2

MILITARY MOBILIZATION
IN CHINA, 1840–1949

Hans van de Ven

The Qianlong Emperor, who ruled China from 1736 to 1799, claimed to have been victorious in ten battles. Some of these, such as the invasions of Burma in the 1760s and of Vietnam in 1788–9, were in reality defeats, but it is nonetheless true that the Qianlong Emperor presided over a prosperous empire of great military vitality. The most important of his victories was the seizure of the 'New Territories' of Xinjiang or Chinese Turkestan in 1756–9, which resulted in the destruction of the Zunghars, a secure western border and a doubling of China's size. Significant too was the defeat in 1790 of the Gurkhas who had invaded Tibet from Nepal. In the eighteenth century, the Qing was an expansionist empire able to sustain large-scale campaigns over enormous distances in inhospitable territory. Napoleon's inability to supply his troops in Russia provides a good foil for understanding China's logistical capacity at the time.

The nineteenth and twentieth centuries are usually cast as a stark contrast. The Qing was defeated by Britain in the Opium War of 1839–42 and the Arrow War of 1856–8; by the French in 1884; and by the Japanese during the first Sino-Japanese War of 1894–5. Following the subsequent scramble for concessions, in 1900 eight countries invaded north China during the Boxer War. Domestically, the White Lotus Rebellion of 1796–1804, the Taiping Rebellion of 1850–64 and the Nian Rebellion of 1853–68 were suppressed only after inordinate bloodshed. Things did not improve after the 1911 Revolution. Warlord armies fought each other regularly while the War of Resistance against Japan, lasting from 1937 until 1945, was a traumatic disaster from which in some ways China has begun to recover only in the last few decades.

It is clearly true that the Qing and its successors were not able to match superior Western and Japanese naval and infantry forces, and that the mobilization of private or local armies to meet foreign and domestic challengers precipitated gruesome cycles of militarization. It is less obviously true that the interpretative frameworks constructed to understand Qing and Republican warfare, in which failure, corruption, backwardness, and a Confucian dislike for the military stand central, are inadequate to the task of explaining China's military record. In these frameworks, the West is associated with modernity, virility, progress, honesty, efficiency, rationality, and a preference for manly combat while China, cast as a declining Oriental civilization, is associated with their opposites. Analyses following this framework have their origins in nineteenth century organicist and essentialist discourses about civilizations and cultures.[1] They have proved persistent for a variety of reasons, including their domestication in China, where they had the added advantage of proving useful to revolutionaries and reformers in criticizing established governments.

In this essay, I analyse China's military weakness not as the result of enduring Confucian cultural traits, although culture certainly mattered, or corruption and backwardness. Rather, I suggest that a radically different security environment and deeply entrenched fiscal problems formed the core problems. At the same time, I suggest a revaluation of the late Qing's self-strengthening efforts, which were not doomed to failure as most historians have argued. I also suggest that domestic mobilizations for nationalist purposes during the War of Resistance were more impressive than critics of the Nationalists and Chiang Kai-shek have suggested.

1 The Qing's weakness in the nineteenth century

China has tended to be militarily powerful when the following conditions obtained. First, because China lacked pasture land, important for breeding horses, as well as other scarce military resources, it needed to maintain alliances with peoples on its frontiers in the north which did possess them. Second, it had to maintain strong forces in frontier zones and keep them loyal through various symbolic and economic systems while, at the same time, to prevent the emergence of powerful regional armies, it needed to demilitarize the interior. Third, the centre needed to be well informed about conditions not just in the interior but also in frontier areas and even further afield. Fourth, because war is above all expensive, a fiscal system able to deliver ample funds needed to be maintained. Even in peace time, the supply of troops in Beijing and along the northern frontier was costly and put a premium on bureaucratic efficiency. Agricultural productivity was low in the north and much of the food supply had to be transported from the south through the Grand Canal or along the coast. In Qing financial accounts, a distinction is made between regular and non-standard costs, the latter often referring to the cost of campaigns. If regular expenditures were met by standard taxation, non-standard costs depended on central Qing reserves and ad hoc measures such as the sale of titles and local procurement by armies on campaign.[2] Finally, Chinese states needed to maintain an innovative advantage in the development of weaponry and strategy.

In the eighteenth century, these conditions existed by and large. The Banner Armies totalling between 200,000 and 250,000 troops were the main military force of the Qing. As Mark Elliot has made clear in his pioneering analysis, the Banners emerged in the seventeenth century in Manchuria when the founders of the Qing Dynasty sought to weaken tribal allegiances, tie local populations to their new state, and establish stable and large military structures.[3] Banners were made up of all members of hereditary military households, and Banner administrations discharged not only military but also economic, political, ritual, and social functions. Not just Manchus, an invented ethnic category, populated the Banners. Mongols and Han Chinese in Manchuria were grouped into their own Banners. This system allowed the Qing to incorporate and exploit the skills and resources of groups critical to its military strength and security. It was combined with Qing claims to universal rulership, in which all ideologies and identities had a place in a well-ordered hierarchical universe defined along ethnic lines with the Qing court at its apex. Qing rulers embodied this principle by variously engaging in Confucian, shamanistic, Mongol, Buddhist, and other ritual practices.

The military role of the Banners was to guard the capital and the Manchu homeland, while they also maintained a number of garrisons along the Great Wall and in several large cities along the Yellow and Yangtze Rivers. Internal order was largely maintained by the Green Standards of around 600,000 troops, with the Banner armies functioning as a backstop. The Green Standards had their origins in Ming armies who had surrendered to or were defeated by the Qing. Its troops too were drawn from hereditary military households. Green Standard troops were dispersed in small units, were not well armed and were paid less than the Banners. They discharged mostly policing functions and were brought together in larger units only to aid in the suppression of rebellions.

The Qing worked hard to demilitarize the interior. It defeated the so-called Three Feudatories in south and south-west China in the 1670s and incorporated the areas they controlled into its administrative structures. Policies such as the prohibition of private arms production and possession, secrecy of militarily sensitive knowledge and the proscription of heterodox societies aimed at preventing the emergence of substantial armed domestic challengers. The Qing also defeated the armed maritime trading empire of the Zheng family based in Fujian and Taiwan. It mobilized a fleet of 300 ships, moved populations from the coast and invaded Taiwan itself. Restrictions on the size of junks and government supervision of overseas trade through a licensing system sought to prevent a resurgence of the threat that the Zheng family had posed.

The financial reforms of the Yongzheng Emperor (1723–35) placed Qing finances on a sound footing. Because the land taxes had been frozen by Yongzheng's predecessor and could not easily be changed, the Qing's financial resources had been consistently straitened. Local governments had circum-vented this problem through fee-taking. The Yongzheng Emperor legalized surtaxes on the land tax and instituted 'honesty' payments to boost official salaries. The Qing's finances also profited from the flourishing eighteenth-century economy. Prosperity resulted from stability, marketization, regional specialization, and the influx of silver from abroad. Population growth, partly made possible by the introduction of crops such as potatoes, peanuts and maize, caused new land to be brought under cultivation and thus increased revenue flows. Surtaxes, licences on foreign trade and the Qing's monopoly on salt production resulted in large financial reserves with which the Qianlong Emperor could finance his expansionist ambitions. Other Yongzheng reforms too were fundamental to Qianlong's military successes. He set up an efficient secret communications system that greatly enhanced his knowledge about local affairs, further centralized power in the Grand Council, which became a body able to make quick decisions on the basis of accurate information, and co-ordinated effectively the activities of central and local government agencies.

In the wake of the defeat in the Opium War, Qing commentators such as the eminent statecraft scholar Wei Yuan (1794–1804) naturally addressed the question of why Qing military prowess had declined.[4] In his analysis, Wei stressed fiscal, bureaucratic and military issues. He noted that after Qianlong, financial surpluses had turned to deficits as a result of increases in the size of the court (from 2,000 to 30,000 since the beginning of the Qing); frequent tax remissions and relief measures that were meant to demonstrate that the Qing was a virtuous dynasty; and laxity in collection, with local officials often not pressed for shortfalls. Wei also discussed the permanent costs resulting from Qianlong's conquests, although he rejected a theory of overextension as the main cause for the fiscal problems of the time.[5]

The Qing could not easily demobilize the Banner or Green Standard armies, which remained constitutionally central to the Qing even when their military usefulness declined and their cost increased.[6] The Qing had proscribed Banner families from seeking employment. The result was that a sizeable and growing segment of the population needed to be supported through central funds. As Mark Elliot comments, 'that one fourth to one fifth of state revenue were set aside every year to pay the living expenses of a conquest military caste that was less than two per cent of the population was certainly one of the more remarkable features of late imperial fiscal structures'.[7] Naturally, many impoverished Bannermen did seek employment, with the result that the martial qualities of the Banner armies declined.

Wei Yuan described an increasingly debilitating fiscal crisis. The contrast with Britain is clear. As John Brewer has argued, the British state developed the excise and customs bureaucracies between 1688 and 1783, which enabled it to tax capitalist agriculture and to use the revenues so obtained to finance the National Debt, instituted in 1694.[8] These revenues enabled Britain to build up its naval forces with which it was able to conquer its overseas colonies. In Europe's mercantilist world, European states competed with each other for the control of international trade routes to secure the trade and hence the treasure that they believed was critical to their power. Britain, once unified, was well positioned to prosper in this world because as an island nation its enemies would find it difficult to invade it; hence it did not need a large land force and could focus on the development of its navy.

In contrast, the Qing sought to finance its war from reserves and remained wedded to an inefficient land tax system that became implicated in abusive local practices because the land and population registers were hopelessly out of date. In addition, the Qing was hostile to armed maritime trade, while its security challenges were in inland frontier zones. In these, success was determined less by powerful artillery than by the ability to form alliances and sustain armies for substantial periods in the field over long supply lines.

During the Opium War, two militaries with very different histories and skills confronted each other. The British prevailed because their superior cannon threw heavier missiles further at a greater rate; because their hand-held guns had a longer range and were shorter than the Chinese ones so that they could be reloaded more quickly; and because their naval ships were better protected and more manoeuvrable. In addition, steam vessels, such as the *Nemesis*, developed in India, could operate against wind and current in shallow waters. During land battles, the British navy could deploy forces rapidly in different theatres along China's coast. The Qing's troops were cobbled together from various areas and were deployed only slowly as they were moved overland. Qing fortifications remained of a type prevalent in Europe before the revolution in fortifications so lovingly described by Geoffrey Parker.[9] Nor were they defended in depth and hence they were vulnerable to attacks by landing parties.

One reason for the Qing's defeat was that its communications system no longer delivered accurate reports. Earlier emperors, such as the tough and shrewd Yongzheng, were well-informed, in part because they collected information from different sources and let local officials know when they had been caught out. During the Opium War, local officials colluded with each other in keeping bad news from the ageing and fickle Daoguang Emperor (1821–50). For a a long period, he appears to have thought that the war was being won. The officials of the time were timid, an attitude fostered by the likely severity of imperial retribution. Most appear to have attempted to survive the war by shifting it elsewhere, by demanding that other provinces sent forces so that the officials of those provinces would be held responsible, or simply awaiting change in the hope that the problem would go away.[10]

In short, the discrepancy between Qing and British military might shown so clearly in the Opium War can be understood in other terms than as a clash between a modern nation state and a stagnant Confucian China or the result of a cultural disdain for military affairs. As Joanna Waley Cohen has shown, the Qing Emperors, who were never simply Confucian, were most definitely interested in Western technological advances. They were quick to make use of new Western cannon-casting techniques and cartography in their wars in the interior.[11] But they feared armed maritime trade and concentrated their military effort on coping with fractious frontiers and domestic rebellions. In addition, the Qing economy was hit hard by the outflow of silver that they believed was a major cause for the economic and financial troubles they faced. They had proscribed opium imports, blocked harbours and burned opium cargoes – the acts that triggered the Opium War – for this reason. The British, on the other hand, had invested in their navy because they depended on armed trade. The conflict, then, was between a large agricultural empire and a small state that depended on armed maritime trade.

2 Military mobilization in the late Qing

The Qing began to make serious efforts to renovate its military not immediately after the Opium War but during the Taiping Rebellion that ravaged south China and the Yangtze provinces from 1850 to 1864. That rebellion, costing perhaps as many as thirty to forty million lives, was led by a man who claimed to be the second son of God and proved as destructive as the nearly contemporaneous US Civil War. The existing scholarship on the rebellion has stressed the significance not of the Qing's regular forces but of mercenary armies raised in the provinces, most famously the Hunan Army of the deeply Confucian Zeng Guofan (1811–72).[12] More recent scholarship, however, has made clear, in the words of K.C. Liu, that 'the Hunan Army's capacity has, in fact, been grossly exaggerated by many admiring chroniclers'.[13] Not only did it suffer serious defeats, its morale declined, and by 1858 its troops behaved 'so badly that local militia corps often engaged them in battle'.[14] Philip Kuhn, the author of the most influential study on the mobilization of regional armies during the Taiping Rebellion, has also written recently that 'the emergence of new military forces led by Han civil élite did not yet mean that the regular Ch'ing [Qing] military system had been supplanted'. According to Kuhn, until 1860 Zeng Guofan 'remained in a relatively minor official status and was hardly able to dominate the Ch'ing military effort'.[15]

It may well be time to explore the Qing's military actions during the Taiping Rebellion anew. Although the Rebellion seriously threatened its survival, its strategy was perhaps more cogent than has been granted by nationalist Chinese historians looking to demonstrate Manchu incompetence. Once it proved impossible to contain the Taiping in the southern province of Guangxi, the Qing seems to have been guided by the idea of preventing the Taiping from capturing the capital and seizing coastal harbours. In this its forces were successful. The Qing appears to have then aimed at maintaining or regaining the support of areas which produced grain surpluses and in which military recruitment traditionally had proved relatively easy. Hunan, Hubei, Jiangxi, Anhui, and Henan were examples of such provinces. The problem for the Taiping, who located their capital in Nanjing, a major city along the Yangtze River not far from Shanghai, was that they had to survive in an area that always had to import food. Cut off from shipments from food-surplus areas in central China and unable to access coastal harbours, the Taiping armies had to go on what were essentially raiding expeditions, something that intensified the divisions in the Taiping leadership which proved so fatal to its military efforts.

To make this strategy work, the Qing had to mobilize regional armies in provinces such as Hunan and Anhui because the Banner armies were not present in great strength in these areas and because the Green Standard armies had become useless. The way the Qing mobilized these armies was culturally specific. It put them under the command of men like Zeng Guofan who were committed to the Qing and fought in the name of upholding the Confucian order. The Qing did not mobilize groups or tribes known for their martial skills. The regional armies were recruited from the settled peasant population under élite supervision. It also should be noted that for their legitimacy, regional armies depended on court sanction and that financially they were supported by transfers from other provinces authorized by Beijing. The mobilization of regional armies was a Qing admission that its regular forces could not on their own cope with the Taiping and amounted to at least a temporary abandonment of the principle of demilitarizing the interior. Nonetheless, if my recapitulation of Qing strategy is correct, and although the mobilization of regional armies carried the risk of putting great power in the hands of men who might move against the Qing, the complementary functions of the Qing's regular armies and the regional armies in overall Qing strategy should also be recognized.

Despite the enormous destruction that the Taiping Rebellion inflicted, it did have positive consequences for the Qing that helped it survive for another half century. The first of these was financial. Because during the Taiping Rebellion the Chinese Customs Service was unable to operate and because the Treaty of Nanjing concluded after the Opium War had stipulated that China's foreign trade would be taxed at five per cent *ad valorem*, the Qing and the foreign powers agreed to establish a foreign-staffed Imperial Maritime Customs Service under Qing control to inspect the collection of trade duties. This became a major source of income for the Qing, delivering from one-third to one-fourth of Qing central revenue. The local transport or *lijin* tax, managed by local élites supposedly under bureaucratic supervision, also became widespread in provinces affected by the Taiping Rebellion. Although Beijing had less control over these, they strengthened local finances. Both sources of revenue improved the financial position of the Qing, with Customs revenues being especially significant for the funding of military modernization and early industrialization projects after the Taiping Rebellion.[16]

Equally significant was the adoption during the latter stages of the Taiping Rebellion of foreign arms and military methods. Following 1860, Britain and France, who until then had remained officially neutral, sided actively with the Qing against the Taiping, believing that the Taiping would not be able to govern effectively and therefore were a threat to trade. Building on initiatives of local officials and foreign residents, the Qing approved the participation in the war of a foreign trained and equipped force, the Ever Victorious Army. Led first by Frederic Townsend Ward and then Major Charles Gordon, who were made part of the Chinese order of battle, it played a significant role in the fighting in the lower Yangtze region.[17] The siege guns supplied by British naval forces proved important in dislodging the Taiping from walled towns and smoothing the way for the Huai Army of Li Hongzhang (1823–1901). That army, which emerged in 1862 and was recruited in Anhui province, became a much stronger force than Zeng Guofan's Hunan Army. Its 40,000 troops possessed 10,000 foreign rifles, had some modern cannon and its 'foreign arms companies' were drilled by Westerners.[18]

The contribution of foreign arms and troops to the defeat of the Taiping led to the emergence of a powerful group of officials in Beijing and in the provinces supportive of military reform along Western lines. Having witnessed foreign arms and troops at close range for several years in the Shanghai area, in 1863 Li Hongzhang invited foreign technical experts to assist with the manufacture of munitions. Two years later, he established the Jiangnan Arsenal. By the end of the decade, its 1300 workers produced small arms, including Remington rifles, ammunition and iron gun carriages. In 1874 a gunpowder plant was added, which produced a ton of gunpowder per day. The Jiangnan Arsenal acquired the largest dockyard in the area, and by 1872 six modern naval ships had been built. The largest was a 3000 ton vessel with twenty-six guns. Except for the propeller shaft and the cranks, it had been built entirely at the Jiangnan Arsenal.[19]

The Fuzhou Naval Yard, too, became an important base for the development of the modern Chinese navy. It was a cooperative venture between Zuo Zongtang, among the three or four most eminent late Qing officials who in the 1870s led the military campaign to recover Xinjiang, and Frenchmen such as Paul d'Aiguebelle and Prosper Giquel. Zuo made contact with these through the offices of the French Customs Commissioner at Fuzhou. Zuo hoped not only to build ships but also to train the naval personnel to man them and educate technical experts and craftsmen capable of producing advanced naval ships independently. The Fuzhou Naval Yard grew into a large complex of dockyards, metal forges, machine workshops, and schools teaching naval construction, design and craftsmanship. Apprentices received three hours of instruction per day in reading blueprints, mathematics and engine manufacture. By 1874 fifteen ships had been built and according to Giquel, the Fuzhou Naval Dockyard had sufficient qualified staff to take over from French advisors.[20]

Efforts were also undertaken to modernize China's land forces. The Peking Field Force was directly controlled by the Qing court. By the late 1860s, this force, commanded by the Manchu Senggelinqin (d. 1865) and drawn from the Banner armies in the capital, had grown to 20,000 men. It was equipped with modern rifles and cannon, and organized and trained along Western models. Its military task was to protect the capital, which it did for instance when a rebel force reached to within eighty miles of the capital, but it also served to maintain Banner and especially Manchu military supremacy.[21] The Qing further began to reform the Green Standard forces. Officials were ordered to eliminate the unfit in the Green Standards and investigate actual troop strengths, which often differed greatly from their paper establishments. With the money so freed up, they were to finance the retraining and re-arming according to Western models of selected Green Standard units. By the end of the century, 60,000 men had been drawn into what was called the Trained Army. If in Qing overall strategy the Trained Army's task was to combat internal rebellion and help safeguard Beijing, that of Li Hongzhang's Huai Army, which had been moved north after the Taiping Rebellion, and his navy was to guard the coast.

The Qing's military modernization efforts took a new turn in the late 1870s. The Qing began to buy modern naval ships in Germany and Britain rather than manufacture them at home. One reason for the shift in policy was that its domestically produced naval craft, which had been designed only to operate along China's coast, had not been able to prevent a Japanese punitive expedition to Taiwan in 1874. Zuo Zongtang too had concluded his victorious but costly campaign to suppress Yaqub Beg's revolt in Xinjiang, during which he had made use of Western rifles, Krupp needle guns and steel cannon. The end of the campaign made it possible for the Qing to spend more funds on its naval build-up and the strengthening of its coastal defences. Given the rapid changes in naval technologies and the limits of China's industrial base, the decision to purchase naval ships abroad was undoubtedly a wise decision.

By the late 1880s, the Qing had a substantial navy of more than fifty ships, of which about half were ocean-worthy foreign imports. This force included two German 7000-ton ironclads each with twenty-two hydraulic guns, machine guns and torpedoes. They could achieve speeds of up to 14.5 knots. There were in addition eight cruisers, some of which were capable of 18 knots, several fast torpedo boats, training vessels, transports, and other usually older gunboats.[22] This naval force was concentrated in north China, where it guarded the entrance to the Gulf of Bohai. Li Hongzhang built coastal defences along both sides of the Gulf along modern lines and armed them with Krupp guns. He also hired William Lang, a British naval officer, to oversee this naval force, and established his own naval academy at Tianjin to ensure a steady supply of cadets.[23]

Military modernization was part of a broad Self-Strengthening Movement. It included such elements as the re-invigoration of the bureaucracy, especially by ensuring that capable, broad-minded and honest officials staffed its offices; the mobilization of local élites in the management of local affairs; and the revival of the rural economy. It also included the development of mining industries, the construction of a national railroad system and a national telegraph system.[24] Translation bureaux, military and naval academies, and institutions such as the Maritime Customs Service were important avenues for the rapid introduction and spread of Western ideas, as was the dispatch of Chinese students abroad.

China's defeat by Japan in 1894–5, resulting in the sinking of China's new navy, and the Allied Expedition, which seized Beijing during the Boxer War, have meant that most historians have examined the weaknesses – rivalries between bureaucratic factions, corruption, divided command lines, and a supposed lack of understanding of the philosophical and social underpinnings of the strength of the West – of the Self-Strengthening Movement. Fundamental problems indeed existed, including a land tax system that was the cause of considerable local distress and abusive behaviour by middlemen.[25] The Qing's Banner system, basic to maintaining the Qing's ethnic and cultural hierarchies and hence fundamental for Manchu dominance, had suited the Qing well in conquering China and expanding the Qing's territorial control during the eighteenth century. But it could not accommodate the new largely Han naval and land forces without upsetting Manchu dominance and was a drain on financial resources.

Even so, it is probably not correct to say that the Self-Strengthening Movement was doomed from the beginning. John Rawlinson, in his study of China's search for naval strength, argues that the Japanese and Chinese navies in 1894 were reasonably well matched, even if the Japanese had the faster ships and the better armaments. He contends that fateful decisions made on the scene in the heat of battle and confusion resulting from differences between Chinese commanders and their Western advisors had a serious impact on the outcome of the battle.[26] One reason for the Qing's defeat was that it had postponed mobilization in order to suggest that Japan was the aggressor and to gain foreign assistance. Decisions taken in the moment of crisis were as important as long-term problems in the Qing's military build-up.

In addition, in evaluating the Self-Strengthening Movement, little attention has been paid to the quality of foreign advice the Qing received. That advice was not always appropriate. Robert Hart, who ran the Maritime Customs Service, was a man of bureaucratic genius, but he had no knowledge of naval affairs. His advice to purchase small unprotected boats with heavy guns was completely inappropriate at a time when ironclads and battleships became the determinants of naval strength.[27] The German Constantin von Hanneken, hired by Li Hongzhang, was a brave man who was present on China's flagship during the naval confrontation with Japan. But he had been dismissed from the Prussian army and had no knowledge or experience of naval warfare. Foreign advice too was offered with the geo-political and strategic interests of the advisor's home country in mind, while individual financial interest too sometimes came into the picture.[28]

It is important to remember as well that the last two decades of the nineteenth century were a period of rapid change in the organization, training, command, and equipment of naval as well as land forces. Furthermore, the rise of newly unified states with fresh imperialist ambitions – Germany, Russia, the USA, and Italy – intensified global conflicts. These conflicts themselves were understood in new ways, partly as a result of Darwinian construals of struggles between nations, but also because Self-Strengthening movements in China and elsewhere suggested that élites in the peripheries of empire were successful in assimilating Western technology while they also adopted more nationalistic stances.[29] Thus, developments around the world and the success rather than the failure of the Self-Strengthening movement led first to Japan's attack on China and then to the Allied invasion.

Finally, to regard the Self-Strengthening Movement simply as a failure ignores its long-term consequences. The great Yan Fu (1853–1921) began his career as Dean of Li Hongzhang's Tianjin Naval Academy. After spending some time at Greenwich, he came to the conclusion that Britain's industrial and military success was less the result of technological supremacy than its liberal political and economic institutions. His translations of British liberal thinkers, including J.S. Mill, deeply influenced reformers and revolutionaries of later ages. In other areas, too, including laying the basis of its communications infrastructure and giving China the Customs Service whose revenues sustained not only the late Qing but also its Republican successors, the Self-Strengthening Movement laid the basis for developments to come. Rather than disappearing together with the Qing's navy, the Self-Strengthening Movement would have a long-term impact.

3 Twentieth-century nationalist mobilizations

The Qing's defeats had serious consequences, one of which was that without a navy China could easily be invaded. Given the cost of naval development and the indemnities imposed after the first Sino–Japanese War and the Boxer Rebellion, amounting to four times the Qing's central revenue, the Qing had little option but to seek to augment its security by building up its land forces, even if that inevitably meant arming potential challengers.[30] After 1900, the Qing initiated a programme to raise a new army of thirty-six divisions, but financial shortages meant that before the crisis of the Russo–Japanese War of 1904–5, which was fought in Manchuria, only a few of these divisions were actually established. Thereafter, provinces were made responsible for financing divisions stationed in their areas, a decision which contributed to military fragmentation and localization. The defeats also provided a powerful stimulus to political movements blaming the Qing for China's problems and calling for radical political change. These two developments came together in 1911, when during the crisis of that year, Yuan Shikai (1859–1916), who had built up the new infantry army, used his military power as well as his access to foreign and especially British sources of finance to convince the last Qing Emperor, Puyi, to abdicate and take power himself.[31] Thus two thousand years of dynastic rule came to an end.

The Republic of China that was then established proved unstable. Its military was divided, while the First World War worsened the fiscal crisis as foreign sources of funding on which Yuan Shikai had depended dried up. Intense conflicts about the form of the new state, the distribution of power, relations between the centre and the province, and more fundamentally, the identity of the new nation, proved unresolvable, while an attempt to reform the tax system also ran into overwhelming opposition. The contest for influence in

China between Britain, Germany, France, Russia, and Japan further destabilized the Republic, while the opium trade put substantial funds in the hands of local contenders for power, making China among the most important markets for arms in the 1920s. The result was that the Republic was dominated by warlords whose armies were as destructive of the economy, the polity and society as they were incapable of defending the nation.

Nationalist mobilizations in the twentieth century therefore had to deal with sizeable warlord armies as well as with foreign aggression. Warlord armies depended for their survival on their ability to collect resources from the areas through which they travelled or in which they had established themselves. These exactions were not only destructive of the local economy, but also of the social order, with local élites increasingly unable to play their traditional mediating role between the state and local society.[32] Social disorder, the opium trade, the disintegration of bureaucratic government, and natural disasters fuelled banditry, while settled society established militias able to defend themselves.[33] Warlordism had deep social roots.

The Republican governments which had to deal with these problems have understandably had a bad press. One consequence of their weakness was that most resorted to murder, drew on bandits and secret societies, made deals with warlord armies, and resorted to irregular forms of extracting money, at the local level by collecting taxes often years in advance or simply allocating contributions to local villages and nationally by demanding large payments from China's nascent capitalist classes.[34] It often made more sense for them to avoid warfare than to throw themselves into a battle which they were bound to lose and which would also give opportunities to their domestic competitors and foreign aggressors.

Historical assessments of these Republican governments, including the Nationalists who ruled China from 1928 until 1949, have been shaped by models based on the emergence of European nation states as well as by the idea of revolution. In these models, central themes are the expansion of a state, administered by a centralized and efficient bureaucracy that increasingly penetrated local society; the widening participation of the population in the political process; and the deepening of national cohesiveness through the spread of education, the media, and a variety of national rituals and practices. The emergence of such a state was often seen as having to be based on radical reform, usually along liberal lines, or on revolution. The failure of Yuan Shikai or after 1928 the Nationalists, for instance, to conform to such models have led many historians to dismiss them as failures. Yet, it should be kept in mind that few European states in the late nineteenth and early twentieth centuries were particularly democratic or were governed by efficient bureaucracies. Many veered from one crisis to the next, were internally divided, did not have efficient administrations, and had to make compromise deals with a variety of vested interests. Arthur Waldron has done much to rehabilitate the Northern Government that dominated China from Yuan Shikai's death in 1916 until

1925.[35] Once we adjust our standards and become more aware of the idealized nature of European models of the state and the virtues of offensive warfare, a similar case can be made for the Nationalists.

The Nationalists came to power after they had built up an army in south China with Soviet assistance and then used it to unify China in a military campaign that lasted from 1926 to 1928. Because they controlled only limited military force themselves, and because even that force included private armies from south China, which were as much a danger as a help to them, their victory could only be achieved by permitting their allies to establish their dominance in a particular region, by seeking further alliances with strong private armies in north China, and by making deals with secret societies in control of Shanghai and other cities.

The Nationalist Government in reality could survive only by making deals with selected warlord forces, powerful regional élites, bandit and secret society leaders, emerging professional classes, rural local élites, and village headmen. But this did not mean that they simply abandoned their nationalist and modernizing agenda aimed at bringing about a modern nation state with a single powerful army, an industrialized economy and a population with a shared commitment to the nation. After Japan seized Manchuria in 1931 and attacked Shanghai in 1932, the Nationalists oversaw a military mobilization and state-making programme of considerable effectiveness. Its major elements were as follows.[36]

First, if until 1931 Chiang Kai-shek (1887–1975) had sought to eradicate his warlord opponents on the battlefield, something had that led to disastrous civil war in which as many as one million troops participated and which made China an easy prey for Japanese expansionism, after 1931 the Nationalists avoided civil warfare and tolerated the largest private armies as long as they confined themselves to their own base areas and paid nominal allegiance to the Nationalists.[37] At the same time, the Nationalists adopted a programme that combined military and civil measures to bring order to the provinces in the lower Yangtze region and firm up their control in these areas. They strengthened bureaucratic rule by eliminating a great number of committees and offices that had fragmented local government. At the local and provincial level, a single bureaucrat was made responsible for all the affairs in his jurisdiction. To wring banditry out of local society, they further revived the system of community mutual responsibility, the *baojia*, in which heads of households were fitted into a hierarchic structure supervised by the bureaucracy. The *baojia* became responsible for the maintenance of local order, informing local society of Nationalist policies and spreading the new image of the nation that the Nationalists hoped to propagate. The Nationalists further established county and provincial Peace Preservation forces. Initially made up of incorporated bandit gangs and militia, the idea was that these forces would serve as a gendarmerie under local civil control and would increasingly be drawn from the local population. Together with an economic blockade and large-scale military operations, the result was that the Communists, who had used the civil wars to establish base areas and increase their military forces, were forced to withdraw. They were pushed to inhospitable frontier areas in north China, where, it was hoped, they would gradually wither away.

The Nationalists simultaneously worked to create an élite military force with help from Germany and to construct a domestic heavy industrial base to supply it with the equipment it needed. German military assistance was provided by Hans von Seeckt, who had masterminded the redesign of the German military after the First World War, and the equally capable Alexander von Falkenhausen. They were important less perhaps for the nature of the advice they offered as for the fact that they lent their prestige to plans that Chiang Kai-shek and his closest associates had consistently pursued, thus helping to overcome the resistance of more conservative military leaders. Von Falkenhausen did indeed have a shaping hand in designing Nationalist strategy after 1935. In addition, German advisors were instrumental in bringing about a barter agreement by which China provided Germany with minerals such as tungsten, a critical hardening agent of which China was a world supplier, as well as certain agricultural products in return for German supplies of military equipment and industrial plants.[38] Without this barter trade, the reform of the Nationalist forces would have been difficult.

The National Defence Planning Council, working closely with German advisors, conducted exhaustive studies of China's economy, its transport systems, mineral supplies, fiscal structures, grain markets, and communications infrastructure. On the basis of the data so collected, a plan was drawn up for the creation of an industrial base capable of supporting sixty divisions, armed and trained according to the latest German practices. Its officers were trained in military academies where instruction was overseen by German supervisors. The troops themselves were to be recruited on the basis of a universal military service obligation. The drive to establish the *baojia* had been accompanied by a population registration drive, which provided the basis for the implementation of universal military service. If the officer corps was to have a national character, the troops themselves were to serve in their own region in a division headquartered there. Those surplus to requirement were to be called up for short periods of military training, in which fostering nationalist sentiments and spreading knowledge about the new state and its history were as important as acquainting the local population with military skills. The new system, then, attempted to reconcile the demands of creating a force closely identified with the nation and drawn from across the population with preserving regional ties and associations. By 1937, on the eve of the war with Japan, China had around thirty divisions that had been recruited in this way.

This military build-up was accompanied by significant economic reforms. China's railway network was extended and repaired. The Nationalists introduced a paper currency that proved stable and ended the chaotic monetary situation that had made orderly finances impossible since the late Qing. A whole series of unauthorized or undesirable taxes, including many of the surcharges that warlords had imposed as well as the *lijin* that hampered trade and drove up the cost of living, were abolished. Education too was rapidly expanded. In the years before the War of Resistance, the Nationalists used their increasing military preponderance, their growing economic strength and their enhanced bureaucratic capacity to extend their control into territories that had remained beyond their reach. They also shepherded warlord forces together into frontier zones, where local scarcities were bound to weaken them. So by 1937, the Nationalists were beginning to enjoy a new popularity as to many it appeared that they had brought warlordism under control, had revived the economy, and had strengthened China.

The War of Resistance against Japan would undo the Nationalists. Much has been said about the failings of the Nationalist military, which has usually been judged by its inability to conduct massed offensive warfare.[39] Given the disparity between the Japanese and Chinese militaries, however, it would have been simply suicidal for the Nationalists to wage offensive warfare. The Nationalists lacked the industrial base, the logistical systems and the bureaucratic organization that are necessary for offensive warfare. The Nationalists adopted largely defensive strategies aimed at avoiding a decisive defeat.

Before discussing these, it is important to note that the Nationalists conducted the War of Resistance with a close eye to the geo-political situation. In the first years of the war, they attempted to draw the Soviet Union into the fighting. Because of the Japanese occupation of Manchuria, the Japanese shared a long border with the Soviet Union. Tensions between the two were exacerbated by Japanese attempts to penetrate westward into Mongolia after 1935. In 1937, war between the Soviet Union and Japan was a distinct possibility, and actual clashes of considerable scale occurred, including the Battle of Nomonhan in 1939, which saw the largest air battle since the First World War. Although the Nationalists did not succeed in drawing the Soviets actively into the war, the latter did provide an airforce as well as many tanks, much artillery, a great number of machine guns, and vast amounts of ammunition.[40] The Nationalists profited from Japanese–Soviet tensions in other ways as well. Fearful of war with the Soviets, the Japanese had decided for a Blitzkrieg war of three months duration, a strategy always unlikely to succeed in a country as large as China. In 1938 the Nationalists escaped a Japanese attempt to encircle and destroy their main forces. They were able to withdraw into a number of inaccessible base areas from which they could continue their resistance.

During the Battle of Nomonhan, the Soviets inflicted a heavy defeat on Japan's Kwantung Army in Manchuria. This made the Japanese hesitant to pursue a war with the Soviet Union, while the Soviets themselves did not want to fight a war on two fronts. The consequence of the resulting Soviet–Japanese Non-Aggression Treaty was that the Nationalists could not count on further Soviet assistance. In addition, Japanese strategy became dedicated to realizing the Great East Asian Co-prosperity Sphere. The Japanese therefore turned south, hoping first to eliminate Nationalist resistance and then destroy European colonies in South and Southeast Asia.

Following the beginning of Japan's southern advance, of which the attack on Pearl Harbour was the spectacular opening salvo, the USA and Britain became active allies of the Nationalists. China would not profit very much from this alliance. What China needed was large-scale involvement of its allies in China itself. However, the USA and Britain did not believe that China could contribute much to the defeat of Japan. They regarded China as useful only to the extent that it could tie down significant numbers of Japanese troops, so that Japan could not attack the Soviet Union, which faced the greatest number of German divisions, or concentrate all their forces against themselves. In 1942 China's allies restricted themselves to largely symbolic gestures such as the despatch of General Harold Alexander, the Hero of Dunkirk, in lieu of meaningful aid. Japan's control of the seas made supplies to China impossible afterwards. Because the Allies decided to defeat Germany first, and because the margins of success were small, the USA and Britain followed a policy of doing just enough to keep China in the war while avoiding serious engagement in the fighting in China itself.

For China, the difficulty was that it needed to maintain its alliance with Britain and the USA. Alone it would not be able to defeat Japan, and it was clear that once Germany was defeated, Japan would not be able to hold out long against the combined might of the USA, Britain and the Soviet Union. The choice facing the Nationalists was to surrender to Japan or to participate in an Allied strategy that was disadvantageous in the short run but would ultimately ensure that they would be on the winning side, with all the advantages that would flow from this. The price the Nationalists paid for joining the Allies was high. The only place in which they could fight together with them in 1942 was Burma. It proved a campaign that was as awkward, in that it required a champion of Asian nationalism to fight to save the British empire, as it would be futile, for the Nationalists lost their best divisions, including their only mobile one. Things would become worse. Although in 1944 the USA and Britain continued to refuse to fight in China or to make significant naval and air forces available to operations in Asia, they nonetheless decided to attack Japanese forces in Burma in an operation to which they attached more symbolic than serious strategic value. They demanded that China once more deploy its best forces there. The result was that a Japanese offensive in China itself, not anticipated by the USA and Britain and for some time belittled, delivered to Japan the grain and recruitment grounds in China on which Nationalist resistance had depended.

Despite their best efforts to involve their allies in the fighting in China, then, the Nationalists were largely dependent on their own efforts to resist Japan in China. In 1937 they launched an assault on Japanese positions in Shanghai, perhaps in the hope that they could score a significant victory there and that the fear of war with the Soviet Union would force the Japanese to the negotiation table. This did not happen, and despite some battlefield victories, within a year and a half the Japanese had taken China's most important coastal cities, the Yangtze River and the most important railway lines. The Nationalists then made Sichuan, a populous and productive province in the inaccessible western part of the country, into their base. They established resistance zones in the rest of the country in areas that were relatively difficult for the Japanese to access but which at the same time enjoyed grain surpluses and were places where military recruitment was relatively easy.

The Nationalists built up a granary system designed to stockpile enough food for its troops for three months at the front and for six months in rear areas. The aim was to make sure that Nationalist forces could be confident that sufficient food supplies were available, but also to prevent those forces from simply settling down and refusing to participate in offensive operations. In their operations against the Japanese, the Nationalists adopted the following tactics. Supply problems for the Japanese were difficult to solve once they moved away from railways and rivers, as they could not carry more than ten days of supplies. The Nationalists therefore sought to lure the Japanese well away from their staging areas, falling back gradually while 'clearing the countryside' so that the Japanese could not live off the land. The Nationalists would then attempt to cut the Japanese rear and attack the Japanese flanks. These tactics brought the Nationalists some significant tactical victories throughout the War of Resistance.

The Nationalists could continue their resistance as long as they were able to hold on to their grain fields and recruitment grounds, and as long as the social and economic order did not disintegrate. After 1942, the Nationalists encountered increasing difficulties in both cases. Before then, they had been able to sustain agricultural productivity by shifting the burden of the war onto the cities and the relatively well-off, by limiting government expenditures, by promoting new seed varieties and different crops, and by promoting trade. The ideal of universal military service was in reality abandoned and armies were recruited mostly from the poorest segments of society. After 1942, the pool of men that could with little pressure be drawn into the armies dried up. The Japanese tightened their economic blockade and conducted military raids into the Nationalists' grain areas. The Nationalists' tax collection system disintegrated as tax collectors were driven from their posts or abandoned them. With markets collapsing and the food supply becoming a serious worry, inflation sky-rocketed. One consequence was that the Nationalists increasingly resorted to violent measures to beat recruits out of the countryside and collect the grain necessary to feed them, thus alienating the population.

The Nationalists ended the War of Resistance in a disadvantageous position. Their best armies were in Burma, far from where they were needed. As the crisis intensified in China itself, the Nationalists had reduced recruitment and ordered most armies to cultivate their own food and secure their own resources, making them militarily useless and socially exploitative. Commanders in many regions no longer had much reason to remain loyal to the Nationalists other than in name only. In short, the Nationalists lost control over the limited forces at their disposal. At the same time, substantial puppet forces had coalesced around the Japanese or the Chinese regime they supported, while the Communists had been able to build up large base areas in China north of the Yangtze River and to expand their armies.[41]

If Japan's surrender in August 1945 brought an end to the Second World War, in China, as elsewhere in East and Southeast Asia, peace did not break out. One of the consequences of the Second World War in these areas was that different groups each with their own vision of the future had become powerful as they had mobilized to resist Japan. Some had profited from Japanese attempts to cultivate local allies, others from Western attempts to do the same, while yet others had been able to do so because of the chaotic conditions in which plenty of arms were available and populations searched for protectors. In China, the Communist victory was not fore-ordained. During the war they had confronted many of the same problems as the Nationalists and their base areas were not the ideal societies sometimes imagined.[42] However, they had not borne the brunt of the fighting against the Japanese and had carefully husbanded their resources. They also profited from the Soviet Union's support in the aftermath of the war, and of the USA's desire to bring the troops home and not become involved in a long and difficult civil war. The Nationalists, meanwhile, had become deeply disliked, had proved incapable of restoring order and reviving the economy, and their armies were often 'paper tigers'. These factors, combined with the disciplines imposed on Communist armies by a tough party, made it possible for the Communists to seize power in 1949.

Conclusion

In this overview of military mobilization and modernization in China during the last two centuries I have first suggested that the Qing was ill-prepared to deal with Britain's naval challenge not because it was a backward country or a Confucian society with little regard for the military, but because it had faced different sorts of military challenges and followed a different path of military development than Britain. I have further argued that the Qing, once it began taking over Western military methods during the Taiping Rebellion, did so with considerable success and with long-term consequences during the Self-Strengthening Movement. Its defeats during the Sino-Japanese War and the Boxer Rebellion had domestic reasons, but were also the result of important changes in the international situation which led European powers, the USA and Japan to transfer their conflicts, and their vastly improved naval and land forces, to China. I have finally suggested that after the 1920s the Nationalists led an impressive mobilization attempt which enabled them to continue resistance against the Japanese invasion for eight long years despite receiving little meaningful outside help. The Chinese contribution to the defeat of Japan, and indirectly that of Germany, is something that deserves greater recognition in accounts of the Second World War that remain heavily centred on Britain and the USA.

This overview will have made clear that warfare and military mobilization were key issues in the history of China during the last two centuries. They have so far received only limited attention. We still lack, in fact, a good English-language history of the Second World War in China. The effects of the search for military strength were profound: they can be seen in the emergence of the command economy, which was not only a product of ideological imperatives but also of wartime scarcities; in the decidedly militaristic tone that was set by the Cultural Revolution in the 1960s and 1970s by the Communists and by the Nationalists during the New Life Movement of the 1930s; and in the organization of daily life, in which at least in urban areas the military-like work unit dominated. Even if China is now at long last emerging from the social and economic consequences of warfare, memories of the War of Resistance especially have gained a new centrality in collective identities.

It is time, then, to integrate China's search for military strength and the wars in which it was involved more fully into our accounts of Chinese history, and of military history more generally. This should be done without either overestimating or underestimating China's military and the governments that mobilized them. It was not able to produce the airforces, infantries and navies essential to modern warfare because it remained a large rural empire that lacked the agricultural surpluses, the industrial base, the communications infrastructure, the bureaucracy, and the fiscal systems that were essential to producing them. Yet it was able, often by using the methods of the past, to sustain resistance, in the case of Japan over many years, and in the process demonstrate the limits of modern offensive warfare. The governments that oversaw these mobilizational efforts had to make deals and compromises, both domestically and internationally, but in this they resembled European states far more than we have tended to acknowledge. To analyse societies solely in terms of their capacity to generate offensive modern warfare, and to base judgments about their states and even their cultures on just this criterion, is both simplistic and can lead to real dangers.

Notes

1 H. van de Ven, Introduction in *Warfare in Chinese History* (Leiden: Brill Academic Publishers, 2000), 1–11 and *War and Nationalism* (London, Routledge, 2003), Introduction.

2 Chen Feng, *Qingdai Junfei Yanjiu* (A Study of Qing Military Expenditures) (Wuhan: Wuhan Daxue Chubanshe, 1992), 48–67.

3 Mark Elliot, *The Manchu Way: The Eight Banners and Ethnic Identity in Late Imperial China* (Stanford: Stanford University Press, 2001), 39–88.

4 On Wei Yuan, see Jane Kate Leonard, *Wei Yuan and China's Rediscovery of the Maritime World* (Cambridge, Mass.: Harvard University Press, 1984) and Philip Kuhn, *The Origins of the Modern Chinese State*, 25–73.
5 Wei Yuan, *Shengwuji* (Record Of Imperial Military Achievements) (Beijing: Zhonghua Shuju, 1984), 470–85.
6 See Kuhn, op. cit.
7 Elliot, *Manchu Way*, 311.
8 John Brewer, *The Sinews of Power: War and the English State, 1688–1783* (London: Unwin Hyman, 1989).
9 Geoffrey Parker, *The Military Revolution: Military Innovation and the Rise of the West, 1500–1800* (Cambridge: Cambridge University Press, 1988), 6–44.
10 Mao Haijian: *Tianchao de Bengkui* (The Collapse of the Empire) (Beijing: Sanlian Shudian, 1995), 155–326.
11 Johanna Waley Cohen, *The Sextants of Beijing* (New York: W.W. Norton, 2000), 92–128. Peter Perdue, 'Military mobilization in seventeenth and eighteenth-century China, Russia, and Mongolia', *Modern Asian Studies*, XXX: 4 (Oct. 1996), 757–93.
12 Kuhn, *Rebellion and its Enemies in Late Imperial China: Militarization and Social Structure, 1796–1864* (Cambridge, Mass.: Harvard University Press, 1970).
13 K.C. Liu, 'The Ch'ing Restoration', in John Fairbank and Denis Twitchett (eds), *The Cambridge History of China* (Cambridge: Cambridge University Press, 1978), vol. 10, 413.
14 Ibid., 414.
15 Philip Kuhn, 'The Taiping Rebellion', in ibid., vol. 10, 290.
16 The best, even if partial, history of the Customs Service during the Qing remains Stanley Wright, *Hart and the Chinese Customs Service* (Belfast: Queens University Press, 1950).
17 Kuhn, 'Taiping Rebellion', 301–7.
18 K.C. Liu, 'The Ch'ing Restoration', 425–31.
19 John Rawlinson, *China's Struggle for Naval Development, 1839–1895* (Cambridge, Mass.: Harvard University Press, 1967), 42.
20 Rawlinson, *China's Struggle for Naval Development*, 41–62.
21 Liu Fenghan, 'Qingji Ziqiang Yundong yu Junshi Chuqi Gaige' (The Self-Strengthening Movement and Early Military Reform', in *Qingji Ziqiang Yundong Yantaohui Lunwen* (Proceedings of the Conference on the Qing Self-Strengthening Movement) (Taibei: Zhongyang Yanjiuyuan Jindaishi Yanjiushuo, 1988), 366–9.
22 Ibid., 375–6.
23 K.C. Liu, 'Self-Strengthening: The Pursuit of Western Technology', in John Fairbank and Denis Twitchett (eds), *The Cambridge History of China* (Cambridge: Cambridge University Press, 1978), vol. XI, 253–8.
24 Besides the above, see also the still classic Mary Wright, *The Last Stand of Chinese Conservatism* (Stanford: Stanford University Press, 1962).
25 Kuhn, *Origins of the Modern State*, 23–4, 84–91.
26 Rawlinson, *China's Search for Naval Development*, 167–85.
27 Ibid., 69.
28 On von Hanneken, see Vera Schmidt, *Aufgabe und Einfluss der europaeischen Berater in China: Gustav Detring im Dienste Li Hung-changs* (Wiesbaden: Harrassowitz, 1984) and Rawlinson, *China's Search for Naval Development*, 175–87.
29 Christopher Bayly, 'The Boxer Rebellion in India: Globalising Myths', paper presented '1900: The Boxers, China, and the World', SOAS, June 2001.
30 For contemporary expressions of such fears, see memorials replicated in Zhonghua Minguoshi Zu (Group for the History of the Republic of China) (eds), *Qingmo*

Xinjun Bianlian Yange (The History of the Mobilization of the New Army) (Beijing: Zhonghua Shuju, 1978), 6–8.

31 See Hans van de Ven, 'Military and Financial Reform in the Late Qing and Early Republic', in Zhongyang Yanjiuyuan Jindaishi Yanjiusuo Shehui Jingjishi Zu (Group for Social and Economic History of the Institute of Modern History of the Academia Sinica) (eds), *Caizheng yu Jindai Lishi* (Finance and Modern History) (Taibei: Zhongyan Yanjiuyuan Jindaishi, 1999), 43–79.

32 Prasenji Duara, *Culture, Power, and the State: Rural North China, 1900–1942* (Stanford: Stanford University Press, 1988), 217–43.

33 Elisabeth Perry, *Rebels and Revolutionaries in North China, 1845–1945* (Stanford: Stanford University Press, 1980).

34 On the first, Duara, op. cit., and on the second, see Parks Coble, *The Shanghai Capitalists and the Nationalist Government, 1927–1937* (Cambridge, Mass.: Harvard University Press, 1980), 29–41, 57–65. Siu, *Agents and Victims*, 74–6, 87, 88–97. See also Helen Siu, *Agents and Victims in South China: Accomplices in Rural Revolution* (New Haven: Yale University Press, 1989) 74–6, 87–97.

35 A. Waldron, *From War to Nationalists: China's Turning Point, 1924–5* (Cambridge: Cambridge University Press, 1995).

36 The following paragraphs are based on Hans van de Ven, *Warfare and Nationalism in China, 1925–1945* (London, Routledge, 2003), chapters 5–7.

37 van de Ven, *Warfare and Nationalism*, ch. 4.

38 Ibid.

39 See for instance Frank Dorn, *The Sino–Japanese War: From Marco Polo Bridge to Pearl Harbor* (New York: Macmillan, 1974) and Ch'i Hsi-sheng, *Nationalist China at War: Military Defeats and Political Collapse, 1937–45* (Ann Arbor: Michigan University Press, 1982).

40 John Garver, *Chinese–Soviet Relations: The Diplomacy of Chinese Nationalism* (Oxford: Oxford University Press, 1988), 38.

41 The best overview is Lyman Van Slyke, 'The Chinese Communist Movement during the Sino-Japanese War, 1937–45', in John Fairbank and Denis Twitchett (eds), *The Cambridge History of China* (Cambridge: Cambridge University Press, 1986), 609–722.

42 See David Apter, 'Discourse as Power' and Chen Yung-fa, 'The Blooming Poppy under the Red Sun', in Tony Saich and Hans van de Ven (eds), *New Perspectives on the Chinese Communist Revolution* (Armonk, M.E. Sharpe, 1994), 193–234 and 263–98. See also Elise De Vido, *The Making of the Communist Party State in Shandong Province, 1927–1952* (Cambridge, Mass.: Harvard University Press, 1995).

3

SOUTH ASIA

Douglas Peers

> Our government of that country is essentially military, and
> our means of preserving and improving our possessions through
> the operation of our civil institutions depends on our wise
> and politic exercise of that military power on which the whole
> fabric rests.[1]

To note that military power was important to British rule in South Asia appears
so obvious as to scarcely merit a mention. But while many commentators have
acknowledged this simple fact, comparatively few have gone beyond noting the
violence which featured in both imperial conquest and imperial rule. What begs
further explanation is how such a small island nation, initially spearheaded by
a commercial company for whom costly wars of conquest were anathema,
was able to establish such a tight military grip on India, and what that in turn
meant for British rule in India, its impact on the peoples of India and on
the successor states of India, Pakistan and Bangladesh. The British Raj was a
conquest state, one that was not only structurally geared towards conquest but
was moreover culturally and ideologically grounded in conquest. The British,
though not without considerable difficulty, were able to establish their military
authority and within the span of just over a century (1740–1860) went from
being a trading power confined to a few enclaves along the coast to the
paramount power in the subcontinent, raising an army of over a quarter million
by the midpoint of the nineteenth century (rising to well over a million in the
First World War and more than two million in the Second), which they were
able to deploy not only to bolster their authority within India and protect its
frontiers, but also as an instrument to assert British power throughout the Indian
Ocean and beyond.

This is not to say that everybody accepted the military's pre-eminence. There
were certainly critics of this situation, but often their objections were ones of
degree rather than outright rejections of the army's centrality to imperial rule.
Certainly it is the case that over time the more overt manifestations of the
military's presence in colonial India diminished. Yet right up until 1947 one of
the most poignant symbols of colonial rule was the British flag flying above the

41

ruins of the Lucknow Residency, the scene of one of the most hard-fought battles in the Indian Rebellion of 1857–8. As one commentator put it, 'We Anglo-Indians [meaning the British resident in India] form, after all, not a nation but a colony; not even a colony but a garrison'.[2] The British decision to leave India in 1947 was in no small part determined by growing alarm that they were losing control over locally-raised military and naval units, and without such authority they really had little else to fall back upon. And finally the situation in contemporary South Asia attests to the military's standing, for not only has the region been rocked by war and the threat of war but in the case of Pakistan and Bangladesh (though not in India) the military has frequently intervened in politics.

Most efforts at explaining Britain's rise to military dominance have fastened on a limited range of explanations, or sometimes a blend of them. For some, the answer lay in innate European superiority. While few scholars today would subscribe to such a blatantly chauvinistic explanation, muted versions of this argument continue to crop up. Another tack was to look at the role of technology, both in terms of more lethal weaponry but also the kinds of political and economic transformations unleashed by more complex weapons systems – so-called theories of a military revolution that have been used to account for the global rise of Western power.[3] A simple calculation based on technology fails to explain British victories adequately. For one thing, clear British superiority in weapons did not materialize until the latter half of the nineteenth century, well after much of the subcontinent had been conquered. Before then, British technological advantages were either rather negligible as Indian powers equipped themselves with similar weapons, or were effectively neutralized by the conditions in which wars were fought or by their opponents' tactics.

The key advantage enjoyed by the British in general over their Indian opponents was that they had the resources to pay and outfit an army that could then be drilled and disciplined in such a way as to maximize its potential. The British conquered India using Indian soldiers, paid for with Indian capital raised from Indian financiers and aided by Indian allies. The end result was a hybrid military culture. Rather than emphasizing differences between Indian and European armies, as has customarily been the case, it is important to acknowledge the very porous boundaries that lay between the British and their Indian opponents and allies. Britain's opponents in South Asia, who were not deficient in courage, technology or skill, all too often lacked the kind of political and economic institutions that enabled large armies to be raised, equipped and maintained over long periods.

Another important characteristic of colonial warfare was that it was often as much a battle against nature as it was one against human opponents. Climate, for example, imposed tight restrictions on how and when campaigns were planned and battles fought. Monsoons often rendered transportation very difficult if not impossible, thereby forcing armies to limit their campaigning to particular seasons. In most of India, this meant that active operations took place between October and May. Moreover, the monsoon season also brought with it a huge increase in water-borne illnesses like malaria and cholera.

> In India there are, with certain local variations, three distinct seasons in the year – the hot season, and the wet season, and the cold season. In the first, if you go to war, you stand a chance of being burnt to death; and in the second of being drowned. The third alone is fit for military operations; and it does not last more than four or five months.[4]

Disease was another persistent problem, in which lay the origins of the macabre toast before battle of 'A bloody war and a sickly season'.[5]

Success in war in India was therefore frequently determined by logistics and good administration. Given that much of India lacked a modern transportation infrastructure and agricultural production was insufficient to meet the needs of armies on the march, armies had to develop means of carrying what they needed with them. Much of the Duke of Wellington's success in India (for which he was derisively dismissed by Napoleon as that 'sepoy general') can be attributed to the care and attention he devoted to questions of supply and transportation. He was able to avoid the problems that were common in Indian warfare when troops were left to fend for themselves.[6] But attention to logistics came at a cost – it slowed down the British by encumbering them with ponderous baggage trains that required troops for their own defence. In the Second Afghan War, there were 15,000 troops guarding the route between Peshawar and Kabul as compared to the 12,000 troops in Kabul.[7]

Equally important in accounting for British success was that while there were tensions within the colonial state, the British fought as a collective, whereas their Indian opponents were often politically fragmented, making alliance warfare on their part exceedingly difficult. The British took advantage of such faultlines by playing factions off against one another. The classic example of this is offered by the Marathas who on several occasions in the 1780s, early 1800s and finally in 1817–19 had posed serious challenges to British interests. They were a loose confederacy of mainly Hindu princes and warlords who ranged across north and west-central peninsular India. Maratha armies were largely cavalry-based, though their preference was for light cavalry, useful for harassing and ambushing, rather than the heavy cavalry, with their shock value, that had been favoured in the Mughal Empire.[8] Frequently depicted as locusts, Marathas armies lived off the land and were accompanied by bands of followers who plundered the countryside. The Maratha Ditch, built in the mid-eighteenth century just outside Calcutta, testifies to their extraordinary range. To this cavalry foundation the Marathas would later add infantry disciplined along European lines (and often officered by Europeans) as well as European-style artillery.[9] All told, it made for a particularly potent combination of military resources, earning them the respect of the Duke of Wellington among others. He claimed in retrospect that the most difficult battle that he had ever fought was the Battle of Assaye (1803), which pitted him against a well-armed and determined Maratha army. The British emerged victorious, but at the cost of nearly 1600 of the 4500 men that Wellington took into battle.[10] Yet while the Marathas could at times best the British on the battlefield, the overall direction of the war all too often turned against them because of a lack of coordination among their various constituencies.

This 'truth' about British rule, namely its dependence upon the military to secure its future, which became manifest in the ideologies and practices of the colonial state, shaped more than simply the opinions and actions of government officials together with their strategic priorities and choice of tactics. In addition to protecting India from attack from without, troops were increasingly used in what the Victorian novelist, essayist and army officer W.D. Arnold described as 'vigorous street constableship.'[11] In 1849–50, some 30,000 sepoys were mounting guard and providing treasure escorts, and in some cases units could expect to do so for periods of up to 15 months.[12] As one officer described it, their duties consisted of 'little action, just a lot of marching and counter-marching to show the flag . . . chivalrously burning two thousand houses lest they should have a shelter for their heads during the rains!'[13] Rendering assistance to the civil power also became a regular demand on the Indian Army following World War One, and there has been an increase of late in such duties in India, Pakistan and Bangladesh.

The military's presence in India was also instrumental in helping to articulate certain images of India in the public mind, for many people came to appreciate India at least in part through the optics of the army. Much of what was known about India during the colonial period was written by military officers and surgeons posted to India, or by observers commenting on military operations. War made for gripping reading, especially when it was set in an exotic location, for it provided dramatic stories of bravery, villainy, comedy, and tragedy. As one author reminded his readers, 'In India every war is more or less popular. The constitution of Anglo-Indian society renders it almost impossible that it would be otherwise.'[14] Such romanticized accounts, however, anaesthetized the public to the brutal realities of colonial warfare. One radical lamented that 'We try to conceal the butchering nature of the business and so spring up in military spectacle . . . clothe war in gayer colours than peace'.[15] Enthusiasm for and interest in dramatic tales of warfare across the far flung empire was made easier by the fact that so few Britons were actually directly affected by all this: it is easier to romanticize warfare when it could be held at such a distance.

The experience of colonial warfare, experienced either first hand or vicariously through the media, also served to buttress increasingly racialized readings of Indian society, the divisions within India as well as the differences between the British and their Indian subjects.[16] British military victories on the Indian subcontinent not only helped to account for the British conquest of India; they also served to rationalize British rule by providing compelling arguments for European superiority.[17] Hence, colonial warfare as well as the people and institutions involved were a defining feature of South Asia under colonial rule, and they have left a legacy for its successor states.

The most striking characteristic of the colonial army in India was its dependence on Indian manpower. As one commentator wryly noted,

> [I]f Queen Victoria engaged in an attempt to govern Ireland by the help of a Romish native army, swarming with Jesuits and officered by Protestants, she would have been in a situation somewhat similar to that of the East India Company relying on a Brahmanic Bengal army for the security and stability of their Empire.[18]

This situation stretches well back into the eighteenth century when the East India Company found that there was a ready supply of Indian recruits at hand, soldiers (known as sepoys from the Persian term *sipahi*) who were cheaper than Europeans, easier to discipline, and better suited to the physical and cultural environment. War was, after all, commonplace to much of India and consequently there was a large population of part-time and full-time soldiers that the British, their allies and their opponents could easily tap into. It has been said that throughout much of India there were but two seasons: planting and campaigning.[19] Many of these prospective recruits could be absorbed into a European-style army without too much difficulty as precolonial armies in India had already begun to adapt some Western forms of organization in addition to Western arms.[20] And what they did not adapt often proved quite enticing to the British, such as the Indian tradition of *silladar* cavalry, an irregular body of light horse in which the recruit either provided his own mount or had one provided by a contractor who had recruited him on behalf of an employer.[21] It is important to recognize this two-way flow of institutions, practices and customs for it helps to account for the hybridized nature of warfare in South Asia as well as the hybridized forms of military culture. But it should also be noted that influences did not simply pass from Europe to India or vice versa. There was also considerable interplay between Indian and Central Asian styles of warfare and military organization that lasted right up to the beginning of the nineteenth century, for as two recent scholars have noted, 'the open plains and plateaus of Northern and Central India, although not very suitable for horse-breeding as such, remained wedded to the nomadic culture of the camp, the horse and the bow'.[22]

The British also came quickly to appreciate that their armies were not only useful in the obvious tasks of overawing the locals and dispossessing truculent chiefs, but could also be employed in a more oblique fashion, namely, by using selective recruiting to incorporate those segments of local society who might otherwise oppose colonial rule and disrupt the stability the British were so eagerly pursuing. The conquest of many of their rivals in North India, for example, had by the early nineteenth century thrown 40–50,000 part-time and full-time soldiers out of work.[23] Sponging up these turbulent spirits became a military priority.

The actual structure of British forces in India went through a number of iterations in the nineteenth and twentieth centuries. In 1800 India was still the responsibility of the East India Company, which used a combination of locally recruited Indian troops (divided into three Presidency armies of Bengal, Madras and Bombay), a small cadre of European recruits under its control, plus approximately 20,000 regular British troops (usually increased during wartime or other times of crisis) that were leased from the British government.[24] One consequence of the Indian Rebellion (1857–8) was the ending of Company rule, and with it went the Company's distinct European force that was eventually and not without some difficulty melded into the British Army.[25] But the principle of having three separate Presidency armies into which the sepoys were recruited continued until 1893 when the three armies were merged into one, in which the attitudes, institutions and personnel of the Bengal Army predominated. The merger came about in part because of a search for economies and in part because the need for these armies became less and less evident as the likely scene of fighting moved further and further away from their borders.

Contemporary writings and consequently some recent works have tended to exaggerate the difference between sepoys and Europeans stationed in India.[26] While the government viewed them as distinct groups and quite deliberately subjected them to different disciplinary regimes, the fact is that for much of the period under review, sepoys served for many of the same reasons as did their European counterparts. The reasons why British soldiers fought included honour, peer pressure, adventure, lack of alternative, money or loot, patriotism, and the fact that in battle retreat was often more dangerous than holding firm. Indian sepoys fought for the same reasons save patriotism, and the importance of patriotism for the British rank and file in India is hard to measure, especially in the nineteenth century.

The most powerful incentive for both sides was pay. For sepoys in particular, the Company unlike most of its Indian rivals paid well and paid regularly.[27] One reason why the state of Mysore had been considered to be such a challenge in the eighteenth century was that it had developed quite sophisticated mechanisms to meet its troops' needs; the same was true for the Sikh army, which was also rated as a serious threat. Initially, pay scales for British sepoys were set at a level that ensured a steady supply of recruits. But this rate remained fixed for over a century, even in the face of inflationary pressures that eroded the sepoys' pay. The base pay for sepoys was seven rupees a month for the entire nineteenth century: it was raised only in 1911 to 13 rupees.[28] Out of this sepoys were expected to feed themselves and it was assumed that food should cost them no more than four rupees a month. There were some exceptions: during times of war they were often fed by the army, or should prices soar too high, the army would intervene and offer a subsidy. Long-serving sepoys could also expect to be rewarded with pensions and sometimes land grants and other gratuities.[29] They and their families secured preferential access to British courts. *Izzat* or honour played an important role as well. For many communities in which military service was both traditional and honourable, service with the British enabled sepoys and their families to maintain their social position which was especially crucial given the upheavals of the colonial era. For example, sepoys had the right to bear arms, which in an increasingly demilitarized society enabled them to reassert their masculinity, status and honour.

The willingness and even alacrity with which their European officers met the sepoys' quest for status and honour contributed to the brahminization or the domination of the Bengal Army before 1857 by high-caste sepoys who secured from the British an agreement that their caste strictures be observed. Religious rites were observed, diet and clothing prohibitions acknowledged, and high-caste sepoys from the central Gangetic Plain were effectively granted a monopoly on positions within the army. Brahminization can also be glimpsed in the reluctance with which the lash was used before its abolition in 1834 – even when it was reintroduced, army officers were loath to use it on Bengal sepoys (though few showed much misgiving when it came to Europeans), for sepoys were seen to be men of honour and hence the best punishment was one that struck at their honour rather than their bodies.[30] The armies of the Madras and Bombay Presidencies were not nearly as exclusive as that of Bengal, and while this led some Bengal officers to view their army as made from much more noble material, its critics could also point to the Bengal Army's greater propensity to revolt.

Confidence in these troops was periodically shaken, never more so than during the revolt of 1857–8. Yet even prior to 1857 there had been doubts about the dependability of the sepoys, for mutinies or near-mutinies had taken place before, including one at Barrackpur in 1824 which drew in most of one regiment. Moreover, there were a series of disturbing breakdowns in discipline among troops dispatched to Sind and the Punjab in the 1840s. The events of 1857 marked a much more widespread reaction against British rule, one that began among discontented sepoys of the Bengal army but soon spread to disaffected elements of the wider population.

Historians continue to debate the long-term causes of the Revolt, but most would agree that they included a growing suspicion on the part of many Indians that the British were about to abandon their earlier promises to respect Indian customs and traditions. The growing numbers of missionaries in India, the way in which Western technologies such as railways and telegraphs were being inscribed on the landscape, Lord Dalhousie's (Governor General 1848–54) annexation of a number of princely states, combined to exacerbate already existing anxieties. To these can be added a series of grievances more specific to the military. Sepoys no longer had the option of volunteering for foreign service (which had in the past entitled them to extra pay). Alterations were made to their uniforms without their consent, and these had religious implications. All of these developments were especially alarming to troops who had with the tacit approval of their officers woven religious and caste practices into the regimental fabric. The breaking point came, however, with the introduction of the new Enfield rifle, which required the use of cartridges that were rumoured to be greased with animal fat. Fat rendered from pork was offensive to Muslims while that which came from cattle was unacceptable to Hindus. The truth of the rumour, even if it could be established, is ultimately irrelevant; the fact that the British were thought guilty of this act demonstrates just how alienated the sepoys had become. And it should be noted that it is the symbolism of the cartridges that matters most, for many sepoys were quite willing to use those cartridges on their officers.

To appreciate the scale and consequences of the Revolt of 1857, it must be remembered that the sepoys were peasant soldiers. Even after having been trained and clothed in a European manner, they retained strong links with their communities, links which the British had been only too willing to encourage in the past.[31] The revolt spread quickly, and it appeared to some that the British could lose India. It was later estimated that some 75 per cent of the adult male population in Awadh (the area from which most sepoys had been recruited) had taken some part in the uprising.[32] Most sepoy regiments had either revolted or were showing alarming signs that they might, which prompted British officers to disarm them. Only twelve of the seventy sepoy regiments in the Bengal Army remained loyal. British rule was most under threat in the six months between the outbreak of mutiny at the large cantonment of Meerut and the subsequent capture of Delhi by the rebels in May 1857 and November 1857, when their strongholds of Kanpur and Lucknow were back in British hands (Delhi having been retaken after a rather desperate attack on 14 September). One newspaper opined,

> Our house in India is on fire. We are not insured. To lose that house would be to lose power, prestige, and character – to descend in the rank of nations, and take a position more in accordance with our size on the map of Europe than with the greatness of our past glory and present ambition.[33]

Yet Britain's military situation did not deteriorate as completely as some had feared. Elements of the Bengal army did remain loyal, more than has often been noticed. Loyal sepoys together with Sikh volunteers made up over half the troops the British used to retake Delhi. The British were fortunate that their armies in the other two presidencies remained quiet, as did most of the population outside the Gangetic heartland. This enabled them to call upon timely military support from the Punjab. Soldiers discharged from the recently conquered Sikh state (1848) readily joined the British, partly in the hope of securing loot from the cities of the Gangetic Plain and partly as a means of avenging themselves on the sepoys who had only recently helped the British to conquer them. The British were also lucky that the rebels lacked a clear plan of action, and that their leadership was fractured and directed towards differing aims. Many of their supposed leaders were somewhat reluctant participants – such was the case, for example, with the Mughal Emperor around whom the sepoys gathered and from whom they expected support. Similarly, the infamous Nana Sahib, who was instrumental in the massacre at Kanpur of British soldiers and civilians, including many women and children, also appears to have been co-opted by the sepoys.[34] While it is clear that there was some degree of coordination among the rebels – illustrated for example in the mysterious circulation of chappatis (unleavened bread) in the weeks before the outbreaks at Meerut and other cantonments[35] – there was no overall plan.

The lack of coordinated action among the rebels, together with their failure to break out of the Gangetic heartland, allowed the British eventually to contain the rebellion, and to come at them from several directions. But victory came at a cost – in human, political and military terms. It had become a very racialized war, one in which both sides engaged in acts of atrocity against each other, unleashing a spiral of violence that was difficult to contain. Tactics were dictated as much by the desire for revenge as by issues of military efficiency. A sergeant at Dinapur wrote home that 'the men are mad, and oh, how they go about swearing and vowing to avenge this atrocity. They are wrought up to the highest pitch of madness, and are burning to go at these murdering monsters.'[36] Similar expressions of rage came from the rebels, Kanpur being perhaps the most famous example. It was also seen in Delhi, where it was reported that 'The hatred of the native population now to the English is something extraordinary, three days after the town being in our possession, two officers went into the magazine and a native quietly put a match in and blew them up in sight of several officers outside who cut him down.'[37] Such feelings lasted until well after the revolt had been suppressed. In 1862, for example, the Viceroy was under intense pressure from British expatriates to grant clemency to a British soldier tried and convicted by an all-white jury for the brutal and premeditated murder of an Indian farmer.[38]

Post-Rebellion assessments of the causes of the sepoy mutinies quickly pointed to Britain's dependence upon sepoys, especially the high-caste recruits of the Bengal army, as the root cause. Consequently the British decided they needed to lessen their dependency. As the Secretary for India informed the commander-in-chief, 'you cannot dispense with the Europeans, and therefore the cutting down must fall on the Natives. What is necessary in them is, enough to do what Europeans ought not to do – or cannot do – so far you must do, but beyond that you must be guided in your numbers by what you can afford to pay for.'[39] Prior to 1857, the ratio of sepoys to European soldiers usually stood at somewhere around four or five to one, though it could stretch as high as seven to one in times of war. The revised ratio was set at two to one – which meant that the numbers of Europeans had to be increased considerably while the sepoys were to be limited. To achieve this, the numbers of European troops stationed in India grew from around 40,000 to 60,000 while the total number of sepoys was reduced from around 230,000 to 120,000. One side effect of this was to raise the cost of the Indian army, for European soldiers worked out to be almost twice as expensive as their Indian counterparts.

The other guiding principle was to continue to frustrate the possibilities of a combined revolt across all three presidencies. The principle of divide and rule became even more entrenched. The Madras and Bombay Armies would continue to be used to counterbalance the Bengal Army, and the Bengal Army would be recast so as to prevent combinations within it. The principle, articulated here by the Secretary for India, was that, 'If one regiment mutinies I should like to have the next so alien that it would fire into it.'[40] The Hindustani sepoys who had previously dominated its ranks would be offset by increasing the flow of recruits from the Punjab, and especially from within the Sikh community. In 1857, Purbiyas (Hindustani recruits from eastern Awadh and western Bihar) comprised 48 per cent of the native army whereas Sikhs, Pathans and Punjabi Muslims made up only 10 per cent. Forty years later these figures were almost reversed with Purbiyas numbering only 9 per cent and Sikhs, Pathans and Punjabi Muslims amounting to 44 per cent.[41] In addition, care was taken to make certain that the sepoys were not given access to the most up-to-date weapons. Their rifles were usually one generation behind those given to British troops and earlier injunctions to prevent sepoys from gaining access to or knowledge about artillery were repeated.[42] Such restrictions would carry over into the twentieth century, partly out of fear that the British should not arm their sepoys too well and partly out of a conviction that the kind of wars that sepoys would fight did not require access to the full panoply of new weaponry. Such precautions meant that sepoys were ill-prepared for the type of warfare that they would find in the two world wars.

There was a consensus that the British would have to lessen their dependence on the high-caste Purbiyas by incorporating other communities. But rather than widen their base of recruitment, the British chose instead to continue to select from a narrow range of what would become known as martial races and castes.[43] Martial race doctrine, at least in principle, rested on the notion that some 'races' were innately more warlike than others. While this doctrine carried most before it, the question of what constituted a 'race' went unresolved as the categories used blended together somewhat haphazardly ethnic, linguistic, religious and occupational criteria. Handbooks describing the martial races and castes were produced under official sponsorship.[44] A key figure was Lord Roberts, one of the more influential commanders-in-chief in India, who insisted that 'In the British Army the superiority of one regiment over another is mainly a matter of training . . . but no comparison can be made between the martial value of a regiment recruited from amongst the Gurkhas of Nepal or the warlike races of northern India, and of one recruited from the effeminate peoples of the south'.[45] Not surprisingly the criteria used to measure martial qualities reflected British values and experiences. With a few exceptions, the Gurkhas for example,[46] the most martial 'races' were those which were fairer skinned, taller, and generally more European in their appearance. There was also a decidedly rural bias, with city dwellers being dismissed as cowardly and clever (cleverness was definitely not an asset in a colonial army).

The persistence of martial race doctrine in the armies of its two successor states – India and Pakistan – is proof of the ability of colonial ideologies to penetrate deeply into colonized societies. The Indian Army of today continues to be dominated by recruits from the same regions as were favoured by the British, though to a somewhat lesser degree. In the 1930s, nearly 40 per cent of the Indians taken as officer cadets came from the Punjab – between 1978 and 1982 that number had dropped to 21 per cent.[47] Yet the population of the Punjab comprises less than 5 per cent of the population of India; thus the so-called martial races continue to be over-represented. In Pakistan there is also a clear preference for Punjabis.

Martial race doctrines also had an impact on the British themselves, for they contributed to the construction of the archetypal British officer. Recruits from the martial races were depicted as sturdy, manly and brave – but they lacked initiative and vision, which meant that their true fighting potential could only be realized once they had been placed under a British officer. As Lord Roberts explained, 'The Natives of India are particularly observant of character, and intelligent in gauging the capabilities of those who govern them'.[48] At issue here is character, an ideal that in some cases undercut the drive towards professionalism. While service in India, like other colonial theatres, frequently allowed junior officers to gain experience more quickly than elsewhere owing to the practice of deploying troops in small packets, it also served as a check on other forms of professionalism. There was an anti-intellectual tradition in the Indian Army, one which privileged character over education as the foundation for the ideal British officer. As the popular novelist G.A. Henty put it, 'Give me a lad with pluck and spirit and I don't care a snap of the fingers whether he can construe Euripides or solve a problem in higher mathematics. What we want for India are men who can ride and shoot'.[49] It is worth noting that intellectual agility was one of the traits invoked in declaring some groups like the Bengalis to be non-martial. Yet not all officers necessarily subscribed to an anti-intellectual culture. There is much evidence of intellectual activity on the part of the officers of the Indian Army; a number fancied themselves as writers and they collectively supported a number of professional journals. In particular, the demands of frontier warfare were the subject of considerable study.[50]

The first question facing decision-makers in the nineteenth and twentieth centuries was whether the colonial army in India was intended to be a colonial gendarmerie in which internal tranquillity and the integrity of India's frontiers were to be given priority (the near unanimous position taken in India), or whether it was to provide an imperial rapid-reaction force designed to shore up Britain's global commitments (a view favoured in London). In his famous aphorism of 1882, Lord Salisbury declared India to be 'an English barrack in the Oriental seas.'[51] One of the major benefits that the British derived from India was the access it gave them to the military resources of the subcontinent. India was unique among British colonies, for not only were the British able to charge the costs of Indian troops against Indian revenues (a legacy of the days of East India Company Rule, 1600–1858), but the British government could also levy fees on India for the use of British troops there. Hence, the War Office squirreled away units of the British Army in India where they were hidden from the scrutiny of politicians eager to reduce the size of the army estimates.[52] The Indian government did try to limit demands made on it and was partially successful in having some of its costs transferred back onto the British Exchequer.[53] Their opposition was based partly on the financial consequences, but was also informed by a different strategic vision. For them, the ultimate purpose of the Indian Army was to defend Britain's Indian Empire, and not necessarily the empire as a whole.

Twice in the nineteenth century (1840–2 and 1857–60) were Indian troops used to force Chinese consumers to accept British merchandise, more particularly opium.[54] Still more would be dispatched during the Boxer Rebellion (1900–1). Indian troops also featured in the the short-lived British occupation of Java (1811–14) and in operations against French possessions in the Indian Ocean. Africa was another destination for Indian troops, with sepoys present in the British invasion of Egypt (1799–1801), the Sudan Campaign (1884–5) as well as making up the majority of the troops dispatched on the punitive expedition sent to Abyssinia (1867–8). There were, however, limits to the use of Indian troops. Crucial among these was the fear of encouraging Indian troops to see themselves as militarily equal to Europeans. Such misgivings gained added currency in the aftermath of the Japanese defeat of Russia in 1905, which suggested that Asians were a match for Europeans. In the First World War, the War Office reluctantly accepted some Indian units for service on the Western Front. Most of the units were offered by Indian Princes and to refuse them would have made for political problems in India. But posting them to the Western Front made for a number of imperial dilemmas. What would happen, for instance, if they proved to be just as good as their opponents? Would this lessen their respect for whites and thereby begin to erode the foundations of British rule? Connected to these concerns was the anxiety that Indian troops might engage in sexual relations with European women, which would only further diminish European prestige.[55] Such reservations were still in place during the Second World War; while the Allies' insatiable appetite for manpower led to Indian troops featuring in all of the major theatres, the British did wherever possible try and limit their use to North Africa and Asia. This was a decision which while justified on such pragmatic grounds as distance and acclimatization also spoke to deeper issues of race and identity in the colonial army.

From an Anglo-Indian perspective, the strategic imperative after 1800 was to secure India from attack, either from within or without. As far as external attacks were concerned, the big question was where India ought to be defended – a forward defence was favoured by many, but the question was how far forward it ought to be. The British in the eighteenth century had reason to fear a seaborne attack, for the French still had designs on India and were actively intriguing with Indian powers. But the potential for a seaborne threat diminished rapidly after 1800 owing to the Royal Navy's growing domination of the Indian Ocean, the defeat of Mysore in 1799 and the fact that French interest in India had waned.[56] This left an overland invasion from the north west as the only serious threat; this was the route through which India had been invaded in the past, and herein lies the origins of what became known as the Great Game. Debate continues as to whether there ever really was a serious Russian threat (probably not), whether contemporaries deliberately exaggerated this threat (some undoubtedly did).[57] Few Russian officials seriously contemplated an invasion of India. But they knew that by gaining influence in Central Asia, they could keep the British off balance and thereby force concessions in Europe. Ultimately, however, the question of whether the Russians (or Soviets) ever intended to invade India, or for that matter whether they had the means to do so, becomes irrelevant: the chief concern was not so much a direct invasion, but rather the belief within the subcontinent that such a possibility existed, for that belief could serve to incite those who wished to rise against colonial rule. Strategic planning in British India could not separate internal and external threats: they were inextricably bound together.

The British consequently directed considerable effort at securing their North West frontier. While some advocated using either the Sutlej or later the Indus Rivers as a natural frontier, others advocated a much more ambitious plan of forward defence.[58] Until 1838 this led some to put their faith in alliances with Persia. After 1838, attention switched to Afghanistan. As a contemporary noted, it was to be a 'strictly defensive war – only the lines of defence are carried more forward'.[59] This is not imperial double-speak: instead, it encapsulates the key strategic principle, namely that it was necessary to establish a firewall between external threats and potentially explosive combinations in India. In the words of the author just cited, 'the farther we can remove the seat of war from India, the safer is India in our hands.'[60]

This emphasis on a forward line of defence was also informed by the degree to which issues of military security had saturated Anglo-Indian society (meaning British residents in India). Throughout its history, British India had many of the hallmarks of a garrison state. As one early and influential Indian governor put it, 'all my notions of Indian politics begin and end in a powerful army'.[61] The considerable though not necessarily uncontested influence enjoyed by the military in India should not be under-estimated, for it fostered a form of colonial militarism. Militarism is a term that can all too easily lead to apoplectic fits among British historians, for they have assumed that of all the characteristics which have come to define the British state, a deeply-rooted suspicion of the army is one of the most persistent, and consequently, they contend, the army in Britain, at least since 1688, has never been as politicized as armies have become in Europe, Latin America or elsewhere.[62] While it is true that colonial forces in India did prefer the barracks to the barricades, this is not the same thing as arguing that they were apolitical. Instead, the military was able to exert a profound influence on imperial policy-making not through conflict with the civil authorities but by being allied with them. One official felt pressed to remind Lord Dalhousie, governor general in 1850, that 'public opinion is essentially military in India. Military views, feelings and interests are therefore paramount'.[63]

The militarization of colonial rule can be attributed to a number of factors. For much of the nineteenth century, Europeans in military dress outnumbered Europeans in civilian clothes. Even when that was no longer the case, the military remained a large and vocal community. Many of the key civil and political offices were manned by seconded military officers. There were also a number of occasions when governors or governors-general were men of military background (for example Hastings, Bentinck and Hardinge in the nineteenth century and Wavell and Mountbatten in the twentieth century). The importance accorded to the army also drew upon prevailing interpretations of Indian history that insisted that Indian society had not reached a state where despotism could yield to civil society. Officials in India were quick to remind observers in Britain that European notions of the separation of the sword from the state, like European notions of a balance of power, were inapplicable to India.[64]

Moreover, military views and influences were bolstered by the tendency to depict India in terms redolent of feudalism and chivalry. By framing India in such a way, the British were better able to justify the hierarchies that bolstered their authority in India.[65] This medieval mania reached its apogee in the 1877 Darbar, a huge gathering of British and Indian notables convened to commemorate the declaration of Queen Victoria as Empress of India.[66] Military themes pervaded its organization and staging, impressing Roberts who proclaimed it a great success.[67] While the more strident manifestations of medievalism ebbed away, British officials were still susceptible to viewing India through sepia lenses. Edward Lutyens exclaimed that India 'makes one very Tory and pre-Tory feudal'.[68] Similar sentiments can be found among twentieth century officers and colonial officials. The soldier-scholar Francis Yeats-Brown, author of *Bengal Lancer*, writing of his experience in interwar India, declared that 'Western civilization bullied and bored me. . . . Here in India I was finding myself'.[69] But beneath the brash confidence which often marked writings on India lay a profound sense of anxiety. Anglo–Indian militarism was paradoxically both a reflection of British confidence and arrogance, and an outlet for deeply rooted anxieties which stemmed from the realization that they were ultimately a beleaguered garrison.

This militarization of colonial rule neither completely pervaded colonial culture nor did it remain at a constant level. Not surprisingly it peaked during times of crisis and was strongest in the earliest phases when the army played a larger role in consolidating colonial authority, a time also when its personnel outnumbered civilians in the Anglo-Indian community. As the number of Europeans in India grew, of whom an increasing percentage were civilians, the military's grip on Anglo-Indian culture and institutions weakened but never gave out. Events like the Indian Revolt of 1857–8 reminded contemporaries of just how vulnerable they were. Even those who were suspicious of the army and its intentions hardly needed convincing of the tenuous basis of British authority. The famed Victorian legal expert Sir James Fitzjames Stephen's enthusiastic support for a moral foundation for law and authority did not extend to India where he declared that British rule was and would remain 'essentially an absolute government, founded not on consent but on conquest'.[70] As noted earlier, the doubts expressed in the 1940s about whether the British could retain their military grip on India – which arose largely from unmistakable signs that the discipline of their Indian military and naval personnel was collapsing – helped hasten Britain's departure.

This is not to say that enthusiasm for the military and for military solutions completely erased the boundaries between civilians and the military. In fact, as events in the eighteenth, nineteenth and even the twentieth centuries have shown, relations were often quite turbulent as officers and civilians fought over their respective rights and privileges.[71] Such struggles reached the highest levels of the government as the authority of the commander-in-chief remained a sticking point throughout the colonial period. To offset the influence of the commander-in-chief, and thereby make the army more accountable, it was decided in 1834 that the governing council would not only include the commander-in-chief but also a military member, chosen by the government, and charged with supervising the administration of the army. Implicit in this model was the idea that the commander-in-chief would deal with questions of command and discipline; the military member would address logistical and organizational matters. While fine on paper, in practice the commander-in-chief and the military member were often at odds with one another, with the commander-in-chief looking to London and the Horse Guards for support and the military member depending on the governor-general. One Viceroy who had experienced this situation described the commander-in-chief as

> a mighty independent autocrat, ruling the vast force which we have in this country, surrounded by devotees of both sexes who depend upon him for promotion, healthy stations, leave of absence, and all that gives security to life or makes it worth living in such a climate, and controlled, in so far as he is under control, by the Gov. Gen. in Council, in which Council the military department is represented by an officer subordinate to himself.[72]

This system persisted until 1906 when the military member was removed after an especially acrimonious row between the Viceroy, Lord Curzon, and the commander-in-chief, Lord Kitchener, which ended with Curzon's resignation. Kitchener's victory, however, was short-lived for he was held responsible for the disastrous Mesopotamian expedition of 1915–16. The Government of India had dispatched an army with the intention of marching up the Euphrates and seizing Baghdad, thereby weakening the Ottoman Empire. Military authorities in India had seriously underestimated the fighting capabilities and determination of their opponents, and logistical support for the expedition was completely inadequate to the army's needs.[73] They were surrounded at Kut-al-Amara by the Turks who beat back all efforts at breaking through to the besieged army. The encircled army of 14,000 eventually surrendered after a siege of nearly five months and many succumbed to disease or ill treatment at the hands of their captors.[74] A committee of enquiry pinned much of the responsibility for this on the organizational changes made by Kitchener to the Indian Army.

Another important consequence that this militarization of Anglo-Indian society had upon British military operations in India is the premium it set on vigorous and decisive action. The rules of the game dictated that even when the British were on the defensive, they could not be seen to be acting defensively. The axiom that the best defence is a good offence acquired a particular resonance in India. As one commander-in-chief put it, 'We are in the position of Champion of England; we must fight whenever neighbouring nations throw down the gauntlet'.[75] Strategically this led to a fixation on the decisive battle; tactically it inclined commanders to adopt the principle of the frontal attack that was targeted at a strategic asset such as the enemy's main army or their capital.

Such frontal attacks often displayed little tactical finesse, with the consequence that casualties were quite high. And when facing a well-armed, well-positioned and determined opponent, such as the Sikhs, victory could be left in doubt. At the Battle of Sobroan (1846), for example, the British were confronted with such a scenario. The commander-in-chief described the Sikh defences as consisting of a 'triple line of breast-works, flanked by formidable redoubts, bristling with artillery, and manned by thirty-two regular regiments of infantry'.[76] Another officer explained that the Sikh position was 'in the shape of a half moon, the flanks resting upon the river, ditch of 4 or 5 feet wide and deep outside and inside nearly all round, with a rampart several feet high, bristling with cannon, upwards of seventy pieces, and defended by 45,000 men who lined the ramparts throughout in many places four and five deep'.[77] An officer in the initial wave recollected a 'storm of grape, canister and musquetry which knocked our poor lads over like nine pins'.[78] The British were successful at Sobroan, and ultimately over the Sikhs, but much of the credit, if it can be called that, goes to the Sikh court, which in an effort to bring their army under control deliberately sought to sabotage its chances of victory.

The need to show an offensive spirit also encouraged risky operations out of fear of losing the momentum. During the Second Afghan War, for example, the commander, Lord Roberts, gambled on a quick march from Kabul to Kandahar with a comparatively lightly equipped force: only 8000 followers for a force of 10,000, as compared to armies in the past that had marched with baggage trains which in some cases had outnumbered the troops by a factor of four to one.[79]

This search for decisive battles proved to be quite elusive when fighting against opponents like the Burmese, the Nepalese or the Pathans who, unlike the Sikhs or before them the Marathas and Mysore, not only subscribed to a different set of strategic principles but lacked the kinds of assets that made for a tempting target. It seems paradoxical at first, but in colonial warfare the stronger and better organized the opponent, the easier they often fell to Europeans. There are exceptions – the Sikh Wars for example – but it was often the case that the most difficult wars of conquest were those fought against societies that had not developed permanent standing armies. Standing armies encouraged rulers to undertake lengthy wars of manoeuvre in which the Europeans had an edge because their pockets were deeper and their resources more extensive. Moreover, standing armies required complex infrastructures, which once destroyed or co-opted could not be easily rebuilt. In other words, the British were stymied as long as their opponents refused a set-piece battle and did not have any strategic assets that could be captured and ransomed.

This was certainly the case with the long-running effort by the British to stabilize India's North West Frontier (the longest land frontier in the British Empire), a region populated by Pathans and other groups who successfully used guerrilla-style tactics to limit British authority over the area. They lacked tight military organization, but this proved to be an advantage for they generally avoided set-piece actions. Instead, their preferred tactics were to control the higher ground, and from there harass the slower-moving columns of the British. Equipped initially with long-barrelled rifled muskets known as *jezails*, which were not only more accurate but had a greater range than anything with which the British were then equipped, and later with more up-to-date rifles of European manufacture, the tribesmen of the North West Frontier successfully limited British inroads into their mountainous hideouts.[80] Sir William Lockhart's address to British regulars in the aftermath of the Tirah campaign speaks to the difficulties of fighting such a foe: 'We must remember that we are opposed to perhaps the best skirmishers and the best natural shots in the world, and that the country they inhabit is the most difficult on the face of the globe'.[81] But when the Pathans were drawn into fixed battles, they generally lost.

The British did develop tactics intended to counter Pathan warfare, and at least in part these were successful. They learned to try to control the high ground, and developed a less cumbersome logistical system that enabled them to move more quickly.[82] In January 1853, for example, redcoats gave way to khaki (which meant that they did not stand out so much), and later officers learned to shed their rank insignia that singled them out for Pathan snipers. The more astute soldiers and sepoys had already learned that they could extend their life expectancy by not standing too close to their officers. The weapons, drill and organization of rifle corps were adopted as the norm. Changes were also made to the artillery: the origins of pack artillery can be traced to this. Eventually air power was also employed. The Royal Air Force was keen to play a role along the frontier, advertising its services as a cost-effective alternative to large columns of troops weighed down with cumbersome supply trains. It even proposed in 1931 that it be given authority over the frontier. But the Government of India was reluctant to turn over too much of the role of frontier policing to the air force, so the RAF was largely confined to supporting the army.[83] The limits placed on the RAF came in part because its methods were seen to be incompatible with the techniques of control used along the frontier – particularly the use of local levies to police their own communities – and partly because of the army's unwillingness to concede too much to the upstart service.

But the British (or for that matter their successors in Pakistan) could never fully overcome Pathan opposition, nor were the Burmese a pushover. This had prompted one commander-in-chief to conclude that 'success in negotiations is of much more importance than success in protracted warfare'.[84] The only alternative, and one which featured more and more in later campaigns in Burma and the North West Frontier, was a scorched-earth policy aimed at denying shelter and provisions to their opponents. In the words of Charles Callwell, the author of the standard work on low-intensity warfare (then called 'Small Wars'):

> But when there is no king to conquer, no capital to seize, no organized army to overthrow, and where there are no celebrated strongholds to capture, and no great centres of population to occupy, the objective is not so easy to select. It is then that the regular troops are forced to resort to cattle lifting and village burning and that the war assumes an aspect which may shock the humanitarian.[85]

But such a strategy had its own risks; all too often it aroused further resentment against British rule.

The combination of factors that had enabled British success in the nineteenth century, and the attitudes that stemmed from such victories, did not prove as useful in the twentieth century. The Indian army was ill-prepared for the nature of combat in the two world wars, its administration and organization had difficulty coping with the huge demands for men and material, and the Army was increasingly out of step with the rapidly changing nature of Indian society. The Indian Army in 1914, while impressively large on paper, was in fact badly prepared for the kind of war in which it would shortly be engaged. There were

155,000 troops under arms, but they were geared towards frontier warfare. They had little by way of artillery support, most of their batteries were of mountain guns, and their training had left them ill-equipped for modern European warfare. The eighteen battalions that were shipped to France in 1914 were doomed to fail. They had not been trained for trench warfare, and they were poorly armed and provisioned. Most had been trained with the North West Frontier in mind – conditions that were about as far from the Western Front as one could get.[86] As the fighting and conditions along the Front ground them down, morale began to suffer and the numbers of self-inflicted wounds grew alarmingly.[87] Moreover, the reasons for their failure had already been well rehearsed – Indian soldiers were just not up to it, and their shortcomings became even more obvious once they were deprived of their officers.

Eventually a total of 1,200,000 Indians were recruited for service in World War I (twice that number would be recruited in World War II, making it the largest volunteer army that the world had yet seen). Yet there was no well-conceived plan to expand the army rapidly following the outbreak of war. The system of caste and class companies, which ensured close cohesion within companies while frustrating combinations between battalions, also meant that soldiers could not be easily transferred. Nor could their traditional recruiting grounds easily meet the cranked-up demand for manpower. The Punjab had been denuded of most of its immediately available manpower. Elsewhere in India recruiters had to compete with agriculture, which was booming, and manufacturing, which had expanded in response to wartime demand. This led to some difficulties at the outset in getting enough recruits, but they eventually managed to raise their numbers without having to stretch too far the definition of 'martial race' (though the definition of 'martial race' came to include 75 groups which had hitherto been excluded).[88] Pressure was particularly brought to bear on the Punjab from whence came nearly 60 per cent of all combat troops raised in India during the war.[89] Local élites assisted British recruiters, identifying and in many cases pressuring recruits, in return for which their own political and economic standing was enhanced. This led the governor to boast that the ratio of soldiers to adult males had gone from 1:150 to 1:44 in one district.[90] The Punjab became even more militarized, a situation which would have profound effects in the future for India and Pakistan.[91]

Outright opposition to the war (such as would become apparent in World War Two) was largely absent. As late as 1918, Gandhi was urging Indians to 'crowd the battlefields of France with an indomitable army of home rulers fighting for the cause of the Allies' which in turn would help the 'fight for our own causes'.[92] Imperial participation was still seen as compatible with nationalist aspirations. But that would quickly change. Rapid demobilization complicated post-war readjustments. An army which had peaked at 500,000 in 1918 was reduced to 120,000 in 1923. The war had also widened the horizons of many Indians who had served under the British; they began to question colonial rule. They came away from the experience with a clearer sense of being

Indian – a national identity, albeit somewhat incomplete and unstable, was a by-product of the war and though this sense of being Indian did not entirely displace other more localized identities, it did help transcend them.

In April 1919 General Dyer responded to growing protests against British authority in the city of Amritsar in the Punjab with the imposition of martial law. A crowd, including veterans and their families, had gathered at Jallianwallabagh apparently unaware that martial law had been declared. Dyer ordered his troops to fire and even conservative estimates place the death toll at 379 with a further 1200 wounded.[93] More would probably have died if narrow lanes had not prevented an armoured car from being brought up or had not the troops' ammunition run out. As he put it to the commission that was struck to enquire into his actions, 'It was no longer a question of merely dispersing the crowd, but one of producing a sufficient moral effect, from a military point of view, not only on those who were present, but more specifically throughout the Punjab'.[94] Dyer was eventually vindicated, but it was a pyrrhic victory. It exposed the flawed logic that had underpinned so much military thinking in India.

The British responded somewhat half-heartedly to nationalist demands that the army be made more accountable with what became known as the policy of 'Indianization', in which Indians were to be slowly introduced into the officer ranks of the Indian Army. Its roots go back into the nineteenth century when some of the more enlightened officers had raised the possibility of allowing Indians to gain commissioned rank in the Indian Army. Native officers had long existed, but these were distinct from and subordinate to British commissioned officers and had become little more than sinecures intended to reward long-serving sepoys. The more far-sighted realized that Indianization would help to win over moderate nationalists. But they fought a constant battle against those who either believed that Indians lacked the 'right stuff' to be officers, or if they possessed it were likely to turn it against their colonial rulers. The end result was a compromise that did little to meet Indian aspirations, as the supply of Indian officers was restricted and their place in the army severely curtailed. Known at first as King's Commissioned Officers, these officers of Indian origin, while initially trained to British standards at Sandhurst (and after 1932 in the Indian Military Academy at Dehra Dun from which they were ranked as Indian Commissioned Officers) could only serve in the Indian Army and even then their options were limited to a few designated units.[95] In addition, the number of Indians admitted to Sandhurst was originally capped at twenty for the cavalry and infantry (initially in 1917 it was set at ten) combined with six more to be divided between the artillery, engineers and signal corps. While these numbers would increase over time, the second-rate status of Indian Commissioned Officers was apparent to the end.

The Indian Army was being pulled in too many directions. It was expected to prepare for modern industrial warfare, it still had to maintain authority along the fractious North West Frontier and it was increasingly called upon to help maintain public order at a time of rising nationalist activity. In order to make the Indian Army more efficient for possible use in a European-style war as well as more acceptable to Indian public opinion, it would have to be modernized and more opportunities created in it for Indians. Yet memories of 1857 still lingered and to upgrade the weapons of the Indian army, or allow more Indians to become officers, was for many colonial officials an unacceptable cost. Even something as minor as electric lighting came to separate British soldiers from Indian sepoys – the formers' barracks were electrified long before sepoy barracks.[96] At the same time, the Indian Army had to fulfil its obligations as an imperial gendarmerie – assisting the civil authorities cope with the growing incidence of popular protest as well as maintaining authority along the explosive North West Frontier. The North West Frontier continued to be ridden with conflict. The Pathans were also becoming better armed. It was estimated in the years after World War One that there were nearly half a million tribesmen, mostly armed with breech-loading rifles. There were even some light machine guns and locally crafted artillery.[97] The limited authority enjoyed by the British in this area became all too apparent when a rebellion in 1936 required the dispatch of a force of 60,000 troops backed by light armoured cars and even air power. These frontier campaigns also revealed just how vulnerable communications could be. Wireless was in its infancy, and landlines could be and were often cut by rebels who realized that telegraphs were not only symbols of colonial rule but instruments of it as well.[98]

Support in aid of the civil authorities became a growing concern for the interwar army, an unpopular service for it tested the discipline and morale of the army. There was little training in appropriate tactics and so officers had to improvise. As one officer recollected from his years in Peshawar, the troops would assemble with weapons ready, 'a bugle would sound and a banner would be unfurled with "Disperse or I fire" written in Hindi and Urdu, at which point many crowds would break up. Should that not be the case, one of the best shots would be directed to shoot one of the leaders, usually in one of the extremities.'[99] One officer complained that battalions that had worked in internal security for three or four years were effectively burned out and unserviceable.[100] If resources limited the Indian Army's capacity to prepare for modern industrialized warfare, apathy appears to have limited its attention to training and preparing for hill and jungle warfare.[101]

In 1939, the Indian Army was decidedly low-tech and ill-suited to the kinds of warfare with which the Indian army would have to contend in the forthcoming war. They were highly trained, but trained and perhaps more importantly equipped to fight the wrong kind of war. Hill warfare was not the only training that troops and officers in India received, but it was the most likely kind of service they would see besides internal security and it was the kind of fighting for which they were equipped.

World War Two witnessed another tremendous increase in both the size of the Indian Army as well as the demands placed upon it. In 1939, there were just over 200,000 troops and officers in the Indian Army plus another 70,000 members of the British Army stationed in India. Three years later there were 900,000 and by the time the war ended, the Indian Army had grown to 2,500,000 men. Yet it found itself overstretched, being called upon to help cover Africa and the Middle East, maintain authority within India at a time of intensified nationalist activity, continue to police the North West Frontier, and eventually contend with Japan's entry into the war. As late as 1944, nearly 38 per cent of the peace-time strength of the Indian Army remained posted to the North West Frontier, so worried were the British that a breakdown of the fragile peace there might spread to the rest of India. Another large chunk of the army was engaged in re-establishing British authority over much of northern India, which had broken into revolt with the Quit India movement of 1942. Some 57 battalions were deployed to deal with these troubles.[102] Even aircraft were used against the protesters.[103] The situation was further complicated by the outbreak of a famine in 1943, which when combined with wartime shortages and the British sequestering of transport and supplies led to an estimated one million deaths.

Other challenges to the Indian Army came with the outbreak of war with Japan. Not only did Japan capture Burma and begin to press on India's eastern frontiers; British defeats in the Malayan Peninsula established the preconditions for the emergence of a nationalist army ranged against the British, the Indian National Army (INA).[104] Established shortly after the fall of Singapore in 1942 by Captain Mohan Singh, an ex-officer in the Indian Army, the INA would eventually expand under the leadership of the charismatic Indian nationalist Subhas Chandra Bose to number some 40,000 recruits, drawn from Indian servicemen captured in South East Asia and from Indian expatriates in Malaysia and Burma. There was even a women's brigade, named the Rani of Jhansi regiment in honour of the rebel hero from 1857. Most recruits to the INA were inspired by nationalism, though it was often tinged by unpleasant experiences of racist slurs and the feeling that they had been shamelessly abandoned by the British. Support for the INA was especially strong in Bengal, in part because that was Bose's political base and also because the INA offered opportunities for Bengalis to prove their martial qualities and masculinity that had been denied them by the prevailing theories of martial race. The actual military impact of the INA was negligible. They were poorly armed and equipped, and the Japanese government had little faith in them. Their only battle experience came late in the war as the Japanese were being forced to fall back from their positions in Burma. Morale collapsed and many soldiers in the INA deserted or surrendered to the advancing British.

The fact that so many Indian troops were willing to join the INA pointed to one of the biggest problems facing the British in World War Two; the degree to which they could not count upon the loyalty of either their Indian soldiers or their Indian subjects. Japanese shipping and air attacks in the Indian Ocean did not trigger widespread resistance to the British in Sri Lanka or southern

India.[105] But there was always a lurking apprehension that should things go badly for the British, their normally loyal troops might turn on them. Some of the army's responses to the challenge of nationalism were quite subtle and sophisticated. Censorship was used on the sepoys, but rather than try to delete all signs of disaffection or disillusionment, the army encouraged sepoys to write frankly. These letters could then be studied, grievances identified and responded to, and propaganda could be more carefully prepared so as to counter rumours and complaints.[106] While these techniques did reduce stresses within the Indian Army and probably helped to prevent the collapse of discipline within the army as a whole, censors' reports clearly revealed that there were limits to the loyalty of Indian soldiers and officers, and that the British would soon be rubbing up against those limits. One such indication came when it was announced that Indian troops would be used in South East Asia to help restore the French and Dutch empires. Lord Wavell, the Viceroy of India, was opposed to this decision but he was overruled by Lord Mountbatten, who was supreme Allied Commander in South East Asia.[107] At the same time, the government was coming round to the view that the growth of popular nationalism was such that it could not be easily contained in the future. The British were able to deal with Quit India in 1942–3 because they were already on a war footing, and hence had the resources and perhaps even more importantly the will and the backing at home to confront the nationalists.

Meanwhile, no matter how unsuccessful the INA was on the battlefield, it did score a tremendous propaganda victory in the immediate aftermath of the war. The British were determined to try members of the INA for desertion and mutiny, which in turn galvanized nationalist opposition.[108] The trials, held in Delhi's Red Fort, began badly for the British. The first three defendants they wheeled out just happened to include a Hindu, a Muslim and a Sikh, suggesting to the viewing public that the INA did represent all of India. These trials were then followed by a series of mutinies in the Royal Indian Navy that took place in February 1946 and which ultimately involved some 78 ships, 20 shore establishments and nearly 20,000 sailors.[109] Much was made by nationalists of these striking sailors, and the mutinies have often been written up as politically motivated. While no doubt some sailors and petty officers were energized by the nationalist activities around them, the underlying motives behind these strikes now appear to be rather more prosaic, involving questions of pay, rank and shipboard conditions.[110]

The Congress leadership opposed the trials and also spoke in favour of the naval protests: they had little choice, for to do otherwise would undermine their nationalist credentials. But it is clear that many in the Congress were of two minds about the INA, wondering what impact freeing them might have on the Indian Army that would shortly be divided between the governments of independent India and Pakistan. Indian officers who had remained loyal to the British and who as nationalists were ready to serve the successor states worried that INA officers might be reinstated and given preference. This was not the case. While Congress and to a lesser extent the Muslim League came out in support of the INA, once the trials were over interest in and talk about the INA fell away. A general amnesty was issued, but members of the INA were not generally welcomed into either of the two successor armies.[111]

Independence brought with it the first in a series of armed clashes between the two successor states. The flashpoint was and continues to be the mountain kingdom of Jammu-Kashmir, a princely state under the British. According to the rules governing partition, princely states were expected to declare for either Pakistan or India.[112] The Maharaja of Kashmir chose instead to dither: he was in an awkward position, for he was a Hindu ruling a largely Muslim population inhabiting lands that lay between India and Pakistan. Pakistan helped incite a rebellion against his authority, and out of desperation he turned to India for help. Assistance, however, came at a cost: India insisted that Kashmir become part of India. Once the Maharaja agreed, Indian troops moved into Kashmir and regained control over two-thirds of the state, leaving the northern third in Pakistan's hands. The war ended with a truce that created a line of control separating the two sides. Pakistan, however, refuses to recognize the line of control and has on a number of occasions attempted to use military force to lessen India's control over Kashmir.

Another legacy of colonialism that has had military ramifications is India's frontier with China, a border which the Chinese government refused to recognize on the ground that it had been imposed by the British. Hints that the Chinese were determined to settle this with force went unheeded in India, where the government of Jawaharlal Nehru showed little interest in military or strategic affairs. The resulting Indo-Chinese War (1962) was an unmitigated disaster for India and for its army.[113] Thousands of Indian soldiers died in the chaotic fighting in the far north west and north east provinces of India, 14,000 square miles of territory were lost, and in fact the losses would have been much greater had the Chinese not halted their advance on their own initiative. The situation seemed so desperate to Jawaharlal Nehru that he called President Kennedy to request American assistance in the form of air cover for India's cities, which he feared would become vulnerable to Chinese attacks.[114] Army and air force units were ill-prepared for the conflict, and the logistical system collapsed as quickly as did the command structure. The search for scapegoats, which began almost immediately, pitted civilians against the military – which only made the direction of the war even more difficult.

In 1965 Pakistan gambled and lost heavily. Believing that the Kashmir issue could be solved only by force, decision-makers in Pakistan decided that the time was ripe for war. India was still reeling from the disastrous Indo-Chinese War and it was felt that any delay would put Pakistan at a disadvantage, for the Indians had commenced an ambitious plan of re-armament. The Pakistan government also seriously over-estimated the degree of support they could expect from the people of Kashmir. The anticipated popular uprisings did not materialize. Moreover, India's defeat at the hands of the Chinese appeared to confirm for many Pakistani officers (most of whom were Punjabi) the truth behind British claims that most Indians were weak and unwarlike.[115] Pakistan's generals were also counting on a short war, one in which they could make the most of their shorter lines of communication. They had assumed that India would not counter-attack quickly, and that when it did the attack would come in Kashmir. Instead, the Indian Army attacked through the Punjab, sending armoured columns into the heartland of Pakistan, threatening centres such as Sialkot and Lahore. At the former city, nearly 600 tanks fought an indecisive battle.

India's victory in the war was not as decisive as post-war propaganda would have us believe. While the official history of the war (along with that of the 1971 war) has yet to be officially released by the Government of India, the *Times of India* did however get hold of a copy and made sections of it available.[116] The litany of mistakes and missed opportunities contained within it hint at a number of colonial legacies. For one thing, there was very poor co-ordination between the services. The Indian Air Force had not been told about the army's planned counter-attack towards Lahore and therefore was not only unable to provide close air support but its aircraft were also dangerously exposed to attacks from Pakistan's air force. Communications and intelligence also failed it, and the line between political and military authority remained very blurred. When asked whether they should continue fighting or agree to a ceasefire, India's chief of army staff urged negotiation on the grounds that they were running out of ammunition and their numbers of tanks had become seriously depleted. In fact, the army had used less than 15 per cent of its ammunition as compared to Pakistan, who had consumed closer to 80 per cent (which meant that many of its 155 mm howitzers were rationed to five rounds per day) and India had double the number of serviceable tanks.[117]

The 1971 war began as internal dissension wracked Pakistan – its eastern half (now Bangladesh) felt that its interests were often sacrificed to those of western Pakistan.[118] Added to this was the fact that East Pakistan was not only Muslim but also profoundly Bengali, and did not identify culturally with West Pakistan. India was able to take advantage of the war to pry apart its long-term rival. Moreover, it had to contend with a serious refugee crisis. As India's involvement in East Pakistan grew, the government in Pakistan decided on a pre-emptive strike. It launched an air attack on India's northern airfields. This time Indian intelligence was up to the task, and combat aircraft had been stashed away in hardened bunkers. Moreover, the Indian Army had prepared itself for such a war, and had been stockpiling ammunition and spare parts for the previous nine months. India's armed forces emerged from the war with a restored reputation, putting to rest many of the doubts that had emerged in the course of the 1960s.

Relations between India and Pakistan heated up again in 1999 (not that they had ever really cooled off, for both sides maintained large garrisons in Kashmir and periodically fired salvoes against each other). Pervez Musharraf, then chief of army staff and now president, embarked on a risky strategy of trying to infiltrate men and supplies into the barren and isolated Kargil sector. Pakistani troops and rebels allied with Pakistan gained control of the higher ground, forcing Indian troops, backed with air support, to fight at altitudes of 16,000 feet and higher. Pakistan's plan appears to have been to re-ignite smouldering resistance in Kashmir. Conflict in South Asia took a more ominous tone as the two great rivals had both acquired nuclear weapons.[119]

Another manifestation of colonialism's legacy in the subcontinent is India's efforts to supplant Britain as the paramount power in the region. This can be witnessed in the Indian Army's intervention in Sri Lanka in an attempt to impose a ceasefire and eventually find a solution to the decade-long war between the Tamil Tigers and the Sri Lankan government. Persuaded to do so both by a sense of ethnic affiliation with the afflicted peoples and as a gesture intended to establish itself as a regional superpower, the well-publicized arrival of Indian peace-keepers quickly became an embarrassment. Their partiality meant that their claim to the traditional neutrality of peace-keepers rang hollow and their use of deadly force also strayed from the norms of peace-keeping.[120] The Indian troops later withdrew without having attained any of their objectives. Subsequently, what had been a vicious yet localized conflict crossed over into India with the assassination of Rajiv Gandhi, the Prime Minister of India.

The ambivalent nature of civil–military relations in colonial India also carried over into the two successor states. The situations in India and Pakistan represent two sides of Anglo-Indian militarism. In the case of India, civil supremacy has been maintained, though it is not as clear cut as once was assumed. While there would not appear to be any imminent risk of a military takeover – with one commentator declaring that 'Indian democracy is more at risk from her own politicians than her soldiers'[121] – relations between the military and their political masters has not always been as smooth as they might first appear. The Indian Army has increasingly been turned to as an instrument of policing within its territories, leading to considerable stress. The government of India appears to have reverted to a colonial model in its predilection for the use of troops to deal with troubles such as those which have rocked Kashmir for two decades, the Punjab for much of the 1980s and sporadically in India's north eastern provinces. This manifested itself most vividly in the aftermath of the Indian government's decision to storm the Sikh temple complex in Amritar (Operation Blue Star), which tested the loyalty of many Sikh soldiers and officers.[122] But a larger crisis was averted and the Indian Army has remained largely under the control of elected officials.

The situation is different in Pakistan, where civil democracy has been repeatedly challenged by military officers. There, the army has shown a frequent willingness, if not eagerness, to leave the barracks and assume political power. Much of this can be accounted for by the pre-eminence of the Punjab within the state of Pakistan. A highly militarized region under the British, in independent Pakistan the coupling together of military values and religious nationalism has proven to be especially potent. A powerful sense of regionalism has enhanced the corporate identity of the officers of the Pakistan army, uniting them at a time when the political infrastructure was proving its fragility. The instability of the political system confirmed its lack of legitimacy, creating a vacuum that the army felt only it could fill. The position taken by the officers in the Pakistan army, and the assumptions which underpin them, would not be unfamiliar to British officers of the early nineteenth century, who were just as convinced that the army had a central role to play in the political economy of the subcontinent.

Notes

1 John Malcolm (1823) *The Political History of India from 1784 to 1823*, 2 vols, London, John Murray, ii, 245.
2 W.D. Arnold (1956) 'Indian Light Literature', *Calcutta Review*, 26, 2.
3 The contours of the military revolution debate have been mapped out in a number of works. See for example Thomas M. Barker *et al.* (1997) 'Geoffrey Parker's Military Revolution: Three Reviews of the Second Edition', *Journal of Military History*, 61, 347–54; Jeremy Black (1994) *European Warfare, 1660–1815*, New Haven, Yale University Press; Kelly DeVries (1997) 'Catapults are not Atomic Bombs: Towards a Redefinition of "Effectiveness" in Premodern Military Technology', *War in History*, 4, 454–70; Victor Davis Hanson (2001) *Why the West Has Won: Carnage and Culture from Salamis to Vietnam*, London, Faber; MacGregor Knox and Williamson Murray (eds) (2001) *The Dynamics of Military Revolution, 1300–2050*, Cambridge, Cambridge University Press; John A. Lynn (1996) 'The Evolution of Army Style in the Modern West, 800–2000', *International History Review*, 18, 502–45; Geoffrey Parker (1996) *The Military Revolution: Military Innovation and the Rise of the West, 1500–1800*, 2nd edn, Cambridge, Cambridge University Press; Clifford J. Rogers (ed.) (1995) *The Military Revolution Debate*, Boulder, Co., Westview.
4 John William Kaye (1852) 'How We Talked about the Burmese War', *Bentley's Miscellany*, 32, 462.
5 F.B. Doveton (1852) *Reminiscences of the Burman War in 1824–6*, London, Allen and Co. More on the impact of medicine on the military history of the British in India can be gleaned from Mark Harrison (1996) 'Medicine and the Management of Modern Warfare', *History of Science*, 30, 379–410.
6 Arthur Wellesley and John Gurwood (1841) *Selections from the Dispatches and General Orders of Field Marshal The Duke of Wellington; by Lieut. Col. Gurwood* (London).
7 Colonel C.E. Callwell (1906) *Small Wars. Their Principles and Practice*, 3rd edn, London, HMSO, 117.
8 Stewart Gordon (1998) 'The Limited Adoption of European Style Military Forces by Eighteenth Century Rulers in India', *Indian Economic and Social History Review*, 35, 229–; Stewart Gordon (1993) *The Marathas, 1600–1818, The New Cambridge History of India*, Vol. II.4, Cambridge, Cambridge University Press. See also Surendra Nath Sen (1958) *The Military System of the Marathas*, 2nd edn, Bombay.
9 Anon (1804) *Brief Remarks on the Mahratta War and on the Rise and Progress of the French Establishment in Hindostan under Generals de Boigne and Perron*, London, T. Cadell; James Grant Duff (1863) *History of the Mahrattas*, Bombay, Exchange

Press; Colonel James Welsh (1830) *Military Reminiscences; Extracted from a Journal of Nearly Forty Years Active Service in the East Indies*, London, Smith, Elder, and Co.; Anon (1839) 'Origins, Services and Present Condition of Scindiah's Reformed Contingent', *East India United Service Journal*, 14, 225–50; Anon (1827) 'History of the Mahrattas', *Naval and Military Magazine*, 2, 476–9.

10 Welsh, op. cit., 177. There has been considerable discussion of Maratha tactics. See Channa Wickremesekera (1998) *European 'Success' and Indian 'Failure' in the Second Maratha War: A Military Analysis*, Vol. 3, Centre of South Asian Studies Working Papers, Clayton, Victoria, Monash University; John Pemble (1976) 'Resource and Techniques in the Second Maratha War', *Historical Journal*, 19, 375–404; R.G.S. Cooper (1989) 'Wellington and the Marathas in 1803', *International History Review*, 11, 31–8.

11 W.D. Arnold (1973) *Oakfield, or Fellowship in the East*, 2nd edn, New York, Humanities Press (first published in 1853).

12 Amiya Barat (1962) *The Bengal Native Infantry; Its Organisation and Discipline, 1796–1852*, Calcutta, Firma K.L. Mukhopadhyay, 155.

13 Anon (1833) 'Campaign against the Pauguls', *East India United Services Journal*, 1, 22.

14 John William Kaye (1851) *History of the War in Afghanistan*, London, Richard Bentley, i, 361.

15 Douglas Jerrold as quoted in Michael Paris (2000) *Warrior Nation: Images of War in British Popular Culture*, London, Reaktion, 25.

16 The racialized nature of much colonial warfare was by no means peculiar to the British. Parallels have been drawn with the US Army in the Philippines. Stuart Creighton Miller (1982) *'Benevolent Assimilation': The American Conquest of the Philippines, 1899–1903*, New Haven, Yale University Press. But not all agree that American forces were that brutal; see Brian McAllister Linn (2000) *The Philippine War, 1899–1902*, Lawrence, University Press of Kansas.

17 G.B. Malleson (1914) *The Decisive Battles of India, from 1746 to 1849 Inclusive*, 2nd edn, London, Reeves and Turner. His contemporary, William Irvine, wrote his history of Mughal warfare in such a way as to demonstrate why the Mughals ultimately failed and the British emerged triumphant. William Irvine (1903) *The Army of the Indian Moghuls: Its Organization and Administration*, London.

18 T. Moegling (1857) 'Indian Crisis of 1857', *Calcutta Review*, 29, 417.

19 Stewart Gordon, op. cit., 13. On the very buoyant nature of the North Indian military labour market, see also Dirk H.A. Kolff (1990) *Naukar, Rajput and Sepoy: The Ethnohistory of the Military Labour Market of Hindustan, 1450–1850*, Cambridge, Cambridge University Press. The degree to which military values and traditions penetrated Indian society is also illustrated in William Pinch (1996) *Peasants and Monks in British India*, Berkeley, University of California Press.

20 Seema Alavi (1995) *The Sepoys and the Company: Tradition and Transition in Northern India, 1770–1830*, Delhi, Oxford University Press.

21 Seema Alavi (1993) 'The Making of Company Power: James Skinner in the Ceded and Conquered Provinces, 1802–1840', *Indian Economic and Social History Review*, 30, 437–66; Broome (1856) 'Bengal Cavalry', *Calcutta Review*, 26, 549–91; Gerald Bryant (1995) 'The Cavalry Problem in the Early British Indian Army, 1750–1785', *War in History*, 2, 1–21; Lieut. G. Malcolm (1847) 'Remarks on Sillidar Cavalry', *Colburn's United Service Magazine*, 2, 583–6; Lieut G. Malcolm (1847) 'Remarks by an Officer of the Scinde Irregular Horse on an Article in the Calcutta Review for March', *Colburn's United Service Magazine*, 2, 230–44.

22 Jos Gommans and Dirk H.A. Kolff (eds) (2001) *Warfare and Weaponry in South Asia, 1000–1800*, Delhi, Oxford University Press, 31.

23 Rajat Kanta Ray, 'Indian Society and the Establishment of British Supremacy, 1765–1818', in P.J. Marshall (ed.) (1995) *The Oxford History of the British Empire: The Eighteenth Century*, Oxford University Press, 508–29.

24 The organization and re-organizing of the Indian Army is dealt with in much more detail in T.A. Heathcote (1995) *The Military in British India; the Development of British Land Forces in South Asia, 1600–1947*, Manchester, Manchester University Press.

25 Peter Stanley (1998) *White Mutiny: British Military Culture in India*, London, Hurst.

26 This is perhaps best exemplified in Philip Mason (1976) *A Matter of Honour: An Account of the Indian Army, its Officers and Men*, London, Penguin.

27 Alavi (1995) *The Sepoys and the Company*, see note 20. See also Barat (1962) *The Bengal Native Infantry*, see note 12.

28 Kaushik Roy (1997) 'Recruitment Doctrines of the Colonial Indian Army: 1850–1913', *Indian Economic and Social History Review*, 34, 321–54.

29 Seema Alavi (1993) 'The Company Army and Rural Society; the Invalid Thanah 1780–1830', *Modern Asian Studies*, 27, 147–78; Kaushik Roy (2002) 'Logistics and the Construction of Loyalty: The Welfare Mechanisms in the Indian Army, 1859–1913', in Anirudh Deshpande and Partha Sarathi Gupta (eds) (2002) *The British Raj and its Indian Army Forces, 1857–1939*, New Delhi, Oxford University Press, 98–124.

30 For the pre-Rebellion period, see Douglas M. Peers (1995) 'Sepoys, Soldiers and the Lash: Race, Caste and Army Discipline in India, 1820–1850', *Journal of Imperial History*, 23, 211–47. The post-1857 disciplinary regime is the subject of Kaushik Roy (2001) 'Coercion through Leniency: British Manipulation of the Courts-Martial System in the Post-Mutiny Indian Army, 1859–1913, *Journal of Military History*, 65, 937–64.

31 Eric Stokes (1986) *The Peasant Armed*, Oxford, Oxford University Press. See also Rudrangshu Mukherjee (1984) *Awadh in Revolt, 1857–1858: A Study in Popular Resistance*, Delhi, Oxford University Press.

32 Christon I. Archer et al. (2002) *World History of Warfare*, Lincoln, University of Nebraska Press, 472.

33 *Illustrated London News*, 31 (4 July 1857).

34 Barbara English and Rudrangshu Mukherjee (1994) 'Debate: the Kanpur Massacres in India in the Revolt of 1857', *Past and Present*, 169–89; Rudrangshu Mukherjee (1990) ' "Satan Let Loose upon Earth": the Kanpur Massacres in India in the Revolt of 1857', *Past and Present*, 92–116.

35 Anand A. Yang (1987) 'A Conversation of Rumours: the Language of Popular Mentalities in late Nineteenth-Century Colonial India', *Journal of Social History*, 20, 485–505.

36 Thomas Malcolm (1891) *Barracks and Battlefields in India; or, the Experiences of a Soldier of the 10th Foot (North Lincoln) in the Sikh Wars and Indian Mutiny*, York, John Sampson, 101–2.

37 Brigadier M.W. Smith to Charlotte Smith, 16 April 1858, MSS Eur B 169 OIOC (Oriental and India Office Collections – British Library).

38 Elgin to Wood, 22 June 1862, MSS Eur F83/3 OIOC.

39 Wood to Rose, 3 November 1861, MSS Eur F78/L.B.9 OIOC.

40 R.J. Moore (1966) *Sir Charles Wood's Indian Policy, 1853–1866*, Manchester, Manchester University Press, 223.

41 A.P. Coleman (1999) *A Special Corps: The Beginnings of Gurkha Service with the British*, Durham, Pentland Press; Roy, 'Recruitment Doctrines of the Colonial Indian Army: 1859–1913', see note 29.

42 Michael Baldwin (1997) 'Arming the Indian Army, 1857–1947', in Alan J. Guy and Peter B. Boyden (eds), *Soldiers of the Raj: the Indian Army, 1600–1947*, London, National Army Museum, 154.

43 The classic text on martial race doctrine is George MacMunn (1933) *The Martial Races of India*, London. More recent studies of this tradition can be found in David Omissi (1999) *The Sepoy and the Raj; the Indian Army, 1860–1940*, London, Macmillan; Roy (1997) 'Recruitment Doctrines of the Colonial Indian Army: 1859–1913', see note 28. It should be noted that this was not unique to India, see Anthony H.M. Kirk-Green (1980) 'Damnosa Hereditas: Ethnic Ranking and the Martial Races Imperative in Africa', *Ethnic and Racial Studies*, 3.

44 For a sampling of these, see *Recruiting Handbooks for the Indian Army*, L/Mil/5/2155–2168, OIOC.

45 Field Marshal Frederick Roberts (1905) *Forty-One Years in India, from Subaltern to Commander-in-Chief*, London, Macmillan, 532.

46 On the Gurkhas, see Lionel Caplan (1995) *Warrior Gentlemen; 'Gurkhas' in the Western Imagination*, London, Berghahn; Tony Gould (1999) *Imperial Warriors: Britain and the Gurkhas*, London, Granta. And see Coleman (1999) *A Special Corps* (note 41) for a history of the early Gurkhas that takes issue with Caplan's conclusions.

47 Stephen Peter Rosen (1996) *Societies and Military Power: India and its Armies*, Ithaca, Cornell University Press, 221.

48 Roberts, *Forty-One Years in India, from Subaltern to Commander-in-Chief*, vii (see note 45).

49 George Alfred Henty (1894) *Through the Sikh War: A Tale of the Conquest of the Punjaub, etc.*, London, Blackie & Son.

50 T.R. Moreman (1996) ' "Small Wars" and "Imperial Policing": the British Army and the Theory and Practice of Colonial Warfare in the British Empire, 1919–1939', *Journal of Strategic Studies*, 19, 105–31.

51 Peter Burroughs (1999) 'Defence and Imperial Disunity' in Andrew Porter (ed.), *The Oxford History of the British Empire: the Nineteenth Century*, Oxford, Oxford University Press, 322.

52 Douglas M. Peers (1995) *Between Mars and Mammon: Colonial Armies and the Garrison State in Early Nineteenth-Century India*, London, Tauris.

53 Keith Jeffery (1982) 'The Eastern Arc of Empire', *Journal of Strategic Studies*, 5, 531–45; Keith Jeffery (1981) ' "An English Barrack in the Oriental Seas"?: India in the Aftermath of the First World War', *Modern Asian Studies*, 15, 369–86.

54 A good overview of the first war is provided in Peter Ward Fay (1975) *The Opium War, 1840–1842*, Chapel Hill, University of North Carolina Press. For the second of these wars, see J.D.Y. Wong (1998) *Deadly Dreams: Opium and the 'Arrow' War (1856–1860) in China*, Cambridge, Cambridge University Press.

55 Gregory Martin (1986) 'The Influence of Racial Attitudes on British Policy towards India during the First World War', *Journal of Imperial and Commonwealth History*, 14, 91–113. Similar anxieties can be glimpsed in the Second World War. See Sonya Rose (1998) 'Sex, Citizenship, and the Nation in World War II Britain', *American Historical Review*, 103, 1147–76. The military's anxieties over the sexual identities and behaviour of its soldiers in India, and the relationship between sexuality, race and class is the subject of a number of studies. See Philippa Levine (1994) 'Venereal Disease, Prostitution and the Politics of Empire: the Case of British India', *Journal of the History of Sexuality*, 4, 579–602; Philippa Levine (1996) 'Rereading the 1890s: Venereal Disease as "Constitutional Crisis" in Britain and British India', *Journal of Asian Studies*, 55, 585–612; Mark Harrison (1994) *Public Health in British India; Anglo-Indian Preventive Medicine, 1859–1914*, Cambridge, Cambridge University Press; Douglas M. Peers (1998) 'Soldiers, Surgeons and the

Campaigns to Combat Sexually Transmitted Diseases in Colonial India, 1805–1860', *Medical History*, 42, 137–60; Douglas M. Peers (1999) 'Imperial Vice: Sex, Drink and the Health of British Troops in North Indian Cantonments, 1800–1858', in David Killingray and David Omissi (eds) *Guardians of Empire: the Armed Forces of the Colonial Powers, c. 1700–1964*, Manchester, Manchester University Press.

56 Gerald Sandford Graham (1967) *Great Britain in the Indian Ocean: A Study of Maritime Enterprise 1810–1850*, Oxford, Clarendon.

57 David Gillard (1977) *The Struggle for Asia, 1828–1914*, London, Methuen; Edward Ingram (1979) *The Beginnings of the Great Game in Asia, 1828–1834*, Oxford, Clarendon Press; Edward Ingram (1981) *Commitment to Empire: Prophecies of the Great Game in Asia, 1797–1800*, Oxford, Clarendon Press; Edward Ingram (1992) *Britain's Persian Connection, 1798–1828: Prelude to the Great Game in Asia*, Oxford, Clarendon; Malcolm Yapp (1980) *Strategies of British India; Britain, Iran and Afghanistan, 1798–1850*, Oxford, Clarendon.

58 Anon (1829) 'Col. Evans on the Practicability of an Invasion of British India', *United Service Journal*, 2, 739–43; Anon (1834) 'On the Overland Invasion of India', *East India United Service Journal*, 1, 220–37; Anon (1839) 'A Brief Survey of the Routes by which Russia may March to the Frontiers of British India', *United Service Journal*, 2, 45–9; Asiaticus (1830) 'Defence of India', *United Service Journal*, 3, 366'; D.D. (1830) 'Overland Invasion of India', *United Service Journal*, 3, 492–9; Frederick Holme (1839) 'Persia, Afghanistan, and India', *Blackwood's*, 45, 93–105; From a German Journal (1830) 'On the Russian Conquests in Asia', *United Service Journal*, 3, 28–31; John McNeill (1839) 'Russia, Persia, and England', *Quarterly Review*, 64, 145–88; Non-Alarmist (1828) *A Few Words on our Relations with Russia, Including some Remarks on a Recent Publication by Colonel de Lacy Evans, entitled 'Designs of Russia'*, London, Baldwin and Cradock; A Company's Officer (1834) 'India, Russia, and Persia', *United Service Journal*, 16, 1–16.

59 *Mofussilite*, 3 February 1857, 77.

60 Ibid.

61 John William Kaye (1854) *The Life and Correspondence of Charles, Lord Metcalfe . . . from Unpublished Letters and Journals*, 2 vols, London, R. Bentley, 149.

62 The debate over militarism and the British Army has been addressed in Hew Strachan (1997) *The Politics of the British Army*, Oxford, Clarendon Press. For an example of just how resilient the myth is of the apolitical nature of the British Army, see John Keegan's review of this book in the *Times Literary Supplement*, 24 July 1998, 26.

63 John Lawrence to Lord Dalhousie, 20 September 1850, MSS Eur F90/3, OIOC.

64 Peers (1995) *Between Mars and Mammon*, especially Chapter 1 (see note 52).

65 Thomas R. Metcalf (1994) *Ideologies of the Raj: The New Cambridge History of India*, Vol. III.4, Cambridge, Cambridge University Press; Douglas M. Peers (1997) ' "Those Noble Exemplars of the True Military Tradition": Constructions of the Indian Army in the Mid-Victorian Press', *Modern Asian Studies*, 31, 109–42.

66 Charles Nuckolls (1990) 'The Durbar Incident', *Modern Asian Studies*, 24, 529–59; Alan Trevithick (1990) 'Some Structural and Sequential Aspects of the British Imperial Assemblages at Delhi, 1877–1911', *Modern Asian Studies*, 24, 561–78.

67 Roberts (1905) *Forty-One Years in India, from Subaltern to Commander-in-Chief*, 331–4 (see note 45).

68 As quoted in Thomas R. Metcalf (1989) *An Imperial Vision: Indian Architecture and Britain's Raj*, Berkeley, University of California Press, 234.

69 Francis Yeats-Brown (1930) *Bengal Lancer*, London, Victor Gollancz, 48–9.

70 Sir James Fitzjames Stephen (1883) 'Foundations of the Government of India', *Nineteenth Century*, 80, 541–68.

71 Raymond Callahan (1972) *The East India Company and Army Reform, 1783–1798*, Cambridge, Mass., Harvard University Press; Douglas M. Peers (1990) 'Between Mars and Mammon: The East India Company and Efforts to Reform its Army, 1796–1832', *Historical Journal*, 33, 385–401.

72 Elgin to Wood, 23 September 1862, MSS Eur F83/4 OIOC.

73 Richard Popplewell (1990) 'British Intelligence in Mesopotamia, 1914–1916', *Intelligence and National Security*, 5, 139–72.

74 Edwin Latter (1994) 'The Indian Army in Mesopotamia, 1914–1918', *Journal of the Society for Army Historical Research*, 72, 92–102, 160–79. See also John Prescott Hewett (1919) *Report for the Army Council on Mesopotamia. By Sir John P. Hewett.* [With a map.], London; and Frederick James Moberly (1923) 'The Campaign in Mesopotamia, 1914–1918. [With maps.]', *History of the Great War Based on Official Documents*, London.

75 Major General Jasper Nicolls, Diary, 5 July 1824, MSS Eur F175/31, OIOC.

76 John William Kaye (1846) 'The War on the Sutlej', *North British Review*, 5, 271.

77 General David Birrell's Diary, 1847, MSS Eur D1026 OIOC.

78 Major Charles Hamilton Fenton to Mary Fenton, 21 February 1846, MSS Eur C 471, OIOC.

79 Roberts (1905) *Forty-One Years in India, from Subaltern to Commander-in-Chief*, 471–8 (see note 45).

80 T.R. Moreman (1994) 'The Arms Trade and the North-West Frontier Pathan Tribes, 1890–1914', *Journal of Imperial and Commonwealth History*, 22, 187–216.

81 Callwell (1906) *Small Wars. Their Principles and Practice*, 320 (see note 7).

82 T.R. Moreman (1998) *The Army in India and the Development of Frontier Warfare, 1849–1947*, London, Macmillan.

83 Tim Moreman (1999) ' "Watch and Ward": the Army in India and the North-West Frontier, 1920–1939', in David Killingray and David Omissi (eds) (1999) *Guardians of Empire*, Manchester, Manchester University Press. See also David E. Omissi (1990) *Air Power and Colonial Control: the Royal Air Force, 1919–1939*, Manchester, Manchester University Press.

84 Paget to Amherst, 27 October 1825, Campbell Papers, Scottish United Service Institute.

85 Callwell (1906) *Small Wars, Their Principles and Practice*, 40 (see note 7).

86 Jeffrey Greenhut (1983) 'The Imperial Reserve: the Indian Corps on the Western Front, 1914–1915', *Journal of Imperial and Commonwealth History*, 12. See also the essays in DeWitt C. Ellinwood and S.D. Pradhan (eds) (1978) *India and World War I*, Delhi, Manohar.

87 See accounts of the war in David Omissi (ed.) (1999) *Indian Voices of the Great War: Soldiers' Letters, 1914–1918*, London, Macmillan.

88 Heathcote (1995) *The Military in British India*, 228 (see note 24).

89 Tan Tai Yong (2000) 'An Imperial Home-Front: Punjab and the First World War', *Journal of Military History*, 64, 371–409.

90 Sumit Sarkar (1989) *Modern India*, London, Macmillan, 169.

91 Tan Tai Yong (1994) 'Maintaining the Military Districts: Civil–Military Integration and District Soldiers' Boards in the Punjab, 1919–1939', *Modern Asian Studies*, 28, 833–74.

92 Brian Lapping (1984) *End of Empire*, New York, St Martin's, 36.

93 Derek Sayer (1991) 'British Reaction to the Amritsar Massacre, 1919–1930', *Past and Present*, 130–64; Amandeep S. Madra and Parmjit Singh (2000) *Warrior Saints: Three Centuries of the Sikh Military Tradition*, London, Tauris.

94 Quoted in Helen Fein (1977) *Imperial Crime and Punishment: the Massacre at Jallianwalla Bagh and British Judgment*, Honolulu, University of Hawaii Press, 21.

95 Chandar S. Sundaram (1997) ' "Martial" Indian Aristocrats and the Military System of the Raj: the Imperial Cadet Corps, 1900–1914', *Journal of Imperial and Commonwealth History*, 25, 415–39.

96 Anirudh Deshpande (2002) 'Military Reform in the Aftermath of the Great War: Intentions and Compulsions of British Military Policy, 1919–1925', in Partha Sarathi Gupta and Anirudh Deshpande (eds) (2002) *The British Raj and its Indian Armed Forces, 1857–1939*, New Delhi, Oxford University Press, 187–8.

97 Moreman (1999) ' "Watch and Ward": the Army in India and the North-West Frontier, 1920–1939', 139 (see note 83).

98 Jeremy Black (2002) *Warfare in the Western World, 1882–1975*, London, Routledge, 20.

99 David Smurthwaite (1997) 'The Indian Army in the Era of the Two World Wars', in Alan J. Guy and Peter B. Boyden (eds) (1997) *Soldiers of the Raj: the Indian Army, 1600–1947*, London, National Army Museum, 170–1.

100 Ibid., 170.

101 Moreman (1999) ' "Small Wars" and "Imperial Policing" ' (see note 83).

102 Heathcote (1995) *The Military in British India*, 248 (see note 24).

103 Sarkar (1989) *Modern India*, 396 (see note 90).

104 For a comprehensive history of the INA, see Peter Ward Fay (1993) *The Forgotten Army: India's Armed Struggle for Independence, 1942–1945*, Ann Arbor, University of Michigan Press. Its fighting capabilities have been studied in Chandar S. Sundaram (1995) 'A Paper Tiger: the Indian National Army in Battle, 1944–1945', *War and Society*, 13, 35–59.

105 S. Nagarajan (1995) 'The Second World War and South Asia: Tamils in South India and Sri Lanka', *Ajiagaku Ronso*, 5, 61–88.

106 Sanjoy Bhattacharya (2000) 'British Military Information Management Techniques and the South Asian Soldier: Eastern India during the Second World War', *Modern Asian Studies*, 34, 483–510.

107 Sarkar (1989) *Modern India*, 419 (see note 90).

108 Raymond Callahan (1977) *The Worst Disaster: The Fall of Singapore*, Newark, University of Delaware Press; Louis Allen (1977) *Singapore 1941–1942, The Politics and Strategy of the Second World War*, London, Davis-Poynter; Fay (1993) *The Forgotten Army* (see note 104).

109 Sarkar (1989) *Modern India*, 424 (see note 90).

110 Ronald Spector (1981) 'The Royal Indian Navy Strike of 1946: A Study of Cohesion and Disintegration in Colonial Armed Forces', *Armed Forces and Society*, 7, 271–84.

111 Stephen P. Cohen (1991) *The Indian Army: Its Contribution to the Development of a Nation*, 2nd edn, New York, Oxford University Press, 155–9.

112 For a brief overview, see Sumit Ganguly (2001) *Conflict Unending: India–Pakistan Tensions Since 1947*, New York, Columbia University Press.

113 Cohen (1991) *The Indian Army*, 175–7 (see note 111). A dated, somewhat polemical but still useful overview of the war is provided by Neville Maxwell (1970) *India's China War*, London, Jonathan Cape.

114 Aparna Kundu (1998) *Militarism in India: the Army and Civil Rights in Consensus*, London, Tauris, 141.

115 Rosen (1996) *Societies and Military Power*, 243 (see note 47).

116 Manoj Joshi, 'Revealed: Official History of 1965 War', *Dawn*, 8 September 2000.

117 Ibid.

118 A very useful overview of the war, its origins, conduct and consequences, can be found in Richard Sisson and Leo E. Rose (eds) (1990) *War and Secession: Pakistan, India and the Creation of Bangladesh*, Berkeley, University of California Press.

119 Ganguly (2001) *Conflict Unending* (see note 112). George Perkovich (1999) *India's Nuclear Bomb: The Impact on Global Proliferation*, Berkeley, University of California Press.

120 Alan Bullion (1994) 'The Indian Peace-Keeping Force in Sri Lanka', *International Peacekeeping*, 1, 148–59.

121 Cohen (1991) *The Indian Army*, 202 (see note 111).

122 Apurba Kundu (1994) 'The Indian Armed Forces' Sikh and Non-Sikh Officers' Opinions of Operation Blue Star', *Pacific Affairs*, 67, 46–69.

4

THE IMPERIAL JAPANESE ARMY (1868–1945): ORIGINS, EVOLUTION, LEGACY

Edward Drea

Priding itself on its warrior heritage, Japan was nevertheless militarily unprepared for the nineteenth century incursion from the West. Despite a fierce demeanour, the Japanese samurai were as antiquated as their swords and ceremonial armour. These warrior-administrators had in fact long neglected the military arts, and the shock of British naval assaults in south-western Japan in the summer of 1863 left an indelible impression – Japan was a weak, divided and isolated nation whose sole hope of maintaining its independence rested on Japanese ability to adopt and adapt the modern military tactics, technology and organization of the West. Japan's emergence as a modern military power is traditionally told in tales of carefully planned expansion characterized by victorious foreign wars against the Chinese (1894–5) and Russian (1904–5) empires, and Japanese expansion into South East Asia and the Pacific through 1942. Yet Japan's Imperial Army (IJA) began with the opposite mission and there was no inevitable design to propel its actions. The development of the Imperial Army was both derivative and original; both pragmatic and unrealistic; both deliberate and uncertain. These conflations appeared in the evolution of the IJA's organization and doctrine, its acquisition and use of technology, its development of imperial defence policy, and its relationship to the larger Japanese society.

Organization and doctrine

Samurai both led and resisted the Meiji Restoration of 1868, a fact that resonated through the IJA for the next fifty years. The winners established an imperial bodyguard consisting of a few hundred ill-trained and ill-equipped samurai drawn from various *han* (fiefs). Three years later, a more imposing imperial guard appeared, this one composed of warriors from the south-western fiefs – Chōshū and Satsuma – that had spearheaded the Restoration. On paper the guards mustered 10,000 men, but the nine infantry battalions, two artillery batteries and two cavalry squadrons perhaps totalled 6,300 troops. Leadership in the Restoration and service in the imperial guard conferred an enduring advantage on samurai from those domains. With the exception of imperial family members, men from Chōshū and Satsuma would monopolize the posts of War Minister or Chief of Staff for the next two generations. While their presence provided much needed continuity in times of domestic and international turmoil, it also spawned the deadly factionalism that plagued the IJA in the 1920s and 1930s.

Soon after taking power, the Meiji leaders dispatched observers to study various European armies. Based on their first-hand assessments, they adopted the French Army system in October 1871, just a month after the devastating French defeat at Sedan. Within the government there was opposition to the choice, but expediency prevailed because of the great pressure to adopt a modern, that is Western, military system as quickly as possible. The French model had practical advantages. Certain of Japan's leaders idealized Napoleonic France and French military advisors had been prominent in Japan before the Restoration, imparting an awareness of French military organization and doctrine. More important perhaps was convenience; the Japanese were familiar with the French language, the indispensable means of transmitting the military knowledge of the West. Thus French instructors founded a number of military institutions in Japan, culminating in 1875 with the establishment of the Military Academy to train and educate Japan's future officer corps.

Four years earlier, the government had organized garrisons (chindai) at four locations, including the new capital at Tokyo and the major commercial city of Osaka. About 8,000 troops, mainly infantry, manned these posts. Early in 1874, however, the chindai were abolished and replaced with six national military districts garrisoned by a total of roughly 15,000–20,000 troops drawn from both imperial troops and conscripts. Each military district featured two or more chindai located at strategic points within the country. Over time these original jurisdictional areas (gunkankatsu kuiki) became the site of divisional head-quarters, and the chindai eventually evolved into the regimental recruiting districts of prewar Japan. The administrative practice was to draft men by geographic region and assign them for training to regiments raised in that same area, subject to a few exceptions. The Imperial Guards Division in Tokyo drew nation-wide for its conscripts. In the case of the two divisions formed in Korea after 1916 and the 7th Division in Hokkaidō, the population of ethnic Japanese was insufficient to support the levees, so they, too, drew nationally for their manpower. Conscripts from the Okinawa regimental district were assigned to regiments in Kyūshū. The Imperial Army stationed its first batch of conscripts at the Tokyo chindai in 1873, and the next year assigned conscripts to Nagoya and Osaka, the latter a mixed force of infantry, artillery and coastal defence troops. The new army's primary mission was to preserve domestic law and order by controlling peasant uprisings and suppressing anti-government revolts led by disaffected samurai.

Japan at the time could hardly be termed a unified nation. The government itself proved so divided over sending a punitive expedition to Korea in 1873 that the intense debate split the Restoration founders. Saigō Takamori, a hero of the Restoration, stormed out of the Grand Council of State and returned to his base in Satsuma, where he attracted pro-war and samurai dissidents. Another samurai, Etō Shimpei, himself a government counsellor, also resigned over the Korea issue, and returned to his home in Saga Prefecture. In 1874 Etō led an unsuccessful uprising of mostly ex-samurai against the government. *Chindai* troops quickly crushed the few hundred rebels. To a struggling government whose nascent army was already heavily engaged in suppressing peasant riots over high taxes, demonstrations against military conscription and protests over inflationary prices, the insurrection made it easy to conjure up an image of a countryside seething with sedition.

To inoculate soldiers from the virus of protest, the government relied on a mythical appeal to imperial sovereignty. The 1872 code of military conduct promoted the myth of the emperor's military role from time immemorial and the notion that all Japanese had once served as the emperor's army. Yamagata Aritomo, himself a leading figure in the Restoration, encouraged such depictions in an effort to develop popular support for a a conscription system that would ultimately rid the government of its risky dependence on samurai volunteers. Many among the 400,000-strong warrior class opposed conscription on the grounds that it was a levelling device that cost them their privileges as a feudal élite. While the government bought off most samurai with stipends, a hard-core of reactionaries from southern-most Kyūshū, the former Satsuma fief, provided the most serious military threat to the Meiji government.

Under the leadership of the charismatic Saigō, thousands of disaffected or disillusioned samurai took up arms against the government. The Satsuma Rebellion of 1877–8 pushed the fledgling Imperial Army beyond its limits. Without a mobilization capability or sufficient reserves to draw upon, the army threw all its available forces into the struggle. Conscription alone proved inadequate to supply the manpower needed to crush the rebellion. About half of the 50,000 government troops were drawn from the imperial guards or conscripts. The others were ex-samurai hastily enlisted as members of the Tokyo Metropolitan Police for the duration.

Conscripts generally were ill-equipped and poorly led. Command and control was virtually non-existent, for the French advisors had instructed Japanese how to organize, train and command units from company to brigade, not those of the higher echelons. Lacking a general staff to plan and coordinate operations, the two field commanders conducted independent campaigns, since neither agreed with the strategic approach of the other.

The distant battlefields of Kyūshū left the army operating at the end of a lengthy line of communication that stretched over the Inland Sea back to Tokyo and depended on dozens of transports and small warships shuttling imperial troops and material to south-west Japan. A lack of supply depots and a service corps compounded the logistical difficulties. On any given day, the army employed 90,000 hastily contracted civilians to load, haul and distribute military supplies, but battlefield consumption still far exceeded government projections and resupply capability.

Outnumbered two to one, the tough, battle-seasoned Satsuma warriors were contemptuous of the army's conscripts and feared only three things: rain (which dampened their musket primers, making the weapons inoperable); red hats (the imperial guard which included ex-samurai sharing a common warrior ethos); and artillery (for its killing power). Firepower, especially artillery where the government forces enjoyed a seven to one superiority, turned the advantage to the army. Losses were frightful on both sides; one in every three government troops was killed or wounded, while one of every two of Saigō's rebels met a similar fate.

After suppressing the rebellion, many Japanese officers, now veterans of 'modern' battle, believed their experience made further foreign instruction irrelevant. Severe budget difficulties – the war cost five times the regular military budget – and implicit blame on the French for operational short-comings led to the cancellation of the French military mission in summer 1879. Six years elapsed before the reappearance of European military advisors in Japan. At that time, the Japanese Army converted to German doctrine and field manuals.

Meanwhile the army's leaders created a general staff, and in characteristic Japanese manner fashioned a hybrid: Western forms and Japanese substance. The Chief of Staff was removed from the War Minister's jurisdiction and for operational matters was placed under the direct command of the emperor, to whom he enjoyed direct access. Henceforth the War Minister was responsible for administration and management of the forces, and the Chief of Staff, exercising the prerogative of the independence of supreme command, became the emperor's chief military advisor on matters of national defence and strategic planning. These general-staff reforms of 1878 pre-dated those implemented by Prussia, but were certainly modelled after contemporary German general-staff concepts.[1]

Yamagata, who emerged as a leader in the Meiji government, engineered this clear separation between political and military affairs to ensure the military's apolitical neutrality would make it immune to the shifting political winds of the day, particularly the grass-roots People's Rights Movement (jiyūminken undō) of the 1880s. He also aimed to eliminate civilian control of the military during wartime, a practice which he believed had interfered with operational planning during the recent rebellion. Appeal to imperial authority was part and parcel of Yamagata's effort to instil national conscious-ness in an emerging national army and to guarantee the military's political neutrality.

To educate officers in operations and strategy, as well as to prepare them for senior staff positions and high command, in 1882 the army established the War College. Patterned after the German model, the War College overshadowed the French-created Military Academy in importance because only War College graduates could advance to the highest levels of the army's leadership. Three years later Prussian Major Jacob Meckel arrived in Japan at the invitation of the government to teach at the War College and advise the general staff. The difficult conversion to the new German military system, new doctrine and a different foreign language followed, but by 1888 the Imperial Army had formally adopted the German field manual. The same year the entire army began to convert its garrison organization into divisions.

As it shifted from fixed garrisons to six mobile divisions patterned on a German mountain division model, the army increased its end strength from 64,000 to 81,700 officers and men by the late 1880s. Japan's square divisions counted two brigades of two infantry regiments each, a cavalry squadron for reconnaissance, a field artillery regiment, plus an engineer and a transport battalion. A standing division's peace-time establishment of infantry was 9,600 and in the Guards Division 5,670. Upon mobilization the wartime establishment roughly doubled. Meckel stressed that a mountain (or light) division was most suited for operations in Japan's rugged mountainous and forested terrain. Indeed the topography of North East Asia would exert a recurring influence on the Imperial Army's operational planning, weapons development and policy formulation for the next sixty years.

Some historians assert that the conversion to mobile divisions demonstrates Japan's aggressive continental ambitions. Contemporary army strategy, doctrine and operational planning did not necessarily bear out that contention. Japan's strategic goal was to repel an amphibious invasion of the home islands. This objective required the rapid concentration of two divisions at the spot of landing in order to contain the invaders within their beachhead. Doctrine then mandated units – that is, divisions – capable of moving rapidly, coordinating deployments by telegraph and railroad, and concentrating forces to repulse enemy landings or contain lodgements. Put differently, for the purposes of national defence, the division echelon with mobile forces complemented the immobile fortress troops.[2] The Imperial Army continued to emphasize coastal defence against a Russian attack, and as late as 1891 the theme of the annual grand manoeuvres was repelling an amphibious invasion. The division organization then was both offensive, because of deteriorating relations with China over Korea, and defensive, because of the emerging Russian threat in North East Asia. It was also a long-considered adaptation of the most up-to-date Western military organization at a time when Japan was striving to master the secrets of the West's success.

More than twenty years of tension between Japan and China over control of the Korean peninsula culminated in the Sino–Japanese War (1894–5). Tokyo fielded seven divisions (174,000 men) and mobilized about 240,000 troops to bring the units to war-time establishment. Logistics still remained chaotic. The army employed 153,000 civilian contractors, labourers and coolies to sustain its war machine. Although receiving extra pay for hazardous duty, they were exempt from military orders and discipline. Coolies deserted in droves, and in one extreme case a battalion commander took responsibility for the delays in moving supplies forward by committing suicide. Moreover strategic planning was inadequate, road and rail facilities were primitive in the theatre of operations, and medical support almost substandard because the army had neglected thorough preparations for field hospitals, field sanitation and epidemic control measures. As a consequence, 12,000 Japanese soldiers (or almost nine times the 1,400 battlefield deaths) perished from illness, the chief culprits being malaria, cholera, dysentery, and beriberi. In this regard, Japan suffered much like its Western counterparts. The United States' ghastly experience during the Spanish–American War (1898) witnessed 2,500 officers and men dead of typhoid, ten times the number killed in battle, and British medical debacles during the Boer War (1899–1902) left nearly three times as many soldiers dead from disease as from enemy action.

On the positive side, command and control displayed improvements. In 1893 the Japanese army and navy recognized the need for a joint staff to conduct war-time military operations. The services accordingly devised regulations for the Imperial General Headquarters (IGHQ), first established in June 1894 to coordinate operations during the war with the Chinese empire. IGHQ would twice reappear; during the Russo–Japanese War (1904–5) and in November 1937 to deal with the escalation of the so-called China Incident. As for tactics, Japanese troops advanced in columns, preferring a frontal assault while seeking an exposed flank to sever the enemy's line of retreat. Several hundred yards from the enemy positions, the columns would break down into companies or even battalions as a skirmish line moved forward to develop the battle. Infantry doctrine clustered troops together at company or even battalion echelon to facilitate command and control and to preserve fire discipline. Troops advanced at close intervals in dense, disciplined ranks. Soldiers moved forward in short rushes, threw themselves on the ground, then arose to repeat the process. Officers led from the front, and suffered correspondingly high losses. One other feature of the war merits comment – the appearance of familiar khaki-coloured uniforms. The infantryman's white summer trousers made tempting targets, showed dirt as well as wear and tear, and by accentuating bloodstains depressed troop morale. After the war the army, as had other world militaries, switched to a khaki-coloured field uniform to replace the summer white. The change was completed by 1902. A newly uniformed and expanded post-war army now numbered thirteen divisions.

Victory in the Russo–Japanese War (1904–5) confirmed Japan's rise to a world-class military power. The army mobilized 1,090,000 troops organized into seventeen standing divisions for the conflict. Some 87 per cent of the army (945,000 troops) deployed overseas, among them 55 per cent infantry

(516,178). Slightly more than 6 per cent were killed in action (60,029) of whom more than 93 per cent were infantry (55,955). Learning from their previous experience, the military organized an auxiliary service corps to transport heavy baggage and artillery. Auxiliaries wore regulation uniforms, were subject to military control and had received three months active duty training followed by posting to an auxiliary reserve for mobilization during wartime. Nonetheless the army still had to press tens of thousands of Chinese and Korean labourers into service to supplement the 260,000 Japanese engaged in keeping the emperor's army fed, resupplied and on the move during the Russian campaigns.

Medical improvements negated the scourges of malaria and cholera, but dysentery, typhoid fever and beriberi still claimed thousands of lives. Japan did manage to mobilize four times as many troops for a longer period of time in the field (twelve versus seven months) and to reduce the one to nine ratio of battle deaths to disease mortality of the 1895 campaign to three to one (60,000 to 21,000) in 1904–5. Still the human cost of the war was staggering. Based on admittedly anecdotal evidence, a single farming village of 520 families and a population of 3,000 sent 15 men to the Sino–Japanese War. All returned safely. The same hamlet sent 105 men to the Russo–Japanese battlefields where sixteen were killed in action.[3] Losses of this magnitude touched families throughout Japan, and convinced many army and civilian leaders that the nation had paid in blood and treasure for special rights in Manchuria.

Certain that it was only a matter of time before Russia launched a war of revenge against Japan, general headquarters retained four wartime provisional divisions in the postwar force structure and outfitted two more for a total of 19 standing divisions and a peacetime establishment of 220,000 men. During the war, the army grew accustomed to using heavy artillery and high tech communications equipment such as telephones, telegraphs, railroads, and observation balloons. This modern technology complemented advances in firepower which in turn mandated greater tactical dispersion, a trend that continued for the next thirty years. The deadly new weaponry of the Russo–Japanese War and the enormous losses of Japanese infantry necessitated a new combat doctrine that would compel the Japanese infantryman to fight on even after he saw his friends killed or wounded.

In the Russo–Japanese War's aftermath, attacks on positions emphasized mobility, superiority of small arms and support by light artillery. Divisions extended their frontages and smaller units stressed individual dispersion that further fragmented companies. Gone were the dense formations, replaced by increasingly dispersed ones – the standard two paces between infantrymen of 1904 stretched to four paces in 1923 and to six by 1940. Increasing dispersion placed more emphasis on platoon and squad tactics, along with greater stress on individual initiative. This development, Japan's military leaders agreed, demanded unquestioning obedience to orders by all ranks. Victory in the Russo–Japanese War also convinced Japanese officers that indigenous values played an essential role in battlefield success. The 1909 revision to the Infantry

Manual emphasized these unique and intangible Japanese values, including the spirit of the attack and the absolute primacy of the offensive. In short, victory or defeat was not necessarily decided by which side had the bigger battalions, but rather by the army with the unflagging offensive spirit and unquestioning resolution to follow orders.

Aside from limited two-month operations against German fortifications in Tsingtao in China, Japan was spared direct involvement in the horrors of World War I ground combat. The army did add two divisions to its force structure for a total of twenty-one, and Japanese officers were, of course, aware of the radical transformation of land warfare and the huge costs of military and industrial mobilization for total warfare. True, during the World War Japan moved from a debtor to a creditor nation, but post-war depressions revealed a fragile prosperity. Moreover, Japan's military appropriations grew from 33 per cent of the total national budget in 1918 to 44 per cent in 1922, mainly to underwrite a naval arms race with the United States.

Certainly the IJA found no glory in its expedition to Siberia (1918–22). The long four-year counter-guerrilla campaign against Bolshevik forces fought over an empty landscape drained the army and the treasury. By 1922 the War Minister cut army rolls by 59,000 personnel and used the 90 million yen in savings to buy modern equipment such as machine guns, heavy artillery and communications gear for the army. These decisions also altered the army's personnel mobilization plans. Henceforth standard practice was to augment each rifle company from 100 to 250 men and to add a fourth rifle company to each of the regiment's three battalions, thus expanding regimental strength from 900 to 3,000 men upon mobilization. Further infusion of reserves fleshed out the division's transport, administrative, sanitation, and supply units.

The massive Tokyo Earthquake of 1923 ruined the army's modernization designs. Government priority on rebuilding the shattered capital city bankrupted the national treasury making it impossible to fund military improvements. For that reason, the following year War Minister Ugaki Kazushige opted to eliminate four divisions from the force structure along with another 33,000 officers and men. Like his predecessor, Ugaki ploughed the savings back into modernized communications equipment, trucks, and new weapons such as a light machine gun, airplanes and tanks. The army in turn established new branches of service to accommodate emerging armour and aircraft technology. The 16-division force structure had an end strength of roughly 250,000 officers and men. Certain Japanese historians see this as a conscious attempt to replace quantity (by cutting force structure) with quality (new, modern weapons) that provided greater firepower.

Modernization did not, however, alter the division design. Experience in the Russo–Japanese War convinced many Japanese staff officers that in the anticipated war against Russia the square division was essential. Japanese planners expected their divisions to conduct independent, sustained operations, a role normally assigned to a corps echelon (two or more divisions). The larger square division's advantages in firepower and manpower, they reasoned, would also overwhelm smaller triangular formations. Thus they retained the huge, cumbersome square division despite the trend in World War I to smaller, more mobile triangular formations. Not until 1936 did the general staff approve the conversion to triangular divisions, although a few square divisions remained in the force structure throughout the Greater East Asia War (1937–45), and in the spring of 1945 Imperial Headquarters formed several square formations for purposes of coastal defence of Japan's home islands.

Doctrine, as might be expected, underwent change after the Great War, but in unexpected directions. The revised Infantry Manual that appeared in 1928 re-emphasized the spirit of the attack, morale and other intangibles of battle as an appeal to uphold the glorious history and tradition of Japanese arms as the means to certain victory. Doctrine stressed the rapid annihilation of the enemy by envelopment or encirclement achieved by a combination of physical and psychological concentration of superior force at the essential point. Doctrine writers accorded primacy to the role of the infantry in modern warfare, and criticized excessive dependence on artillery supporting fire as symptomatic of materialism or defeatism. In other words, the IJA depended on élan (attack à l'outrance) to compensate for material deficiencies. As a result, the post-1925 army force structure eliminated the artillery brigade echelon and had fewer artillery batteries, fewer artillery regiments and fewer heavy artillery units. The 1928 rewrite of Tōsui kōryō (Principles of Strategic Command) went so far as to strike the words for 'surrender', 'retreat', and 'defence', from the manual because of their negative psychological connotations for troop morale.[4]

Since the Russo–Japanese War the IJA had maintained a military presence in China's north-eastern provinces collectively known as Manchuria. In 1919 the army upgraded this constabulary to a 10,000-man force designated the Kwantung Army. Standing IJA divisions deployed units to Manchuria on a rotating basis to provide the Kwantung Army's establishment. By 1930 the notion of a Manchurian lifeline had caught the popular imagination, and the unilateral Kwantung Army military operations that began in September 1931 with the so-called Manchurian Incident and concluded, or so the Japanese thought, with the seizure of all of Manchuria in early 1932, were wildly popular at home. Manchuria offered the bright promise of solving Japan's domestic problems of overpopulation, high unemployment, lack of natural resources, and so forth.

Yet the Kwantung Army's seizure of China's north-eastern provinces had actually created a strategic salient thrust deep into Soviet Far East. This development left the IJA with a new contingency of defending hundreds of miles of largely ill-defined and disputed border areas running along a contested frontier. This time the opponent was not a weak and divided China but the strong and tightly controlled Soviet Union. The Red Army reacted to Japanese aggression by reinforcing its Far Eastern forces, and IJA planners hastily responded by strengthening the Kwantung Army. Beginning in the 1920s and continuing for two decades, the IJA shaped a doctrine designed to defeat the Soviet Union. Army planners knew that Japan could not fight and win a war of attrition against the Soviets, and so refined their tactics during the 1930s to wage a rapid, short, and decisive campaign (*sokusen sokketsu*). The objective was to encircle the enemy's main forces and then annihilate them. Tactics placed a premium on mobility, initiative, concentration of forces, night attack and night movement, close cooperation between artillery and infantry, and, above all, the spirit of the offensive.

By 1937 the Soviets had 20 divisions and 1,500 aircraft in the Far East and the numbers kept growing. The Kwantung Army expanded from one brigade to six divisions and about 200 aircraft. Japanese army efforts to create buffer zones in North China to shield Manchuria from Chinese interference sparked a series of crises between 1932 and 1937. In each case, local Chinese officials backed down when threatened with Japan's military might, but with Manchuria as the focus of Chinese irredentist passions, its status became the issue between China and Japan that defied a political or diplomatic settlement.[5] Yet another minor skirmish outside Beijing in July 1937 seemed to fit the previous pattern, but to the surprise and consternation of the Japanese, the Chinese fought back. Although senior Japanese army leaders were divided over dispatching large numbers of troops to China, more hawkish generals and colonels escalated the fighting by insisting that if Japan gave an inch, the Chinese would take a mile. Other hawks saw the opportunity to knock out Chinese military power in North China as a means to secure a strategic flank for future operations against the Soviet Union. Soon Tokyo found itself bogged down in a full-scale, though undeclared, ground war in China.

Operational and tactical doctrine applied against Chinese armies from 1937 onwards brought success, but insistence on the offensive exacted a high cost – more than 700,000 Japanese dead or wounded in the China fighting by December 1941. When applied against a better equipped, more modern Red Army, Japanese doctrine and tactics proved wanting both on a small scale engagement (division minus) in 1938 at Changkuofeng, a dot on the Korean–Soviet border, and the following year on a larger scale border war (multi-divisional) on the remote Mongolian steppes near Nomonhan.

Manchuria, then, provided opportunity and danger, and IJA planners found themselves confronted with a dilemma: strategy and doctrine predicated a short, decisive war, but by the mid-1930s Japan's hypothetical opponents included not only the Soviet Union and the United States but also China and Great Britain. Japan had little hope of forcing a decisive battle against the Western powers and so had to consider the possibility of a protracted conflict. Prolonged warfare in turn required larger ground and air forces, 20 standing divisions, 50 total divisions and 140 aerial squadrons. These numbers became the IJA's goals for 1942 as laid down in its 1936 Rearmament Plan.

A central feature of the Rearmament Plan called for the conversion of square to triangular divisions. The triangular configuration enabled the IJA to field more divisions – the supernumerary fourth regiments of the square divisions merged to form new triangular ones – and to redesign the divisions to meld machine gun companies and mountain artillery sections in each infantry battalion. Requirements in China, particularly counter-guerrilla operations, spurred the establishment of light triangular divisions. Stripped of heavy artillery and motorized transport, these units protected strategic points and lines of communication in the occupied zones, maintained stability in the Japanese-held rear areas, and 'mopped up' the elusive communist guerrilla forces fighting in North China.

Stalemate in China and defeat at the hands of the Red Army did not prove salubrious for the IJA. Burdened with the costs of the China fighting, the army could not afford the far-reaching technological and doctrinal reforms proposed by various post-mortem official boards of inquiry after the Nomonhan debacle of 1939. By December 1941 the IJA had 51 divisions in its force structure, of which 27 were engaged in China operations and 13, arguably among its best, were stationed in Manchuria eyeball-to-eyeball with the Soviet Union. An additional eleven divisions remained in homeland reserve, but five of those were newly activated and not considered combat-ready. The IJA also found itself diverted from its continental focus by the navy's designs for war against Britain, the US, and the Netherlands. The army's objectives were regions closest to the Asian mainland: to secure Malaya to open the path to the resources of the Netherlands East Indies; to seize the Philippines to protect its strategic flank in South East Asia; and to occupy Burma, initially in order to protect the Malaya–Thai flank and eventually to sever the allied line of communication resupplying China. This continental strategy required eleven infantry and two air divisions. The infantry formations came from China or French Indochina (eight) and homeland reserve (three), not the borders of the Soviet Union. IGHQ's *Confidential War Diary* entry for 15 October 1941 encapsulated the IJA's attitude. 'War should be avoided. The army does not want a war with the United States any more than the navy or the government. In its heart of hearts, however, the army is even willing to fight a hundred years war to settle the China Incident.'[6]

For the Imperial Army, operations against the West in Asia were a diversion from its main theatre in China and for preparations for its long-anticipated war against the Soviet Union. Indeed, the general staff fully expected that by the spring of 1942 it could recycle 200,000 troops used in the southern operations against the West's colonies in Asia back to Manchuria, where they would be refitted and re-equipped for war against the Soviet Union. Nor did the IJA have any means to win the war against the West. The army could and did seize territory, but its victories would amount to the creation of a defensive perimeter behind which it would fight a war of attrition. Unique Japanese values and fighting spirit made the IJA perfect for such a role because the Western powers, deemed to be decadent democracies, would prove unable to endure the bloodletting, and would ultimately agree to a compromise settlement leaving Japan in control of vital strategic resources. Or so Tokyo estimated.

It was, however, the navy that pulled the army into the far reaches of the Pacific – to the killing grounds of Guadalcanal, New Guinea, the Marianas, the Aleutians. As the strategic offensive passed to the Americans and Australians in the Pacific theatres, on sea from June 1942 (Midway) and on land from January 1943 (Guadalcanal and Battle of Bismarck Sea), Japanese forces found themselves overextended and undersupplied. Instead of providing a coherent defence, Japanese garrisons in the Pacific were destroyed piecemeal, albeit at great cost to the Allies in the Central Pacific campaigns and the Philippines. Unable to concentrate forces on its Pacific front, but anxious to retake the strategic offensive, IGHQ and Prime Minister General Tōjō Hideki finally approved the Fifteenth Army's thrust to India in early 1944. Japan's legions launched ground offensives against the Allies that climaxed in the early summer of 1944 at Imphal-Kohima. Disaster followed in the greatest land defeat to date in the IJA's history, exacerbated by a criminal disregard for logistical support of the advancing Japanese army. Forced on the strategic and operational defensive in the Pacific and India fronts, in early 1945 the IJA saw China as the theatre for offensive operations. Intact Japanese forces in China could destroy American airfields there to prevent Allied air attacks on home soil. They could also open and maintain an overland line of communication from Saigon in French Indochina to Pusan in Korea, immune to the devastating Allied submarine and air attacks that had gutted Japan's merchant marine.

Beginning in 1943, IGHQ had redeployed more and more divisions from China, as well as the élite formations stationed in Manchuria, to the Pacific front. By 1945 the once mighty Kwantung Army was reduced to a hollow shell easily cracked open by the Soviets' well-executed August blitzkrieg. Even after two atomic bombs obliterated the cities of Hiroshima and Nagasaki, the Imperial Army's leaders remained defiant, convinced the still five million-strong army could continue the war through 1945 and inflict enough casualties on the Allies, especially if an invasion of the home islands was attempted, to secure a negotiated settlement to the conflict on the army's terms. Imperial intervention was required to overcome the army leaders' dogged refusal to consider unconditional surrender.

Technology and modernization

Emperor Meiji's new government inherited a bewildering assortment of European and American small arms from the armouries of the Tokugawa *bakufu* (the military and political authority), but by 1874 had standardized weaponry by equipping its regular infantry with Enfield rifles. Conscripts continued to make do with older Sneider rifles. As for artillery, only obsolete French bronze cannon were available, although the government did procure several Krupp-manufactured steel guns for the Guards' artillery unit. The outdated French guns proved effective in the Satsuma Rebellion due solely to weight of numbers. Of greater moment was the experience of handling and transporting artillery pieces during the civil war.

The absence of decent roads in the rugged, mountainous island of Kyushu and the scarcity of draft horses in Japan made it difficult for the army to bring field artillery to bear. For example, it took four dray horses to pull a field artillery gun, but only two smaller pack horses to carry the lighter mountain gun. Mountain artillery's greater mobility made it the weapon of choice for gunners, and mountain guns fired 80 per cent of the artillery ordnance expended by government forces during the rebellion. From the outset then, rugged topography and terrain as well as the underdeveloped road and rail routes of North East Asia exerted considerable influence on the development of Japan's modern weapons.

Another influence of geography on weapons production was Japan's lack of natural resources. Military leaders understood the advantages of German-made steel artillery weapons, but iron ore deposits in Japan were scarce and iron and steel mills virtually nonexistent. These conditions left the Imperial Army dependent on manufacturing Italian bronze artillery cannon under licence at the newly built Osaka arsenal. Japanese arsenals produced both field- and mountain-versions of the 75 mm artillery gun, and after 1887 all artillery units were equipped with these weapons which saw action in the Sino–Japanese War. As for small arms, Tokyo arsenal produced the domestically designed Murata rifle that used smokeless powder and became standard equipment, for the Guards initially and for the rest of the army gradually.

Dependence on foreign sources for weapons design, technology and manufacture was seen as a necessary evil. After all, the army had to rely on imported weapons to fight the Satsuma rebels, but what if the enemy had been a foreign one? Such thinking led to the post-war promotion of 'weapons independence' (heiki dokuritsu). The catch phrase did not mean independent development of weapons, especially artillery, but rather the study of foreign technology and production techniques in order to adapt foreign-made weapons to Japanese requirements. In other words, copying and modifying foreign weapons for domestic production would result in independence within the scope of Japan's own industrial and technological capabilities. Obviously the munitions factories and arsenals became centres for the absorption and dissemination of modern techniques and skills, and the government retained strategic industries such as metallurgy, machine tools and shipbuilding along with the arsenals, dockyards, machine shops, and wool and clothing factories that produced the sinews of war for the military.[7]

The 1882 military budget doubled the size of the infantry branch, but the heavier expense was the outfitting of modern combat engineer, cavalry and artillery units. An average of 16 per cent of the national budget went for defence between 1883 and 1887, much of it to re-equip the army with modern weaponry. Engineers were especially in demand to improve roads and bridges as Japan developed a national transportation network. In 1891 army leaders managed, through supporters in the House of Peers, to fund a military construction bill to expand national railroads, a strategic initiative designed to facilitate rapid concentration of forces and their arms and equipment either for purposes of coastal defence or overseas deployment. The resulting railway boom vastly increased track mileage, although Meckel complained that the new track often ran too close to existing coastal routes making it susceptible to interdiction by hostile naval gunfire.[8] To Japanese officers, however, construction inland through precipitous mountain ranges would be technically more difficult and enormously more expensive than following a coastal route. In short, pragmatism prevailed because it was better to have some railway communication line, even an exposed coastal one, than none at all.[9]

Coinciding with the conversion to division echelons, Army reforms undertaken between 1884 and 1887 eliminated the obsolete French artillery and replaced it with newer, more powerful Italian weapons. But weapons technology was in the midst of a sweeping revolution during the last decade of the nineteenth century, and the danger existed that today's wonder weapon would be tomorrow's museum curiosity. After the Sino–Japanese War, the new quick-firing artillery pieces using smokeless powder and an improved recoil mechanism were manufactured at Osaka arsenal. Rapid advances in artillery technology soon superseded these early models, whose range and accuracy was inferior to more sophisticated Russian artillery. Desperate to achieve parity with its most likely hypothetical enemy, Japan purchased more than 600 artillery pieces from German (Krupp) and French (Sneider) firms in 1899 and 1900. Great secrecy shrouded these arms sales, for Japan's leaders did not wish to expose the nation's industrial and technological weaknesses to potential enemies. Military budgets reflected the enormous expense of an expanded force structure and new weapons, particularly artillery: between 1894 and 1902, 45 per cent on average of the national budget went on defence.

The IJA used its foreign manufactured artillery to great advantage during the Russo–Japanese War. Battlefield consumption of artillery shells, however, far exceeded the army's projections and Japan's industrial capacity. At Nanshan, the first major engagement of the conflict, Japanese gunners fired 30,000 shells in a single day, an amount equal to two full months' supply of the army's artillery stocks. Munitions factories in Japan could not keep up with demand, quality control deteriorated and dud rounds became common. Seeing row after row of unexploded Japanese artillery ordnance lined up by Russian soldiers at Mukden, one Japanese staff officer remarked, 'We fire at the enemy, but our shells take a nap'.[10] Again the government had to look overseas for assistance, and by floating foreign loans purchased millions of rounds of artillery shells, shell casings, fuses, and cordite.

Manufacturing shortcomings affected more than armaments. Beriberi resulting from a lack of vitamin B1 again plagued the Japanese foot soldiers. The army knew from its experience with the disease during the Sino–Japanese War ten years earlier that barley mixed with polished rice could prevent outbreaks. Unfortunately Japanese factories could not process barley in large enough quantities to fill the rations of all the mobilized forces. Beriberi alone killed almost 6,000 Japanese troops. Moreover the inability of Japan's manufacturing sector to process sufficient fresh vegetables for the field armies' rations resulted in vitamin C deficiencies among the troops.

The war did confirm the value of mountain artillery in rugged, roadless terrain. Light artillery, though, proved unable to breech hastily built field fortifications, much less permanent ferro-concrete ones. Thus heavy artillery, heretofore considered a defensive weapon for static coastal defence fortifications, underwent a metamorphosis to an offensive weapon following the war.

Fearful that the Russians would sooner rather than later seek revenge for their defeat, Japanese military planners considered the post-war era not a peace but merely an extended armistice preceding the next round of fighting. Tokyo's defence appropriations swelled to between one-quarter and one-third of the national budget in order to underwrite a modernization of artillery, small arms and communications equipment needed for the next war. A redesigned Type 38 (1905) 75 mm field artillery piece was introduced to the forces, along with improved field telephones that enhanced fire direction capabilities. Modernized and expanded telegraph and telephone lines in Japan and Manchuria facilitated command and control of ground forces. The Japanese government also subsidized private stock companies to expand Japanese-controlled railroads in Korea and Manchuria in order to improve strategic transportation and logistical support in the likely theatres of future operations.

Japan was spared the horrors of World War I, but the army paid close attention to the conflict. Most apparent was Japan's great inferiority vis-à-vis the West in terms of weapons technology, munitions production and manufacturing potential. To match the great powers of the West meant modernizing a weak industrial base to support advanced military technology. Up-and-coming middle-grade Japanese officers saw the revelation of World War I as the advent of total war that mobilized the entire resources – human and material – of the nation for the struggle. Their views gained prominence during the mid and late 1920s as the army grappled with means to fight such a war. Military planners dreamed of laying the groundwork for war-time expansion of key strategic industries through mobilization planning and basic applied research to develop a new generation of indigenous weapons. The army now demanded equipment to fight a war of movement as well as one of position, and the resolution of that paradox occupied its best thinkers for the next two decades.

Money for modernization was hard to come by in the tight post-war economic conditions of Japan. The short-term solution, as with most military organizations, was to cut personnel and put the savings into equipment. Reforms in 1922 eliminated troops, but added new or improved weapons and equipment to the force structure. An improved Type 38 field artillery piece boasting increased range and separate charge and projectile entered the forces in 1926, forming with the Type 10 105 mm howitzer and 75 mm pack mountain artillery the standard division's artillery complement. The heavier guns reduced mobility because they required teams of draft horses whose numbers extended road march columns and slowed deployment off the march for a meeting engagement. The army still wanted to move light and fast, unencumbered by a lengthy baggage train of impedimenta, and deploy rapidly off the march. To achieve these requirements, army leaders eliminated the fourth artillery battery of each regiment, thereby compressing road march formations. Thus the Japanese army sacrificed firepower for speed and mobility.

Japanese military thinkers recognized that the World War I revolution in weaponry – tanks, poison gas, and advances in weapons like machine guns, aircraft and so forth – had occurred, but they did not blindly rush to incorporate the new technology into the forces. Rather, adaptation and integration proceeded according to the unique requirements of North East Asia's geography and the empire's industrial capability and capacity. Field artillery, for instance, relied on lighter, more mobile and smaller calibre weapons. A special report prepared in July 1940 dramatically portrayed the deficiencies in large calibre weapons. Japan had only 150 artillery weapons larger than the Type 15 150 mm cannon and could produce only five heavy artillery weapons annually. It took Japanese industry eight months to manufacture one Type 15 cannon and 18 months to produce a Type 24 240 mm howitzer. Similar industrial and manufacturing backwardness influenced trends in motorization and armour.

Motorization was costly, dependent on foreign supply and of dubious value on the inferior road networks of Manchuria, North China and the Soviet Far East. Not until 1933 did Japanese industry manufacture more than 1,000 automobiles per year, leaving the army as reliant on animal transport for mobility as it had been during the Russo–Japanese War. Even by 1940 there were a total of 220,000 automotive vehicles in the entire Japanese empire, most of those imported. Japan had the industrial capacity to produce only 30,000 trucks per annum at a time when operations in China alone demanded a minimum of 100,000 military trucks. Planning estimates that a total of 250,000 trucks were needed to put the army on wheels necessitated annual production of 130,000 trucks, far beyond Japan's minuscule automotive manufacturing capability. By way of comparison, in 1940 alone the United States *produced* 3.7 million passenger cars and more than 750,000 trucks.

The same reciprocal issues of terrain and industrial capacity influenced armour design and doctrine. The IJA had imported a tank from Great Britain in 1918 to study its technical characteristics and properties, and activated its first light tank regiment in 1925. Japan opted for light tanks for several reasons. First, armour had to be deployed overseas, making size and weight vital considerations for the loading and off-loading capacity and capability of transport ships. Light (10 tons or less) and medium (16 tons) tanks were seen as the ideal for the limited road network of North China and Manchuria. They could, for example, cross unbridged rivers on pontoons or ferries so long as their weight was restricted. It was also thought vital for tanks to be able to surmount trenches and obstacle ditches, and a boxy, wider body design achieved this result. Doctrine mandated that tanks support infantry attacks by preceding the infantry, suppressing enemy opposition and destroying enemy field works. Speed was therefore not a paramount consideration, because as infantry support vehicles tanks could move at the pace of the advancing foot soldiers.

Limited combat experience in Manchuria after September 1931 revealed that tanks drew enemy fire, resulting in casualties to accompanying infantry-men. Doctrine writers then positioned tanks to the flanks of the attack and decreed that if enemy positions were not protected by obstacles, there was no need for armour to spearhead assaults. The Spanish Civil War (1936–9) confirmed Japanese suspicions about terrain limiting the effectiveness of tanks. Once Italian tanks moved off-road, they either broke down mechanically from the pounding or became bogged down, snared by natural obstacles that impeded movement and disrupted the tempo of the advance. The disabled tanks made easy stationary targets for Republican gunners. Finally, Japanese industry just could not produce masses of tanks. As late as 1939, two years into the China Incident, factories were manufacturing an average of 28 tanks (all models) per month. Production did increase after mid-1940, but only to about 40 or 45 tanks monthly.

Aircraft development by the Imperial Army followed a similar path of initial purchase of aircraft from foreign firms, adaptation of aircraft technology to Japan's requirements, doctrinal development and indigenous production. In 1920 imperial orders established the Army Air Force Department (JAAF) with an aerial reconnaissance mission. Five years later organizational reforms made possible by reductions in other branches added fighter, bomber and balloon squadrons to the air order of battle. The formal Army Air Force Branch appeared in 1925, but it took another eight years for an air doctrine manual to see the light of day. JAAF doctrine originally emphasized the role of air power for reconnaissance as well as control of the airspace above the battlefield. Neither close air support of infantry nor strategic bombing attracted many adherents in the JAAF. Nor, for that matter, did aerial air defence. Japanese staff officers did not foresee aerial bombing supplementing, much less replacing, artillery bombardment, and in fact the army never, from lack of technical ability, produced an effective bomber.

Unlike the cases of artillery, small arms and tank manufacture, the army relied on civilian industry – chiefly Nakajima, Mitsubishi and Kawasaki – for serial aircraft production and development of military aircraft. The expansion of the civilian Japanese aviation industry in turn depended on military contracts. Government protection, subsidies and guarantees also encouraged the development of the civilian aircraft industry. By the early 1930s, the JAAF's mission was to support ground operations by conducting reconnaissance, bombing enemy targets and achieving air superiority. At the time the army possessed about 650 aircraft, roughly 450 of which were operational. For comparative purposes, their hypothetical opponent marshalled at least 750 aircraft in the Soviet Far East alone. Total military aircraft production rose from 445 planes in 1930 to 4,768 in 1940, and to a wartime peak of 47,900 in 1944. The JAAF stressed high levels of training and turned out only about 750 pilots annually up to December 1941. Training emphasized pilot skills, and other flight instruction was left to the new pilot's tactical unit.[11]

Japanese aviation developed later compared to the West, but by 1935 had reached world technical standards in single-engine aircraft, chiefly by borrowing and adapting foreign technology, especially from Germany. Standard practice was to purchase a single aircraft model from abroad for testing, comparison and technical innovation. Aircraft were manufactured under licence, and Japanese private companies kept abreast of the latest developments in foreign aircraft industries and aerial technology. The army made only one large foreign purchase – 82 Italian Fiat heavy bombers in 1937–8, which in the event proved clumsy firetraps in the skies of China.

For the Japanese, air defence relied on pre-emptive strikes. Mid–1930s war plans envisioned launching surprise air raids to destroy Soviet air bases and vital installations around Vladivostok, in order to prevent Soviet air attacks on the homeland. In 1937 the General Staff formalized plans to open hostilities against the Soviet Union with air attacks on Soviet air bases. Following the initial phase, Japanese airmen would continue their air superiority mission, with only the minimum number of aircraft assigned to direct support of ground operations. The air arm's slogan, 'Air superiority prerequisite for ground operations' (chijō zettai kōkū yūsen), was put to the test in the 1939 summer fighting against the Red Army at Nomonhan. The campaign witnessed an unauthorized and illegal cross-border Japanese air strike on Soviet air bases at Tamsag, Outer Mongolia, and continuous air battles that destroyed hundreds of Soviet aircraft. Moscow, however, not only replaced losses but also threw in seasoned reinforcements, veteran airmen of the Spanish Civil War, whose combined weight of numbers and improved pilot skills gradually wore down the numerically smaller JAAF, denying it the local air superiority it desperately sought to attain.

At war with China since 1937, the government resorted to legislation, culminating in the General Mobilization Law of 1938, to restructure the economy to put it on a war-time basis. Put simply, industries deemed non-essential for the war effort such as rayon, paper and textiles, were hamstrung by regulations that limited resources capital, and labour while military related industries such as automotive, steel, chemicals, and petroleum benefited from government contracts, favourable legislation, and access to capital and natural resources as well as guaranteed supply of labour.[12] The controlled economy did indeed greatly improve armaments production and accelerate the development of heavy industry in relative terms. However, the initial base line was so low to begin with that in absolute terms the increases were minuscule compared to what the West would prove capable of achieving.

Increased industrial output could not even meet the army's demands on the China front, much less the needs of a wider conflict. Production problems appeared early and, despite all the government's and army's efforts, persisted and worsened during the war against China and the West between 1937 and 1945. By the conclusion of the Wuhan operation in central China in November 1938, the Imperial Army had lost its flexibility to continue large-scale operations in China. At that time the IJA had mobilized 34 divisions, but its four-month strategic reserve of small arms ammunition sufficed for only 30 divisions. Stocks of artillery shells, the perennial Japanese shortcoming, were sufficient to support operations of a mere seven divisions.[13] Fighting the Red Army at Nomonhan in the summer of 1939, the Japanese had to withdraw both of their committed tank regiments after their first battle because of unexpectedly heavy losses. Beyond replacing the destroyed tanks, difficult enough for Japanese industry, the army needed its small armour force as the cadre for its envisioned future expansion of tank corps in Manchuria. Further losses of matériel thus became unacceptable. By 1943, in order to manufacture anti-aircraft artillery guns and especially aircraft for homeland defence, Japan actually manufactured fewer tanks, fewer artillery weapons and less ammunition than the previous year.

Even so, air defence emphasized civil defence, not military countermeasures, and placed the burden on civilian involvement at the neighbourhood levels. Government-directed air raid drills had been conducted as early as 1928, and these exercises continued through the 1930s. Yet there was little government spending on the programme and few official attempts at mobilizing strong public commitment. Tokyo's basic premise was that Japan's distance from potential opponents afforded the best protection because few aircraft had the range to reach specific targets in the home islands from faraway overseas airfields. Once Allied technology invalidated that premise, Tokyo reacted with tactics more suitable to the nineteenth than the mid-twentieth century. The main defensive measures announced in late 1943 and acted upon in 1944 were first to evacuate children from the threatened cities and second to level blocks of buildings in crowded urban areas to open fire breaks during air raids.[14] Factory and industrial workers meanwhile remained tethered to their machines.

There were six major government arsenals employing more than a quarter of a million workers by 1945, and they drew support from another thousand plus civilian factories employing about 350,000 workers. Government arsenals manufactured artillery, automatic weapons and tanks, while civilian factories produced two-thirds of the ammunition and almost all signal and optical equipment used by the army.[15] Civilian industry also provided uniforms, rations and medical supplies to the fighting forces.

The fundamental problem Japan's strategic industries faced, of course, was that access to natural resources depended on a merchant marine that was already overstretched in December 1941, before it suffered any serious battle losses.

The destruction of Japan's surface commerce primarily by US submarines and Allied aircraft further obstructed military and government attempts to achieve self-sufficiency. What they did achieve was an unbalanced economy that left the majority of Japanese civilians initially without the creature comforts of life (matches, polished white rice, gasoline, cosmetics, permanent waves, stylish clothing) and ultimately by the summer of 1945 devoid of basic necessities of sufficient food, clothing and shelter.

By the mid-1930s, Japan had the arsenal of weaponry – essentially late World War I era technology – with which it would fight the East Asian war. True there would be further technological advances, especially in aircraft manufacture, but by and large the imperial army fought its final war armed with weapons at least a generation old. So equipped the IJA was nonetheless successful in early 1942 fighting against Allied forces similarly armed. Against the modern weapons developed by the Allies, especially the United States, during the course of World War II, from 1942 onward Japan was outranged, outgunned, and outclassed at every level. Beyond the material aspect of a massive reorganization of the forces whose costs the empire was unable to bear, there was the psychological conundrum of adapting an army and its traditions to modern, more impersonal weapons. Even if materially possible, such wrenching changes to Japan's infantry doctrine and its military training and officer education system might have fatally disrupted the army's ethos and culture.

National policy development

From the Meiji Restoration into the mid 1880s, Japan looked inward. The main presumed opponent, Imperial Russia, existed more for planning purposes than for anticipated field operations because Japan was too weak in every sense to resist foreign military advances. By the late 1880s, Tokyo's attention turned to China, land of turmoil and competitor for the strategic Korean Peninsula. Yamagata's *Opinions on China* (1884) called for Japan to strengthen its military forces, expand Japanese influence in East Asia and help re-impose order in Imperial China. Six years later he elaborated on the two paths to national independence: first, to defend national sovereignty from outside aggression; and second, to defend a forward line of overseas interests as vital national advantages. Put differently, Yamagata proposed to extend the Japanese empire's national prestige and sovereignty to the defence of colonial possessions as legitimate means to defend national interests. The cause of his ruminations was twofold. First, Russia would complete construction of the Trans-Siberian Railway in four or five years, and the rail line would carry Moscow's influence into East Asia. Second, China was meddling in Korea, the paramount Japanese 'overseas interest', and this development, if not checked, made a clash of arms between the two competing regional Asian powers inevitable. Still, Japanese operational planning was defensive in nature, premised as it was on defeating an advancing Chinese or Russian army in order to protect Japan's overseas' interests.

Only after the Russo–Japanese War did Japan's generals and admirals craft a national defence policy, and even then it was to align military and political goals and their attendant shares of the national budget with the overall economy. The naval general staff remained cool about formulating any policy that relegated their service to a secondary role, so in 1906 army leaders appealed to the throne to order the chiefs of staff of both services to prepare a policy for national defence. The resulting compromise document, completed in April 1907, contained the following premises: first, the essence of national defence lay in offensive striking power, an idea rooted in the notion that barbarians (*iteki*) should never be allowed to violate imperial soil; second, Russia was Japan's primary hypothetical opponent; third, preservation of the Anglo–Japanese alliance and simultaneously actively seeking other alliances was essential; fourth, national defence necessitated sufficient imperial forces to oppose the Russians and the Americans in offensive operations. These standards required 25 standing divisions and 50 war-time divisions, or roughly double the size of the Russo–Japanese War army. Imperial defence then formally mandated the protection of overseas rights in Manchuria and Korea, which in turn dictated that Japan had to depend on forward offensive operations conducted overseas for its security. Operational plans that emphasized offensive campaigns against Vladivostok and the Ussuri River area received official approval in the 1907 National Defence Plan. While the navy engaged and destroyed the enemy fleet on the high seas, the army would annihilate the opponent's ground forces by a series of rapidly conducted offensive operations on the Asian continent. Japanese military strategists scripted a decisive battle to replicate a Cannae-like double envelopment and annihilation of the opposing force.

The first revision to imperial defence policy occurred in 1918. Russia remained Japan's primary future opponent, but the United States along with China were added to the list. Significantly, the army henceforth focused its planning and budget requirements on a campaign against Russia (and the successor Soviet Union) while the navy designed war plans and crafted its ever-increasing budget demands based on a conflict with the United States. Strategists retained the traditional short-war concept, defined as gaining a decisive battlefield victory in the opening phase of a conflict, but incorporated a provision acknowledging the necessity of preparations for and resolution to endure a protracted war. In theory this revised strategy equated to capitalizing on the initial military successes to create strongly defended and self-sufficient bases for protracted warfare along with the capability to fight decisive battles on several fronts.

Anti-war sentiment and economic retrenchment in the years immediately following World War I forced the army to drop its wartime requirement to 40 divisions. Shortly afterwards the throne again sanctioned a revision of defence policy, this time in response to the international disarmament trend exemplified by the Washington Naval Conference of 1922. In the 1923 version of imperial defence policy, the United States, by virtue of its possessions in East Asia, its rejection of the League of Nations, its promotion of the China market, and its racial exclusion policies, became the paramount threat to Japan's ambitions to secure the resources of Asia and the Pacific. Moreover the collapse of Imperial Russia left the United States by default the status of the IJA's main hypothetical enemy. Strategic policy envisaged joint operations to seize the Philippines and Guam at the outset of hostilities. Japan would forge alliances where possible in order to avoid international isolation and would employ its total national resources to achieve its war aims rapidly, but, as necessary, would also be able to sustain a protracted war.

The third and last revision of defence policy came in 1936 in anticipation of the advent of the non-naval treaty era. The document was as notable for its appeal to the mysticism of the imperial house as to the fundamental principles of national defence. The theatre of operations included East Asia and the western Pacific reflecting Japan's hypothetical opponents – the United States, the Soviet Union, Great Britain, and China. Defence policy still hinged on a quick, decisive war, fought with advanced weapons, in order to avoid a protracted conflict of attrition. The accompanying force structure to implement this strategy appeared in the armaments replenishment plan, drafted in 1936, that envisioned 50 war-time divisions along with 140 air squadrons. Thus the army expected to mobilize the entire nation for a total war and between 1937 and 1942 to completely re-equip and modernize its forces for the inevitable conflict.

Japan's military takeover of Manchuria in 1931–2, its aggressive behaviour in North China, its industrial and commercial exploitation of China's resources, and Tokyo's incessant demands on the Chinese Republic naturally kindled Chinese resentment and resistance. Just as the IJA was about to embark on its Five-Year Rearmament Programme, a minor clash of Chinese and Japanese forces at the Marco Polo Bridge on the outskirts of Beijing rapidly escalated into a full blown, if undeclared, continental war. As a generalization, Japanese staff officers in the War Ministry and the General Staff who favoured rearmament and a national defence state for the purposes of total war were willing to settle the incident locally. Others, however, believed that Chinese resistance would crumble after the IJA delivered a single punishing blow. Some 200,000 reservists were quickly mobilized and three divisions brought to war-time strength deployed to North China in late July 1937. Contrary to conventional wisdom in the ranks, the Chinese did not cave in before Japan's military onslaught as fighting not only continued in the north but also spread to Central China. A second wave of mobilizations in mid-August threw 300,000 more troops into Shanghai to crush Chinese resistance. Instead the IJA found itself in exactly the war it never wanted – a protracted war of attrition in the streets of Shanghai. Five reserve divisions were mobilized in late August and rushed to the the central front. Japan's force structure now counted 24 divisions, 16 of them engaged in operations in China. The grandiose scheme for rearmament went out the window.

Japanese losses in the three-month-long bloodletting around Shanghai amounted to 40,000 troops and produced a popular expectation at home that the sacrifices would bring huge concessions, indemnities and other rewards from China. But the fighting dragged on with no achievable end in sight. Imperial General Headquarters, established in November 1937, expected that the capture of the Chinese Nationalist capital at Nanjing would end the war. Instead it produced one of the most notorious war crimes of the twentieth century. Bogged down in the wrong war, at the wrong place, at the wrong time, against the wrong enemy, the IJA next attempted a vast encirclement campaign in central China designed to envelop and annihilate China's field armies. It too failed, serving only to draw Japan deeper into the Chinese mainland, and left the over-committed Imperial Army mired in a war it could neither win nor quit.

Ignoring the suffering of the private soldier (a trademark of its later Asia and Pacific campaigns), the high command in Tokyo fought its battles on maps and pressed field commanders to hurl units forward as if the swampy, marsh-like terrain around Wuhan or rugged hills further west did not exist. Advancing in 100-degree heat without proper equipment and handicapped by severe shortages of personnel, equipment, ammunition, medicine, and food (also all too familiar characteristics of Japan's later campaigns in Asia and the Pacific), envelopment operations against Changsha and Wuhan witnessed outbreaks of cholera and malaria in the ranks while malnutrition also stalked the field forces. As an indication of its logistics problems, the army eventually switched to light infantry formations, who parked their field artillery in garrison in exchange for the extra mobility needed to trap Chinese forces retreating as part of a strategic withdrawal and scorched-earth policy. Left to their own devices, Japanese infantry regiments relied for supporting fire on organic battalion mountain artillery, and often resorted to unsupported infantry attacks because of a break-down in logistical support. Similar infantry tactics for similar reasons resurfaced during the Pacific and South West Asia fighting.

Badly overextended, supply lines in chaos, with cholera epidemic and no end to the war in sight, IJA planners pondered their next move. They could neither withdraw unilaterally from China nor continue their ambitious rearmaments plan. Thus in December 1941, on the eve of Japan's attack on the West, the IJA had suffered 700,000 casualties in China and another 25,000 in two border wars with the Soviet Union. It was in this context that US Secretary of State Cordell Hull's demand that Japan pull out of China provoked War Minister Tōjō Hideki to exclaim, 'What would we ever tell the war dead?'[16]

Society

The Imperial Japanese Army had a Tommy Atkins-like relationship with the larger society. When the nation–state was threatened, a concept that had not impinged on the popular consciousness until the Sino–Japanese War, the army's prestige rose. Government war-time propaganda and appeals to patriotism and chauvinism mobilized popular opinion for wars against China and Russia. But the same emotional calls could backfire by creating false expectations, as happened during the treaty riots of 1905 following the Russo–Japanese War. The military, moreover, could not sustain its war-time popularity during the stretches of peace between 1905 and 1930. Still, throughout its existence the army was a central feature of general Japanese society and popular culture.

From samurai to soldiers

Families of samurai stock accounted for between 5 and 6 per cent of Japan's estimated 30–2 million population in 1868, or roughly two million individuals. They were, of course, the most powerful social group, and in 1872 when the Meiji government abolished the four social classes only the samurai retained their status as *shizoku* (warriors). Nevertheless, for the sake of national unity parochial loyalties to individual feudal lords and fiefdoms had to be eliminated, and to re-establish domestic law and order a national army filled by conscripts had to be created. Popular reaction to both measures was often violent. The Satsuma uprising was the great samurai death throe, but peasant unrest was an issue that successive Japanese cabinets dealt with into the 1930s. Rural uprisings in the 1870s against conscription involved thousands of people nation-wide as peasants denounced the draft as a blood-tax and a revival of the hated corvée of Tokugawa *bakufu*. More than fifteen major riots erupted, mainly in western Japan, where peasants attacked and burned government offices, schools, and police stations. Troops quelled the disturbances, and the government subsequently executed the ringleaders as well as punishing at least 20,000 others involved.

Draft resistance stemmed partly from ignorance – rumours abounded in the countryside that the army authorities would drain conscripts' blood to obtain the red dye for military trousers, caps and blankets or give the blood to foreigners to drink (red wine) – and partly from a long-standing resentment of the haughty warrior class that most peasants had no desire to join or emulate. At root, however, conscription not only disrupted the individual's life but also threatened the survival of the entire peasant family by denying it a vital source of young, healthy manual labour in a labour-intensive farming economy whose back-breaking work provided only a marginal existence for most peasant families. Finally, outside a minority living in the great cities, the concept of a nation-state was vague and appeals to membership in a larger entity fell on deaf ears.

The Sino–Japanese War produced a clearer definition of the emperor as commander-in-chief of the armed forces and a more coherent notion of national unity. Emperor Meiji showed the way in September 1894 by moving from his Tokyo palace to Imperial General Headquarters located in Hiroshima. Leaving behind his entourage, wife and concubines, the emperor appeared daily in full military regalia, projecting a manly appearance and idealizing a spartan existence. Meiji's focus on his troops was part of the emerging imperial myth that required the emperor to be shown in personal command of forces. As Stewart Lone observed, however, the throne was something like the Wizard of Oz – awesome in imagination, weak in reality.[17] Meiji had no place in war councils and there is no evidence he initiated any policy, although his public image confirmed Japan's role as leader of Asia under a benevolent emperor figure. The close association between emperor and army continued during the Russo–Japanese War as Meiji presented regimental colours to the War Minister who in turn passed them to regimental standard bearers. Before and after the war, the Meiji emperor officially attended various military ceremonies and observed reviews and military manoeuvres. Imperial attendance at the annual autumn manoeuvres became institutionalized and evolved into an important feature of Emperor Hirohito's relations to his armed forces. During World War II, Hirohito went one better than his famous grandfather by personally presenting regimental colours to the standard bearers at highly ritualized palace ceremonies.

In like fashion, leaders of the new government sought incentives to develop loyalty, discipline and obedience in the new conscript army. Fifty days after a revolt by an imperial guards' unit, the so-called Takebashi uprising of August 1878, the government promulgated the *Gunjin kunkai* (Admonition to Servicemen). Written in stilted language that made it difficult for commoners to understand, the injunction enjoined officers to cultivate the derivative, and largely fictional, samurai virtues of loyalty, bravery, courage, and obedience to orders. Obedience became the bedrock of a military institution renowned for its severe discipline to indoctrinate recruits.

The 1882 Imperial Rescript to Soldiers and Sailors targeted a different audience – the enlisted ranks. It took direct aim at the popular rights movements in a conscious effort to keep the military out of domestic politics. Its straight-forward, unadorned language emphasized to the ranks that the national army was the emperor's army. The link between the army and the throne meant that obedience to the orders of one's superiors was synonymous with obedience to the direct command of the emperor. The preamble to the *Rescript* drew on myth to elaborate the imperial control of military forces dating from antiquity, and identified the five military virtues of loyalty, courtesy, bravery, fidelity, and frugality for all to emulate. Sons of the royal family also served in the military, a fact the army used to its advantage to further identify itself with the throne.

Another distinction for the military services in society came in 1879 when the government enshrined its war dead in the newly renamed Yasukuni Shrine across from the Imperial Palace in Tokyo. The War Ministry defrayed the shrine's annual upkeep and the war dead in turn became spirits guarding the nation. Thus the notion that the military were a unique group in society received official status that reached far beyond the service institutions themselves. Tying the military virtues, especially obedience, to society, the *Imperial Rescript on Education*, issued in 1890, inculcated an orthodox philosophy of state with strong Confucian overtones of hierarchical personal relationships. The *Rescript* emphasized that the Japanese nation was a family, possessed of unique moral values and ruled by a divine emperor.[18] These officially approved civic virtues clearly complemented the officially promulgated military values.

Military service gained greater acceptability among ordinary Japanese following the Sino–Japanese War. Success bred acceptance. The terrible losses in the Russo–Japanese War for seemingly paltry gains, however, produced a backlash of popular protest. Rioting engulfed Tokyo's Hibiya Park following the government's announcement of the terms of the Portsmouth Treaty. Ignorant of the actual battlefield conditions – Japan being short of junior officers, ammunition, medical supplies, and money – the popular outburst was essentially anti-government, not anti-foreign or anti-military in nature. Forced to declare martial law, the government called out troops to restore order in the capital city, a traditional and familiar mission for the army. More significant, the army authorities were never candid, even among themselves, about the tenuousness of Japan's victory over Imperial Russia. Official military histories extolled the tactics employed and Japan's unique fighting spirit, an idea that seeped into popular awareness. Suppressed was the unpleasant reality of Japan's serious logistical and strategic shortcomings, and only a handful of selected officers at the Imperial War College each year were even made aware that such documentation existed. Instead the army embellished tales of Japan's uniqueness to explain Japan's military success – a national myth that became increasingly interwoven into the fabric of the larger society.

Through such glorification of wartime exploits, the Japanese military claimed a special relationship with the emperor, a closeness to the throne and a selfless attitude that placed the military above the crass commercialism, political opportunism and individual self-indulgence of the day. At the popular level, patriotism replaced people's rights movement.[19] Finally, participation by larger and larger numbers of young Japanese males in the expanding post-war army gave the institution greater exposure throughout society. Professional soldiers may have replaced hereditary samurai, but society continued to rely on tales of modern warriors emulating their ancestors.

The Ministry of Education, for instance, promoted the heroes and heroics of the Russo–Japanese War as paragons of Japaneseness in primary school history and ethics texts. To commemorate the Fall of Mukden in 1905 (present Shenyang), 10 March was thereafter designated Army Day, a national holiday, while the government fixed Navy Day on 27 May in honour of Admiral Tōgō Heihachirō's victory at Tsushima Straits. The army's prestige waxed in the immediate post Russo–Japanese War years, and military authorities capitalized on the growing number of reservists by founding the Imperial Reservists Association in 1910. The association gained a prominent social and political role, especially in rural villages, enabling the army to spread its values to the local populations. Following the personnel reductions of 1922, the Education Ministry placed 2,000 seconded officers throughout middle schools, where they supervised military training courses in the curriculum.

Conscription and society

Japan's initial conscription ordinance drafted youths at age twenty for three years active service followed by two years each in the first and second reserves respectively. Modelled on the French system, the legislation originally allowed paid substitutes to serve in place of the putative conscript and contained numerous exemptions from military service. Japanese authorities initially honoured primogeniture so as not to upset the traditional social order. Besides heirs, heads of households, government officials, and students were also exempted from military service. Conscription reform in 1883 abolished paid substitutes and eliminated most other exemptions as well. Further reform six years later eliminated all exemption clauses related to households, but provided for extended deferments from entering active service according to family circumstances and for students.[20] The first cohort of conscripts, though, were mainly second and third sons, who were likely to come from farming families given the demographic structure. From these men, who stood to inherit nothing, came the cadre of the army's career non-commissioned officers (NCOs). This pattern persisted into the 1930s and 1940s as army personnel officers remained reluctant to recommend first-born sons for NCO training. By 1891, 12 per cent of conscripts were high school graduates or had equivalent work experience; 28 per cent primary school graduates or equivalent work experience; 34 per cent had a limited ability to read and do arithmetic; and fully 26 per cent were illiterate.[21]

Conscription was not initially pervasive because the army needed relatively few young Japanese males to fill its small 36,000-man force structure. Until the second revision of the conscription ordinance in 1889, the actual number of those drafted versus those liable for military service was relatively insignificant – 3 per cent of those eligible in 1875, and roughly 6 per cent annually through 1890. Even after the reforms and the Sino–Japanese War, by 1897 only about 11 per cent of qualified young men were inducted. Following the Russo–Japanese War and further expansion of the army, that figure more than doubled to 23 per cent and remained at that level into 1937. In 1906, as part of an economy drive, the War Ministry reduced the term of active service from three to two years, a move when combined with the expansion of the army doubled the percentage of inductees. This meant about 100,000 twenty-year-olds were called to the colours annually to replace those leaving active service. The discharged soldiers in turn went directly into the reserves, thereby doubling the number of veterans returning to their communities each year.

After reaching their twentieth year, youths reported for their pre-induction physical examinations, normally conducted in April and May at a local primary school or regional assembly hall. On 10 January of the following year, those conscripted reported to their regiments. Army medical examiners graded the recruits: A = taller than 51 inches and B = taller than 50 inches were the prime candidates for induction during peace-time. The men in the A group became the pool from which the army drew men for active duty service. Those in the B group were placed in the First Replacement Pool, otherwise fit for active duty, but excess to the army's current active duty personnel requirements. For example, in 1912, 256,754 young men were inducted into the army and 4,931 drafted for the navy (which depended on volunteers for its smaller, more élite service). Of these, 103,684 (the A Group) were conscripted for a full two-year term on active duty in the army. Another 153,070 (the B group) were assigned to the First Replacement Pool where they received about 120 days of basic military training after which the army discharged them from active service but retained their military skills with a lengthy reserve obligation.

By 1937, the draft age remained at age twenty with a two-year active service obligation, five years four months first reserve commitment and a ten-year second reserve obligation. Those classified B1 and B2 formed replacement pools of fillers liable for twelve years for recall to active duty. In April 1941 manpower demands terminated the second replacement pool and in 1944 the government lowered the conscription age to nineteen. Likewise, the authorities abolished student deferments in the autumn of 1943 in hopes of obtaining technical expertise and high-quality officer stock from the universities. One of the most poignant visual records of Japan's last war remains the film footage of thousands of mobilized students wearing their school uniforms, shouldering their antiquated rifles and marching behind their school flags during a driving October rain as they pass in review before thousands of spectators filling Tokyo's Meiji Stadium. Given their education, some of these student-soldiers went into aviation branches of both services where some ended their lives as kamikaze flyers. As late as October 1944, however, Japan had mobilized not more than 6.3 per cent of a population of 73 million whereas Germany, the Soviet Union, and the UK had by that time 18 to 20 per cent of their citizens in uniform. Even the United States had 8 per cent of its population in uniform.

Training the force

Enlisted training involved repetitive exercises by individual soldiers to master a single new technology – machine gun, artillery piece, engineering equipment, and the like. Non-commissioned officers (NCOs) served as models for army life and were the purveyors of military technical expertise. Company-grade officers acted as instructors during the first year of recruit training, but almost never interfered directly with the internal squad affairs. Indeed, aside from the officer of the day, officers stayed out of the barracks, which were the preserve of the NCO. Unit training typically involved battle drills designed to produce instinctive reaction to anticipated tactical situations. Discipline was harsh, obedience to superiors absolute. Corporal punishment was not only condoned but also approved as a means of strengthening the recruits' martial resolve and promoting the values of Japanese spirit. Such practices gradually became accepted conduct in the barracks and army following the Russo–Japanese War.

The 1908 revision of the army handbook (*guntai naimusho*) established a *naimuhan* (a grouping of soldiers in the barracks for purposes of administration and discipline). The group was a reinforced squad echelon that mixed together about fifteen to twenty enlisted men, composed of first-, second- and third-year draftees plus their NCOs, all of whom shared a common barracks. The purpose was to improve the supervision and oversight of daily life, as well as to instil spiritual indoctrination (*seishin kyōiku*) in conscripts. Armed with new regulations that stressed discipline as the lifeblood of an army, the *naimuhan* became the mechanism to enforce unquestioning obedience to orders among conscripts. Revised regulations also described the army as a family that together shared its joys and sorrows. The *naimuhan*, then, was the surrogate family whose NCOs and officers became parents to the conscripts. And just as parents might justify punishing children, so, too, the NCOs or the 'older brothers' (the second-year soldiers) might justify punishing recruits for mistakes that embarrassed or shamed the *naimuhan* 'family'.

Besides official rules and regulations, the Imperial Army, like the larger society, relied on a series of informal standards to achieve conformity, discipline and obedience. Most noticeable was barracks life controlled by second-year soldiers, who resorted to a combination of hazing, physical violence, kangaroo courts, and threats to ensure that new recruits adapted to the army's culture. Violence was pervasive in the barracks where, away from officers' eyes, recruits suffered physical abuse for making mistakes on the drill field, for not following instructions to the letter and for all the minor infractions that basic training dwelled on to transform a civilian into a soldier. Having endured this year-long rite of passage, the recruits in turn inflicted the same regimen on their successors in the barracks. Violence in the barracks became institutionalized.

Critics assert that physical intimidation common to the barracks was the only way the army could guarantee the iron-clad obedience it demanded. It is true that corporal punishment, the object of which was to instil unquestioning obedience as a reflex or habit in the soldier, was pervasive, but more than brute force and intimidation was needed to forge squad unity and martial spirit. The conscious efforts by civilian and army leaders to link the army inseparably to the throne by appeals to a mythical past connection gave larger meaning to the privations and indignities of the barracks. The familial pattern gave a context to the routine daily activities of army life. Indignities were stoically accepted by the many as part of the army experience, which in turn was an accepted part of life as more and more Japanese gravitated to an unquestioning belief in unique national virtues identified with the unbroken imperial line.

The officer corps

Officers matriculated from the military academy, usually via officer cadet preparatory schools (*yōnen gakkō*) whose numbers varied from six to one depending on the army's requirements and budgets. Officer education emphasized tenacious military spirit and the fostering of rigid military discipline in the ranks. Tactics dominated the curriculum at both the Military Academy and at the War College. Subject matter relied on memorization of facts, and initiative and determination became more prized than objective assessments of a given situation. Instructors reinforced the notion that the margin between victory and defeat in battle was razor thin, so the side willing to endure the greater hardships and privations would be the more likely to emerge victorious. Officers were groomed as commanders, and the army assigned its best to combat arms – infantry, cavalry, artillery. Less capable ones were shunted off to duller postings as logisticians, a career whose appeal may be gauged by a contemporary army saying: 'When baggage handlers become soldiers, telephone poles will sprout flowers'.

The military academy graduated on average about 250–300 cadet aspirants annually, but the total of course fluctuated according to the army's needs, swelling to a high of 882 graduates in 1907 and a low of 117 in 1930. After 1941, classes averaged more than 1,500. Upon graduation cadets spent four months with their assigned unit before receiving a commission. These numbers were insufficient for the demands of mobilization, so in 1883 Japan adopted a reserve officer system. Henceforth a qualified young man might volunteer for a one-year active duty stint which, if successfully completed, gained him a reserve commission. These specially trained men became the source of the officers mobilized for Japan's wars.

The aspiring reserve officer had to be a middle-school graduate and had to pay out of his own pocket all expenses associated with his active training.[22] These qualifications limited the potential pool of officer candidates to a small strata of society and were well beyond the dreams of almost all Japanese. Only in 1933 did the army abolish the personal payment requirement. The need for large numbers of junior officers from mid-1937 onwards necessitated further changes to the reserve officer system. Potential officers still had to be middle- or high-school or university graduates. After three months of basic training, the army tested conscripts with these qualifications to measure leadership aptitude. Three months later, after service in a troop unit, a second, written test on military skills and tactics followed. Successful candidates were divided into two groups: A for officer training courses and B for NCO training. Cadet aspirants underwent eleven months of officer training and four months service as a cadet with a field unit before receiving their reserve commissions. NCOs received one year of training in branch speciality schools and promotion upon graduation. Of Japan's 67,500 officers, 36 per cent were regulars by 1939, but that percentage dropped to about 10 per cent by 1945 – 21,500 regulars in an officer corps numbering 202,000. Only 22 per cent of all 50,000 lieutenants were regulars in 1939, meaning that the IJA already depended on reservists to supply nearly 80 per cent of its company grade officers two years before the outbreak of the Greater East Asian War.

The army and domestic order

Certainly the early years of the army's existence gained it little popularity with the citizenry – quite the opposite. Troops repeatedly appeared to suppress riots, quell popular demonstrations, break labour strikes, or dissolve public protests. Enlisted soldiers were politically active, passing out petitions, for example, and recent research suggests that the then current popular rights ideology influenced the Takebashi mutineers. In 1884 a ten-day uprising by 6,000 peasants in the Chichibu region of central Japan protested against the government's refusal to allow a moratorium on usurious loans by attacking loan sharks' offices and government buildings. Soldiers called out to crush the rioting arrested 3,000 demonstrators, including five alleged ringleaders who later were convicted and hanged. After the Sino–Japanese War, labour troubles afflicted Japan's corporations as underpaid and poorly treated workers sought a measure of dignity and a living wage. Troops again moved in to restore order, notably in the Ashio mining strike of 1907.

The new age of Taishō (1912–26) witnessed a striking decline in military prestige occasioned by a clumsy attempt to use the throne to force through a huge military budget, precipitating the so-called Taishō political crisis of 1913. In 1907 the army had increased its force structure by two regular divisions as a first step towards reaching a goal of 25 standing divisions. Attempts to add two more divisions in 1912 precipitated political deadlock. Prime Minister Saionji Kin'mochi was sympathetic to the proposal but the condition of the government and the national treasury rendered such a large increase in the military budget unaffordable. Heavy-handed attempts by the army's leaders to use the throne to compel the Imperial Diet to pass the military appropriation budget included the resignation of the War Minister, which led to the fall of the Saionji cabinet. The unexpected popular backlash to the army's machinations, however, doomed the successor cabinet's attempts to supplement the military budget and dimmed the army's lustre in the popular mind.

Corruption scandals involving navy contracts further tarnished the military's supposed aloofness from personal gain. Moreover new or revitalized ideologies – socialism, Marxism, anarchism, and communism – added to Japan's intellectual ferment during the period. Their prescriptions to redress the imbalance in economic and social life between town and county often ran contrary to the military's values and the emerging official formulation of *kokutai* (the structure of Japan's polity under an unbroken imperial line). The years between 1912 and 1926 witnessed rapid change – a demographic shift to the cities, a boom-and-bust economy, domestic population pressures, and international dangers from a newly established Soviet Union, a resurgent Chinese Republic and a discriminatory United States.

Rice riots in the summer of 1918 lasted three months and spread nationwide, involving more than 700,000 people in 60 cities, towns and villages. Again the army mobilized troops against the demonstrations, and in large cities such as Kobe and Kure soldiers fired on demonstrators to suppress the outbreaks. The following year witnessed large-scale labour disputes. Strikes at the army's Osaka artillery arsenal, at copper mines and at the Kobe shipyards again pitted imperial troops against strikers. By the advent of the 1920s, the reservoir of goodwill of civilian society toward the army seemed to have run dry.

Feeding on the myths of Japanese uniqueness to formulate its post Russo–Japanese War doctrine, the army's reaction to the new styles of political expression and swirling social currents of the Taishō era was to redouble efforts to stress spiritual education in its ranks. This re-evaluation was evident in the 1921 edition of the army Squad Regulation Handbook (*guntai naimusho*), which ascribed the source of the Japanese Army's strength to the imperial institution. Obedience to superiors' orders manifested resolution, understanding and loyalty to the imperial institution as defined by *kokutai*. Army authorities consciously sought to reinforce reverence for the monarchy at what they saw as a critical juncture, given the recent collapse of the Russian, German, Austro-Hungarian, and Ottoman empires. Identification with the throne reinvigorated the status of army.

Added to this reaction was the military's rejection of Taishō liberalism. Distinct from society and possessing a higher ethos and superior values, the military portrayed itself as above the venality and corruption of party politics or the crass commercialism of capitalism, as well as the decadence of modern, urban society. An early manifestation of potential implications of appeals to Japan's uniqueness occurred in the aftermath of the Great Tokyo earthquake of 1923, when a military police captain strangled the anarchist agitator Ōsugi Sakae, his wife and six-year old nephew to remove poisonous threats to *kokutai*.

During Japan's Roaring Twenties, however, few Japanese agreed with the army's self-image. Derided as tax thieves by the press, officers stopped wearing their uniforms in public in large cities during the early 1920s, and large personnel reductions put thousands of officers and enlisted men out on the streets. Many of the redundant officers soon found employment as instructors, for by 1925 compulsory military training in schools spread military ideology to the most impressionable members of society. The Manchurian Incident of September 1931 reinvigorated public support for the army. The Kwantung Army's bold action in seizing Manchuria had, so the public believed, secured Japan's 'lifeline' and asserted Japanese rights against 'unruly' Chinese and discriminatory Western imperialist powers.

Japan's army itself was in turbulence during these transitional years. The founding generation was retired, dead or dying off, and younger officers literally fought among themselves to replace their leaders. As the army grew distant from the larger society during the 1920s, extremists within the officer corps believed the military alone embodied the true values of Japan. Anti-militarism, societal decadence, greedy capitalists, and the impoverished condition of farming villages (the source of conscripts) radicalized certain junior officers, who turned to violence to achieve their version of a Shōwa Restoration. Factionalism grew rampant in the Japanese Army and spawned deadly violence.

Under Yamagata's patronage, officers from the former Chōshū fief had dominated the top positions in the army until the 1920s. At that time, middle-grade staff officers – majors and colonels intrigued by the notion of a national defence state – used their connections to gradually exclude officers from Chōshū from the War College, in effect ending Chōshū's predominant influence in the army. Attempts to undermine the Chōshū clique in turn created multiple factions committed to a variety of programmes, ranging from preparations for total war to direct imperial rule. The former, generally known as the Control Faction, and the latter, identified as the Imperial Way clique, waged a Mafia-like struggle of sub-rosa plots to overthrow the elected cabinets, conducted inflammatory and vituperative pamphlet campaigns, and organized the assassination of leading political and military figures. The climax was the great military mutiny of 26 February 1936 when radical young officers murdered the Finance Minister, Lord Keeper of the Privy Seal and the Inspector General of military education as 1,400 officers and men of the 1st Division simultaneously took control of central Tokyo. A tense stand-off ensued over four days as armed troops faced each other across the capital's snow-covered streets. The rebellion collapsed because Emperor Hirohito steadfastly refused to negotiate with the rebel officers, despite the pleas of certain of his senior military advisors who sympathized with the mutineers. Martial law remained in effect in Tokyo until mid-July 1936 as the Control faction consolidated its power and purged its rivals from top posts in the army. The military also gained ascendancy in political cabinets after the so-called 2–26 Incident by virtue of reinstating a 1901 provision that required the service ministers (War and Navy) to be general officers on the active list. Without the army's approval, no cabinet could be formed. Henceforth the army had the power of life and death over the civilian cabinet.[23]

Military ascendancy was the denouement of the institutionalization of the concept of the independence of the supreme command (tōsuiken dokuritsu), whose origins in the late 1870s were more benign. At that time, the purpose was simply to separate the concentration of military and political power in a single man's hands, in order to prevent the reappearance of a Saigō Takamori-like figure who simultaneously commanded imperial troops and in the highest counsels of state also set national policy for the units he commanded. Later the notion evolved as a device to prevent senior officers from being manipulated by political factions and to inoculate officers from the popular rights movement of the 1880s. Article Eleven of the 1889 Meiji Constitution stated that the emperor was the supreme commander of Japan's military forces and that the respective chiefs of staff were to 'assist' his imperial majesty without regard to the cabinet or Imperial Diet. With the passage of time, independence of the supreme command left the military unrestrained by the civilian government.

To check the growing power of political parties, in 1900 the Yamagata cabinet also formalized the right of the service leaders to enjoy direct access to the throne in operational matters. By the late 1920s, however, field commanders in North China, invoking the right of supreme command and the time-honoured principle of command authority, appealed to these prerogatives to justify their unilateral, and illegal, conspiracies designed to provide *casus belli* for military intervention on the continent. The assassination of a Manchurian warlord in 1928 followed by the fabricated incident along the South Manchuria railway outside Mukden in September 1931 opened the way for Japanese military aggression in north Asia. It was not simply disregard of civilian authority. It was just as often defiance of the War Ministry and General Staff in Tokyo, as occurred during the border war with the Soviet Union at Nomonhan in the summer of 1939. Insubordination also spread within the Imperial Army as junior and middle-grade officers plotted and executed *coup d'états* designed to restore direct imperial rule as they interpreted it.

One might conclude that, in an odd sense, both the Control and Imperial Way factions were winners in the aftermath of the 2–26 Incident. The Control group finally seemed to have the power to institute the military, economic and social reforms to recast Japan into a controlled and economically self-sufficient economy. Yet the army's political ineptitude at home and the diversion of scarce resources to underwrite the outbreak of war in China ended any possibility of remaking Japan into a self-sustaining national defence state. As for the Imperial Way members, although temporarily discredited, their ideology trumpeting the intangibles of spiritual power and imperial mysticism remained embedded in the forces.

Total war

Japan's undeclared war with China that began in July 1937 quickly degenerated into a stalemate whose implications soon appeared on the home front. More and more of the nation's slender resources went to military production; less and less to the domestic consumer market. Home-front rationing began with gasoline in 1938 and by 1942 clothing and food were also restricted. Inflation took hold because in 1937 the government, expecting a short war, had from 1937 financed the extraordinary military expenditures by bond issues for two years. That decision sowed the wind that reaped the inflationary whirlwind of paying for a protracted general war. Price controls served only to hold down real wages and impoverish workers. Rice production fell steadily between 1937 and 1944 for a combination of reasons. Labour was scarce in farming villages because the army had called so many young men to the colours, fertilizer was lacking because ammunition factories needed the ingredients to manufacture explosives and farming implements were in short supply because factories had converted to manufacture military goods. The average citizen consumed fewer and fewer calories as the war continued, and by mid summer of 1945 the population in the cities was slowly starving to death.

By the end of 1937, the IJA counted 16 divisions, with two-thirds of its force structure and roughly 700,000 troops fighting in China. Eighteen months of operations from July 1937 to December 1938 claimed a quarter of a million soldiers killed, wounded or dead from disease. As the force structure expanded to meet war-time needs, more and more men were needed to fill the 41 regular divisions formed by 1939. As of January of that year, one village in north-east Japan with about 500 households listed 202 recalled reservists and 81 regulars on active service. Eleven had already been killed in action or died of wounds or illness, and seven more had been wounded in the fighting or felled by illness. The war also made soldiers of 182 of the village's farmers, eleven of its merchants, nine of its labourers, sixteen of its civil service workers, nineteen of its day labourers, two of its priests, and three of unspecified occupations. Even the temporary loss of this cross-section of skills seriously impaired the local community's social and economic infrastructure.[24]

To expand the force structure for the undeclared war and to replace its losses, the army mobilized its reserves and increased draft calls. This only siphoned off still more male labour. As of 1 August 1938, 11 per cent of soldiers serving in China were regulars (20–24 years old), 22 per cent recalled from the first reserve (25–30 years old), 45 per cent recalled from the second reserve (30–37 years old) and 21 per cent from the replacement reserve (untrained or partially trained fillers 22–33 years old).[25] Reservists called to active duty in the summer of 1937 marched off to war confidently, assuring their wives and children that they would be home to celebrate New Year's Day. Troop morale plunged after heavy losses and meaningless victories in a seemingly endless struggle. The cavalier attitude of staff officers toward the lower ranks contributed to discontent. 'Use soldiers up as you please', ran one cynical refrain, 'they only cost the price of postage for their draft notice'. This attitude seemed pervasive. General head-quarters routinely blamed defeats on cowardly soldiers, not their ill-conceived and unrealistic operational plans. The aphorism

> For officers it was a business,
> For NCOs it was a hobby,
> Only for enlisted troops was it for the sake of the nation

revealed a mentality that squandered soldiers' lives with little concern.

Japan's civilians also suffered from military neglect. Besides the vicissitudes of double-digit inflation and declining real wages, protection of civilians had never ranked high with the military. As a consequence, air defence emphasized civilian involvement at the neighbourhood level, not military defence. Although demographic shifts in the early years of Shōwa translated into 33 per cent more Japanese living in densely packed cities by 1940, the main homeland defence action announced in late 1943 and acted upon in 1944 was to create fire breaks by tearing down blocks of wooden buildings in the major cities.[26] *Sokai* (evacuation) became government policy in 1943, and in January 1944 school children living in Tokyo and Nagoya began to be resettled in rural areas. By June *sokai* touched more than 400,000 primary-school students. As military-age men and children left the cities, the government, with great reluctance because of prevailing sexist attitudes, mobilized young women into factories to replace male labour. At least 500,000 women were mobilized for war work, but only as an emergency measure. Japan's cities, nevertheless, remained woefully undefended and eventually served as the tinder for the indiscriminate urban bombing and fire raids that levelled city after city from March 1945.

The Japanese soldier

The interaction between strategy, doctrine, technology, equipment, society, and ideology produced a Japanese infantryman who by 1939 standards was suitably armed and equipped, well-trained and indoctrinated, and capable of suicidal perseverance and barbaric behaviour. He carried nearly 30 kilos of personal equipment, ammunition and rations on his back. Tramping through China in his hobnailed boots, he wore his field cap and lashed his steel helmet to his backpack. Inside the pack were extra socks, underwear, shaving and washing utensils, and an A or B emergency field ration. The A field ration included rice, canned meat, salt, miso, and soy sauce, while the B ration substituted hardtack for rice. His mess kit as well as a pair of *tabi* (rubber-soled canvas socks) were attached to his backpack. Two rolled sheets of shelter canvas, a rolled overcoat, shovel, canvas haversack, canteen, and tent peg festooned the soldier's back. He may or may not have carried a gas mask and bag strapped to his chest, but certainly had a utility belt with two ammunition pouches on each hip, each holding 60 rounds of 6.6 mm ammunition, as well as a cartridge case with another 180 rounds around his waist for his eight-pound Type-38 bolt-action rifle bearing the imperial crest. A two-foot-long bayonet and scabbard completed his regulation equipment. Extra rations, ammunition, hand grenades and the like added to his burden. Normally carrying about 40 per cent of his body weight, the infantryman was routinely expected to march 24 kilometres per day, and many more if the operational situation so dictated. Baggage trains, mainly horse-drawn carts, carried heavy weapons, additional small arms plus artillery ammunition and rations. Larger dray horses pulled artillery guns along the route of march. Division transport was usually some combination of horse-drawn vehicles supplemented in most cases by a limited number of military trucks.

Well-trained and indoctrinated, convinced he was a fighter, like soldiers in any life and death situation he was subject to a complex of emotions and motivations. Grandiose concepts such as fighting for the emperor or for the sake of the nation, while not totally absent, counted for little. For most soldiers, more immediately tangible things mattered in battle – self-preservation often meant kill or be killed. Others persevered because they refused to let their comrades down. Most intriguing of all, many fought for the honour of their family name, suggesting the familial bond that the army exploited in basic training held fast during battle.[27]

This notion of individual honour was embedded in the Field Service Regulations of 1941, which enjoined soldiers to avoid the disgrace of being taken prisoner. There is no question that Japanese soldiers fought on beyond the bitter end, but the larger question is not why they fought so desperately but why they died so recklessly. It is fashionable these days to ascribe the Allied troops' racial loathing of the Japanese and their unwillingness to take prisoners (both true in varying degrees) as inducements for the imperial soldier to fight to the death. Yet the almost total annihilation of Japanese garrisons occurred on isolated islands from Attu to Iwo Jima. Where the army had room to manoeuvre or had an intact line of communication, shattered units did withdraw (New Guinea, Luzon and Burma are examples) or were evacuated (as at Guadalcanal or Kiska). Even in these cases where there was opportunity to retreat, large numbers of Japanese soldiers still killed themselves and their wounded. The Japanese soldier died in great numbers because of his unquestioning obedience to unimaginative or desperate orders, his belief in the superiority of his race and culture, and his brutalized training constantly reinforced by field experience.

The IJA produced rock-ribbed soldiers capable of fighting to the death, but it also manufactured an army whose institutionalized brutality forever stamped its legacy. It is one thing for desperate soldiers fighting with their backs to the wall to resort to desperate measures, but how can one explain Japanese conduct in victory? Brutality did not begin at Nanjing, China, in December 1937. When Japanese infantry overran Port Arthur in 1895, they rounded up and executed hundreds, perhaps thousands, of Chinese prisoners, civilians and deserters, allegedly in retaliation for the Chinese mutilation of the corpses of fallen Japanese soldiers. The army was on its best behaviour during the Boxer Intervention (1900) and the Russo–Japanese War (1904–5), possibly because in both cases its senior leaders realized that the Western powers were monitoring and evaluating Japanese conduct. Counter-guerrilla operations against Bolsheviks in Siberia between 1918 and 1922 produced atrocities on both sides, but the story remained more or less forgotten in the remote Siberian hinterland. The army's conduct in China after mid summer 1937 could not be concealed from the world.

The gruesome events in central China – systematic murder, rape, arson – culminated with the notorious Rape of Nanjing. But Nanjing was hardly the exception. Japanese troops murdered tens of thousands of overseas Chinese living in Singapore in 1942; killed and starved more than 10,000 Americans taken captive in the Philippines plus 30,000 Filipino troops and another 100,000 Filipino civilians between 1942 and 1945; mistreated, malnourished and overworked 13,000 Allied prisoners of war to death along the Burma–Siam railway line, and even that staggering number pales beside the estimated 330,000 indigenous labourers who perished building the railway. Tens of thousands of natives conscripted by the Japanese as labourers simply vanished during the war.[28] And then there was North China, scene of the IJA's ceaseless 'mopping-up' counter-guerrilla campaigns grimly nicknamed 'Three lights' by the Chinese Communists: 'kill all, burn all, loot all'.

Violence against women was so widespread in China that senior officers issued tougher field orders as early as 1940 to prevent it, and reports of rape in Malaya 'although likely to be British propaganda' found their way into an interpellation in the House of Peers in 1942.[29] By that time, rape was apparently so commonplace and tolerated that the army penal code was amended in February 1942 to provide harsher penalties for the crime. Both to uphold the army's reputation and to prevent the spread of venereal disease, the IJA resorted to so-called 'comfort women' – no one knows how many, but estimates range from 50,000 to 200,000 – mostly young Korean girls, whom the army forced into prostitution at military-administered field brothels.[30] What accounts for the late Louis Allen's description of 'the curious mixture of spartan ideals and sybaritic behavior' in the imperial Japanese army?[31]

Racist contempt for Chinese and other Asians played a part, as did revenge and reverse racism directed against Caucasians. Japanese attitudes towards women and convictions of superiority did too. But these generalizations do not fully explain basic brutality that continued right up until the end of the war. During July 1945 Australian patrols in New Guinea, for instance, reported finding the mutilated, half-eaten or dismembered corpses of Australian soldiers. At that point in a lost war, exactly whom did the Japanese soldier think he was going to intimidate?

Tough as he was as an infantry fighter, the strengths and weaknesses of the Japanese infantryman derived from his homeland. He accepted the myths of superiority and offensive spirit, and would carry them to irrational ends. He, like his nation, was poorly equipped for mid twentieth century warfare and tried to compensate for material deficiencies with the intangible of fighting spirit. His army training coupled derivations from modern weaponry and tactics with a fundamental and increasingly doctrinaire appeal to Japan's mythical ancient origins and supposedly unique characteristics. His army's pragmatic development in the late nineteenth and early twentieth centuries gave way to a more aggressive style of leadership that insisted Japanese spirit could, if not overcome, at least compensate for material deficiencies. When substantive weaknesses were transformed into imaginary strengths, the soldier paid the difference in blood. The deliberateness that had been the watchword of the founding generation gradually unravelled, and from 1937 the war with China permanently rent the fabric of military decision-making. The demands of fighting that war set Japan's army on an uncertain course, during which expediency became the watchword and militarization of society occured. As the army gained ascendancy, more and more of its emphasis shifted to alleged traditional values, perverted into the suicide tactics of the kamikaze, not the modern and increasingly scientific techniques of conventional and atomic warfare in the mid twentieth century.

Bibliographic note

Aside from the sources footnoted in the text, I have relied on a variety of Japanese language materials when writing this essay. Selected, general works include former Imperial Army staff officer Katogawa Kotarō's *Sanjūpachi hoheiju* (The Type 38 Infantry Rifle), Shirogane shoten, 1975 and *Teikoku rikugun kikōbutai* (The Imperial Army's Mechanized Corps), Hara shobō, 1981. Among his numerous works on the Japanese Army and its relationship to society, I relied on Ōe Shinobu's *Nihon no sanbō honbu* (Japan's General Staff), Chūkō shinsho, 1985, *Shōwa no rekishi* (A History of the Shōwa Reign), Vol. 3, *Tennō no guntai* (The Emperor's Army), Shōgakkan, 1982, *Nichi-Rō sensō no gunjishiteki kenkyū* (Research into the Military History of the Russo-Japanese War), Iwanami shoten, 1976 and *Nichi-Rō sensō to Nihon guntai* (The Russo-Japanese War and the Japanese Military), Rippu shoten, 1987. Fujiwara Akira, another dean of study of the Imperial Army, has likewise written extensively on the subject. His *Nihon gendaishi taikei – Gunjishi* (An Outline of Modern History – The Army), Tōyō keizai shinpōsha, 1961, later expanded, is still useful while later works like *Taiheiyō sensō shiron* (Treatise on the Pacific War), Aoki shoten, 1982 and his studies during the 1990s of the Japanese military's conduct in China are always thought-provoking. Hata Ikuhikō's publications and knowledge of the history of the Imperial Army in the twentieth century are unrivalled. *Nitchū sensō* (The Sino–Japanese War), Kawade shobō, 1961 was a path-breaking monograph, and *Nankin jihen* (The Nanking Incident), Chūkō shinsho, 1986, though provoking controversy, was an attempt to analyse the Nanking Incident as history, not emotion. Among a series of monographs published in the early 1980s by historians at the National Institute for Defence Studies Morimatsu Yoshio *Daihon'ei* (Imperial General Headquarters), Kyōikusha, 1980 and Ikuda Makoto, *Nihon rikugunshi* (A History of the Japanese Army), Kyōikusha, 1980 are very good overviews. Akiyama Monjiro and Mitamura Kei, *Rikugun kōkūshi* (History of the Army Air Force), Hara shobō, 1981 offer a fine general history of the development and doctrine of the army's air arm to 1937. Another former IJA officer turned historian Matsushita Yoshio's *Nihon kokubō no higeki* (The Tragedy of Japan's National Defence), Fūyō shobō, 1976 and *Meiji no guntai* (The Army of Emperor Meiji), Shibunsho, 1963 although dated are still helpful especially in combination with Hara Takeshi's careful examination and analysis of the Imperial Army's operational planning in *Meijiki kokudo bōeishi* (A History of National Self-Defence during the Meiji Period), Kinseikai, 2002. Kaneko Tsunenori, *Heiki to senjutsu no Nihonshi* (A Japanese History of Weapons and Tactics), Hara shobo, 1982 analyses the relationship between weapons technology and the army. Kuwada Etsu and Maebara Toru (eds), *Nihon no sensō – zukai to deeta* (The Wars of Japan – Maps and

Data), Hara shobō, 1982 is a very helpful general reference work containing detailed campaign maps accompanied by order of battle and other statistical information for Japan's wars from 1895 through 1945. In the English language, the late Alvin D. Coox's voluminous works on the imperial army, particularly his magisterial *Nomonhan* volumes, Stanford: Stanford University Press, 1985 set standards that have yet to be surpassed. Lastly, Richard Frank's *Downfall: The End of the Imperial Japanese Empire*, New York: Random House, 1999 places the last months of the imperial army in a diplomatic and military context that goes far to explain the United States' decision to use atomic bombs against Japan.

Notes

1 Ernst L. Presseisen (1965) *Before Aggression: Europeans Prepare the Japanese Army*, Arizona: Tucson, University of Arizona Press, 63–4.
2 Hara Takeshi (2002) *Meijiki kokudo bōeishi* (A History of National Self-Defence During the Meiji Period), Tokyo: Kinseikai, 156.
3 Ōe Shinobu (1988) *Heishitachi no Nichi-Rō sensō* (Private Soldiers of the Russo–Japanese War), Asahi sensho, 7.
4 Leonard A. Humphreys (1995) *The Way of the Heavenly Sword: The Japanese Army in the 1920s*, Stanford, CA: Stanford University Press, 106.
5 Usui Katsumi (2002) *Nitchū sensō* (The Sino–Japanese War), Tokyo: Chūkō shinsho, new rev. edn, 6.
6 Gunjishi gakkai (eds) (1998) *Daihon'ei rikugunbu sensō shidōhan, Kimitsu senso nisshi (jō)* (IGHQ Army Department, War Guidance Section, Confidential war diary) (1), Kinshosha, 170.
7 Janet E. Hunter (1989) *The Emergence of Modern Japan: An Introductory History Since 1853*, London: Longman Group UK Ltd, 111; Mikiso Hane (1982) *Peasants, Outcast, and Rebels, The Underside of Modern Japan*, NY: Pantheon Books, 141.
8 Presseisen, op. cit., 122.
9 Hara, op. cit. 251.
10 Katogawa Kotarō (1996) *Rikugun ni hansei (jō)* (Reflections on the army) (1), Bunkyō Shūppan, 98.
11 Alvin D. Coox (1980) 'The Rise and Fall of the Imperial Japanese Air Forces', *Aerospace Historian*, 27:2, 81; Alvin D. Coox (1988) 'The Effectiveness of the Japanese Military Establishment in the Second World War', in Allan R. Millett and Williamson Murray (eds) *Military Effectiveness*, Vol. III, Boston: Allen & Unwin, 6.
12 Coox (1988) 'Effectiveness', 5.
13 Handō Kazutoshi (1998) *Nomonhan no natsu* (Nomonhan summer), *Bungei shunjū*, 12, 14.
14 Gordon Daniels (1976) 'The Great Tokyo Air Raid, 9–10 March 1945', in W.G. Beasley (ed.), *Modern Japan: Aspects of History, Literature and Society*, Tokyo: Charles E. Tuttle Co., 121, 124.
15 Coox (1988) 'Effectiveness', 6–7.
16 Cited in Tobe Ryōichi (1998) *Nihon no kindai*, Vol. 9, *Gyakusetsu no guntai* (Japan's Modern Times, The Paradox of the Military), Chūōkōronsha, 308.
17 Stewart Lone (1994) *Japan's First Modern War: Army and Society in the Conflict with China 1894–1895*, London: St Martin's Press, 78–9.
18 Hunter (1989), op. cit., 171.
19 Lone (1994), op. cit., 179.
20 Naoko Shimazu (2000) ' "The Myth of the 'Patriotic Soldier'": Japanese Attitudes Towards Death in the Russo–Japanese War,' *War & Society*, 19:2, 74.

21 Yui Masaomi, Fujiwara Akira, Yoshida Yutaka (eds) (1989) *Nihon kindai shisō daikei*, Vol. 4, *Guntai heishi* (An Outline of Modern Japanese Thought, The Military and the Soldier), Iwanami shoten, 473–4.

22 As of 1938 there were 3,000 middle schools enrolling 1.4 million students; 200 higher schools with 120,000, and 45 universities with 70,000. *Shōwa 18 nen Asahi nenkan* (1943 Asahi Almanac), Tokyo: Asahi shimbunsha, 457.

23 The provision was amended in 1913 to include general officers on the inactive list, but in fact none were ever appointed.

24 Fuijiwara Akira (1982) *Shōwa no rekishi*, 5, *Nitchū zenmen sensō* (A History of the Shōwa Reign, The Full Scale Sino–Japanese War), 226.

25 Fujiwara, *Nitchū zenmen sensō*, 226.

26 Daniels, 124.

27 Kawano Hitoshi (2001) *Gyōkusai no guntai, seikan no guntai* (An Army of Death Before Dishonour: An Army of Returning Alive), Kodansha, 38. Kawano's findings lend support to sociologist Eiko Ikegami's contentions in *The Taming of the Samurai: Honorific Individualism and the Making of Modern Japan*, Boston: Harvard University Press, 1995.

28 Kisaka Jun'ichirō (1989) *Shōwa no rekishi*, 7, *Taiheiyō sensō* (A History of the Shōwa Reign, 7, The Pacific War), Shōgakkan, 232–5.

29 Kisaka, op. cit., 235.

30 Yoshimi Yoshiaki (2000) *Comfort Women: Sexual Slavery in the Japanese Military During World War II*, trans. Suzanne O'Brien, New York: Columbia University Press, 29.

31 Louis Allen (1984) *Burma: The Longest War, 1941–1945*, New York: St Martin's Press, 599.

5

THE UNITED STATES MILITARY,
1815–2000

Spencer Tucker

In 1815 the United States relied on a dual military system consisting of a small professional establishment and a militia. This was very much in keeping with British tradition that regarded standing armies as a threat to liberty, but it also sprang from the fact that in 1815 the US did not face any substantial continental enemies.

Militia service had been the practice since colonial days, and according to the Militia Act of 1792 all adult males between the ages of 18 and 45 were required to enrol in militia formations of their particular state. These roughly paralleled regular army formations but were under state control. Although rare by the early nineteenth century, militia were supposed to train regularly. Under the terms of the act the men were to provide their own weapons and could be called to service for only three months out of the year and in no case could be compelled to fight outside US territory. Indeed, during the War of 1812 some militia units had refused to cross into Canada.[1]

In both the War of American Independence and the War of 1812 the nation had relied on large numbers of militia. These, however, had given indifferent service. Although militia performed some useful functions, when employed in a pitched battle they could not stand against regulars, and time and again they simply broke and ran, as in the August 1814 Battle of Bladensburg ('The Bladensburg Races'). Nonetheless it was popular cant in the US that militia, rather than regular forces, had won both the War of American Independence and the War of 1812 against British regulars.

At the beginning of the War of 1812 the US Army had numbered only about 7,000 men and the navy just 13 vessels, none of them larger than frigates, along with 160 small gunboats. The latter, conceived by Thomas Jefferson, were the naval equivalent of militia on land. The navy, despite its small size in numbers and lack of any ships of the line, had performed well in the war against the Royal Navy. The US Army had begun the war abysmally but by 1815 had grown into a well-trained and well-led force of 34,000 men that had proven itself in stand-up contests against British regulars in the 1814 Battles of Chippewa and Lundy's Lane in Canada, and at New Orleans in 1815.

At the end of the war, with no potential enemies on the horizon, the US embarked on the nation's first major naval building program, the Gradual Increase Act of 1816. It provided for construction of nine 74-gun ships of the line, 12 frigates and three steam floating batteries (the US Navy was the first in the world to have a steam warship, the *Demologus* in 1814). Congress also voted to erect a system of coastal fortifications.

The immediate post-war economic boom turned into a depression and these defence plans were soon shelved. Ships were laid up and naval construction was largely limited to the gathering of supplies. The first of the coastal forts, Fortress Monroe at Hampton Roads, Virginia, was not begun until 1817.

Congress also set the army to 6,000 men. Secretary of War John C. Calhoun (1817–25) lost his bid for an expansible army, top-heavy in officers that could readily expand in time of war without diluting its abilities. Calhoun had more success in other areas. He reformed the command structure, creating a staff system for the army and establishing the position of commanding general. He also established numerous small forts in the West and created the army's first branch school, the Artillery School of Practice at Fort Monroe in 1824. In 1827 Calhoun's successor founded an Infantry School of Practice at Jefferson Barracks, Missouri.[2]

In 1821 Congress fixed the regular army at seven regiments of infantry and four of artillery. Cavalry was abolished but a Corps of Engineers was retained to train the cadets at the US Military Academy, West Point, founded in 1802. Although the army fought two wars with the Seminole Indians in this period (1817–18 and 1836–42), it relied heavily on militia to buttress the numbers of regular troops.[3]

Despite the military's small size, there were efforts to promote professionalism. France was then the military model and in 1826 West Point superintendent Sylvanus Thayer sent instructor Dennis Hart Mahan to study there. Mahan returned to West Point in 1830 to teach military engineering and instruction in the 'art of war'. Through his teaching and writing Mahan began the American branch of the study of military theory. Mahan stressed fire and movement and the Napoleonic big battle. His writings, and those of his pupil Henry Halleck, formed the basis for tactics both North and South during the Civil War.

This period also witnessed the establishment of professional journals, such as the *Military and Naval Magazine* (1833–6); the *Army and Navy Chronicle* (1835–44); and the *Military Magazine* (1839–42). In 1849 Major Alfred Mordecai published the first systematic and accurate description of US Army artillery, *Artillery for the United States Land Service*.

The navy also underwent reform. In 1815 it created the Board of Naval Commissioners and then in 1842 a system of five naval bureaux to standardize and improve procedures within the service. In 1845 Congress established the US Naval Academy, at Annapolis, Maryland.[4]

During this time the navy had a regular presence in the Mediterranean, was active off the coasts of Africa in the suppression of the slave trade and carried out a number of exploring missions. Charles Wilkes led an expedition to the Pacific during 1838–42 and Commodore Matthew Perry opened Japan to the West in 1854.

The navy also experimented with new ship designs and naval innovations, including steam warships. The steam sloop *Princeton*, which entered service in 1843, was the first propeller-driven steam warship on the naval list of any nation and the first to have her machinery entirely below the waterline. In 1842 Congress had appropriated money for Robert L. Stevens to build the world's first sea-going ironclad vessel, but the Stevens Battery, as it came to be called, was never completed. The navy also experimented with new and more powerful guns and exploding shell.

The Mexican–American War

From 1846 to 1848 the US fought a war with Mexico, its first with a foreign power since 1815. The outbreak of the war found the US Army with only about 8,000 men. The Mexican Army, a well-trained European-style force, was four times as large. On the seas it was a different story. The US Navy had 70 ships while Mexico had virtually no navy. Control of the seas was vital in the war for the US, offsetting the disadvantage of conducting offensive operations far from its home bases.

The US Navy carried out an effective blockade of Mexico's coasts, denying it imports of weapons. It also supported army amphibious operations, most notably at Veracruz, where on 9 March 1847 it put ashore 10,000 men, their horses and equipment in the largest amphibious operation in US history until World War II. The navy also resupplied troops ashore. During the conflict the superiority of steam warships to sailing vessels, especially in the movement of supplies over distance became clear.

The Americans postulated a quick success, for which volunteers would suffice. Congress authorized 50,000 volunteers, as well as an increase in the regular army to 15,000 men and eventually to 32,000. A total of 104,000 American troops were raised during the war: 60,000 volunteers, 32,000 regulars and 12,000 militiamen, the latter employed only briefly. Over half the troops served for periods of 12 months or less, a major problem for generals in conducting campaigns. Despite this the practice of short-term enlistments continued into the Civil War. The war did prove to be a training arena for the leading generals on both sides of the Civil War a generation later.

Although percussion cap muskets were then coming available, the army fought the Mexican War largely with the wildly inaccurate and unreliable flintlock. The US artillery was more efficient and better served than its Mexican counterpart and proved decisive in a number of battles, including Buena Vista and the Mexico City campaign. The war ended in a victory for the

US in 1848. The Mexican government recognized the loss of Texas, and it gave up New Mexico (the future New Mexico, Arizona, Colorado, Utah, and Nevada) and California to the US.[5]

The two chief developments in land warfare in the first half of the nineteenth century were the Minié ball and the percussion cap. The army was slow to embrace them, but under Secretary of War Jefferson Davis (1853–7) the army adopted the Minié ball. Davis also ordered that new infantry units be armed with percussion-cap, muzzle-loading rifled muskets, and that the national armouries make only rifles and began conversion of old smoothbores into rifles.

In artillery during the 1850s Robert P. Parrott of the West Point Foundry Association, developed a muzzle-loading rifled cannon, which appeared in a variety of sizes and became the preferred rifled artillery piece of both sides during the Civil War. It consisted of a cast-iron gun with wrought-iron rings shrunk on over the breach, the point of greatest strain. For the navy, Lieutenant John A. Dahlgren developed an efficient boat howitzer and then perfected a system of heavy smoothbore guns, 9-inch guns for broadside use and heavier 11-inch guns for pivot mounts. These were the preferred guns of North and South during the Civil War, when the navy also cast these highly reliable guns in 13-inch and 15-inch sizes.[6]

The Civil War

In April 1861 the long anticipated Civil War began. Material factors all favoured the North. It had a 3:1 population advantage (22.3 million to 9.1 million for the South, four million of whom were slaves) and 85 per cent of the pre-war national manufacturing resources. It also had a developed rail network (which the South lacked), essential in the quick movement of men and supplies.[7]

Still, the US military was hardly ready for the war. At the onset the regular army numbered only about 16,300 men. The regular army was in fact kept small during the war. The bulk of troops raised for the conflict, North as well as South, were volunteers. Thus some excellent officers of the professional army, such as General Philip Sheridan, did not get their chance until late in the war.

The South got the jump on the North, when on 6 March 1861 Jefferson Davis, president of the Confederate States of America, called for 100,000 volunteers to serve for 12 months. On 15 April US President Abraham Lincoln called for 75,000 volunteers, to serve three months. Both sides were plagued during the war by short-term enlistments. The South, with far less manpower, went to conscription in 1862; the North adopted it a year later. Southern leaders hoped to outlast the North, wearing down Northern resolve by simply standing on the defensive. Northern advantages, especially in population and manufacturing were simply too great for the South to overcome.

Hopes of both sides for a short war were dashed, and ultimately Lincoln adopted the 'Anaconda Plan' that had been suggested by old General-in-Chief General Winfield Scott at the start of the war. This centred on a blockade of southern coasts and then using large Union armies, in conjunction with the navy, to bisect the South along its great rivers, especially the Mississippi and Tennessee. Ultimately this strategy brought victory.

Generalship, North as well as South, was on a par with that of Europe, but Lincoln did have a terrible time finding the right field commander. He went through a succession of generals until settling on Ulysses S. Grant, an uncommonly able and unflappable commander who was able to see the entire situation clearly and who made destruction of the Southern armies through attrition tactics his goal. The US Army also created a superb staff system. Ultimately effective Union generals commanding large, well-equipped, better trained, and disciplined field armies overcame Southern resolve and zeal.

Davis made a number of poor appointments for top command positions. Robert E. Lee, commander of the Army of Northern Virginia from July 1862, was not one of them. The Confederates, although they had some uncommonly able commanders, were neither as well supplied or equipped as the 'Yankees'. They lacked almost everything, including shoes, although the Confederacy never lost a battle for want of ammunition. The Southern railway system, inadequate in peace, broke down entirely during the war.

The 40 US Navy vessels in commission when the war began were scattered around the globe. Counting those in reserve, the US Navy numbered only about 80 ships. Most naval officers remained with the North, and the South had only a few ships at the onset of the war. Shortly after the beginning of the war, Lincoln proclaimed a blockade of the more than 3,500 miles of Confederate coastline. The blockade steadily grew in effectiveness. Although the US Navy was never able to completely halt blockade runners from getting in and out of southern ports, the blockade ruined Southern trade and denied the Confederacy much-needed imports such as weapons, steam locomotives, railroad track, and manufactured goods.

The US Navy met its great need for vessels to maintain the blockade by purchasing merchant vessels and converting them into warships, and by new construction. By 1865 the US Navy had grown to nearly 700 vessels and was second in numbers only to Great Britain. The Navy not only operated along the Confederate coast, but also conducted riverine operations in conjunction with the US Army, and hunted down Confederate commerce raiders on the high seas.[8]

The Confederates, vastly outnumbered on the seas, turned to new weapons. They developed ironclad vessels, experimented with mines and built 'torpedo boats' (vessels to carry a spar-torpedo, a mine on the end of a long pole). Although both sides experimented with submarines, only the Confederacy employed them. On 17 February 1864, the CSS *Hunley* approached the USS screw sloop *Housatonic* off Charleston, South Carolina, and planted a spar-torpedo in her hull. The explosion sank the *Housatonic*, but the *Hunley* also sank while returning to base. This was, however, the first time in history that a submersible craft had sunk a warship.[9]

The Confederates also sent to sea commerce raiders, a number of which were built in British yards. The most successful of these was the CSS *Alabama*, which took 66 Union prizes before being sunk in an engagement with the USS *Kearsarge* off Cherbourg, France, on 19 June 1864. Despite Confederate hopes, its *guerre de course* failed to break Northern resolve by driving up insurance rates, although the campaign did lead to the flight of many US merchant ships to foreign registry.[10]

The war also saw the first clash of ironclad vessels in history, when on 9 March 1862, off Hampton Roads, Virginia, the CSS *Virginia* (ex-USS *Merrimack*) battled the USS *Monitor*. Both sides liked what they saw in their respective vessels. The vast majority of subsequent Union ironclad were turreted vessels of the *Monitor* type, while the Confederacy built far fewer casemated rams loosely patterned after the *Virginia*.

The South, strangled by the blockade, was also bisected by powerful Union armies. Its economy in ruins, the Confederacy finally surrendered in April 1865. Following the war, the United States again disarmed. The US Army went from a million men under arms at the surrender to a mere 25,000 by 1867. It remained at that strength until the Spanish American War.

The Indian Wars

Troops of the US Army continued in garrison in parts of the South until 1877, but beginning in the late 1860s and continuing throughout the 1880s the army fought numerous Indian 'wars'. These were brought about by settler encroachment onto Indians lands. The Indian Wars saw more than 1,000 combat actions, in which the army sustained an estimated 2,000 casualties and killed some 6,000 Indians. The forces on the frontier were always small, only a little more than a third of the army, and most Indian fights involved isolated garrisons of no more than a company.

Many of the Indians had traded for or otherwise secured the repeating Winchester rifle, while the soldiers for the most part were armed with the single-shot trap-door Springfield. The army also had the Colt 1872 0.45 calibre 'Peacemaker' revolver, while the artillery piece of choice was the two-pounder Hotchkiss gun.

The result of these wars was a foregone conclusion. Many of the tribes reached accommodation with the whites and agreed to move onto reservations. Probably the 'hostiles' numbered only about 100,000 people, and they were rarely able to combine into groups larger than a clan or tribe. In addition to far greater numbers, the army had the advantages of the railway and superior organization. The wars ended by 1890.[11]

The end of the nineteenth century saw renewed interest in a post-graduate military education. In 1881 Commanding General of the Army General William T. Sherman (1869–83) established the School of Application for Infantry and Cavalry at Fort Leavenworth, Kansas. This grew into today's

Command and General Staff College. The Naval War College was founded in 1884. Professional organizations and journals also appeared, including the *Cavalry Journal* (1888) and the *Journal of the United States Artillery* (1892).

In the decades after the Civil War the navy languished. By 1880 the navy consisted largely of fourteen old 'sea-going' twin-turreted monitors mounting 15-inch smoothbore muzzle-loading guns. The US Navy was inferior to those of all other major powers and even to that of Chile. This sorry state of affairs changed with the growth of US overseas trade, the rise of imperialism and the efforts of navalists such as Alfred Thayer Mahan.

The son of Dennis Hart Mahan, Alfred Thayer Mahan became a professor at the Naval War College and then its president (1886–9 and 1892–3). His book, *The Influence of Sea Power upon History, 1660–1783* (1890), is often referred to as the most influential study of naval warfare ever written. Mahan believed that world power meant naval power and that only battleships could win control of the seas, in decisive fleet actions. This flew in the face of the traditional US Navy *guerre de course* strategy.

The support of key Congressional leaders helped fuel demand for new, powerful ships. The modern steel navy dates from 1883 when Congress authorized construction of three new cruisers, the *Atlanta*, *Boston* and *Chicago*, and a gunboat, the *Dolphin*. These so-called 'ABCDs' were constructed of steel and had a steel deck for protection from plunging fire. Driven by new compound steam engines, they mounted new breech-loading rifled guns. From 1885 to 1899 Congress authorized 30 new warships of different classes, aggregating nearly 100,000 tons of construction.

The Spanish–American War

The navy played the key role in the 1898 war with Spain, the nation's first with a foreign power since Mexico a half century earlier. The cause of the war was popular sentiment in the US to free Cuba from Spanish control. As usual the army was unready, and the navy quite literally won the war in only two battles. The Spanish Navy, which appeared formidable on paper, consisted largely of older ships and was poorly trained. Commodore Thomas Dewey's victory in May over a Spanish squadron at Manila Bay and Rear Admiral William T. Sampson's victory in July at Santiago Bay cut off Spanish garrisons in the Philippines and Cuba from reinforcement.

The wiser course would have been simply to maintain a naval blockade until Spain agreed to peace, but public opinion demanded an immediate descent on Cuba and 150,000 volunteers were called to the colours. While the regulars were armed with modern 0.30 calibre Krag-Jorgensen repeating rifles (Spanish troops in Cuba had the superior Mauser), the volunteers had to make do with old black-powder trap-door 0.45 calibre Springfields. Equipment of all types was lacking and the volunteers went to the tropics in blue wool uniforms. Trained horses were in short supply, so much of the cavalry fought on foot, including Theodore Roosevelt's 1st Volunteer Cavalry (the 'Rough Riders').

Training was wretchedly inadequate and men died in larger numbers in the camps than in the fighting in Cuba. Transporting the nearly 17,000 men of Major General William Shafter's V Corps to Cuba was more complicated than sending more than two million men to France during World War I, although the late July descent on Puerto Rico by 5,000 men under Major General Nelson Miles went very well indeed.

The Americans were fortunate in that the Spanish commander on Cuba failed to take advantage of his considerably larger numbers, and on 1 July the Americans won the key land battles of San Juan Ridge and El Caney, largely from bravado and superior numbers. These battles gave them control over Santiago.

In reasonably short order Madrid recognized the inevitable and agreed to give Washington all it demanded. Cuba became independent, but the US took Puerto Rico, Guam and the Philippines. America now had an empire, although little thought was given to the responsibilities that went with this, for acquisition of the Philippines set up the subsequent confrontation with Japan.[12]

Following the war the US had to fight to subdue Filipino nationalists, already at war with Spain. The Philippine–American War (1899–1902) ended in an American victory, although it took 75,000 American troops to achieve it. The US also participated in the relief of the foreign embassies in Beijing (Peking) during the 1900–01 Boxer Uprising, the first time that the US had waged coalition warfare since the American War for Independence.[13]

Its record in the Spanish–American War benefited the navy. It continued to expand, becoming the world's third largest by 1917. In the two decades that followed the war the army also received modern equipment, including the 0.45 calibre pistol (which remained in service for 70 years) and the superb 0.30 Model 1902 Springfield rifle. The army also received the quick-firing three-inch gun. It also underwent reorganization with the re-establishment of a true general staff, replacing an antiquated bureau system. The post of commanding general of the army, filled by the senior-ranking general of the army who had then held it until retirement, was abolished and replaced by a chief of staff of the army, who served a fixed term. In 1901 the Army War College was established and Congress set the regular army at 30 regiments of infantry, 15 of cavalry and a corps of engineers. Total army strength could vary between 60,000 and 100,000 men, depending on the President.

In 1903 the Dick Act repealed the old Militia Act of 1792 and in effect created two militias, with the wholly volunteer National Guard as the first-line military reserve. The mass of adult males between the ages of 18 and 45 constituted the second militia. The Act also provided for more federal super-vision of Guard training in return for Federal subsidies.

Following the victory against Spain the US intervened a number of times in Latin America, the Caribbean and in Mexico. In 1916 Brigadier General John

J. Pershing led 6,000 men into northern Mexico in an unsuccessful attempt to capture Mexican revolutionary Pancho Villa, who had raided across the border into Columbus, New Mexico and killed a number of Americans. This operation, while it failed to capture Villa, led to a call-up of the National Guard along the Mexican border and provided useful lessons in mobilization. The army also experimented with truck transport and with aviation.[14]

Troubles with Mexico and the Great War in Europe were the impetus behind the National Defense Act of 1916. It authorized expansion of the army to 175,000 officers and men over a five-year period, with the National Guard to increase from 100,000 men to 400,000. It also provided for greater army supervision over the training of the Guard, established fixed drill periods and provided that the Guard could be federalized for the duration of a war rather than the previous maximum of three months. The Act also created the Reserve Officer Training Corps (ROTC) and army officer and enlisted reserves.

World War I

The US entered World War I in April 1917, almost three years after the start of the conflict. Although most Americans favoured the Allies against the Central Powers, the prevailing sentiment was to stay out of the war. Events in 1917, especially the German decision to resume unrestricted submarine warfare but also the infamous Zimmermann telegram and German sabotage activities in the US, brought a declaration of war by the United States against Germany.

The American entry into the war was a tremendous morale boost and financial lift for the hard-pressed Allied side, but it was many months before the US was able to do anything militarily. It took the country a year to train and transport sufficient troops to Europe to have significant influence. When the United States declared war, the regular army numbered only 127,000 men, with an additional 66,000 National Guardsmen in federal service along the border with Mexico. The navy was in better shape, but many of its 360 ships, including 151 warships, were undermanned and in need of repair.

In May 1917 Congress passed the Selective Service Act, requiring all males between the ages of 21 and 30 to register. In 1918 this was extended to ages 18 to 45. Ultimately 24 million men were registered, and between April 1917 and November 1918 the Army grew to 3,685,458 men. Of this total, almost 2.2 million were conscripts. But of 29 divisions (1,000 officers and 27,000 men each) that saw action in France, only 11 were draftee divisions; the remainder were volunteers, seven regular and 11 National Guard divisions.

General John J. Pershing commanded the army and US Marine Corps contingents that made up the American Expeditionary Forces (AEF) in France. A capable commander, Pershing insisted on rigorous training. One of the strongest military personalities of the war, he sought US control over a sector of the front.

The navy was better prepared than the army. Rear Admiral William Sims, in Britain for talks at the time of the declaration of war by the United States, immediately assumed command of US naval forces in European waters. He also insisted on the introduction of a convoy system. In April 1917 US destroyers were sent to Queenstown, Ireland, as convoy escorts and to take part in anti-submarine patrols under British command. By July there were 34 American destroyers there, the first time that US warships had operated under foreign command. A destroyer flotilla also went to Brest in France, to escort troop transports to the continent.

Expanding the army was relatively easy when compared to the logistical nightmare of training and equipping it. Taken together, the army, navy and Marines only had 11,000 officers in April 1917, and at least 200,000 were needed in the expanded military. Training facilities were also totally inadequate. The army had to construct more than 30 temporary camps to train the men before they were shipped to France. Despite the superb efforts of Secretary of War Newton Baker and others, serious shortcomings lasted to the end of the war.

Naval operations were geared to support the army, with its chief task that of transporting US soldiers, their equipment and supplies to France. The government requisitioned and purchased ships to build 'a bridge to France'. It also began an expanded shipbuilding programme, and 109 interned German vessels were pressed into service. Still, almost half the ships used in this work were British. Only six transports were sunk by U-boats, all in European waters, and four of these were on the return voyage. The convoy system insured the safe passage of American troops and supplies.

The 1st Infantry Division arrived in France by July 1917, but it was soon broken up for training. At the end of 1917 Russia dropped out of the war and Germany was able to shift substantial resources to the Western Front. In March 1918 the Ludendorff Offensive registered tremendous gains, and the Allies appealed for more American troops. In July, alone, more than 300,000 were shipped to France.

The AEF used mostly French and British equipment. A majority of its artillery was French and no American-made aircraft or tank saw action on the Western Front. The small Army Air Service was amalgamated with American volunteers flying for the French as the Lafayette Escadrille. They began combat duty in March 1918 under Colonel William Mitchell, who became the foremost US proponent of air power after the war. Soon the Americans had three air squadrons. The army had only 55 planes when the war began, but at its end the United States boasted 3,227 de Haviland 4 aircraft. The navy flew Curtiss float planes to assist in locating submarines.

The navy also sent a battleship division to join the British Grand Fleet at Scapa Flow, but it did not see action because following the 1916 Battle of Jutland the German High Seas Fleet stayed largely in port. Some 120 submarine chasers sent to France did provide useful training for junior officers destined for higher command in World War II.

Before spring 1918 most American troops in France were largely behind the lines undergoing rigorous training for trench warfare. Until May 1918

American casualties were slight and only 163 soldiers had been killed in action. From the end of May to November the AEF entered the battle in full strength. The big question for Pershing was how the AEF would be employed on the Western Front. To avoid being bound to the Allied agreements on territory to be taken from the Central Powers, President Woodrow Wilson instructed Pershing that in military operations the AEF was to 'cooperate' with other forces fighting the Central Powers but that US forces were a separate and distinct component of the combined forces, and that their identity was to be preserved. To Pershing, this meant that the Americans should fight in a distinct army, holding its own section of the front, and not be amalgamated in, or assigned to, British and French units. Under the pressure of the Ludendorff Offensive, however, the British and the French pleaded for American troops as fillers in threatened sectors of the line, stiffened by their own tested units. Under the pressure of the German offensive and Wilson's orders, Pershing gave way, although US troops were committed as divisions. The Supreme Allied commander Ferdinand Foch promised in turn that once the German drives had been blunted, the Americans would receive responsibility for a sector of the front.

American forces were vital in turning the tide. They proved they were the equal of the Germans in fighting at Cantigny, Château Thierry and Belleau Wood. American forces also played a key role in the last major German offensive of the war, the Second Battle of the Marne, at Reims in mid July 1918.

The Allies then went on the offensive and Foch reluctantly agreed to Pershing's demand for an American attack in the St. Mihiel Salient. Pershing wanted to continue the drive to Metz but, in a stormy session, Foch refused. American forces then took part in the general Meuse–Argonne Offensive that began at the end of September and lasted the remainder of the war. It was the greatest battle in which American troops had ever fought.

The fighting ended with an armistice on 11 November 1918. It is hard to see how the Allies could have won without American help. American losses were small in comparison to those of other powers; out of some 1,390,000 American troops and sailors who saw active combat duty, 49,000 were killed in action or died of wounds; 230,000 more were wounded. Another 57,000 died from disease, largely the result of an influenza–pneumonia pandemic that swept the camps in America and France in the autumn of 1918.[15]

Following World War I the US retreated into isolation. The US Senate failed to ratify the Treaty of Versailles and the US did not join Wilson's cherished League of Nations. Congress also enacted neutrality legislation that would prohibit the sales of arms to belligerents once a war had been declared.

World War II

When World War II began in Europe in September 1939 the US Army ranked nineteenth in the world; its 190,000 men put it just after Portugal. The US Navy was, however, one of the world's two most powerful, with 15 battleships in commission in September 1939. It also operated five fleet carriers, one light carrier, 18 heavy cruisers, 19 light cruisers, 149 destroyers, and 71 submarines. Still, it would be hard pressed to fight on two oceans simultaneously. Most of the Navy's admirals anticipated great battles involving surface warships in gunnery duels as the naval war of the future. In June 1940 Congress appropriated $4 billion to build a two-ocean navy and more than double the fleet's combat shipping. The plan included building 20,000-ton Essex-class carriers, but it would be at least three years before appropriations could be translated into ships at sea.

In September 1940 Congress approved the Selective Training and Service Act (the Burke–Wadsworth Act), the nation's first peace-time draft. It provided for registration of all males between the ages of 21 and 35, and the induction into the armed forces of 800,000 draftees.

Gearing up military production took time, and much of what was being produced was going to Britain to keep that nation in the war. Army Chief of Staff General George C. Marshall's draftees trained with broomsticks for rifles and logs representing artillery pieces. Trucks bore signs with the word 'tank'.[16]

President Franklin Roosevelt was especially anxious to expand US air power. In early 1939 Congress approved Roosevelt's request to more than double the size of the Air Corps from 2,320 aircraft to 5,500. Manpower would increase apace, but this plan was rendered obsolete by the outbreak of war in Europe.[17]

In 1940 US steel production was 67 million tons or 82 per cent of capacity. By 1944 it was full blast, at 89 million tons, a figure that was about half of the world's total. This translated into vast numbers of weapons. Roosevelt announced plans to build 50,000 aircraft in 1943 and Hitler scoffed. In fact, the US built more than 85,898 planes in 1943 and 96,318 in 1944. During the period from May 1940 to July 1945, the US produced 297,299 aircraft, including 99,742 fighters and 97,592 bombers. Of this construction, some 185,000 went to the Army Air Forces, 60,000 to the Navy, 33,000 to Britain and Commonwealth nations, 18,000 to the USSR, and 4,000 to China. The US also manufactured 86,333 tanks, 650,000 Willys 'jeeps', and 12,573,000 rifles and carbines. The army had so many vehicles that it could place every man and woman in the service in them at the same time and still have room left over.

American shipyards launched 14 million tons of warships, including 88,000 landing craft and 8,812 major naval vessels (147 aircraft carriers). During the war the Ford Motor Company alone produced a greater value of durable goods than did the entire nation of Italy. America's war-time industrial capacity provided the nation with tremendous strategic flexibility and allowed it to conduct warfare worldwide, while also supplying the British Empire, the Soviet Union and China through Lend Lease.

By way of contrast, from 1940 to 1945 Germany manufactured 109,586 aircraft, 56,000 tanks and 1,255 submarines of all types. Japan made a major effort but built only 74,656 aircraft, 4,571 tanks and 568 major naval vessels. In other words, the US out-produced Germany and Japan combined, 3:2 in aircraft and 4:3 in tanks. The imbalance in warship tonnage was far greater. The significant Soviet weapons production should also be noted. From 1940 to 1945 it manufactured 146,929 aircraft, 102,301 tanks, and 14,631 rifles and carbines.[18]

On 1 September 1939, Roosevelt had appointed Brigadier General George C. Marshall as Army Chief of Staff. Marshall was junior to some 60 other general officers. A brilliant appointment, he came to be known as the 'Organizer of Victory'. Marshall stressed firepower and manoeuvre. To Marshall this meant not only tanks but that the entire army would be mechanized and motorized to a degree beyond that of any other military in the world. It would also enable the army to make effective use of the 'triangular' concept, worked out while Marshall was deputy commander of the Infantry School at Fort Benning, Georgia from 1927 to 1932. The army went from large, foot-bound four-brigade divisions of 28,000 men to highly mobile three-brigade, 15,000-man divisions. This triangular concept extended to the lowest level. One manoeuvre unit would fix an enemy formation in place while another turned its flank and the third manoeuvre unit remained in reserve.[19]

In July 1941 Roosevelt called for an estimate of the forces required to defeat 'potential enemies'. Given this assignment, Major Albert C. Wedemeyer estimated that by the end of 1943, Germany and its allies might field 400 divisions. Conventional wisdom held that attacking forces needed a 2:1 ratio to overcome defenders, and Wedemeyer thus put the requirement at 800 divisions. Leaving out the Soviet Union, which he believed might not be able to withstand the German onslaught, he calculated that other allies could provide 100 divisions, which meant the United States would have to raise 700. Counting support troops, this would mean a total US military of 28 million men. But the population of the United States was only 135 million, and industrial production requirements, which experts believed would limit any military to a maximum of 10 per cent, meant that the armed forces could be no more than 13.5 million men, of which the army would get 8.8 million: 2.05 million in the air forces and 6.75 in the ground forces. The latter were to be formed into five armies, three purely offensive task forces and two defensive. Wedemeyer postulated 215 manoeuvre divisions, of which 61 were to be armoured, 61 mechanized, 54 infantry, four cavalry, ten mountain, and seven airborne. He thought that with overwhelming air superiority, firepower, heavy armoured components, and a high degree of mechanization and motorization, such a figure would be sufficient. Transporting such a force to Europe would require 1,000 ships of 7,000 tons each, and building these alone would take two years, as would raising, equipping and training the troops.[20]

As it worked out the US Army fell far short of this figure in the so-called '90-division gamble'. Actually the army numbered only 89 divisions: 66 infantry, one cavalry, 16 armour, five airborne, and one mountain. The United

States committed only 60 divisions to the struggle for the European continent, and it turned out that the number was sufficient.[21]

The US Army in World War II was to that point in time the most-mobile, best-equipped, most-educated, and highest-paid army in history. Many of its best officers were not in the infantry, however. The Air Corps and specialist branches, such as Rangers, commandoes and paratroops, and the service staffs were permitted to cream off too high a proportion of the best-educated and fittest recruits. The infantry rifle companies called upon to fight the Wehrmacht, the most skilled army of modern times, were made up of men who were in all too many cases the least impressive material America had called forward. Despite this, the US Army lost only one major battle to the Wehrmacht – its first – at Kasserine Pass in February 1943.

The army worked on developing new high-firepower weapons. These included remodelled Browning automatic rifles, the Browning air-cooled light-weight 0.30 calibre machine gun, the Mark 2 0.50 calibre machine gun (which remains in use), and the superb M-1 Garand infantry rifle with an eight-round clip. The M-1, designed by John C. Garand and adopted by the army in 1936, fired 40 rounds a minute in the hands of the average rifleman, but an expert could get off 100 rounds over the same time. It had 40 per cent less recoil than the Springfield '03 it replaced and had only 72 parts, compared to 92 for the Springfield. The Garand could be entirely broken down using only one tool: a 0.30 calibre round. There was also the light-weight (5 lbs) M1 Carbine, which was issued to officers instead of a handgun. Later the army introduced the M3 submachine gun, most of the parts of which were stamped out. It was capable of a rate of fire of 450 rounds per minute. The artillery developed new techniques to minimize the time necessary for all guns in a battery to fire on a target.[22]

The army was not so efficient in other areas. Congress had abolished the Tank Corps in 1920 and relegated tanks to the infantry. Not until 1931 did the cavalry, which still employed horses, receive light 'tankettes', known as 'combat cars'. The US Armoured Force came into being only in July 1940, after the defeat of France, and its M3 Grant, designed hurriedly in 1940, was obsolete before it was built.[23]

Despite shortcomings, the US Army had greater firepower than any other army in the world. It was not only the quality and quantity of military equip-ment and supplies produced that was significant, but the speed with which new weapons came on line. The bazooka anti-tank weapon, for example, went from development to production of 5,000 units in only 30 days.[24]

The US Army was not only the best armed in the world; it was also the best supplied and it had superior communications and unparalleled mobility. In early 1943 Marshall reorganized the army into three major components: the Army Ground Forces; Army Service Forces; and Army Air Forces. In personnel the army grew by April 1945 to 8,157,386 men and women, of whom 1,831,091 were in the 16 Army Air Forces.[25]

The navy, Marines and air force all grew apace. The navy incorporated the US Coast Guard, the cutters of which proved invaluable in hunting submarines. The Marines, which came under the navy, expanded to six divisions and more than 485,000 men and women. Until 1943 the Navy took volunteers only, but Marshall protested to Roosevelt that the navy and the air forces were skimming off the best personnel, leaving only the dregs for the infantry, and in that year the navy began taking some draftees. Total navy personnel strength grew to 3,408,347 men and women by August 1945. The navy had 1,099 vessels of all types in June 1940. By 1944, in numbers of ships alone, it was larger than all the rest of the world's navies combined. In February 1945 the five carrier task groups operating against the Japanese home islands included 119 warships, yet only four of these ships had been in service before 7 December 1941. In August 1945 the US Navy had in commission ten battleships, 27 aircraft carriers (CV and CVL), 111 escort carriers (CVE), 47 cruisers, 370 destroyers, 504 destroyer escorts, 217 submarines, 975 minecraft, 1,915 patrol ships and craft, 1,612 auxiliary ships, 66,055 landing craft, and 3,053 district craft (yard craft).[26]

After Japan's attack on Pearl Harbor on 7 December 1941, Britain and the US pooled their resources and developed a common strategy. Their leaders concluded that the more formidable opponent, Germany, should be defeated first. But because of a shortage of shipping and landing craft – a chronic problem for the Western Allies in both the European and Pacific theatres – and the need to tame the submarine menace and win the Battle of the Atlantic, no invasion of the European continent was possible in 1942. This allowed military assets to be sent to the Pacific theatre faster than had been envisaged.

The only way the US could effectively get at Germany in 1942 was via the air, and this meant strategic bombing. In the period between the two world wars Army Air Corps leaders believed that the long-range bomber offered the best chance to carve out an offensive role and the best chance for an independent air force. The airplane chosen for that role was the Boeing B-17 'Flying Fortress'. A rugged and excellent bombardment platform, the B-17 mounted a dozen 0.50 calibre machine guns and was very much in keeping with Italian air theorist Guilio Douhet's notion of a self-defending 'battle plane'. The Air Corps sold the B-17 to Congress in 1934 as a coast defence weapon.

Air Corps emphasis on the long-range bomber adversely affected development of fighter aircraft. Air Corps leaders believed that fighters could not intercept bombers and were in effect obsolete. Early US fighters in the war lagged far behind those of the RAF and Luftwaffe.

The Army Air Corps underwent tremendous expansion during the war, growing from fewer than 20,000 men at the start of the conflict. General Marshall, an air power advocate, fully supported these increases. During the war the USAAF put 194,000 men through pilot training and another 300,000 men through gunnery school. They were also not rushed into combat. American airmen received far more flying time before combat than their German or Japanese counterparts.

Army Air Forces commander General Henry 'Hap' Arnold and most of his key subordinates opposed British terror bombing of civilian centres, partly on moral grounds but primarily because they believed it would not work. The Americans favoured daylight precision bombing of key German industrial targets.[27]

General Arnold and the 'Bomber Barons' believed it would be possible for vast bomber armadas to conduct pin-point raids against precisely selected German targets in daylight. This optimism was based on the defensive firepower of the B-17 as well as the highly accurate Norden bombsight. The British reiterated that such bombing would not work against stout German defences; they pointed out that the Germans had failed in 1940 in their daylight precision bombing attempts against British defences.[28]

US bomber units began arriving in Britain in the summer of 1942 and conducted their first strategic bombing operation of the war in mid August. At the January 1943 Casablanca Conference, British and US leaders agreed to an 'around the clock' bombing campaign, known as the Combined Bomber Offensive. In effect, the British and Americans went their separate ways. The Americans would carry out precision day-time raids on German industrial targets while the British conducted night-time area raids on civilian centres to break German morale. The USAAF Eighth Air Force flew from British bases to strike Germany, while the Fifteenth Air Force operated from bases in North Africa and then in Italy. Allied planners thought that attacking the Reich from two directions would stretch thin its air defences.[29]

The US shifted its targeting to include cities, and ultimately to focus on them. It had its origins in pragmatism rather than military dogma. Daylight bombing of heavily defended German industrial targets simply did not work. It was not the fault of the air crews but rather of the circumstances in which they had to drop their bombs, including bad weather and the lack of fighter protection. Harassment from German fighters and anti-aircraft fire simply made level bomb runs largely impossible. Thus the Americans no less than the British bought into Douhet's thesis that the way to win the war was to shatter civilian morale by area bombing of cities. Ultimately the addition of two superb long-range fighter aircraft, the P-51 Mustang and the P-47 Thunderbolt, turned the tide against the German fighters.

While the air campaign went forward, US ground strength steadily increased. The costly British raid on Dieppe of August 1942 showed that the Allies were not ready to undertake a cross-Channel invasion of Europe that year, or even in 1943. But Roosevelt had promised Soviet leader Josef Stalin that the Allies would mount a major invasion before the end of 1942, and he pushed for the invasion of French North Africa. It took place in November 1942 at three sites in Algeria and Tunisia. The American landing at Casablanca, which sailed from Norfolk, Virginia, was the greatest distance travelled by any expeditionary force to that point in history. At the same time the British Eighth Army broke out at El Alamein and drove west.

In the spring of 1943 North Africa was cleared of Axis forces, and the Allies then invaded Sicily in July and Italy in September. British Prime Minister Winston Churchill wanted a concentration on the central and eastern Mediterranean, but Roosevelt and US military leaders insisted on the cross-Channel invasion of France. This occurred in June 1944, with the commitment of three Allied airborne divisions. The Americans had employed airborne forces in the invasion of North Africa and in Sicily and Italy, but this was on a far greater scale.

Thanks to Allied deceptions, overwhelming air and naval resources, and the French Resistance, the landings were a success, although it was July before the British and Americans were able to break out from their shore lodgement. The Western Allies then drove east, as the Soviets, who had over-run central Europe, reached Germany from the opposite direction.

A series of missteps, including failures to close the Falaise–Argentan Gap and secure the Scheldt River, meant that the war in Europe dragged on into 1945. Another difficulty was the failure of the US to deploy a heavy tank in the fighting quickly enough. US armour formations had to take on superior German tanks with the M4 Sherman medium tank. The M4 was both under-gunned and thinly armoured. Dubbed by its crews the 'Ronson' for its tendency to catch fire easily (the Ronson cigarette lighter was sold with the motto 'Lights every time'), the M4 had only a 75 mm gun and 3.5-inch armour. The German tanks had heavier frontal armour and a much higher velocity gun; the Tiger, for example, mounted an 88 mm gun. The German *Panzerfaust* anti-tank weapon could easily knock out the Shermans, whereas the US 2.36 inch Bazooka was effective only against German tank side armour.

In the course of 1944–5 the 3rd Armoured Division alone lost 648 Sherman tanks completely destroyed in combat and another 700 knocked out, repaired and put back into operation: a loss rate of 580 per cent. The United States lost 6,000 tanks in Europe in World War II, while the German Army never had more than 1,500 tanks. The M26 Pershing heavy tank was not available until after the Battle of the Bulge.[30]

In December 1944, in a last-ditch effort, Hitler flung his legions against the Americans in the Ardennes. The resulting Battle of the Bulge caught the Americans completely by surprise and was the biggest battle fought on the Western Front in World War II. With 600,000 US troops engaged, it was also the largest engagement ever fought by the US Army.

The Western Allies did not get across the Rhine until March 1945. Meanwhile the Red Army closed on Berlin from the east. The Germans fought on, surrendering unconditionally to the Allies in May 1945.

In the Pacific theatre the Japanese ran riot for the first six months of the war, taking the Philippines, Malaya, Singapore, Hong Kong, the Netherlands Indies, and much of Burma, at only minimal cost to themselves. The Japanese easily secured their planned defensive ring. But the ease of their conquests and the desire not to adversely impact morale by going over on the defensive led them to press beyond it. Australian and US forces, however, defeated the Japanese on land on Papua/New Guinea and Gaudalcanal, while at sea the Americans checked the Japanese in the Battle of the Coral Sea and soundly defeated them in the Battle of Midway.

The Allies now went on the offensive, with the Marine Corps taking the lead in island-hopping operations in the central Pacific. In the 1920s the Corps had come under siege. The largest amphibious operation of World War I, the Allied invasion of Gallipoli in Turkey in 1915, had been a failure, and many, especially in the army, wanted to do away with the Corps. Many observers concluded that the days of assaults on fortified positions from the sea were over. Others, particularly Marine Lieutenant Colonel Earl H. 'Pete' Ellis, believed that the key to winning a war in the Pacific would be base seizure and defence. Although Japanese outpost bases would be difficult to capture, Ellis believed that the marines should prepare to 'execute opposed landings and attacks on denial positions ... with the greatest rapidity'.[31]

By 1921 Ellis had outlined the problems of conducting assaults in the Marshall and Caroline Islands, but he was also confident that with proper training the Marine Corps could take a defended beach-head. An opposed landing could succeed if there was rapid ship-to-shore movement by waves of assault craft and it was supported by concentrated naval gunfire and air power. Securing the beach would be the key. Assaulting troops would require high-firepower weapons but also new landing craft or vehicles armed with machine guns and light cannon. Close-in naval gunfire could help neutralize enemy shore positions. Ellis disagreed with those who advocated night assaults to minimize casualties. Ellis believed the attacks would have to occur in the day-time, in order to minimize confusion. To be successful, such assaults would require careful planning, preparation and coordination.[32]

Building on Ellis's theories the Marines began experiments and training for amphibious operations, and contracted for specialized landing craft. These latter came to include the incredibly successful LSTs (Landing Ship, Tank) and LSIs (Landing Ship, Infantry) and smaller LCIs (Landing Craft, Infantry) that were so important in the war, especially in the Pacific. The Marines also utilized LVTs (Landing Vehicle, Tracked, or Amtrac), which were true amphibians, to carry their forces and supplies from troop ships across the beaches of Japanese-held islands. Such operations became the *raison d'être* of the Corps.

Beginning in November 1943, Marines and Army infantry divisions carried out a series of amphibious assaults in the Central Pacific, taking selected islands in the Gilberts, Marshalls and Marianas chains. Capture of Saipan, Guam and Tinian in the Marianas allowed the US to establish bases for its heavy B-29 bombers, which then began sustained bombing of Japan.

At the same time US forces under General Douglas MacArthur returned to the Philippines. Control of these islands would sever the Japanese from their southern resource base of the Dutch East Indies and especially its oil. As a consequence the Japanese fleet sortied in force. The resulting October 1944 Battle of Leyte Gulf was history's largest naval engagement. The 282 vessels involved (216 US, 2 Australian and 64 Japanese) outnumbered the 250 ships in the 1916 Battle of Jutland. The battle engaged nearly 200,000 men and was fought over an area of more than 100,000 square miles. It included all aspects of naval warfare – air, surface, submarine, and amphibious – and it saw the deployment of the largest guns ever at sea, the last clash of the dreadnoughts and the introduction of kamikazes (Japanese suicide aircraft). Although the war at sea was not yet over, Leyte Gulf finished off the Japanese surface navy as an organized fighting force.

Following the capture of the Philippines, army and Marine forces landed on the islands of Okinawa and Iwo Jima. Okinawa was taken as the base for a projected invasion of Japan. The Japanese threw into the fight a large number of suicide aircraft (kamikazes), which inflicted significant damage. The Japanese lost 770 aircraft, while the US Navy suffered 4,907 men killed and 4,874 wounded, a total higher than all the other battles fought by the navy put together. The navy also lost 38 ships sunk and 368 damaged.[33]

Meanwhile, Marianas-based B-29s were hitting Japan. Although these raids were having some effect, in March 1945 the attackers began fire-bomb raids against Japanese cities. On 9–10 March, in the single most destructive raid in the history of warfare, 334 B-29s flying at 7,000 feet dropped 1,667 tons of incendiary bombs against a city built largely of wooden structures. Widespread firestorms destroyed 15 square miles of central Tokyo. More than 83,000 people died and 100,000 were injured.[34]

Over the next months B-29s hit the largest Japanese cities, one after the other. Of 64 major cities, 63 were struck; only the shrine city of Kyoto was spared. Hundreds of thousands of Japanese died. Iwo Jima, halfway between the Marianas and Tokyo, was taken as a fighter field and emergency landing point for crippled B-29s.

At the same time Japan was being subjected to air attack and strikes by carrier aviation, US submarines were ravaging Japanese shipping. At the beginning of the war Japan had 6 million tons of merchant shipping, only a marginal capacity. Japan constructed another 2 million tons during the war, but US submarines sank 5.32 million tons of merchant ships (1,113 vessels). From the beginning the United States waged unrestricted submarine warfare.

US submarines also took a heavy toll of Japanese navy ships, sinking 201 totalling 577,000 tons. The top priority targets for the US submarines were aircraft carriers and then tankers. The Japanese were so short of aviation fuel by 1944 that they could scarcely train pilots; Japanese aviators had only about 120 hours of flying time before combat whereas US pilots had 300–400 hours. Although US submariners lost about 3,506 officers and men, a casualty rate of almost 22 per cent and the highest for any branch of the military, it was far less than the totals for Germany or Japan.[35]

Japan concluded peace in August 1945. Japan was brought to ruin by the triad of USAAF strategic bombing, including the mining of Japanese waters, carrier task forces able to operate at long distances from their bases and submarine warfare, well before the atomic bombs were dropped on Hiroshima and Nagasaki.

US casualties in World War II were relatively light. The US lost only 292,100 military dead and 571,822 wounded. Military dead for other powers included at least 7,500,000 for the Soviet Union, 2,850,000 for Germany, 1,506,000 for Japan, and 398,000 for Britain.

Following the war the US followed its traditional pattern of disarmament, its leaders believing that the Communist world would not risk nuclear destruction. With the coming of the Cold War, attitudes began to change but the military was still in appalling shape in June 1950 when the Korean War began. It had gone from 12 million men and women in 1945 to only 1.6 million in 1950; the defence budget dropped from $80.9 billion to $16.5 billion. The army was down to only nine divisions and 630,000 men and was short of equipment, including tanks. The air force lacked aircraft and the navy was short of ships.[36]

The Korean War

The four US divisions in occupation duty in Japan in 1950 were both poorly trained and lacked equipment, including rifles, but Far East commander General Douglas MacArthur cannibalized one division and got the remaining three to Korea to fight within two weeks of the North Korean invasion of South Korea. The navy and air force played key roles in the war. The navy kept open the vital sea lanes to Japan and the US. It also carried out key amphibious landings and evacuations, provided offshore gunfire support, and conducted carrier operations. The air force established air superiority early in the war, helping to ensure that United Nations Command (UNC) forces would not be driven off the peninsula in the summer of 1950. The air force conducted strategic bombing of North Korea and supported troop operations on the ground. Its heavy bombing of the North in 1953 helped bring the war to a conclusion that July.

US ground forces did not fare well early in the war. Many of the men were poorly trained: some soldiers were rushed into combat in a matter of a few weeks after induction, being expected to learn to fight in actual combat. The Marines welcomed the chance to prove their utility in amphibious assault. The September 1950 Inchon invasion, spearheaded by the 1st Marine Division, was one of the most important operations of the war.

With the North Koreans failing to achieve a quick victory, the Americans and South Koreans, supported by their allies, were able to build up their strength and dominate at sea and in the skies. With the UNC threatening to conquer all North Korea, China entered the war, chiefly because it feared a US military presence on the Manchurian border. The massive Chinese intervention caught MacArthur by surprise and drove UNC forces back across the 38th Parallel. In 1951 the front stabilized in a war of position. Peace talks opened that year but became bogged down on the issue of prisoner repatriation. Finally the war ended in an armistice, although the border between the two Koreas remained one of the world's flash points. In 2000 the US still maintained some 37,000 military personnel in South Korea.

In the war the United States sustained 36,914 war-related deaths from all causes. Massive UNC artillery fire had helped to offset Chinese numbers. The war saw extensive experiments with the helicopter, which was deployed not only in search-and-rescue operations and medical evacuation but also in resupply and the movement of troops. The war also speeded up desegregation of the armed forces. The effectiveness of the military in this impacted the Civil Rights Movement of the 1960s.

The Korean War had profound effects on the military. After previous conflicts the US had disarmed, but this did not happen after Korea, marking the transition to a permanent garrison state. President Dwight D. Eisenhower, elected in 1952 on a mandate of ending the war, was nonetheless wary of skyrocketing defence costs. He instituted a policy of heavier investment in nuclear weapons, a policy that came to be known as Massive Retaliation or 'more bang for a buck'.

The Vietnam War

The Cold War expanded the military commitments of the United States world-wide, especially in Western Europe. It also brought Washington's commitment to the doctrine of Containment of Communism, which led to a plethora of American military advisory groups abroad, including South Vietnam, where an insurgency had begun by 1959.

The US had taken over the French role in South Vietnam in 1954 and immediately created a conventional style military establishment for the Republic of Vietnam armed forces. Washington failed to understand the nationalist nature of the struggle. Washington also completely failed to understand the degree of punishment to which the Communist government of North Vietnam was willing to subject its people in order to achieve military victory and reunification.

Both sides gradually escalated the conflict in Vietnam as the US committed increased numbers of advisors, then helicopter pilots and finally, in 1965, ground troops. The US also began to bomb North Vietnam in 1965. A year earlier it had begun the secret bombing of Laos. These campaigns, which saw more bombs dropped than in all of World War II, failed to accomplish their goals of causing Hanoi to give up its support for the southern insurgency and halting the infiltration of men and *matériel* along the Ho Chi Minh Trail through eastern Laos into South Vietnam.

Both sides, meanwhile, built up their military personnel and equipment in South Vietnam. By 1968 the United States had over 500,000 military personnel in South Vietnam. Even this number was not sufficient. Washington's fears of a Chinese intervention as in Korea led to a strategic decision not to invade the North, a tremendous advantage to Hanoi in developing its own military options.

Contrary to popular belief, the US military was not caught off guard by the Communist Tet Offensive of January 1968, but it was surprised both by the precise timing during the Chinese Lunar New Year celebrations and by its intensity. Virtually the entire Communist military strength of 85,000 men was committed to the operation. Although the Communists failed in their objectives of bringing about a general uprising of the civilian population against the Americans, the Tet Offensive led to profound disillusionment over the war in the United States, and from early 1968 onward Washington sought a way out of it. The determination of Presidents Lyndon Johnson and Richard Nixon to achieve 'peace with honour' meant that the war continued, however.

Although the US military found much to criticize in Washington's policies of denying it certain strategic options and the failure to declare war and extend combat tours, many of the problems it faced in fighting the Vietnam War were self-inflicted. These included the six-months combat tour for officers, inefficient use of resources with only about 10 per cent of troops actually in combat, wasteful concentration on creature-comforts, and a reliance on firepower at the expense of manoeuvre. Command and control problems proliferated at all levels, as was shown even in the last American battle of the war, the so-called Christmas Bombing of the North in December 1972.

The Vietnam War finally ended for the US in January 1975. In the war US forces sustained 47,382 killed in action and 10,811 non-combat deaths. A total of 153,303 personnel were wounded in action.[37]

The US armed forces emerged from that conflict in terrible condition. The Vietnam War had wrecked both discipline and morale. The services were rife with racial problems, insubordination and a general permissiveness that led to careerism or 'ticket punching' among the officer corps and abrogation of authority by non-commissioned officers. During the mid-1970s all branches of the services, particularly the Army, suffered from underfunding and congressional and executive neglect.

The Army sought an all-volunteer force. Its Volunteer Army Project (VOLAR), begun in 1970, received President Nixon's support. Embracing the plan as a means of ending middle-class opposition to his Vietnam War policies, he abolished the draft in 1972. A year later the US Armed Forces were all volunteer.

Recruiting standards were upgraded and discharge programmes rid the force of drug users and those not suited for military life. The services targeted 1975 as the first year that no one would be accessed without a high school diploma. They also began a massive education programme to eradicate perceived and actual racial discrimination. The number of African-American officers increased and promotion boards ensured that minorities were promoted equally, based on percentages of numbers of those serving. Other initiatives such as barracks' renovation and involving the enlisted force in ideas to improve quality of life ended many irritants of the draft era. Another major change was allowing women increased opportunities in the US Armed Forces, to include combat roles, air force and navy pilots, and command positions aboard ships.

The next phase of armed forces reorganization was focus on missions. Efforts were made to define purposes and emphases of the military forces. The Cold War had always centred on Europe, where the North Atlantic Treaty Organization and the Warsaw Pact confronted one another. The watchword became 'professionalism'. Rather than attempt to bury lessons from Vietnam, the services studied every aspect of the conflict from helicopter tactics to media relations. New doctrines emerged in the form of 'active defence' on the ground in Europe to forward positioning of support facilities. The Air Force studied not only tactical air warfare but heavy airlift and newer aircraft designs.

Post-Vietnam military operations

The first test of the post-Vietnam military came in Operation Urgent Fury in Grenada in 1983. This military intervention, mounted by the Reagan administration, was to forestall a Soviet military presence on the island. Initially the navy and Marines received the task of evacuating Americans and restoring the political situation. However, interservice rivalry led to participation by all the services. What should have taken 48 hours took five days. Coordination was poor, not only between the military and political leadership but also within the services themselves. Most US losses were to 'friendly' fire. This fiasco led to more study and real joint operations.[38]

The proof of the reforms came in Operation Just Cause, the December 1989 invasion of Panama. This time joint operations worked well. Within a week Panama had been secured. Objectives had been clearly defined and the politicians deferred to the military once the decision to use force had been taken. New weapons, including the F-117 (Stealth) fighter and AC-130 gunship had also performed well.[39]

The Gulf War

The final test of the post-Vietnam military came in the war with Iraq. In August 1990 Iraqi dictator Saddam Hussein ordered his forces into Kuwait, quickly over-running that country. Caught off guard by the Iraqi action, President George Bush resolved to fight, in order to prevent Iraq from controlling the world price of oil and dominating Saudi Arabia, which supplied Western Europe with the bulk of its petroleum. Officers who had served in Vietnam, such as Chairman of the Joint Chiefs of Staff General Colin Powell, resisted having to fight another unpopular war in a faraway country. Most certainly the Pentagon over-estimated Iraq's military prowess.

President Bush put together a formidable international coalition and held it together, while in Operation Desert Shield the Allies built up a sizable force in Saudi Arabia. The US, the largest element of the coalition forces, provided in excess of 500,000 military personnel, 110 ships, 4,200 tanks and armoured personnel carriers, 1,800 fixed-wing aircraft, and 1,700 helicopters.

Operation Desert Storm began in January 1991 with a massive month-long air campaign, followed by the ground war. Iraqi forces were completely overwhelmed in the ground war which lasted just 100 hours. The war cost the Allies 300 casualties, most occurring from accidents or 'friendly fire'. The Iraqis lost at least 50,000 dead. A cease-fire was concluded on 3 March, with Kuwait free and Iraqi armed forces prohibited south of the 37th parallel. It was a remarkable renaissance of American forces from the 1970s, but it also left Saddam Hussein in power. A decade later it appeared as if the US would have to undertake another military operation against Iraq, which they successfully did in 2003.[40]

In the nearly two centuries between 1815 and 2000 the US military had emerged as the strongest in the world. As the only superpower in the world in 2000, the US also had no serious military rival.

Notes

1 Dave R. Palmer, *1794: America, Its Army, and the Birth of the Nation*, Novato, CA: Presidio Press, 1994, p. 217.
2 Allan R. Millett and Peter Maslowski, *For the Common Defense: A Military History of the United States of America*, rev. edn, New York: Free Press, 1994, pp. 126–8.
3 See Robert Remini, *Andrew Jackson and His Indian Wars*, New York: Viking Penguin, 1991.
4 Charles O. Paullin, *Paullin's History of Naval Administration, 1775–1911*, Annapolis, MD: Naval Institute Press, 1969, pp. 167, 210.
5 On the Army in the war see Richard Bruce Winders, *Mr. Polk's Army: The American Military Experience in the Mexican War*, College Station, TX: Texas A&M University Press, 1997; on the Navy see K. Jack Bauer, *Surfboats and Horse Marines: U.S. Naval Operations in the Mexican War*, Annapolis, MD: Naval Institute Press, 1969.
6 On land artillery see James C. Hazlett, Edwin Olmstead and M. Hume Parks, *Field Artillery Weapons of the Civil War*, Newark: University of Delaware Press, 1983 and Edwin Olmstead, Wayne Stark and Spencer C. Tucker, *The Big Guns: Civil War Siege, Seacoast and Naval Cannon*, Alexandria Bay, NY: Museum Restoration Service, 1997. On US naval ordnance of the period see Spencer C. Tucker, *Arming the Fleet: U.S. Navy Ordnance in the Muzzle-loading Era*, Annapolis, MD: Naval Institute Press, 1989.
7 A good overview of the background and war is James M. McPherson, *Battle Cry of Freedom: The Civil War Era*, New York: Oxford University Press, 1988.
8 On the sea war see Spencer C. Tucker, *A Short History of the Civil War at Sea*, Wilmington, DE: Scholarly Resources, 2002.
9 See Brian Hicks and Schuyler Kropf, *Raising the Hunley: The Remarkable History and Recovery of the Lost Confederate Submarine*, New York: Ballantine Books, 2002.

10 Spencer C. Tucker, *Raphael Semmes and the Alabama*, Abilene, TX: McWhiney Foundation Press, 1996.
11 For a good overview see Robert M. Utley, *Frontier Regulars: The United States Army and the Indian, 1865–1891*, New York: Macmillan, 1973.
12 See David F. Trask, *The War with Spain in 1898*, Lincoln: University of Nebraska Press, 1981.
13 See Brian M. Linn, *The Philippine War, 1899–1902*, Lawrence: University Press of Kansas, 2000.
14 See Herbert M. Mason, Jr., *The Great Pursuit*, New York: Random House, 1970.
15 See Edward M. Coffman, *The War to End All Wars: The American Military Experience in World War I*, Madison: The University of Wisconsin Press, 1986; and John S.D. Eisenhower, *Yanks: The Epic Story of the American Army in World War I*, New York: The Free Press, 2001.
16 See Geoffrey Perret, *There's A War to be Won: The United States Army in World War II*, New York: Random House, 1991.
17 Mauer Mauer, *Aviation in the US Army, 1919–1939*, Washington, DC: Office of Air Force History, 1987, p. 436.
18 I.C.B. Dear (ed.), *Oxford Companion to World War II*, New York: Oxford University Press, 1995, pp. 610, 1060, 1181–3, and 1216; Angelucci, *The Rand McNally Encyclopedia of Military Aircraft*, pp. 165, 167; Perret, *There's A War to be Won*, p. 109.
19 Perret, *There's A War to the Won*, pp. 12–18, 26.
20 Ibid., p. 32.
21 Shelby L. Stanton, *Order of Battle: U.S. Army, World War I*, Novato, CA: Presidio Press, 1984), p. 4.
22 Perret, *There's A War to be Won*, pp. 83–5.
23 See George F. Hofmann and Donn A. Starry, *Camp Colt to Desert Storm: The History of the U.S. Armored Forces*, Lexington: The University Press of Kentucky, 1999.
24 Ibid., pp. 86–8.
25 Dear, *Oxford Companion to World War II*, p. 1192.
26 Ibid., pp. 1198–9; H.P. Willmott, 'World War II at Sea: Pacific Theater', *Naval Warfare: An International Encyclopedia*, edited by Spencer C. Tucker, Denver, CO: ABC–CLIO, 2002, III: p. 1120.
27 Robin Neillands, *The Bomber War: The Allied Air Offensive against Nazi Germany*, New York: The Overlook Press, 2001, pp. 157–8.
28 Thomas M. Coffey, *Hap: The Story of the U.S. Air Force and the Man Who Built it, General Henry H. 'Hap' Arnold*, New York: The Viking Press, 1982, p. 251.
29 Neillands, *The Bomber War*, pp. 200–2.
30 See Belton Y. Cooper, *Death Traps: The Survival of an American Armored Division in World War II*, Novato, CA: Presidio Press, 1998.
31 Allan R. Millet, *Semper Fidelis: The History of the United States Marine Corps*, New York: Macmillan, 1980, p. 321.
32 Ibid., p. 326.
33 Ian Gow, *Okinawa, 1945: Gateway to Japan*, Garden City, NY: Doubleday, 1985, p. 195.
34 On this campaign see E. Bartlett Kerr, *Flames over Tokyo: The U.S. Army Air Forces' Incendiary Campaign Against Japan, 1944–1945*, New York: Donald I. Fine, 1991.
35 Clay Blair Jr., *Silent Victory: The U.S. Submarine War against Japan*, Philadelphia, PA: J.B. Lippincott, 1975, p. 877.
36 Millett and Maslowski, *For the Common Defense*, p. 656.

37 For a short survey of the war see Spencer C. Tucker, *Vietnam*, London: University College London Press, 1999.
38 Lee E. Russell and Albert Mendez, *Grenada, 1983*, London: Osprey, 1985.
39 See Ivan Musicant, *The Banana Wars: A History of United States Intervention in Latin America from the Spanish–American War to the Invasion of Panama* (New York: MacMillan, 1990).
40 See Michael R. Gordon and Bernard E. Trainor, *The Generals' War*, Boston: Little, Brown, 1995.

6

WAR IN MODERN
LATIN AMERICA

Miguel Angel Centeno

The military plays an important role in our images of Latin America. Both popular media and academic analyses assume that the military has been and remains the critical state actor. It would be hard to imagine a region more associated with a strong military tradition or one where armed conflict was apparently so central.[1] Yet, while Latin American militaries have interfered in politics and often served as repressive policemen, they have rarely functioned as the more traditional roles of soldiers.

Since independence in the early nineteenth century, Latin America has been relatively free of major *international* conflict. In the twentieth century the record is truly remarkable, especially in light of the experience of other regions of the world. During the same two hundred years, however, Latin America has also experienced a great deal of internal strife, ranging from persistent but limited rebellions to almost apocalyptic revolutions and social conflicts. The distinction between these two types of conflict is critical. They are both violent and both involve mobilization of some sort and a great deal of destruction. But their origins and consequences *may be* radically different.[2]

War is not simply acts of military violence or banditry (Latin America has had more than enough of both). Rather, war is a special form of *organized* violence with clear political goals. War is different from other violent acts in that it involves the 'existence, the creation, or the elimination of states'.[3] I would add that wars are different from what we may call 'militarized disputes' in that they involve lengths of time and amounts of resources requiring a substantial organizational commitment on behalf of at least one of the actors. That is, wars are concerted efforts requiring a minimal level of organizational and strategic commitment.[4] Thus, war is 'a substantial armed conflict between the organized military forces of independent political units'.[5]

There is no question that Latin Americans have tried to kill each other. There are too many examples of brutal and bloody conflicts to deny this. The Creole population of Guanajuato was massacred in 1810 while the Yaquis of Northern

Mexico, the Mayas of Yucatan and Guatemala and Mapuches of Chile (to name just three examples) were pursued with practically genocidal fury throughout the nineteenth century. The War of the Triple Alliance almost depopulated Paraguay and the Chaco War cost nearly one hundred thousand lives. The Mexican Revolution included many of the defining elements of modern war: civilians treated as combatants and cities as battlefields; railroads took men to battle where they faced barbed wire and machine guns. On an individual level, wars in Latin America also witnessed the degradation and transformation of humans into wild beasts. How else to explain the atrocities of Colombia's Violencia of 1948–55?

Yet, in general, South America has experienced low levels of militarization, the organization and mobilization of human and material resources for potential use in warfare. (Central America may represent an exception and will be discussed separately.) Latin Americans *have* tried to kill each other on numerous occasions, but they have generally not attempted to organize their societies with such a goal in mind. The region has experienced what we may call a violent form of peace. It has largely been spared the organized mass slaughter into which modern warfare developed over the past two hundred years, but it has also been subject to ferocious chaos.

How much war?

There is little question that the last two centuries have seen an unmistakable global increase in the ferocity of war. The number of actual conflicts may have declined and the number of years when the globe has known peace may actually have increased, but so has brutality of war. All indications of war's destructive capacity – absolute number of deaths, percentages of population affected, military versus civilian casualties – have dramatically increased.[6] Measures such as the number of men under arms (expressed either in absolute terms or as percentage of the population) have also increased. Some of these trends reflect the twentieth century's 'Thirty Years War' from 1914 to 1945. There is enough evidence on either side of these dates, however, to contradict the notion that this is an isolated phenomenon and the product of a geopolitical quirk.

In this context, Latin America seems unique. The last two centuries have not seen the same level of warfare common to other regions. No matter how measured, Latin America appears remarkably peaceful. The nations of Europe and North America, for example, have had nearly four times the number of men in their armed forces on a per capita basis, have killed tens of millions more people, and at a much faster rate. Latin America, with 150 more years of independence than Africa, has had roughly the same order of conflict as that continent. The Latin American figures would look even less bellicose but for the demographic disaster of the Paraguayan War of the 1860s. One might say the same about the world wars in Europe, but these conflicts both reflected the history of the region and had much more effect on subsequent societies than the limited Latin American wars. Again, Central America may represent a possible exception to this pattern.

The particularity of the continent is most evident if we distinguish between civil and international wars. Latin American states have only rarely fought each other. What is most striking is that Latin America appears to become more peaceful over time – the twentieth century saw episodes of warfare, but was generally non-violent. Even when looking at civil conflicts, moreover, Latin America appears benignly peaceful. Depending on which measure we choose, other regions have been at twice as violent.

The individual wars were geographically and historically concentrated. The greatest number and by far the most significant international wars occurred in the nineteenth century.[7] The twenty years after 1860 were particularly bellicose, with almost every country in the region invading a neighbour or defending itself. International conflicts were concentrated in three zones: Northern and Central Mexico; the La Plata basin shared by Brazil, Paraguay, Uruguay, and Argentina; and the mid-Pacific littoral where Bolivia, Peru and Chile meet. These wars were largely 'land grabs' by more powerful neighbours seeking to increase their access to resources. None of the international wars experienced by Latin America featured the intensity of ideological, nationalistic or ethnic hatreds that were so much a part of the history of other parts of the globe.

Civil conflicts followed the same pattern of decline in the twentieth century. Overall, however, there is much less periodization. There was a trend in the reasons for and natures of the civil conflicts. The first hundred years saw domestic wars largely defined by challenges to central authority and ideological or commercial disputes between élite factions. The twentieth century saw many more 'popular' revolts involving class struggles and a general intensification of the level of violence. Geographical concentration was again quite pronounced. Colombia, Mexico and Argentina suffered the most from this type of conflict, but no country was immune. In Central America, on the other hand, civil conflict became much more acute in the late twentieth century.

The degree of internal conflict that continues to dominate Latin America is both a cause and an indication of the relative inability of these states to fight each other. Internal violence was a reflection of both the absence of international enemies and of political powerlessness. Alternatively, there was not enough external conflict to draw attention away from internal divisions. Perhaps the best evidence of this condition is the relative importance of civil as opposed to international wars during the twentieth century. Moreover, in a notable departure from the European pattern, we see little evidence of internal struggles enveloping neighbours.[8] Violence rarely crossed borders.

In general, Latin America has largely fought what I call *limited* war. To understand what I mean by this, first consider a definition of contemporary total war.

This form of conflict may be said to have begun with the military revolution of the seventeenth century, to have achieved new levels of destruction and social consequences with the French Revolutionary and Napoleonic wars, to have developed into its modern counterparts beginning with the Crimean and US Civil wars, and to have culminated in the two World Wars. Total wars may be characterized by (a) increasing lethality of the battlefield, (b) the expansion of the killing zone to include not only hundreds of miles of front lines but also civilian targets, (c) association with a form of moral or ideological crusade that contributes to the demonization of the enemy, (d) the involvement of significant parts of the population either in direct combat or in support roles, and (e) the militarization of society, in which social institutions are increasingly oriented towards military success and judged on their contribution to a war effort.

Such efforts require that states therefore be able to (a) amass and concentrate large amounts of men and *matériel* in a relatively short time, (b) be able to expand their efforts across hundreds if not thousands of miles, (c) prescribe some form of coherent ideological message, (d) convince significant numbers of the population to accept direct military authority over their lives, and (e) transform their societies to be able to meet these challenges.

Limited wars, on the other hand, (a) involve short overall duration of conflict with isolated moments of ferocity, (b) are restricted to few and small geographical areas, (c) are between states with shared ideological or cultural profiles and originate in economic or frontier clashes, (d) are fought by either professional mercenary armies, or those made up of small numbers of draftees from lower classes, and (e) may be practically ignored by the typical civilian. They do not require dramatic fiscal or personal sacrifices, or a strong state to impose these. Most important, they do not require the political or military mobilization of the society except (and not always) in the euphoric initial moments. Because of these limited needs, such conflicts leave little of the historical legacy associated with total wars. The streets are not filled with veterans, the state is not a post-bellum Leviathan, and economic wealth is barely touched by fiscal authorities. Life goes on much as before. As I will make clear in what follows, the limited war pattern has largely defined the Latin American experience.

Possible exceptions to this pattern, namely Paraguay in the nineteenth century, and Nicaragua, Guatemala and El Salvador in the twentieth reflect exceptional circumstances largely absent from other regions and times.

Latin America at war

Clearly, Latin America has been violent but the largest part of political conflict occurred within states, not between them. The following pages provide a summary of the major conflicts in Mexico and South America over the past two centuries.

The Wars of Independence

The most significant wars in Latin American history occurred at practically the very birth of the new states.[9] It is impossible to classify these as international or civil, for they contained elements of both. Formally fighting an external power (Spain), the wars were often conflicts between different groups within the élite or even (at their bloodiest) between social classes and castes. The fact that the most momentous wars for the continent were fought prior to the establishment of states is significant. Violence was not between states but oriented towards the creation of a new political order. This pattern would be repeated over the next century.

The Wars of Independence originated both in the internal conditions of the colonies and in events in Europe. In part, they were the culmination of centuries-old tensions between colonies seeking greater autonomy and a weakened empire that had only recently attempted to re-establish centralized control. Social divisions paralleled institutional ones. Whites born in the colonies (*criollos* or creoles) suffered from systematic discrimination in favour of Spanish-born subjects (*peninsulares*). Attempts to reform economic policies or political institutions were often read as benefiting one or the other of these two élite factions. The alliance of subaltern groups to one side or another of the élite depended on region and specific circumstances.

The confusion produced by the Napoleonic invasions of Spain in 1808 provided the spark and the opportunity for Latin American independence. The legitimacy of the empire resided in the person of the king. With his abdication, the already strained political apparatus fell apart. By 1810, colonial juntas had been declared in Caracas and Buenos Aires, and with the exception of Peru and Cuba, the entire continent witnessed the rise of independence movements. The Independence Wars can be divided into three major fronts: Mexico, Southern Cone and Northern Andes.

The Mexican independence movement represents a war model subsequently followed by the rest of the region. It began with the most socially radical agenda of any in the Americas, but produced little other than the collapse of the central state. As such it is emblematic of the generic fate of all the successful independence movements: none reformed the colonial structure of their societies and all failed to quickly institutionalize authority.

The struggle for independence began in 1810 in the Bajío region.[10] There, Father Miguel Hidalgo led a poorly armed mass of largely Indian and mestizo soldiers through some spectacular early victories, infamous massacres, and an early defeat as the discipline of the colonial army wore the insurgents down. Hildalgo's successor, José María Morelos, was more successful at creating a viable military and even managed to call the Congress of Chilpacingo to draw up a model for the new post-independence Mexico. Once again, however, the greater resources and organization available to the Spaniards were decisive, and Morelos was captured and executed by 1815. The rebellion was largely dormant for the next five years. When independence did come in 1821 it was thanks to the reformist efforts of Agustín Iturbide's Army of the Three Guarantees, whose emphasis on maintaining links with Spain and the Catholic Church marked a clean break with the much more radical movements of Hildago and Morelos. Iturbide's victory also brought about the independence of Central America (despite substantial ambivalence among the élite) and the creation of a Federation ruling the isthmus until the 1830s.

Critical to an understanding of the failure of the first stage of the Mexican revolt and subsequent events is the fact that Hidalgo's and Morelos' armies did not merely oppose Spanish political rule; they also expressed hatred of all of the institutional legacies of the Spanish Conquest of three centuries before. The fight against the rebellion soon evolved into much more than a defence of colonial rule. Many criollos originally sympathetic to independence chose to fight against any threat to their social position.

The defeat of Hidalgo's and Morelos' forces led to several critical developments. First, it marginalized the Indian masses from what was to become increasingly an intra-élite struggle. Second, the white élite came to fear the potential for social violence and sought to limit opportunities for such explosions to flare again. In a lesson to be repeated again and again throughout the continent, criollos appreciated that whatever differences may exist between whites necessarily came second to the need for preserving the colonial social order.

In the Southern Cone,[11] the Independence Wars began in Buenos Aires in May 1810 and in Santiago in September of the same year, with the establishment of juntas claiming to replace the royal authority of Spain. Unlike the Mexican case, these events did not generate calls for radical changes in social structures. (This was not the case in Uruguay, where José Artigas led a much more popular rural force.) While the Buenos Aires junta was unable to hold onto Paraguay (which established its autonomy by 1812) or Upper Peru (Bolivia) (which was re-conquered by local troops from Peru), it never faced a serious royalist threat to its own independence. Instead, in a pattern that was to be repeated for the next fifty years, its main military efforts were oriented towards maintaining other provinces under its control. Revolutionary Santiago had no such luck with weak royal forces, being retaken by loyalists in 1814.

On the northern coasts,[12] the pattern was the same as in Chile. Original enthusiasm in Caracas faced provincial resistance, fears of social upheaval and determined royalist opposition. Control over the area shifted, but by 1815 Bolívar was exiled in Jamaica and royalists were exacting their revenge in all the major cities.

The first five years of the Independence Wars serve as a model for the pattern of wars that would dominate the continent over the next century. First we find a pattern of substantial destruction with limited logistical complexity. The armies that fought in these wars were not large, but they left behind them a considerable wake of death and destruction.[13] Second, everywhere one sees squabbling élites. The first cut was clearly between *peninsulares* and *criollos*, but even beneath these divisions we see ever shrinking factions and battles between supposed allies. Sides are switched, loyalties betrayed, ideologies overturned in a dizzying cadence. Finally, hanging over all the battles, we detect the terror of race and class war motivating élites to go to one side or another depending on local conditions. The sub-text running throughout the Independence Wars was the fear that a political battle would be transformed into a social one. Only when enough of those in power felt secure of their future (or Spain began to represent a potentially greater threat to the social status quo), could the revolutions proceed.[14]

José de San Martín and Simón Bolívar led the rebellion's comeback. San Martín had been an officer in the Royal army, but had joined the rebellion upon his arrival in Buenos Aires in 1812. Convinced that the key to the success of the war lay in capturing loyalist Lima, he lobbied for an invasion through Chile, as opposed to the already failed route through Upper Peru (Bolivia). San Martín's campaign is notable on several counts. There is of course the sheer military bravado of the Andes crossing, and the strategic intelligence that San Martín displayed at Chacabuco, Maipu, and later the siege of Lima. For our purposes, the most important aspect of the campaign is one that makes it practically unique in the Independence Wars. Prior to crossing the Andes in the winter of 1817, San Martín gathered forces and *matériel* in Mendoza, Argentina. There he established the kind of organizational and logistical centre typical of armies in the contemporary period. His forces were not a semi-organized rabble, but a disciplined and relatively well-supported army. With this, he was able to defeat loyalist troops left in Chile, invade Peru by sea, and capture Lima in 1821. The administrative and financial support enjoyed by San Martín prior to and during his Chilean campaign meant that the final conquest of that country was not undertaken by semi-autonomous and divided bands, but by a centralized power that used the occasion to reassert its authority.

Bolívar's war was equally triumphant, if somewhat more complex. Returning from exile in 1816, he benefited from resentment of the newly victorious *peninsulares* and their draconian policies. He won his first victory in the small port town of Angostura, which allowed him access to supplies and volunteers coming via the sea. With this new victory in hand, Bolívar allied himself with the *llaneros* cavalry of José Antonio Páez and together they began the difficult invasion of New Granada across the northern tip of the Andes. Following the victories of Boyacá and Carabobo, Bolívar now ruled a combined 'Gran Colombia' which would soon also include Ecuador. Conquering Quito in 1822, Bolívar and his lieutenant Sucre moved on to Peru and the decisive defeat of the Spanish at Ayacucho on 9 December 1824.

Several aspects of Bolívar's campaigns deserve attention. First, in an early hint of tensions that would characterize the next century, efforts to recruit non-élites and non-whites into the army met various obstacles and produced resentment among local *criollos* and within the army itself. The question of who could be trusted with the citizenship implied by military service was never resolved. Second, the various congresses and meetings organized by Bolívar during the campaign betrayed the ambivalence between what would come to be called Conservative and Liberal views on the formation of the new states and their relationships with their societies under their rule. The extent to which the population could be trusted with its own affairs, the state's relationship with the church, and the autonomy of the various parts of the newly liberated continent were never adequately determined. In the absence of a hegemonic political vision with an accompanying enforcement capacity, claimants arose in each of the distinctive regions. These did not necessarily reflect the respective social and political status quo, but relied on their military resources to establish their rule. The Bolívarian project produced neither the unitary state that the *Libertador* had sought, nor coherent smaller political entities.

The most important consequence of the wars was the fracturing of political power. Not only did the Spanish-American Empire dissolve into several nations (a process that continued through the 1820s), but even within the new borders, governments exercised little authority and had even less control. Civilian administration was destroyed throughout the continent. Its opposition to the Wars of Independence weakened the other major institution, the church. The Wars also did a great deal of sheer physical damage to the economic infra-structure of the Latin American economy, especially the mining sector.[15] Unlike the case of Europe where the end of the Napoleonic Wars provided a political base for a hundred years of political consolidation and economic growth, the Independence Wars left a legacy of violence and destruction that still haunts Latin America.

International wars[16]

All of the major Latin American wars may be characterized as involving territorial swaps motivated by fairly simple geopolitical competition.[17] While the territorial adjustments made to the colonial map have been relatively small, the acquisition and defence of territory has been the dominant historical trope. While this may seem unsurprising or even universal, it is critical to recognize the kinds of international wars that Latin America has avoided. No countries have fought each other as representatives of an ideology or a religious faith. That is, the Latin American nation-states (with the possible exception of Cuba after 1959) have never mounted crusades on behalf of an abstract principle. Invasions and wars have, of course, been justified with rhetorical claims to justice (and even here we find surprisingly little of the political self-justifications associated with international conflict), but the flags carried by the respective armies were theirs and no one else's. This is particularly interesting in light of the legacy of the Independence Wars, when armies of one region did seek to export their notions of liberty and autonomy. To a surprising extent (and with some exceptions noted below) the individual countries have respected each other's autonomy (even when lusting after or pursuing a neighbour's property).

The wars have also been relatively short and with simple linear narratives. Few wars have been decided by more than one or two decisive battles. In almost all cases (the French invasion of Mexico is an exception) the stronger country and the one winning at the start of the struggle was victorious at the end. Bibliographic accounts of the wars are remarkably simple. There is often no need for more than one strategic map, battles can be described in a single paragraph and whole wars summarized in a few pages. Not surprisingly, by contemporary standards, the wars involved relatively few men and minimal equipment. What is also surprising is the absence of tribalistic hatred in most of the wars (exceptions include Paraguayan views of Brazilians and Peruvians of Ecuadorians). Soldiers fighting each other (often for the first and last time) do so without the form of collective hatred so common in other parts of the world. They meet and kill each other with an apparently desultory attitude. It often appears as if participants and observers had already accepted the marginality of their actions. Looking back on nearly 200 years of global violence, one can find few incidents as apparently meaningless.

The Battle for La Plata[18]

From the 1820s to the 1850s, the Rio de la Plata saw a series of struggles over which country would control the river and dominate the regional economy.[19] The conflict had a long history going back to the contests between Portugal and Spain. The early development of Buenos Aires and the establishment of the Vice-Royalty of La Plata in 1776 were at least partly due to this rivalry. Within the Spanish territories, Buenos Aires and Montevideo competed for dominance. Up river, the future territory of Paraguay was already a land apart with the heritage of Jesuit missions and the demographic survival of the Guaraní indians. In the north, cattle ranchers in southern Brazil sought greater pastures and, like all the players, access to the River Plate. The region was the site of a classic geopolitical competition, as well as some of the bloodiest wars in the continent's history.

During much of the first part of the nineteenth century, Brazil was the strongest player, either occupying the eastern bank of the river (what it called the Cisplatine Province and is now Uruguay) or controlling the politics of that country after its independence. In 1825, a revolt by a group of Uruguayan exiles from Argentina (the famous '33 orientales') soon led to the official incorporation of the 'Banda Oriental' into the Argentine Republic. The Brazilians responded with a blockade of the river. Two years of considerable naval and land warfare followed which exhausted the fiscal and military capacity of both sides. By 1827, Argentina seemed to have the upper hand, but the collapse of the Rivadavia government and the pressure of the British (whose merchants were suffering from the interruption in trade) led to the acceptance of the independent buffer state of Uruguay. At least in the case of Argentina, the war accelerated the disintegration of central authority while simultaneously beginning the long-term financial dependence on British capital. In Brazil, however, the wars arguably helped consolidate centralized rule.

Ten years later, the conflict resumed. Internal divisions in Uruguay drew in Juan Manuel de Rosas, dictator of Buenos Aires. The resulting complications produced (in rough order) a French intervention, revolts in the Argentine littoral, a ten-year siege of Montevideo, a British intervention, the entry of Brazil, and the fall of Rosas. While arguably signalling the beginning of the process that would lead to Argentine consolidation, and again strengthening the Brazilian state, the war was a disaster for Uruguay and sentenced that country to fifty more years of *caudillos* and chaos. The end of this conflict sealed the 'entente' between Argentina and Brazil, which is perhaps one of the most remarkable aspects of intra-regional relations in Latin America. Despite the continuing tensions between the two most obvious potential super-powers, they never fought a war against each other after mid-century.

The War of the Triple Alliance[20]

The origins of this war may be traced to a variety of sources: the colonial legacy of imperial rivalry and vague borders; international competition for trade; geopolitical struggles for control over the La Plata River system; long-standing Brazilian–Argentinean intervention in Uruguayan politics; British support for the creation of a new economic system in the Southern Cone; domestic instability in both Argentina and Uruguay; and the personal dementia of the Paraguayan leader Francisco Solano López. While Brazil and Argentina were obviously the more powerful states, Paraguay had developed an independent manufacturing capacity in small arms and ship repair. Using all the resources available to a state monopolizing the country's economy, López sought to finish the long-standing quarrels with his neighbours and create a new South American Empire. He believed that in conjunction with his internal allies in both Uruguay and Argentina, and with the likely Argentinean opposition to shedding blood on behalf of the slave monarchy in Brazil, the alliance between the two regional giants would not survive a single Paraguayan victory.

As in the earlier conflicts along the River Plate, the weakness of the Uruguayan state was the immediate cause of war. The possible entry of Paraguay into the geo-political mix was not welcomed by either Brazil or Argentina. The Brazilian Empire had an interest in keeping Uruguay and Paraguay compliant and weak in order to assure free passage on the Paraguay River to the increasingly important province of Mato Grosso. Argentina saw the continued existence of Paraguay (a breakaway province from the former Viceroyalty of La Plata) as an incentive for separatist *caudillos*. López hated and feared both larger neighbours. Uruguay was essentially a passive observer in a war ostensibly fought over it.

In 1864 Brazil marched into Uruguay to support its clients in the Colorado Party. López responded by commandeering an Imperial steamer and then successfully invading Brazil. But he then made the critical error of entering Argentina to 'improve' his strategic position. This brought Argentina into the war on the side of Brazil (despite the expected distaste at finding itself allied with a slave state). Within a few months, Paraguay had lost two major battles and most of its navy. Lacking support from potential allies such as Bolivia and Chile, Paraguay soon faced a completely defensive struggle. López increasingly committed the entire Paraguayan society to the defence of the Republic and allowed for the continuation of the war even after disastrous military defeats in 1866. These battles usually consisted of recklessly brave Paraguayan soldiers assaulting strong Allied positions and suffering massive casualties. Paraguayan resistance shocked the Allies, but it also meant that the country soon began to run out of bodies that could be thrown at the cannons. In part because of the Allies' overestimation of Paraguayan resources, in part because of the cholera epidemics that caused havoc, in part because of López's ability to mobilize the entire society in a defensive struggle, the war dragged on for three more years and did not end until López was killed in 1870.

The War of the Triple Alliance is unique in many ways. In terms of length, passionate intensity, logistical challenges, and consequences, it has no equal on the continent. This is as close as we come to the modern notion of 'total war' in Latin America. The destruction caused by the war removed Paraguay from the geopolitical map (and almost removed the entire country and its population from the globe). It was the most difficult post-independence military challenge faced by Brazil and Argentina and the consequences of their campaigns were significant. As the one dog of war that definitely did bark, the War of the Triple Alliance sets off the rarity of the continental experience in a clearer light and, if nothing else, allows us to better appreciate the good fortune of the continent.

Wars of the Peruvian–Bolivian Confederation and of the Pacific[21]

Given their very close economic and administrative links during the colonial era, the early separation of Bolivia and Peru was in many ways a political fiction. In part because of their historic and economic connection and in part because of the rising strength of the Chilean state, the Bolivian president General Andrés Santa Cruz sought to establish closer connections between two halves of the old Vice-Royalty of Lima. In alliance with some Peruvian *caudillos*, he invaded Peru in 1835, and in October 1836 he declared the establishment of the Peruvian–Bolivian Confederation. This union did have some popular support, but the division of Peru into two provinces and the selection of Lima as the capital alienated élites in both countries. More importantly, the union threatened the geopolitical position of Chile and in Argentina. Both countries viewed a strong Peru as challenges to their predominance. The first declared war in December 1836, the latter in May

1837. Despite some early failures, the Chilean army, in alliance with Peruvian forces opposed to the union, were able to defeat Santa Cruz in the Battle of Yungay in January 1839, leading to the dissolution of the Confederation.

Chile's victory over Peru and Bolivia in the 1830s established its reputation as the regional 'Prussia' and further solidified the political institutionalization begun under Diego Portales (who was assassinated at the very beginning of the war). If any war 'made' Chilean exceptionalism, it was this one, as it provided a rare legitimacy while also establishing a stable civil–military relationship. For Peru and Bolivia, defeat appears to have accelerated the process of economic and political fragmentation begun with independence. (Peru did have one successful military adventure in the nineteenth century. Following the Spanish invasion of the Chincha Islands, Peru repelled the Spaniards in the war of 1864–6.)

Beginning in 1840 various international companies began the exploration of the Bolivian coast in order to make use of the guano and nitrate deposits there. The exploitation of silver beginning in 1870 led to an economic boom. During this decade Chile and Bolivia appeared to resolve a series of quarrels by increasing the influence of the former in the disputed region. But disagreements over taxes and the nationalization of Chilean mines in the Peruvian desert in 1875 maintained the tension. Following some diplomatic efforts to resolve a new set of crises, Chile declared war in April 1879. Given a Peruvian–Bolivian alliance, this involved Chile in a war with both northern neighbours. The war quickly became a contest for plunder as each side sought control over the nitrate fields and the coast.

None of the countries was prepared for war, although Chile had a significant advantage in naval forces. More importantly, the Chilean state retained its institutional solidity while both Peru and Bolivia suffered from internal divisions. Chile occupied the Bolivian littoral, then Tarapaca in 1879, and Tacma and Arica and most of Northern Coast in 1880. By this stage the Chilean Army had increased significantly, with an invasion force of 12,000 men. International pressure from both the United States and European powers forced the two sides into negotiation, but the Chileans sought complete victory. In 1881, with an army now numbering 26,000 men, the Chileans entered Lima. They did not leave until 1884, annexing the province of Tarapaca forever and the provinces of Tacna and Arica until 1929. Chile also took the entire Bolivian coast (Atacama).

The victory helped determine the future professional character of both the Chilean and Peruvian militaries, as well as partially defining the development options of the three countries. Chile enjoyed an economic boom as well as unprecedented patriotic euphoria, both of which helped dissolve the gloom of the 1870s. Despite the relative shortness of the war, Peru suffered severe casualties and the destruction of much of its coastal infrastructure. The war may also be seen as the best example of the military formation of a new national identity, as the Peruvian and Bolivian memory of their defeat continues to play a large role in their respective nationalisms. The Bolivian defeat deprived that country of a great part of its wealth and left it contained within the *altiplano* (in which Chile had no interest). The war did help decrease the political influence of the military and helped consolidate the rule of a civilian oligarchy dominated by mining interests.

The War of the Chaco[22]

In many ways this was the most tragic of all the international conflicts, involving as it did two extremely poor and autocratic societies in which the military already played important roles, Paraguay and Bolivia. The war arguably originated in earlier defeats of the two participants. For Bolivia, the Chaco promised access to the sea (lost to Chile) through the Paraguay River. For Paraguay, control of the Chaco served to ameliorate the pain of the López catastrophe. Unfounded hopes of natural wealth only served to heighten the tension.

The two countries had been in a low-intensity conflict over the region since the early twentieth century. Thanks to military autonomy, sheer political inertia and rumours of oil, clashes in 1928 were followed by all-out war in 1932. At first, the Bolivians appeared to have the advantage with their early assault on Fort López, but under the leadership of José Felix Estigarribia, Paraguay united behind the war effort with the army growing to over twenty times its peace-time strength. Over the next three years, the armies fought in some of the most inhospitable terrain in the world. By 1935, the Bolivian Army had collapsed and Paraguay was awarded the disputed territory.

Both victory and defeat produced long-term changes. The failure of the Bolivian Army embittered a whole generation of junior officers, who were to lead a series of pseudo-radical experiments in the following years. More importantly, it weakened the political legitimacy of the mining oligarchy that had run the country for so long. In Paraguay, victory led to the end of the Liberal regime that had dominated in the twentieth century and prepared the setting for a civil–military alliance through the Colorado Party that would culminate in the dictatorship of Stroessner. Yet, while it was one of the bloodiest wars in Latin American history, the Chaco conflict was relatively marginal to the continent. Much as geopolitical events in Latin America made little difference to the larger world, the results of a squabble between Bolivia and Paraguay mattered little to even their own neighbours.

The invasions of Mexico[23]

In terms of geography and global historical impact, the US–Mexican War was no doubt the most important of the conflicts fought by a Latin American country. To a large extent, the war may have been unavoidable, given the economic and ideological pressure of US expansion as well as the particular political needs of slavery. While it is undeniable that Mexico could not have been worse served than by the leadership of General Santa Anna, it is difficult to imagine any other outcome given the very different military and political capacities of the two states.

The origins of the war may partly be traced to the political instability of post-independence Mexico, particularly after 1827. This instability (and the aborted Spanish invasion of 1829) paved the way for the rise to power of General Antonio Santa Anna. His attempted imposition of greater centralized control from Mexico City led to revolt in the northern province of Texas. Despite his opening bravado and early victory in San Antonio, Santa Anna was unable to put down the rebellion. Following his capture by the rebels, he had to recognize the independence of the new Texan Republic. The southern province of Yucatan also tried to escape increased centralized control (and to obtain more effective military support for its system of caste slavery) later in the decade, but was unable to secure its independence.

Santa Anna remained a key player in the increasingly chaotic Mexican political scene in the early 1840s, often relying on military bombast and threats to declare war on the United States should it attempt to annex the Texan Republic. Despite European efforts to mediate in the dispute, the momentum of 'manifest destiny' and Southern slavery politics led to the annexation of Texas by the United States in February 1845. The United States also made it clear that its ambitions would not be satisfied with Texas, that it desired all the territory north of the Rio Grande as well as California. Despite early efforts to avoid a war (few Mexicans had any illusions about the capacity of the army to withstand an invasion), public opinion and military pride led to Mexican refusal to accept annexation.

Three months after the beginning of hostilities in May 1846, the US army occupied most of Northern Mexico. In part because of continuing instability requiring the participation of the army in civil unrest in Mexico City, the United States was able to land in Veracruz in March 1847. Proving that war does not necessarily unite, much of the Mexican military effort was expended on domestic struggles. States would not support the federal government, which in turn did not trust the cities that had to bear the brunt of the US invasion. When the Mexican government was able to produce an army to fight the US invaders, it was largely defeated by the absence of logistical support. Artillery was outdated, powder was limited, the men were untrained, and the officers seemed to care little and know less about strategy. By September 1847 US troops were overcoming the last Mexican resisters in Chapultepec Castle (the famed 'Halls of Montezuma' of the US Marines).

The Treaty of Guadalupe Hidalgo left Mexico without half of its territory. It may have also contributed to the rise of the new Liberal party that under Benito Juárez would begin the construction of contemporary Mexico. For the

United States, the war brought glory and heartache. The acquisition of so many resources and the trans-continental expansion provided the basis for its future power. The control over vast territories also intensified the competition between the Southern and Northern views on the union.

A decade later, Mexico had to defend itself again.[24] The Wars of Reform (1858–61), the culminating conflict between Liberals and Conservatives, had left not only continued divisions among the élite and weakened government but also an economic disaster. Finding himself bankrupt, President Benito Juárez refused to pay back immediately some of the debts and claims held by European citizens. The French Emperor Napoleon III was interested not merely in payment, but also sought to recreate an empire in the Americas. In December 1861, his troops (temporarily accompanied by British and Spanish) began the occupation of Veracruz.

The French were generally welcomed by the defeated Conservatives and particularly by the Church. Despite an early Mexican victory in Puebla (the famous *Cinco de Mayo* of 1862), by early 1863 the French and their Conservative allies had occupied Mexico City. They were followed by the new Imperial Court of Maximilian and Carlota (chosen by Napoleon as the carriers of European civilization). The French–Conservative royal government appeared to succeed in finally destroying the Liberals and for two years the Habsburg court attempted to establish its legitimacy. But the withdrawal of French troops beginning in 1866 and the end of the American Civil War meant that Maximilian had lost his protector while Juárez gained new support. The end was relatively quick with the Liberal army easily defeating the now-isolated Conservatives and finally capturing the Emperor in May 1867. With the fall of the city of Queretaro and Maximilian's execution, Mexico's independence as well as the Liberal hegemony were firmly established.

Two characteristics of the international wars fought by Mexico deserve special attention. The first was the absence of any sense of élite unity prior to the ultimate victory by Juárez. Whether arguing among themselves as the US troops conquered huge territories, or cooperating with a foreign invader, the Mexican political élite was unable to establish either a general consensus regarding the form of government or securely establish its control over the entire country. This resulted in the second key aspect of the wars: despite the bloodletting (the war against the French lost 50,000 lives) the armies that fought over Mexico were never logistically complex. The Liberals won in 1867 with little but antiquated rifles and the government of Mexico was never able to muster enough authority or will to field anything approaching a modern army.

Some exceptions[25]

We may identify three important exceptions to the geographical and chrono-logical distribution of international wars in Latin America.

During much of the nineteenth century, Central America witnessed a series of wars between the various republics, beginning with the dissolution of the Federation by 1840, continuing through the subsequent Conservative and Liberal hegemonies and followed by the anti-communist crusades of the post-war era. Uniquely in the Western hemisphere, the countries of the isthmus have had a consistent policy of military animosity and have sought to interfere in each other's political decisions. In the last three decades of the twentieth century, this tendency took a particularly bloody turn. First, in 1969, Honduras and El Salvador fought what has been derisively called the 'Soccer War'. While the military actions were limited, the resulting deaths may have numbered in the thousands. In the 1970s and 1980s, the various civil wars, interventions by the United States and regional competitions blended in a regional struggle that consumed billions of dollars and killed more than 100,000. The latter conflicts approached our earlier definition of 'total' war, but they were largely driven by the concerns and resources of the United States. Once the superpower lost interest, the wars and their victims withered with neglect.

Cuba's adventures in Africa are unique in that a regional power was able to project itself militarily across an ocean. With Soviet assistance, the Cuban army fought both conventional and guerrilla wars in Angola and Ethiopia. The latter conflict occurred in 1977–9 in support of Mengistu Haile Mariam's regime, specifically against incursions by Somali forces. The Cuban involvement was largely limited to armoured units and air forces, with relatively small numbers of infantry. In Angola, on the other hand, the Cuban commitment was much larger, with several divisions fighting at one time and in non-specialized units. Casualties in the two conflicts totalled thousands and help define the Cuban military in subsequent years (with a potential threat to the Castro regime thwarted by the late 1980s). The African wars also helped create Cuba's new role in the global arena as ambassadors of socialism and helped consolidate the island's leadership among Third World countries. These activities also helped to exacerbate US–Cuban relations even before Ronald Reagan's presidency. The autonomy of the Cuban forces vis-à-vis Soviet authorities, their relationships with African troops and the role played by the United States in inciting these incursions remain topics for debate.

The final exception to a general pattern is Argentina's invasion of the Falklands/Malvinas in 1982 and the subsequent 'war' with the British expeditionary force. Largely conceived as a classic tactic for generating domestic support, Argentina's invasion followed more than a century of contention regarding the ownership of the islands. In the end, the conflict merely showcased the logistical, tactical and strategic limitations of the Argentina military and led to the downfall of the last junta. Resulting in the death of nearly a thousand men, the Falklands War may be the best example of the marginal role to which Latin American militaries have been assigned in any geopolitical calculus.

Civil wars[26]

Latin America has experienced much more internal or civil conflict than conflict of an external, international kind. The number of wars and the complexity of their historical and social origins make it difficult to give any summary description here. As Loveman notes, it is impossible to exhaustively list all the civil conflicts. This is especially true if we wish to count coups, *cuartelazos* and *pronuncamientos*. Bolivia, for example, suffered thirteen military uprisings in four months in 1840, Colombia had eleven major rebellions in the nineteenth century, and Mexico 49 administrations in just 33 years.[27] We may distinguish five general types of civil war that students of Latin America need to consider.

Regional rebellions

This first type of conflict dominated the nineteenth century and largely involved struggles over the establishment of central authority or provinces rebelling against control by the capital. Practically every country suffered from such wars. In Argentina, the fight within and between provinces (or between *unitarios* and *federalistas*) lasted much of the century. The first 25 years after independence witnessed innumerable battles between the various Independence War generals, and then between Rosas and autonomous *caudillos*. In the 1850s, the Confederation and Buenos Aires continued to fight. Even after the victory of Mitre in 1861, central authority was not absolutely secured until 1880. Uruguay was for many years practically two countries, Montevideo and the rural hinterland, each fighting the other for either control or autonomy. During the 1830s, only two of the Brazilian Empire's eighteen provinces did *not* rebel. Particularly serious were uprisings in Maranhão (1831–2), Bahia (1832–5), Minas Gerais (1833), Mato Grosso (1834), Pará (1835–7) and Rio Grande do Sul (1835–45). In Central America, similar processes produced the independent 'city-states' of today by 1840.

Regionalism continued as a political force well into the twentieth century. Mexico's version of the Federalist versus Centralist battle took up much of the first half of the century and arguably still played a role in the second half. Peru was divided into North and South, and Coast and Sierra, while Ecuador was torn between Guayaquil and Quito, and Bolivia's altiplano was isolated from the rest of the country. Finally, recent events in Colombia indicate that that country's traditionally weak state has not been able to impose assumed centralized control even after almost two hundred years of independence. The central government has essentially recognized the sovereignty of two guerrilla armies over country-sized swathes of its territory.

While these conflicts were often quite bloody (in part because they often combined racial and class elements with the more geographical disputes) they usually involved small armies and irregular troops. In many cases, it would be difficult to distinguish between civil wars and police actions against banditry. In this way, regional struggles are the prototypical Latin American wars: nasty, brutish, and short.

Ideological battles

Often indistinguishable from the regional rebellions, these conflicts persisted well into the twentieth century. The nineteenth century consisted of almost universal squabbles between Liberals and Conservatives (often paralleling divisions between Federalists and Centralists respectively). Liberals believed in free trade, the elimination of special *fueros* or corporate rights and property ownership, and favoured an expansion of citizenship rights (at least theoretically). Conservatives were protectionist, favoured the Church and looked back to the colonial past for some of their inspiration. Mexico may be the extreme example of this kind of conflict. The Conservatives dominated for much of the first thirty years of independence, the Liberals for most of the next twenty, but each had to expend huge amounts of time, energy and resources in fighting the other. These divisions were acute throughout Central America, where Conservatives and Liberals fought each other across international borders. Ecuador experienced similar divisions, as did Colombia, continuing into the twentieth century. In the latter case, the struggle began with the War of the Supremes in 1839 (in part a regionalist squabble), continued for fifty years of almost perpetual conflict, and culminated in the extremely bloody War of the Thousand Days (1899).[28] This struggle became so institutionalized that competition between political parties and their adherents became more important than the original points of dispute. Histories of conflict bred their own ferocity, resulting in the infamous *Violencia* of the 1940s and 1950s.

In some cases, the ideological divisions focused on relations with the Church. This was clearly an element in the Mexican case (not resolved until the 1920s) as well as in Chile, where the antagonism over anti-clericalism belied the notion of a Chilean political consensus. More recently, the doctrine of National Security and subsequent 'dirty wars' against 'communist subversion' may be seen as the heirs of such splits. These had their bloodiest expression in the civil wars of Central America in the 1970s and 1980s.

Obviously both what I am calling ideological and regional wars reflected underlying social and economic conditions and inequalities. Regional struggles in Brazil in the nineteenth century were often less about where power resided and much more about which social sector wielded it. Often, concerns over trade policy, protectionism and the status of slavery were more important than the call for local autonomy. The Brazilian *Farroupilha* Rebellion of 1845 was arguably more about class than geography. Both types of civil war reflected the inability of post-independence governments to establish the hegemony of a single political and ideological regime. These wars arose not because the state was so important and so powerful, but precisely the opposite. It was the marginality of state power and the absence of a clear élite project that gave rise to so many struggles.

Caudillo wars[29]

Wars fought on behalf of *caudillos* or popular military leaders were the most common form of conflict during much of the nineteenth century. In some areas, they remained part of the political landscape well into the twentieth. I wish to distinguish these from the two types described above, for they had little or no social basis. That is, these conflicts did not reflect social divisions on the ground, but rather were the product of simple squabbles over government privileges or booty. This is not to say that *caudillos* were completely endogenous to their respective societies, but it is important to distinguish between social conflicts that were led by military strong-men and conflicts that were about little but personal ambition. While these may be the most popular image of military struggles in Latin America, I would argue that they are the least significant. Rather than a cause of the political instability that they symbolized, they were the products of the failure to institutionalize political authority. Perhaps the prototypical examples are the careers of Generals Gamarra and Castilla of Peru or that of General Santa Anna in Mexico during the first fifty years of their independence.

Race/Ethnic Wars[30]

The most important of these occurred during the Conquest and so before independence. In the course of the Conquest, the vast majority of the pre-Colombian population was either killed or died from disease and overwork. While the Conquest itself is outside the purview of this chapter, its legacy overshadows the centuries discussed. The very success of the Conquest and the fact that it occurred centuries before the formation of the independent states left ethnically divided populations and ambivalent national origins. Though it may be obvious, it is too often forgotten that much more so than any other case outside of South Africa and the United States, the states that arose in the nineteenth century had a clear racist component.[31] To a large extent, the new governments were seen as white institutions maintaining control over an Indian, black, or mixed population. As we shall see in subsequent chapters, the history of Latin American wars cannot be understood without reference to this fundamental division.

In the eighteenth and nineteenth centuries, rebellions in Peru and Mexico sought to win back the region from the European population. These uprisings contributed to an atmosphere of white fear that helped determine how wars were fought, against whom, and how they would involve their respective societies. The genocide of the Indians continued as well, as frontier wars culminated with the expulsion, killing or subjugation of native populations in Chile, Argentina and Mexico during the last quarter of the nineteenth century. It may not be coincidental that these three states (along with Brazil arguably the most institutionalized polities in the region) led assaults on Indian territories and populations precisely at the critical points in the consolidation of centralized authority. These campaigns not only served to unite white opinion but also often provided new resources and territories that could be distributed so as to consolidate consensus. More recently, the civil war in Guatemala during the 1970s and 1980s took on the characteristics of a race war as the government identified Indians as automatic enemy sympathizers. The rebellion in Chiapas in 1994 and the Sendero Luminoso insurgency in Peru during the 1980s and 1990s indicate that this war will continue well into the next century.

Revolutions[32]

A final type of civil war is that generated by revolution. These conflicts may combine aspects of the first three with an organized effort to remake the social and economic rules of the respective countries. These wars are not so much over territory as over the distribution of a social and economic pie. As a military struggle, the Mexican revolution (1910–20) deserves pride of place. In length (ten years), destruction (a million dead, more than 5 per cent of the population), tactics and logistics (barbed wire, railroads, artillery), and sheer narrative complexity, this conflict ranks as one of the great wars of the twentieth century. Arguably it also heralds the next half-century of 'great' revolutions throughout the globe.[33] For contemporary Latin America, however, the Cuban revolution of the 1950s (despite its military marginality) may be the most important case. Other examples include Bolivia in 1952 and El Salvador and Nicaragua in the 1970s and 1980s.

Latin American revolutionary wars tend to have a similar origin and structure. They begin with the conjunction of long-term popular discontent, rising middle-class political aspirations, and (perhaps most importantly) weakened repressive regimes. An early 'honeymoon' period when all those in revolt can agree on the need (if not the form) of change, is followed by the collapse of reformist governments and battles between those wishing to preserve aspects of the status quo ante and more radical forces.

The civil wars that devastated Central America were all characterized by this pattern. Early reformers such as Guatemala's Arbenz (1954) are pushed aside by right-wing forces allied with the United States. Parts of the ruling class continue to treat the countries as their individual fiefdoms, such as the Somoza family in Nicaragua (1933–79). Middle-class leaders such as El Salvador's Duarte (1979) or the pre-1980 Nicaraguan opposition seek to heal political breaches, but fail to deal with rampant social inequality. Violence and brutality then yield to more of the same leading to the exhaustion of all parties, the destruction of economies and permanent social divisions. All these in turn make it difficult for democracies to rule effectively, thereby creating authoritarian temptations that may begin the cycle over again.

The Independence Wars remain the unfortunate prototype: despite a great deal of violence, rarely does the post-bellum social order look much different from its predecessor.[34]

Explaining Latin America at war

Why the Latin American exceptionalism? The geopolitical tendency towards peace and the underdevelopment of the state are closely linked and need to be analysed within a historical context.

Political autonomy in Latin America was largely the result of the collapse of the Spanish Empire rather than the internal development of new political forces. As the new Latin American states appeared in the first third of the nineteenth century, they enjoyed little centralized authority and certainly could not enforce a monopoly of the use of violence. It is important to remember that before wars could serve as stimuli for Western European development, the proto-states had already established their military dominance. Thus, when those states required the resources with which to fight in the new type of wars, especially following the Peace of Westphalia of 1648, they were already equipped with the organizational and political capacity to impose these needs on their societies. This was not the case in any Latin American country, with the possible exceptions of Chile and Paraguay prior to the last third of the nineteenth century. (The bellicosity of these two states would indicate at least a correlation between greater state capacity and likelihood of war.) The wars that did occur did not provide an opportunity to establish state power over the society precisely because the wars were 'limited' and the new states lacked the organizational and political base from which to do so.

Equally important was the domestic social context in which the Latin American republics arose. As in much of the post-colonial world, states preceded nations in Latin America. With limited possible exceptions, we find little evidence of a sense of nationhood paralleling the future state boundaries. While there was a sense of vaguely defined 'American-ness', it was generally limited to the minuscule white élite. For the vast majority of the population, belonging to a newly independent state meant very little. While at first some subaltern groups saw the independence movement as a possible avenue for changes in the social and economic status quo, these hopes were dashed by the *criollo* reaction to early radical claims. By 1820, 'American' merely meant the imposition of military duties to complement already heavy fiscal demands. Even such early promises as the abolition of special Indian taxes and tributes were broken.

None of the newly independent states (again with the possible exception of Chile and Paraguay) could easily define the nation that they were supposed to represent. Whether divided by race, caste, class, or a combination of all three, Latin American populations did not possess a common identity. Because the construction of such an identity was so fraught with political conflict, states hesitated to follow the 'nation-building' efforts of Western European and North American counterparts. The struggle to define the nation and the rights and obligations of citizens consumed most of the nineteenth century in Latin America. For the past two centuries the class and racial 'enemy within' has been much more important a target than any threat from the outside. Latin America's path was set by wars between and across a myriad of social boundaries that ultimately defined the Latin American states, not by struggles between territorially compact, cohesive political units, as in Europe.

The stunted development of Latin American states and the frailty of their respective nations reflect the key, but too often neglected aspect of the development of the continent's nation-states. The Wars of Independence produced fragments of empire, but not new states. There was little economic or political logic to the frontiers as institutionalized in the 1820s – they merely were the administrative borders of the empire. The new countries were essentially mini-empires, with all the weaknesses of such political entities. Oscar Oszlak has captured the situation in describing a 'national state established in a society that failed to acknowledge fully its institutional presence'.[35]

The final element that is key to understanding the Latin American cases is the geopolitical or international context in which these countries arose. The Latin American region was born as a whole; the countries were surrounded at birth by states very similar to themselves in terms of immediate history and even social structure. Contrast this with the situation in Western Europe (the United States for the moment must retain its exceptional status). On that continent, states preceded each other in a complex chronology. This produced forms of both competition and emulation not available in Latin America. Moreover, Latin America as a whole arose as a geopolitical entity in a world where the distribution of power was extremely asymmetrical. The ability of any Latin American country to challenge the geopolitical status quo was limited. Unlike Italy and Germany, for example, Latin American states could not even aspire to play a role in imperial competition. They were born in the third rank of nations (at best) with a low probability of moving up. If we think of these nascent nations as city-states, they had little opportunity to expand beyond their previously assigned zones of influence.

The Latin American peace is also in many ways the ultimate expression of *dependencia*. The absence of international conflict in part reflects the irrelevance of immediate neighbours for each country's political and economic development. Latin American states often directed their attention not to their immediate borders, but to metropolitan centres half a globe away. These foreign 'powers that be' also provided the continent with a hegemonic balance of power, thus assuring that no individual regional military giant could arise. This avoided the geopolitical competition responsible for much contemporary warfare. However, it also deprived the region of significant geopolitical autonomy.

The weaknesses of the Latin American state restricted the continent to limited wars and long stretches of peace. This in turn deprived the states of a potentially important impetus for development. A close look at Latin American cases prompts us to rethink the geopolitical competition between the various European countries and the resultant forms of political authority that developed on that continent. It seems that their development was in no sense inevitable, nor did it reflect a universal political trend. Instead, the interaction of particular societies and a particular set of events best explains the differences observed.

Notes

1 And yet, it is the rare book on or guide to general military history that even mentions the continent. See Robert Cowley and Geoffrey Parker (eds), *The Reader's Companion to Military History*, Boston: Houghton Mifflin Company, 1996; R. Ernest Dupuy and Trevor N. Dupuy, *The Encyclopedia of Military History*, New York: Harper & Row, 1970; and J. Keegan, *A History of Warfare*, London: Hutchinson, 1993.

2 For a more detailed discussion of these themes, see Miguel Angel Centeno, *Blood and Debt: War and the Nation-State in Latin America*, University Park, PA: Penn State Press, 2002.

3 Michael Howard, *The Causes of War*, Cambridge: Harvard University Press, 1984.

4 A simple way of measuring this commitment is the number of casualties. I use Singer & Small's threshold of 1,000 deaths per year (J.D. Singer and M. Small, *Resort to Arms*, Beverly Hills: Sage, 1982). Below that level, we cannot expect to see the type of state action which is the subject of a large part of this study.

5 Jack S. Levy, *War and the Modern Great Power System*, Lexington, KY: University Press of Kentucky, 1983, p. 51. The notion of independence does not necessarily require formal international recognition. My definition includes civil wars as long as these are more than armed squabbles. Incorporating these does represent some problems. I do so in the case of Latin America in part because it increases the relevant sample, making systematic study more feasible. More importantly, the distinction between civil and international wars can create problems of anachronistic application. For example, we treat conflict between the King of France and the Duke of Burgundy as an international war. Similarly, wars between Italian cities are judged to be inter-state. Why not, then, the struggles between the various provinces of early Argentina?

6 Keegan, *History of Warfare* and Charles Tilly, 'State-Incited Violence, 1900–1999', *Political Power and Social Theory*, 9, 1995, pp. 161–79.

7 There was some concern that the region was 'heating up' in the 1970s and 1980s, but international stability appears to have returned. See Michael Morris and Victor Millan (eds), *Controlling Latin American Conflicts*, Boulder, CO: Westview Press, 1982; and Walter Little, 'International Conflict in Latin America', *International Affairs*, 63, 4, 1987, pp. 589–602. For a dissenting view, see David R. Mares, 'Securing Peace in the Americas in the Next Decade', in Jorge Domínguez, *The Future of Inter-American Relations*, New York: Routledge, 2000, pp. 35–48, and David Mares, *Violent Peace: Militarized Interstate Bargaining in Latin America*, New York: Columbia University Press, 2001.

8 The obvious exceptions here were US interventions and more recent Cold War struggles.

9 For the best narrative of the military campaigns see John Lynch, *The Spanish-American Revolutions, 1808–1826*, Norton, 1986. For more analytical depth see Jaime E. Rodríguez, *The Independence of Spanish America*, New York: Cambridge University Press, 1998. See also Jay Kinsbruner, *Independence in Spanish America*, Albuquerque: University of New Mexico Press, 1994. For a fascinating comparison of the Independence Wars in the US, Haiti and Latin America, see Lester D. Langley, *The Americas in the Age of Revolution, 1750–1850*, New Haven: Yale University Press, 1993.

10 For Mexico see John Tutino, *From Insurrection to Revolution in Mexico: Social Bases of Agrarian Violence, 1750–1940*, Princeton: Princeton University Press, 1986; Timothy Anna, *The Fall of Royal Government in Mexico City*, Lincoln: University of Nebraska Press, 1978; Brian Hamnett, 'The Economic and Social Dimension of the Revolution of Independence, 1800–1824', *Iberoamerikanisches Archiv*, 6, pp. 1–27; Hamnett, *Roots of Insurgency: Mexican Regions, 1750–1824*, Cambridge: Cambridge University Press, 1986; Christon I. Archer, *The Army in Bourbon Mexico: 1760–1810*, Albuquerque: University of New Mexico Press, 1977; Archer, 'The Royalist Army in New Spain: Civil–Military Relationships, 1810–1821', *Journal of Latin American Studies*, 13, 1, May 1981, pp. 57–82; and Archer, 'The Army of New Spain and the Wars of Independence, 1790–1821', *Hispanic American Historical Review*, Vol. 61(4), 1981, pp. 705–14.

11 See Tulio Halperín-Donghi, *The Aftermath of Revolution in Latin America*, New York: Harper Torchbooks, 1973; Halperín-Donghi, *Politics, Economics, and Society in Argentina in the Revolutionary Period*, Cambridge: Cambridge University Press, 1975; Halperín-Donghi, *Guerra y finanzas en los orígines del estado argentino, 1791–1850*, Buenos Aires: Editorial de Belgrano, 1983; Simon Collier, *Ideas and Politics of Chilean Independence*, Cambridge: Cambridge University Press, 1969; John Street, *Artigas and the Emancipation of Uruguay*, Cambridge: Cambridge University Press, 1959; and John Hoyt Williams, *The Rise and Fall of the Paraguayan Republic: 1800–1870*, Austin: Institute of Latin American Studies, University of Texas, 1797.

12 The literature for this area is sparser at least in English. Unfortunately, the Spanish language literature is dominated by hagiography or mind-numbing military detail. See Gerhard Masur, *Simon Bolívar*, Albuquerque: University of New Mexico, 1969; Lynch, 'Bolívar and the Caudillos', *Hispanic American Historical Review*, 63, 1983, pp. 3–35; David Bushnell, *The Santander Regime in Gran Colombia*, Newark: University of Delaware Press, 1954; Timothy Anna, *The Fall of the Royal Government of Peru*, Lincoln: University of Nebraska Press, 1979; Vicente Lecuna, *Bolívar y el arte militar*, New York: The Colonial Press, 1955; and general works cited above.

13 In the first stage of his campaigns in 1812–13, Bolívar had no more than 500 men and the royalist army he faced less than 900. Bolívar's ultimately triumphant Peruvian campaign began with 2,100 men and only grew to 4,900 over the course of the campaign. San Martín's armies ranged from 4,000 to 6,000. The Royalist army in Peru had 20,000 men of which 7,000 were Spaniards. The battle of Ayacucho, arguably the largest and most decisive battle of independence, involved no more than 17,000 men total on both sides. Armies were slightly larger in Mexico, but Iturbide's triumphant Army of the Three Guarantees, combining practically all organized military forces in the area, had less than 40,000 men in 1821. See Centeno (2002), *Blood and Debt*, Chapter 5.

14 In order to better grasp the importance of this issue, imagine a Hundred Years War or a War of the Roses fought within the context of an ever-threatening revolt in England against Norman rule.

15 Brazil largely escaped the dislocations of a military struggle. The Royal House of Portugal had moved there from Lisbon in 1808 in order to avoid the fate of the Spanish crown. Even after João VI moved back to Portugal in 1821, his son Dom Pedro remained in Rio de Janeiro. The immediate cause of independence came, not from within Brazil (where the dominant landowners felt well represented by the crown), but from changes in Portugal and that country's feeble attempts to return to the status quo ante. The Brazilians were able to establish their independence in late 1822 with little violence

16 For summary accounts of the wars see Brian Loveman, *For la Patria: Politics and the Armed Forces in Latin America*, Wilmington, DE: Scholarly Resources, 1999; Tulio Halperín-Donghi, *The Contemporary History of Latin America*, Durham: Duke University Press, 1993; David Bushnell and Neill Macaulay, *The Emergence of Latin America in the Nineteenth Century*, New York: Oxford University Press, 1988 and the *Cambridge History of Latin America*, especially Volume III. For an excellent discussion of the geopolitics of the continent during the transition into the long peace see João Resende-Santos, 'Anarchy and the Emulation of Military Systems: Military Organization and Technology on South America, 1870–1930' in *Security Studies*, 5, 3 (Special Issue: *Realism: Restatements and Renewal*), 1996, pp. 194–260.

17 See Gordon Ireland, *Boundaries, Possessions, and Conflicts in South America*, Cambridge: Harvard University Press, 1938; Jack Child, *Geopolitics and Conflict in South America*, New York: Praeger, 1985; and Stephen Clissold and Alistair Hennessey, 'Territorial Disputes', in Claudio Veliz (ed.), *Latin America and the Caribbean*, London: Blond, 1968.

18 See Fernando López-Alves, *Between the Economy and the Polity in the River Plate: Uruguay, 1811–1890*, Research Paper 33, London: Institute of Latin American Studies, 1993; and 'Wars and the Formation of Political Parties in Uruguay, 1810–1851' in Eduardo Posada-Carbó (ed.), *Wars, Parties and Nationalism: Essays on the Politics and Society of 19th Century Latin America*, London: Institute of Latin American Studies, 1995; Tulio Halperín-Donghi, *Historia Argentina: De la revolución de independencia a la confederación rosista*, Buenos Aires: Paidós, 1972; Felix Luna, *Historia Integral de la Argentina*, Vol. 5, Buenos Aires: Editorial Planeta, 1995.

19 A good start on this topic is Halperín-Donghi, *Politics, Economics, and Society in Argentina in the Revolutionary Period*, Cambridge: Cambridge University Press, 1975. For the Brazilian side see Ron Seckinger, *The Brazilian Monarchy and the South American Republics*, Baton Rouge: Louisiana State Press, 1984.

20 See Thomas Whigham, *The Paraguayan War*, Lincoln: University of Nebraska Press, 2002; John H. Williams, *The Rise and Fall of the Paraguayan Republic*; Pelham Horton Box, *The Origins of the Paraguayan War*, NY: Russell & Russell, 1967; Charles Kolinski, *Independence or Death. The Story of the Paraguayan War*, Gainesville: University Press of Florida, 1965; José María Rosa, *La guerra del Paraguay y las montoneras argentinas*, Buenos Aires: Hyspamerica, 1986. For an example of the more polemical treatment see Leon Pomer, *La guerra del Paraguay: Estado, política y negocio*, BA: Centro editor de América Latina, 1987. For a discussion of the demographic results of the war see Vera Blinn Reber, 'The Demographics of Paraguay: A Reinterpretation of the Great War, 1864–1870', *Hispanic American Historical Review*, 68, 2, 1988, pp. 289–319; Thomas Whigham and Barbara Potthast, 'Some Strong Reservations: A Critique of Vera Blinn Reber's "The Demographics of Paraguay: A Reinterpretation of the Great War"', *Hispanic American Historical Review*, 70, 4, 1990, pp. 667–76; Thomas Whigham and Barbara Potthast, 'The Paraguayan Rosetta Stone: New Insights into the Demographics of the Paraguayan War, 1864–1870', *Latin American Research Review*, 34, 1, 1999, pp. 174–86.

21 See William F. Sater, *Chile and the War of the Pacific*, Lincoln: University of Nebraska Press, 1986 for an exhaustive analysis. There is no equivalent for the Peruvian side, but one may consult Heraclio Bonilla, 'The War of the Pacific and the National and Colonial Problem in Peru', *Past and Present*, 81, 1978; Florencia E. Mallon, *The Defense of Community in Peru's Central Highlands: Peasant Struggle and Capitalist Transition, 1860–1940*, Princeton, NJ: Princeton University Press, 1983; and *Peasant and Nation*, Berkeley: University of California Press, 1994).

22 See Bruce W. Farcau, *The Chaco War: Bolivia and Paraguay, 1932–1935*, Westport, Conn: Praeger, 1996; Herbert Klein, *Bolivia: The Evolution of a Multi-Ethnic Society*, New York: Oxford University Press, 1982; David Zook, *The Conduct of the Chaco War*, New Haven: Yale University Press, 1960; and H.G. Warren, *Paraguay: An Informal History*, Norman, Oklahoma: Oklahoma University Press, 1949. The Chaco War may also be responsible for much of the international imagery of war and the military in South America. For a fascinating (and telling) depiction see Tintin's adventure *The Broken Ear*, 1940.

23 Gene M. Brack, *Mexico Views Manifest Destiny, 1821–1846*, Albuquerque: University of New Mexico Press, 1975; John H. Schroeder, *Mr. Polk's War: American Opposition and Dissent, 1846–1848*, Madison: University of Wisconsin Press, 1973; Charles A. Hale, 'The War with the United States and the Crisis in Mexican Thought', *The Americas*, 14, 1957, pp. 153–73; and Ramón Ruiz, *The Mexican War: Was it Manifest Destiny?*, New York: Holt, Rinehart and Winston, 1963. For an excellent narrative see Jan Bazant, *A Concise History of Mexico from Hidalgo to Cardenas, 1805–1940*, Cambridge: Cambridge University Press, 1977; and Daniel Cosío Villegas, *A Compact History of Mexico*, Los Angeles: Media Production, 1974. See also the following website for the great PBS documentary on the war: http://www.pbs.org/kera/usmexicanwar/mainframe.html

24 For the background to the French wars, the best source is Nancy Nichols Barker, *The French Experience in Mexico, 1821–1861: A History of Constant Misunderstanding*, Chapel Hill: University of North Carolina Press, 1979. Again, see Bazant, 1977 and Cosío Villegas, 1974.

25 For Central America, see James Dunkerley, *Power in the Isthmus: A Political History of Modern Central America*, London: Verso, 1988; Ralph L. Woodward, *Central America, a Nation Divided*, 2nd edn, New York: Oxford University Press, 1985; James Mahoney, *The Legacies of Liberalism: Path Dependence and Political Regimes in Central America*, Baltimore, Md.; London: Johns Hopkins University Press, 2001; Piero Gleijeses, 'Reflections on Victory: the United States and Central America', *SAIS Review*, 10:2, 1990, pp. 167–76; Leonard Thomas, 'Central America, US Policy, and the Crisis of the 1980s', *Latin American Research Review*, 31:2, 1996, pp. 194–211; David Stoll, *Between Two Armies in the Ixil Towns of Guatemala*, New York: Columbia University Press, 1993. On Cuba see Louis A. Perez, *Cuba: Between Reform and Revolution*, 2nd edn, New York: Oxford University Press, 1995; Carlos Antonio Carrasco, *Los cubanos en Angola, 1975–1990*, La Paz: Centro de Estudios Internacionales, Universidad Andina, 1996; Jorge I. Dominguez, 'Cuban Operations in Angola', *Cuban Studies/Estudios Cubanos*, 8:1, 1978, pp. 10–21; Nelson Valdés, 'Cuba's Involvement in the Horn of Africa', *Cuban Studies/Estudios Cubanos*, 10:1, 1980, pp. 49–80; William LeoGrande, *Cuba's Policy in Africa, 1959–1980*, Berkeley: Institute of International Studies, 1980. On the Falklands/Malvinas, Peter Calvert, *The Falklands Crisis: the Rights and the Wrongs*, New York: St Martin's Press, 1982; The Sunday Times of London, *War in Falklands: the Full Story*, New York: Harper and Row, 1982; Carlos Landaburu, *La Guerra de las Malvinas*, Buenos Aires: Circulo Militar, 1989.

26 A wonderful new book on the nineteenth century is Rebecca Earle (ed.), *Rumours of Wars: Civil Conflicts in Nineteenth-Century Latin America*, London: Institute of Latin American Studies, 2000.

27 Loveman, *For la Patria*, p. 43

28 Charles Bergquist, *Coffee and Conflict in Colombia, 1886–1910*, Durham, NC: Duke University Press, 1978.

29 John Charles Chasteen, *Heroes on Horseback: A Life and Times of the Last Gaucho Caudillos*, Albuquerque: University of New Mexico Press, 1995; John Lynch, *Caudillos in Spanish America, 1800–1850*, New York: Oxford University Press, 1992; Enrique Krauze, *Siglo de caudillos: biografía política de México (1810–1910)*, Barcelona: Tusquets Editores, 1994.

30 See Mallon, *The Defense of Community in Peru's Central Highlands* and her *Peasant and Nation* (see note 21); and Nelson Reed, *The Caste War of Yucatan*, Stanford: Stanford University Press, 1964. For a discussion of race and state creation and comparisons see Anthony W. Marx, *Making Race and Nation: A Comparison of South Africa, the United States, and Brazil*, New York: Cambridge University Press, 1998; Mark Thurner, *From Two Republics to One Divided: Contradictions of Postcolonial Nation-making in Andean Peru*, Durham, NC: Duke University Press, 1997; Ada Ferrer, *Insurgent Cuba: Race, Nation, and Revolution, 1868–1898*, Chapel Hill: University of North Carolina Press, 1999.

31 Obviously, what may be called 'racial' hierarchies existed in Europe. An obvious example may be the Norman/Saxon distinction in Medieval England (and later ones between English, Welsh, Scots, and Irish) or the special caste claims of the Polish and Magyar nobility.

32 For Mexico see Alan Knight, *The Mexican Revolution*, 2 vols, New York: Cambridge University Press, 1986; for Cuba see Hugh Thomas, *Cuba or The Pursuit of Freedom*, New York: Harper & Row, 1971; for Bolivia see James Dunkerley, *Rebellion in the Veins: Political Struggle in Bolivia, 1952–82*, London: Verso, 1984; and for Central America see James Dunkerley, *Power in the Isthmus: A Political History of Modern Central America*, London: Verso, 1988.

33 But note how that 'honour' is usually assigned to the Bolshevik revolution in Russia in 1917.

34 For a discussion of Latin American inequality, see Kelly Hoffman and Miguel Centeno, 'The Lopsided Continent', *Annual Review of Sociology*, Vol. 29, 2003.

35 Oscar Oszlak, 'The Historical Formation of the State in Latin America', *Latin American Research Review*, 16, 2, 1981, pp. 3–32.

7

SUB-SAHARAN AFRICAN WARFARE

John Lamphear

Pre-colonial warfare

Reconstructing traditional African warfare[1]

The pre-colonial military history of sub-Saharan Africa has received less scholarly attention than virtually any other inhabited part of the world. When it has been considered at all, it often has been portrayed in terms of antithetical stereotypes. This is due in part to ideological factors. In the period before, during and after the Scramble for Africa, Western observers often described a 'dark continent' of incessant conflict waged by savage warriors. Such depictions, the very essence of imperialist propaganda, demonstrated the need for the 'pacification' of these 'barbarous' lands.[2]

The advent of Independence in the mid twentieth century ushered in a radically different perspective, however. In their efforts to re-establish the integrity of African civilization, revisionist scholars sought to refute the allegations of rampant violence. Notions of traditional warfare were scaled back by some to the point that it was denied that Africans had participated in bona fide warfare at all. In some depictions, African conflict was portrayed as ritualistic and harmless; a notch above an athletic contest.[3] Even museum curators refrained from displaying African weaponry for fear of perpetuating notions of African savagery.[4] While informed reconstructions of traditional African social, economic, environmental, and gender history appeared, little serious attention was paid to military history. Except for a few fine studies of West African, South African and Ethiopian states,[5] and a smattering of useful contributions for East Africa,[6] military history remained an ambiguous, little explored area, regarded by many as politically incorrect. Recently, a handful of more sophisticated treatments have begun to appear. But while this modest increase of interest in traditional warfare is welcome, attention continues to be focused on larger states, which, while often exhibiting similarities to warfare in other parts of the world, were by no means typical of a great many other African societies.[7]

Formidable problems of historical reconstruction remain. Until recently, many sub-Saharan African societies have been extra-literate, so the sorts of written documentation that are taken for granted in other parts of the world are often absent. Nevertheless, from the time of the Scramble a significant body of written documentation did begin to appear, largely in the form of travellers' accounts, colonial records and ethnographic treatments. With rare exceptions, however, it is tinged with deep ethnocentric bias, and considerable care is needed to deconstruct the colonial voice. Likewise, these treatments embody a timeless functionalism, making diachronic change difficult to perceive. Additional information on traditional warfare can be found in a growing corpus of African oral history gathered, often incidentally to the main research, in the fieldwork of Africanist scholars over the past several decades. Again, however, great expertise is required in the interpretation of this complex mode of communication.

Compounding such methodological problems is the spatial magnitude and diversity of Africa. In this chapter, only sub-Saharan Africa below approximately latitude 15° north is considered. Even so, this area constitutes two-thirds of the continent and is more than twice the size of the United States. Though punctuated by mountains, uplands and great river basins, the region can best be visualized as a vast plateau. While Africa is the most tropical continent, with the equator dividing it into two nearly equal halves, there are substantial climate and vegetational differences. In the humid equatorial latitudes of western Africa are rain forests, mainly in the Congo River basin and along the Guinea coast, which however comprise less than ten per cent of the continent's vegetation. Far more common are savanna grasslands and acacia woodlands, sprawling away to the north and south. Proceeding further from the equator, rainfall generally diminishes so that dry savannas eventually give way to the Sahara in the north, to semi-desert lowlands in eastern Africa and the Horn in the north-east, and to the Namib and Kalahari Deserts in the south-west. In contrast, many of the highland regions of eastern Central Africa, Ethiopia and South Africa provide well-watered temperate environments.

Within these vast and varied regions, African societies displayed remarkable adaptations and developed a myriad of political organizations. Although Africa certainly had its share of centralized states, a great many Africans also lived in decentralized, stateless societies where political authority was diffused among councils of lineage elders, age classes or secret societies. There were bands of hunter-gatherers, dispersed nomadic pastoralists, matrilineally-based chiefdoms of shifting cultivators, and large, bureaucratic kingdoms of sedentary agriculturalists. Literally hundreds of individual languages, belonging to four major language families, were spoken.

Despite such great diversity, one may still identify some key factors which served to shape modes of traditional African warfare. Demographically, it appears that much of the continent was relatively sparsely populated until recent times. Certainly fission and migration were important dynamics of political processes in many areas until well into the twentieth century. The control of people and resources, therefore, rather than the control of territory per se, was generally more important in determining the nature of African conflict. There were, likewise, essential geographical determinants. While in some exceptionally fertile regions it was possible to produce food in abundance, the typical subsistence agriculture of the drier savannas yielded little surplus, making the mobilization of large numbers of fighting men for any but very short periods extremely difficult. Tropical diseases also played an important role. For example, trypanosomiasis, endemic to huge areas infested with tsetse flies, precluded the rearing of horses and draft animals so integral to the armies of temperate regions of the globe. These and other factors, such as the near impossibility of manoeuvring bodies of fighting men during annual rainy seasons – or through rain forests during any time of the year – served to create severe logistical problems.

The social and cosmological fabric of African communities also served to define the nature of traditional African conflict and helped distinguish it from warfare common to other parts of the world. While some African states (and sometimes stateless societies, too) could and did wage wars featuring organized campaigns and set-piece battles – an activity that will be termed 'campaigning war' here – African conflict frequently took the radically different form of raiding cycles to capture livestock, foodstuffs or women and children. Even the largest of military operations were seldom protracted and their essential goal was to seize resources rather than methodically to annihilate enemy opposition. Indeed, Robert Smith, one of Africa's few truly prominent military historians, endorses the notion that for even the most centralized African states traditional warfare was most fundamentally an 'investment decision'.[8]

In many places, boundaries between African societies were fluid and indistinct. While this often permitted a controlled flow of commodities, ideas and peoples between neighbouring groups, it could also produce serious instability. In times of stress, struggles for survival could bring escalating violence. Individuals, often imbued with deeply engrained 'warrior traditions', were able to launch small-scale operations against their neighbours. This form of conflict, termed 'primitive war' by an earlier generation, has been widely misunderstood. Similar to the Africanist view discussed above, it has been seen as a ritualistic, limited activity, well below the horizon of true war.[9] Some recent studies, however, have suggested important revisions applicable to Africa and other parts of the non-Western 'tribal' world.[10]

Far from being merely ritualistic games, a 'skulking way of war' involved small but frequent raids that struck at the very bases of enemy subsistence and reproduction. Quests for blood revenge, in addition to militarized economic acquisition, might perpetuate raids and counter-raids for generations. Under such conditions differences between 'combatants' and 'civilians' became blurred, as all elements of a population were exposed quite directly to the horrors of war. It is important to stress that in many, perhaps most, cases, powerful political mechanisms worked against escalations of such cycles. But the intensity and lethality of this type of traditional conflict, which is termed 'raiding war' here, should never be underestimated. Although it has received little systematic attention, it surely would be incorrect to see it as static and unchanging. It should also be emphasized that in some respects this form of conflict bore a disconcerting similarity to the Western concept of 'total war', as well as to contemporary instances of 'ragged' war.

Military evolution in the nineteenth century

African armies at the beginning of the nineteenth century were, with few exceptions, infantry forces. Except in parts of the western and central Sudanic belt, some regions of the Horn and portions of the South African veldt, tsetse infestation precluded cavalry troops. Navies of war-canoes plied some coastal, riverine and lacustrine areas, but only Swahili city states of the Indian Ocean coast possessed armed ocean-going sailing vessels.

In terms of military organization, many communities had militia systems where every able-bodied man capable of doing so served as a part-time citizen soldier. Such militiamen protected homelands or raided enemies as the need arose, but would then revert to normal pursuits of farmers or herdsmen when operations ceased. Militia contingents might be composed of kinsmen, age-mates or neighbours. Leadership was informal; men who demonstrated superior military skills might attract an armed following, functioning as a raiding party or as a unit of a larger conglomerate army fighting, temporarily, in some wider 'national' cause. In some centralized states, individual leadership was based on privilege, as hereditary chiefs brought contingents together into ephemeral state-wide armies under the command of the paramount ruler or officers of the central government.

Some parts of Africa witnessed important changes as the century progressed, however. Sometimes, military factors underlay dramatic political and economic expansions; conversely, they contributed in other cases to severe social disruption. In the Sudanic belt of West Africa, expansions of political scale were fuelled by ideological forces. Early in the century, Uthman dan Fodio, an adherent of Sufi mysticism, preached Islamic reform and declared a jihad against local Hausa ruling élites. In parts of these tsetse-free Sudanic grasslands, traditional armies had included cavalry, but Uthman's Fulani forces were at first largely infantry archers who beat back enemy assaults from defensive squares. Gradually a cavalry arm, élite shock troops who wore quilted and chainmail armour and fought with lances and swords, was added. His jihad spread over a wide region and at his death in 1817, his Sokoto empire was consolidated by his able son, Muhammad Bello. Later in the century, other Islamic reformers, including Seku Ahmadu Lobo and Al-Hajj Umar, followed Uthman's lead and employed their own armies to create imperial states elsewhere in the western Sudan.[11]

Other significant enlargements of scale, while not driven by the same ideological factors, took place elsewhere. Before the nineteenth century it is likely that most African militia armies were marked by loose discipline and weak unit cohesion. In the Natal region of South Africa, however, standing armies based on a regimental organization produced an entirely new military structure. The impetus here was derived from ecological and demographic pressures experienced by small Bantu-speaking Nguni chiefdoms. As competition for resources increased, conflicts intensified until two chiefdoms, Mthethwa and Ndwandwe, emerged as the main rivals. In both, earlier initiation practices were employed to form more cohesive bodies of fighting men. By about 1820, Shaka, a brilliant young Mthethwa commander, had begun the creation of his own Zulu military state. His army, composed of age-based regiments, each with its own prescribed uniforms, traditions and powerful esprit de corps, was honed through constant drill and rigid discipline into an astonishingly mobile fighting force. The regiments, fighting at close range with hide shields and short, deadly stabbing spears, held assigned positions in a tactical formation, the 'Horns of the Beast', designed to envelope and destroy enemies in the field.[12] In addition, Shaka devised a new system whereby fighting men were segregated from the rest of society in permanent regimental barracks maintained by the state, becoming thereby a standing, professional force of 4,000 well-trained troops always at the disposal of their king. A master of strategy and tactics, Shaka rapidly created one of Africa's mightiest empires. The process, termed locally the *mfecane*, the 'crushing', involved a complex mix of expansion, conquest, absorption, and disruption.

Migratory warriors founded new states in many places, including present-day Mozambique, Zimbabwe and even Tanzania, over a thousand miles to the north. To varying degrees, these new states reflected original Nguni models and often employed age-regiments as a means of incorporating conquered foreigners into burgeoning new kingdoms such as Gaza, Ndebele and Ngoni.[13]

Regimental organizations emerged elsewhere too, for example among the Nilotic-speaking Maasai and Turkana in East Africa. Here the transition was all the more remarkable as these were decentralized societies strongly committed to nomadic pastoralism. In these instances, it was hereditary prophet/diviners who supplied centralizing leadership and won control over the age–class apparatus. Before this, age systems in eastern Africa often had functioned as mechanisms by which councils of elders curbed the aggressive tendencies of younger men. The emergent centralizers, however, deriving personal benefit from shares of the spoils brought in from military operations, had no qualms about conflict escalations. Curbs on youthful violence could give way to enthusiastic encouragement for newly-initiated teenagers to attack rivals. Competitors were displaced or assimilated, often *en masse*. As with the Zulu, age-sets became corporate military units. The Maasai even developed a *manyatta* ('barracks') system similar to Shaka's, by which a standing regimental organization was created. Previously loose cultural confederations were thus afforded a stronger collective identity as their control was extended over the pastoral resources of wide areas, and small-scale raiding gave way to coordinated operations.[14]

Not all enemies were destroyed, dispersed or assimilated in the expanded warfare of the nineteenth century, however. Some societies fought back successfully, though often by altering their own military structures and conceptualizations of war. In West Africa, for example, the Bornu leader, Al-Kanemi, reversed the decline of his once powerful state by constructing a new military force to check the eastern advance of Uthman dan Fodio's *jihad*. In present-day Kenya, Nandi managed to resist the Maasai by also bringing their armed forces under the direction of prophet/diviners. In Tanzania, a number of previously loose-knit communities, including the Hehe, Sangu, Bena, and Wangu, developed stronger notions of centralization and revamped armies to check Ngoni invasions. In many instances, it is likely that the transitions were more psychological than tangible, however, involving the inculcation of new military attitudes rather than specific institutions or weaponry. In many parts of sub-Saharan Africa, fortifications were developed as effective defences against enemy raids. In northern Zambia, formerly autonomous Bemba chiefdoms achieved new political unity and constructed strings of stockaded villages to deflect Ngoni advances in the 1850s, while in Lesotho the brilliant statesman Moshoeshoe built a confederation of chiefdoms, absorbed *mfecane* refugees and waged stubborn defensive operations from natural mountain strongholds. In both these latter cases, however, enhanced military power was derived from the adoption of firearms.[15]

This alien technology introduces another important nineteenth-century military adjustment. The rise of most of the military forces just examined rested almost entirely on the use of indigenous weaponry, but in certain parts of the continent imported military technology had long been in use. Since the fifteenth century, European mariners had been trading along the coasts of sub-Saharan Africa. Among the goods flowing from Europe into coastal 'factories' were immense numbers of firearms. By the dawn of the nineteenth century, many thousands of muskets were in use in West Africa. The significance of this foreign armament to the conduct of war has been much debated. Some have suggested that it underpinned a veritable military revolution, while others point out that in many places few firearms were actually in use before the late nineteenth century, and even when there were, they often were poor-quality 'trade guns', which failed to supplant traditional weapons.[16] Some firearms were also being imported into parts of the Horn, and Boer settlers were carrying limited numbers from the coast into the High Veldt in South Africa. A few were present in East Africa as well, though these were outdated matchlocks relegated to the Swahili coast.[17]

As the nineteenth century progressed, firearms became increasingly wide-spread. The British-inspired abolition of the slave trade early in the century and the new focus on 'legitimate' commerce brought a huge expansion of African overseas trade. African entrepreneurs supplied more and more of the raw commodities required by Western factories, even as their European counter-parts marketed the surpluses of the industrial revolution in return. African appetites for foreign goods, including new and improved European armaments, increased apace. In all, over 16 million firearms were imported into Africa in the nineteenth century.

While rather simplistic notions of self-sustaining 'slave–gun' cycles have been revised, expanding commerce certainly helped shape the nature of conflict in many places. In some cases, inland societies, such as the Asante kingdom, sought access to European coastal stations by military means. Having already built a formidable militia army of musketeers in the previous century, from the early nineteenth century the Asante sought to eliminate Fante rivals situated closer to European Gold Coast entrepots. Throughout Africa, long-distance trade routes developed, linking hinterlands with coastal markets. As overseas demand increased, well-armed caravans of traders and hunters scoured interior regions for ivory, gums and other products.

In addition, while abolition theoretically had ended the slave trade, the capture of slaves in some areas actually increased. In East Africa, the Omani Arab-dominated Sultanate of Zanzibar, in partnership with coastal Swahili and backed by Indian bankers, took control of hinterland trade routes and dispatched caravans – some of more than a thousand musketeers – deep into the interior. Such massive bodies of men often faced severe logistical problems and resorted to foraging and pillaging, becoming, in effect, mobile, predatory armies. From their trading stations, they disseminated coastal goods, including large stocks of guns and ammunition, which sometimes enhanced the military power of hinterland peoples. Among the Nyamwezi and other western Tanzanian peoples, for example, there now emerged leaders who understood that expanding trade, political activity and military might could be mutually reinforcing. Building on new notions of warfare, which had been introduced into the region by the Ngoni, these leaders gathered personal followings of *ruga ruga*, professional mercenaries recruited from prisoners, fugitive slaves and outlaws who affected outlandish costumes and extreme demeanours calculated to terrify and intimidate their adversaries. Some commanders of *ruga ruga* were no more than local bandit chiefs while others were truly gifted politicians and soldiers, including Mnwa Sele (or Mnywa Sera), who challenged the commercial dominance of the coastal caravans in the 1850s, and Nyungu-ya-Mawe, a Nyamwezi, who established a conquest state among neighbouring Kimbu in the 1870s. Most notable of all was Mirambo ('Maker of Corpses'), a military genius (the adventurer H.M. Stanley called him the 'African Bonaparte'), who built a 7,000-man army of *ruga ruga* reinforced by levies. With it Mirambo absorbed neighbouring chiefdoms into an empire stretching between Lakes Tanganyika and Victoria Nyanza, and fought a five-year war with the Zanzibaris from 1871 to 1876 for control of interior commerce.[18]

The development of a huge domestic market for slaves stimulated predatory military expansion in other parts of the interior. By mid-century, musket-armed slave raiders proliferated; petty Zigula and Yao warlords, for example, who had long practised small-scale raiding warfare, used personal followings to attack and capture their neighbours. In the 1860s, Msiri, a Sumbwa trader from western Tanzania, invaded parts of Zambia and Congo with a private army, methodically collecting slaves, ivory and copper. By the 1880s, Tippu Tip, a Swahili, was doing much the same thing on the upper Congo River. He assembled a force of several thousand riflemen with whom he pillaged a wide area before finally establishing a harsh but effective administration over much of eastern Congo. Inland from the coast of West Central Africa, caravans of well-armed Ovimbundu expanded northwards, sometimes trading guns for ivory and slaves to interior peoples. Obtaining muskets from them, Chokwe hunters and raiders pushed the process further into the hinterland, overrunning much of northern Angola. By the 1880s, the unfortunate Luba were being simultaneously attacked by Chokwe from the west and Tippu Tip's forces from the east, so that waves of commercially fuelled violence now spread from coast to coast across central Africa.[19]

Although not linked so directly to aggressive commercial expansion, firearms were also increasingly adopted by other African polities as the century progressed. In interlacustrine East Africa, Mutesa, king of the Buganda state, used imported firearms to transform his army into a regional superpower by the 1870s. In West Africa, the Dahomey kingdom developed a standing army equipped with rifles, including an élite corps of female soldiers, the famous 'Amazons', which finally ended the long domination of the neighbouring Oyo empire in the mid nineteenth century. Savanna states, which had been slow to acquire firearms, partly because of the almost universal distaste with which Islamic cavalry viewed them, also finally began to adopt guns in quantity, sometimes facilitating the emergence of standing professional armies. As early as the 1850s, Al-Hajj Umar, launching a *jihad* in the western Sudanic belt, sought to modernize his Tukolor forces by building an army of infantry musketeers.[20]

While in many cases firearms were merely grafted onto pre-existing military structures, there were some attempts to institute sweeping military reforms based on Western models. In Ethiopia at mid-century, a former bandit chief named Kassa worked tirelessly to unify autonomous petty princes, until finally he was crowned as Tewodros II, king of kings of an enlarged Ethiopian empire in 1855. To end the pillage of civilians by predatory armed bands, he sought to create a disciplined, salaried army of 70,000 provided for by the state and trained by Turkish and European military advisers along Western lines. He engaged Western technicians to create an arms industry. Ultimately, he was unable to curb the predatory behaviour of his troops, however, and by the 1860s he was instead using them to wage huge plundering expeditions. His fledgling arms industry, while producing a few monstrous pieces of artillery, never came close to achieving self-sufficiency. His successor, Yohannes IV, created an even more modernized force in the 1860s, though deep logistical problems remained. A similar attempt at modernization took place on the island of Madagascar. Here, the unification of the Merina kingdom in the early nineteenth century ushered in a new era of military expansion, and the reform-minded Radama I, with the assistance of British advisers, remodelled his army in terms of its weapons, organization, discipline, and even uniforms, along European lines by the 1820s. The new force rapidly brought most of the island under Merina control, and a burgeoning munitions industry was producing quantities of gunpowder, small arms and artillery. In West Africa, the great Mandinka soldier and statesman, Samori Toure, created a well-ordered empire. Samori acquired up-to-date firearms for his *sofa* infantry and also made a bid for self-sufficiency in weapons by establishing arsenals employing hundreds of craftsmen to produce gunpowder, repair guns and even laboriously to manufacture a few breechloaders from the 1880s. To achieve something of European-style discipline, he sent men to enlist clandestinely in the French *tirailleurs* and recruited ex-colonial soldiers to train his troops. Some of his units learned to fire volleys, respond to bugle-calls and were dressed in French-style uniforms.[21]

Evolutionary processes were by no means uniform, however. Ominously, some professional forces began to take the form of 'personal' armies composed not of 'national' forces, but of foreigners and individual mercenary soldiers. In addition to roving caravan armies and *ruga ruga*, similar warbands appeared throughout much of sub-Saharan Africa. In East Africa, the Bunyoro Kingdom relied on *bukedi* mercenaries, the Sultans of Zanzibar hired contingents of Baluchis, and the Wanga Chiefdom employed entire age-sets of Maasai warriors. In the Zambezi valley of central Africa, *Chikinda* private armies of *Prazeros* plantation owners created virtually autonomous states for their masters. In West Africa, personal mercenary armies became the mainstays of Yoruba towns who vied for ascendancy in the aftermath of the collapse of the Oyo Empire. Earlier militia structures were abandoned as upstart warlords, whose authority transcended traditional warchiefs and even subverted the power of kings, assembled client armies of professional gunmen. All too often, those who assembled these new standing forces found themselves controlled by them. The only sure means of retaining their loyalty was to keep them constantly occupied: to leave them idle risked having them switch allegiance to patrons who could offer better economic prospects, or even worse, having them turn against their creators themselves.[22]

Logistics also continued to present immense problems. Many of the largest, most decisive campaigns of the nineteenth century were essentially huge raids. The predatory nature of caravan armies is obvious. Likewise, Nguni migrations were most fundamentally long-range razzias. In their essence, Maasai and Turkana expansions were well-coordinated cattle raids extending over large territories. Much of Asante and Dahomey warfare took the form of pillaging expeditions. In the West African *jihads*, religious fervour typically devolved into raiding forays in frontier areas. Even those that came closest to emulating Western models, such as the Ethiopian and Merina empires, regularly were obliged by their rudimentary logistical systems to become predatory scavengers. And, there were of course many African societies that continued to engage mainly in small-scale 'skulking wars' where pillaging was endemic. Nevertheless, although they have been little investigated, there was certainly constant innovation and refinement on this level, too.[23]

Thus, the nineteenth century witnessed tremendous African military evolution. Certainly the African military experience was far richer and more complex than stereotypical notions of unchanging ritualized conflict or chaotic savagery suggested. Undoubtedly, when more systematic and macrocosmic studies of traditional conflict finally are undertaken, they will show that warfare was just as important in shaping the historical experience of Africa as any other part of the world.

Of huge importance was the reshaping of traditional modes of warfare themselves. Where only raiding war had been practised in much of southern, central and eastern Africa, there were now instances of campaigning war. Stronger unit cohesion, accompanied by new sorts of training and discipline, transformed the individualized identity of militiaman and raiding warrior into the collective identity of regimental soldiers. A very different sort of military psyche began to appear. Sometimes pitched battles now culminated in decisive victories that curtailed cycles of reciprocal raiding. There were increasing distinctions between soldiers and civilians, and often the latter became less directly affected by organized violence. Some societies, through enlargements of scale and the creation of increasingly efficient military structures, appear to have been moving away from demonstrations of 'force' (that is, direct applications of armed might) toward the application of 'power' (a subjective phenomenon existing in the perception of others). In some instances, this enforced pacification, although sometimes decidedly imperialistic, amounted to the application of effective conflict resolution over wide areas. But any such African initiatives were soon to be irrevocably interrupted by a rather different sort of 'pacification' by outside forces.[24]

Colonial Africa

Wars of resistance[25]

Throughout the nineteenth century, European interest in Africa increased, culminating finally in the formal partitioning of the continent among the imperial powers. Military conquest at first proceeded slowly, as European policy generally opposed direct involvement in African affairs, and even when individuals did seek to extend the few toe-holds of European control, they faced daunting problems. Usually little manpower could be mobilized and any attempt to push far from secure bases entailed huge logistical problems. Moreover, until the second half of the century, Europeans often had no clear superiority in armaments. While in some instances, inferior 'trade guns' especially designed for African trade were exported, in other cases Africans were well supplied with essentially the same muzzle-loaders being used by European armies. Logistical difficulties, especially problems of transport, generally prevented the effective employment of field artillery.

In the final decades of the century, European conquest began to accelerate, however. By 1885 the Berlin Conference had institutionalized the partition. Coming as it did at a time of unusual peace in Europe, colonial powers could approach the conquest with a unity of purpose, allowing them to concentrate on fighting Africans rather than each other. Likewise, the Western technological revolution of the later nineteenth century gave the imperialists important – though seldom decisive – advantages over African opponents. In addition, the colonialists began to tap new sources of manpower. With rare exceptions, high mortality rates among European troops operating in tropical climates and the sheer expense of dispatching them to and maintaining them in far-flung colonial regions prevented the deployment of the metropole's regular forces for imperial ventures. Instead, European units specifically designed for colonial service were created (such as the French Foreign Legion and *Chasseurs d'Afrique*), troops were brought in from other colonial areas (for instance British West Indian and Indian Army contingents), and, most importantly, large numbers of Africans were recruited. These were of two main sorts: either irregular allies and levies, or forces organized, armed and trained along European lines (such as French *Tirailleurs Senegalais*, Belgian *Force Publique* and British KAR and WAFF). Considered the most expedient and cheapest alternatives, these African forces came to form the backbone of 'European' imperial armies.

Ultimate imperial victory, however, was not derived entirely from Western superiority – technical, organizational or otherwise – but also from the legacy of the African historical experience itself. Nineteenth-century military evolutions had, of course, occurred in response to indigenous challenges. Relatively modest improvements in organization, discipline or firepower could bring easy victories. Few saw any need to maximize the efficiency of alien weaponry. Even African states with impressive arrays of firearms tended to employ them ineffectively. In the latter stages of the century, African armies began to obtain large numbers of breech-loaders. Often, the adoption of more sophisticated weaponry actually proved detrimental, as it was far more difficult for Africans to repair and reproduce them than simpler flintlocks and percussion muskets. Ammunition, too, tended to be in chronically short supply. African dependence on outside sources of weaponry thus became greater than ever before. Ironically, the very societies that had been the most militarily dominant and most likely to employ set-piece battles to crush indigenous enemies now became the most vulnerable. Massed bodies of zealous religious

179

disciples, regiments of well-drilled age-mates, or companies of rifle-toting mercenaries could decisively overwhelm opponents whose military traditions were of informal militias and small-scale raids. But to engage colonial forces face-to-face usually ended in catastrophe.

There is a tragic similarity to scenarios played out again and again throughout sub-Saharan Africa. At Ulundi in 1879 Zulu regiments were mowed down by the disciplined volleys and machine gun fire of a huge British square that had no flanks or rear which the 'Horns of the Beast' might envelop; the same fate befell Gaza warriors attacking a Portuguese square in Mozambique nearly 20 years later. Near the village of Amoafo in 1874 Asante forces, some firing nails and bits of scrap metal from their trade muskets, sought to rely on the dense forest for protection but were blown to shreds at close range by high-velocity British rifles and artillery fire. At Youri in the Western Sudan in 1897, a Tukolor army tried to turn the tables by forming a European-style square of its own, but was routed by the steady volleys of French *tirailleurs*. The list of similar disasters is a long one. The handful of African victories – the Zulu obliteration of a British column at Isandhlwana; the Ethiopian defeat of the Italian invasion at Adowa – were all the more spectacular for their rarity, and typically reflected European overconfidence and incompetence as much as African military skill. Likewise, fortifications, which had once provided confident security, became death traps for garrisons defending them against the barrages of European siege guns and the determination of colonial assault troops.[26]

Even more important was the fragmentation of the African response. All too often, African rivals continued to be perceived as more immediate threats than the imperial invaders. Lacking any sense of an African collective identity that might have provided a semblance of unity, Africans resisted society by society, while Europeans supported (but ultimately betrayed) the enemies of each of their major opponents in turn. It was this ability to 'divide and conquer' that enabled so few European actors to conquer vast territories. Underpinning all this were, again, perennial problems of logistics. African economies, many of them further weakened by increasing foreign dependency, simply could not sustain long-term campaigning war. Protracted combat created tremendous stress, even rapid disintegration. Logistical problems were acute for the colonialists, too, but were ameliorated by water transport and railways facilitating huge transfers of war materials even to theatres of operation deep in the hinterlands.

There is a perception that the colonialists increasingly resorted to economic warfare, especially as African opponents turned more to guerrilla tactics during the later stages of the conquest. Frequently this has been seen as indicative of the brutal 'total war' Europeans introduced into the continent. Certainly such warfare was brutal, often atrociously so: villages were burned, food and livestock taken, civilian populations killed. Operations, such as those of the Germans against the Herero and Nama in South-West Africa, were essentially genocidal.

Nonetheless, it is important to locate colonial economic warfare in the wider military experience of African raiding war and rudimentary logistics. In fact, in many expeditions, most attacks on civilian economies were carried out by African contingents allied to the colonialists who were fighting traditional enemies in traditional ways. In the process, logistical dilemmas were also solved, as invading forces supplied themselves at the expense of their enemies. Despite misgivings about using levies who carried out fierce personal vendettas against traditional enemies, they continued to be employed throughout the entire era of 'pacification'. In the 1890s French Bambara auxiliaries actually outnumbered resisting Tucolor armies. In German East Africa allies played vital roles in the initial conquests in the 1890s and again in quelling the Maji Maji Rebellion in 1905. As late as 1918, large contingents of levies were recruited for British operations against Turkana in northern Kenya.[27]

The imperialists held an inherent advantage in this sort of economic warfare. Whereas African societies possessed livestock, crops and homes that became the targets of razzias, Europeans and their African regulars did not. Remarkably, some of the more effective instances of African resistance involved innovative attempts to overcome this deficiency. The gifted Samori Toure in West Africa concocted one ingenious solution. Despite his attempts to remodel his army, he understood that it was foolhardy to engage the colonists in set-piece battles. Instead he resorted to guerrilla-like tactics, including ambushes and the use of terror. Eventually he took the extraordinary step of physically shifting his entire state to the east, employing a brutally effective scorched-earth policy that left utter devastation in areas from which his forces were withdrawing and into which his French adversaries were advancing. Eventually, though, hemmed between French and British spheres, he ran out of territory to surrender and his own logistical system dissolved.

The Turkana, nomadic pastoralists from semi-desert northern Kenya, provide another example. They too had remodelled their military system, obtaining breech-loaders and creating a corps of professional *Ruru* riflemen. The Turkana also understood it was suicidal to meet British forces in open battle, and sought to utilize traditional mobility and raiding skills to their advantage. If the British and their KAR askaris had no resources to be raided, the 'pacified' peoples who served as auxiliaries certainly did, and so, under the inspired leadership of their Diviner, Loolel Kokoi, and his commander, Ebei, they returned to the familiar tactics of raiding war – though now on a grand scale – in 1917, driving traditional enemies back into areas of European settlement. In the end, this brought on even heavier raids by the British and their allies, until, as with Samori, Turkana logistical structures collapsed.[28]

Colonial armies[29]

The establishment of colonial rule radically changed African military development and practice. Warfare between societies – in particular raiding – was forbidden and colonial armies became the only officially sanctioned forces. In many cases they functioned as gendarmeries enforcing law and order, although operations against recalcitrants could be decidedly coercive.[30] Inexorably, though, colonial regimes ruled through application of 'power' rather than 'force'. While military policies differed from colony to colony, some general patterns emerged.

There was, for instance, a tendency to recruit from societies touted as 'martial races' so that colonial armies often reflected a particular ethnic composition. Colonial regimes also constructed effective mechanisms to control dissent among colonial forces. Within the context of their integration into the colonial political economy, the troops certainly were mercenary, but older images of their serving colonial regimes out of some deep sense of loyalty have been rejected: discipline and *esprit de corps* should not be mistaken for collaboration. Colonial governments imbued their soldiers with a sense of superiority and physically insulated them from mainstream society. They were afforded many perks. To keep them from identifying with the faintest stirrings of organized anti-colonial sentiment, armies were kept strictly apolitical. Colonial forces therefore became more closed and separate military establishments than those that had existed before, most fundamentally, of course, because they were copies of systems born out of a totally foreign military experience grafted onto artificially concocted colonial states.

African colonial forces saw considerable combat experience in the two World Wars. In both cases, armies were hugely expanded, especially in British and French areas. In the First World War, British forces mainly battled German *Schutztruppe* askaris in East Africa. Typically, logistical problems were immense and thousands of civilian carriers were pressed into service, many of them perishing from neglect and mismanagement. Over 171,000 French *tirailleurs* served in France itself, losing over 30,000 in action. Even greater numbers of Africans saw service in the Second World War. This time those from British territories served in Ethiopia, Madagascar, the Middle East, and Burma, while French *tirailleurs* fought in the defence of France in 1940 (thousands were captured and spent the rest of the war as German PoWs), later for the Vichy and finally the Free French. In the post-war era, *tirailleurs* served in Algeria, Indo-China and in the Suez Crisis, while British askaris fought in Malaya in 1951.[31]

Independent Africa[32]

There is a general awareness that endemic violence has been rending sub-Saharan Africa since the coming of the Independence Era. Grim images of limbless children, rivers choked with corpses and human tides of starving refugees appear regularly, though fleetingly, on television screens. Mass-media portrayals of African conflict tend to be brief depictions of 'tribal feuds' and horribly genocidal 'ragged wars'. The brutality, devastation and ubiquity of low-intensity conflicts (LICs), in all their infinite variety, are particularly perplexing, as they seem to bear scant similarity to any Western notions of 'real warfare'.

For the first couple of decades of the era, however, things were generally not quite so catastrophic. It was possible, for a while, to distinguish different categories of organized violence, some of which resembled conventional twentieth century conflict. There was, for instance, a rash of relatively bloodless military coups that swept across the continent in the immediate aftermath of independence. These revealed, above all, the inherent fragility of infrastructures inherited from the colonialists. The metropolitan authorities had expected a perpetuation of colonial military structures, but the old checks and balances often proved inadequate to manage the soldiers of newly independent states. As full citizens, soldiers expected greatly improved conditions of service. 'Martial races' sought to perpetuate their exalted status. New regimes, anxious that their armies embrace new ideologies, made fatal mistakes in politicizing and expanding them, frequently also co-opting them as instruments of narrowly defined policy and patronage. At first mainly apolitical expressions of dissatis-faction, military coups soon became the easiest way to oust incompetent, corrupt or autocratic civilian regimes, transforming the soldiers into 'khaki politicians'.

A second form of conflict were anti-colonial liberation struggles, beginning as early as the 'Mau Mau' Emergency in Kenya (1952–6) and extending until the attainment of majority rule in South Africa in 1994. In most instances, initial transitions to independence that swept through Africa in the late 1950s and early 1960s, although underpinned by strident political activism, essentially had resulted from diplomatic negotiation. By the mid 1960s, however, this first wave of independence was over, leaving just a few territories, mainly clustered in the southern third of the continent, still under colonial rule. Often controlled by die-hard white-minority regimes, the transition here involved prolonged armed violence.

At first disorganized and poorly armed insurgents were overwhelmed by colonial might, but as the nationalists embraced new ideologies, such as Marxism or the subversion strategies of Mao Zedong, they gained inexorable momentum. As Cold War rivalries extended into Africa, they received massive support from Eastern Bloc nations, while their colonialist opponents were supplied by Western allies, or, in the case of South Africa, through domestic industrial production. In the Portuguese colonies of Angola, Mozambique and Portuguese Guinea, on-going liberation struggles caused such war-weariness that the metropolitan government fell to a military coup in 1974, paving the way for the establishment of independent Marxist governments in all three territories. Another prolonged independence war raged in Rhodesia (to be renamed Zimbabwe) until 1979. Even in South Africa, home of the most powerful white minority government of all, internal opposition to odious racial policies of apartheid escalated into an undeclared civil war by the later 1970s, and there was stiff resistance to South African attempts to annex the UN Trust Territory of South West Africa (to be renamed Namibia at independence).

There were also wars of secession, in which ethnic, regional or religious dissent threatened to tear apart fragile African states. Thus, wealthy Katanga Province tried to separate itself from the Congo within weeks of Independence in 1960; Muslim Eritrea began its long struggle to break free of Christian-dominated Ethiopia from 1962; in Kenya's Northern Frontier District the 'Shifta War' (1963–7) was waged by separatist Somalis; the oil-rich Eastern Region of Nigeria, largely comprising an Ibo population, attempted to become the independent Republic of Biafra in the cataclysmic Nigerian Civil War, 1967–70. Other civil wars were fought, not with the aim of secession but so that a particular faction might emerge as economically and politically dominant. In the newly independent state of Angola, for instance, one of the hottest theatres of the Cold War developed as the Soviet- and Cuban-backed MPLA government forces faced off against UNITA rebels supported directly by South Africa and indirectly by Western powers. Similarly, South Africa backed RENAMO rebels against the Marxist regime in Mozambique. Most ominously, Hutu–Tutsi violence in Rwanda and Burundi flared throughout the 1960s and 70s. Although often characterized as 'ethnic' conflict, the two groups were not in fact separate ethnicities, but distinct socio-economic strata of the same society – Tutsi aristocratic pastoralists and Hutu commoner peasants – whose differences had been exaggerated by Belgian colonialism. In addition to secessionist wars, there were also a few examples of international wars, notably a struggle between Ethiopia and Somalia (1977–8) over the disputed Ogaden (again embodying Cold War rivalries) and the Tanzanian invasion of Uganda (1978–9) to oust dictator Idi Amin.

Most of these conflicts featured aspects of low-intensity guerrilla struggles, but many also displayed properties of large-scale 'conventional' war, including protracted campaigns and battles featuring mechanized infantry, heavy armour and air power. In the Nigerian Civil War, the Federalists assembled an army of 120,000 reasonably well-trained and equipped soldiers. There was also ever-increasing involvement by outside powers. Massive state-to-state, or state-to-insurgent, transfers – especially from the super powers – involved artillery, tanks, helicopters, and jet fighters. By the early 1960s there were direct French, Belgian, British, and American interventions, and individual soldiers of fortune were recruited. By the 1970s, thousands of Cuban troops were fighting in Angola and the Horn; French soldiers were deployed from permanent African bases to a dozen different wars; and South African forces made forays into neighbouring states. UN peacekeeping contingents attempted to mediate in several conflicts. African states, including Tanzania, Zambia, Guinea, and Nigeria, and later Mozambique and Angola, actively supported insurgents against white-minority regimes. Libyan and Algerian troops fought in Chad; Libyans, Moroccans and Tanzanians fought in Uganda.[33]

From about 1980, sub-Saharan Africa experienced even more frequent and catastrophic outbursts of violence. In a few instances, earlier patterns persisted for a while. Into the late 1980s the Angolan civil war and the Eritrean–Ethiopian war, for example, continued to display aspects of 'conventional' war, including massive tank battles and air strikes. As Cold War rivalries dissipated with the fall of the Soviet Union, and as South Africa moved toward majority rule, there were great changes, however.

The most common form of conflict now became LICs, the products of the collapse of basic infrastructures. There were many causes: global economic crises; the failure of inappropriate institutions bequeathed by colonialism; pervasive mismanagement, corruption and greed; the continued exploitation and interference of outsiders. It became difficult to distinguish any clear 'types' of sub-conventional war. Coups, civil wars, attempted secessions, and ragged wars of terrorism and ethnic cleansing all blended into nightmarish cultures of violence. Often, LICs exhibited similar characteristics. In many cases, combatants were not state forces, but an infinite variety of private armies, guerrillas, militias, and even the employees of European, American and South African 'security companies'. Factionalism was rampant as armed bands – sometimes ethnically composed, but as often not – constantly fragmented and fused into new configurations. By the late 1990s in Somalia, for example, 25 clan and sub-clan armies vied for power. Political entrepreneurs played deadly games of 'Warlord Politics', building local sovereignties in place of failed state-wide institutions. Although professing lofty goals to mask selfish personal ambition, ideologies were frequently shallow.

Another marked similarity was the increasing role of civilian populations. Having been excluded from military activities during the colonial era, civilians were again immersed in the experience of war as they had been in pre-colonial times. Often they became the targets of undisciplined warlord armies who plundered villages more often than they fought each other. But civilians also became active participants, forming irregular militias for the defence of rural settlements and urban neighbourhoods, and sometimes hiring themselves out to competing factions. Desperation born of economic collapse provided endless supplies of man (and woman) power. Alienated youth, especially huge numbers of homeless orphans, were recruited or kidnapped, and transformed through brutal initiations and coercion into child soldiers. Dressed in bizarre costumes and well-supplied with drugs and alcohol, they became mainstays of fighting forces from Uganda to Sierra Leone. Over 40,000 under the age of fifteen served in Liberia alone.

The proliferation of small arms became another common feature of LICs. With the end of the Cold War, state-to-state transfers of heavy weaponry practically ceased, though huge amounts from earlier aid packages now passed into private hands. Instead, a massive trade in small arms commenced, especially cheap, outdated Soviet AK-47s and RPGs very useful in sub-conventional war. The quantities marketed by a wide array of gun dealers were immense, though detailed records from which to gauge even approximate numbers are entirely lacking. Still, estimates (even if significantly inflated) of six million AK-47s in Mozambique alone, and as many as 100,000 in remote, sparsely populated Karamoja District in Uganda, where they are used largely for cattle raids, give some hint of the magnitude. While technological determinism by itself certainly cannot adequately explain the expansion of contemporary violence, the ready availability of small arms definitely has created a powerful 'gun culture' in many areas, and facilitates the expansion of trivial incidents into full-blown warfare.

The most horrifically obvious characteristic of LICs, however, is the sheer scope of mind-numbing atrocity and suffering that typifies them. The studied application of terrorism and brutality certainly had been a feature of pre-1980 conflicts, as well: at least 200,000 civilians had been killed in earlier Hutu–Tutsi violence, and diabolical dictators such as Amin and Jean-Bedel Bokassa had murdered thousands of their own people. But as states proved unable to maintain a semblance of law and order, perpetual cycles of raids, murder, terrorism, and starvation now produced stark anomie. 'Low intensity' in terms of the simplicity of arms – sometimes machetes, spears and agricultural tools are employed – these conflicts are catastrophically intensive in terms of casualties: a half million deaths in the Angolan Civil War; 250,000 killed in Somali inter-clan struggles; 800,000 dead in Uganda; close to a million slaughtered in Rwanda in just a few months of 1994 alone. Staggering numbers also have been displaced: there are currently well over six million African refugees, a third of the world's total. Unquestionably Africa has been enduring genocidal horrors comparable to the Holocaust and Cambodian Killing Fields. Tragically, recent LICs have witnessed a grim transition from a situation just a short time ago when a few brutal dictators slaughtered defenceless people, to one in which whole populations have participated in orgies of killing and destruction.

Much of this can be understood as stemming from very basic struggles for resources. As states decayed, often the only means of obtaining resources was through violence. Sometimes this involved wholesale 'asset stripping' by major armed factions. Angolan rebels and Sierra Leonian government forces both financed their military operations through illicit diamond sales. In Burundi, the army was funded partly by gold and heroin smuggling; in Liberia rebels traded iron ore and timber for guns. On a more basic level, quests for resources became individual struggles for survival. Colonial nation-states came to have less and less relevance to local communities; guerrillas and refugees violated their boundaries with impunity. Warlords gained adherents by providing essential commodities for them and lost them if they could not. As with traditional raiding wars, conflicts were waged not to secure decisive victories but to gather booty. For peasants and the urban poor, violence often provided the only path to survival. Under such conditions, conventional strategies of peace resolution had little chance of success.[34]

Indeed, on-going attempts by outsiders to impose solutions largely failed. From the 1980s, international financial agencies fostered programmes of economic liberalization that, in seeking to diminish autocratic centralized control, as often facilitated the emergence of autonomous strongmen who built private client networks. Humanitarian support of NGO relief agencies was co-opted by warring factions for their own uses. Food itself became a powerful weapon. United Nations peace-keeping forces met with little success. Their counter-insurgency operations were thwarted by immense logistical problems. The diversity of competing factions made peace negotiations on a 'national' level all but impossible. All too frequently, outside intervention had the effect not of quelling violence but of preventing victory. In places such as Somalia and Rwanda, peace-keeping forces admitted failure and withdrew. The French, who had often undertaken unilateral operations, were by the late 1990s also having to reappraise their policies after major failures. Likewise, the imposition of the American 'New World Order' proved unworkable. Africa's crumbling infrastructures, teeming refugee camps and endemic ragged wars were simply not compatible with an imagined brave new world of capitalist free markets and spontaneous outbursts of Jeffersonian democracy. After the failed intervention in Somalia in 1993–4, a deep disillusionment set in. As African LICs posed no serious security or economic threats to big power interests, they were increasingly ignored. Western media and Western scholarship now pay far more attention to Middle Eastern and Balkan conflicts, although their casualty figures are dwarfed by the seven-figure mortality rates of African LICs.

In place of external intervention, some stronger African states have recently begun to play the role of regional powers. Increasingly, for all their inherent parochialism, some LICs are simultaneously exhibiting wider international dimensions, and as a result, aspects of conventional warfare have begun to recur in some instances. In West Africa, in response to the anomic and atrocious violence of Liberia and Sierra Leone, a multi-national peace-keeping force dominated by Nigeria and Ghana, ECOMOG, has intervened. While Nigerian and Ghanaian commanders have certainly followed their own agendas, and while their counter-insurgency operations have had only mixed success, they have managed to restore sufficient order that Sierra Leone could hold a semblance of national elections in 2002. In East Africa, Yoweri Museveni has adopted a proactive policy of intervening in neighbouring states to create a 'zone of pacification' around his war-torn country. The collapse of the long-lived Mobutu regime in the Democratic Republic of the Congo (formerly Zaire) in 1997 has fundamentally altered the power balance in Central Africa, so that states including Rwanda, Uganda, Angola, and Zimbabwe are now all playing active regional military roles.[35]

Ultimately, solutions to Africa's contemporary violence will have to be African ones. One important step will be the achievement of a better under-standing of pre-colonial African warfare. It is plain that there is an important continuity between recent LICs and traditional modes of war, although certainly many traditions have become hideously debased, and the scale of contemporary violence must be infinitely greater. Still, the low-level militarization and prolonged cycles of conflict that were the essence of African raiding war are obviously reflected in contemporary ragged wars. So too is the intimate involvement of civilians and the ultimate goals of winning resources rather than decisive battles. Traditional recruitment of teenagers into militarized age-sets finds distorted replication in today's armies of child soldiers. Similarly, nineteenth-century mercenary companies who used their firearms to intimidate, pillage and provide bailiwicks for their warlords are uncomfortably similar to privatized contemporary warbands. Likewise, floods of imported arms continue to shape the course and escalation of violence. On other levels, traditional oathings and initiations ensure the loyalty of present-day fighting men. Spirit mediums still enlist the support of ancestors and supernatural forces; diviners use prophetic dreams to plan military strategies. Traditional charms give invincibility to APCs and medicines are sprinkled on soldiers to ensure their invulnerability to bullets. Young men join guerrilla units to acquire the wealth and power to elevate their status in traditional society.[36]

Until a clearer comprehension of Africa's military past is gained, any satisfactory understanding of the present or effective planning for the future will continue to be elusive. To some extent, the revival of traditional mechanisms for regulating violence – the re-empowerment of councils of elders, perhaps – may hold the key. On a wider level, though, solutions may lie in Africa's ability to make the transformation from chronic demonstrations of 'force' to new perceptions of 'power', as regional, multi-national and even pan-African cooperation allows the sorts of enlargements of scale and conflict resolution that were apparently under way in parts of the continent before they were interrupted by colonialism.

Notes

Abbreviations:
JAH Journal of African History;
IJAHS International Journal of African Historical Studies

  1 Much of the data for this section was collected as part of a larger project, the writing of a monograph: *A Pre-Colonial Military History of East Africa*. This has received generous funding from the Harry Frank Guggenheim Foundation, the University of Texas and the Dora Bonham Fund, whose support I gratefully acknowledge.
  2 Typical examples abound. See, among many others, any of the works of H.M. Stanley, Frederick J. Lugard or Harry Johnston.
  3 See, among others, M.S.M.S. Kiwanuka, 'Bunyoro and the British: A Reappraisal', *JAH*, 1968, 9, 4; J. Fadiman, *Mountain Warriors* (Athens: Ohio University Press, 1976); H. Kjekshus, *Ecology Control and Economic Development in East African History* (Athens: Ohio University Press, 1996).
  4 C. Spring, *African Arms and Armor* (Washington, DC: Smithsonian Institution Press, 1993), pp. 12–13.
  5 These include, for West Africa: R.S. Smith, *War and Diplomacy in Precolonial West Africa* (London: Methuen, 1976); R.A. Kea, 'Firearms and Warfare on the Gold Coast and Slave Coast from the Sixteenth to the Nineteenth Centuries', *JAH*, 1971, 7, 2;

J.P. Smaldone, *Warfare in the Sokoto Caliphate* (Cambridge: Cambridge University Press, 1977); for Ethiopia: M. Abir, *Ethiopia: the Era of Princes* (London: Longmans, 1968); D. Crummey, 'The Violence of Tewodros', *Journal of Ethiopian Studies*, 1971, 9, 2; R.A. Caulk, 'Firearms and Princely Power in Ethiopia in the Nineteenth Century', *JAH*, 1972, 13, 4; for South Africa: J.D. Omer-Cooper, *The Zulu Aftermath* (London: Longmans, 1966); J. Gump, *The Formation of the Zulu Kingdom* (San Francisco: Edward Mellen, 1990).

6 These include D.A. Low, 'Warbands and Ground-Level Imperialism in Uganda', *Historical Studies*, 1975, 16, 65; G.N. Uzoigwe, 'Kabalega's Abarusura: the Military Factor in Uganda', *Proceedings of the University of East Africa Social Science Conference* (Nairobi: 1968); B.A. Ogot (ed.), *War and Society in Africa* (London: Frank Cass, 1972). Important contributions by social scientists include A. Mazrui, *The Warrior Tradition in Modern Africa* (London: E.J. Brill, 1977); K. Fukui and D. Turton (eds), *Warfare Among East African Herders* (Osaka: National Museum of Ethnology, 1979).

7 Among others, J. Thornton, *Warfare in Atlantic Africa* (London: UCL Press, 1999); R. Reid, 'Mutesa and Mirambo', *IJAHS*, 1998a, 31, 1; and his 'The Ganda on Lake Victoria: A Nineteenth Century East Africa Imperialism', *JAH*, 1998b, 39, 1.

8 Smith, op. cit., p. 37.

9 H.H. Turney-High, *Primitive War* (Columbia, SC: University of SC Press, 1949), pp. 21–38; J. Keegan, *A History of Warfare* (New York: Vintage, 1993), pp. 94–115.

10 Among others, L. Keeley, *War Before Civilization* (New York and Oxford: Oxford University Press, 1996); P. Malone, *The Skulking Way of War* (Baltimore and London: Johns Hopkins University Press, 1991).

11 Smaldone 1977, op. cit.; M. Last, *The Sokoto Caliphate* (New York: Humanities Press, 1967).

12 There is, however, a debate as to how much credit actually belongs to Shaka, as opposed to some earlier innovator, and there have been radical reinterpretations of Shaka's alleged ruthlessness. See, among others, J. Gump, op. cit.

13 Omer-Cooper, op. cit.; T. Spear, *Zwangendaba's Ngoni, 1820–1890* (Madison: University of Wisconsin Press, 1972); I. Knight, *The Anatomy of the Zulu Army* (London: Greenhill, 1995).

14 The fullest account of the Maasai is still R. Waller, 'The Lords of East Africa: the Maasai in the mid-Nineteenth Century', unpublished D. Phil. Thesis, University of Cambridge, 1979; an important revision is C. Jennings, 'They Called Themselves Iloikop: Early Missionary Sources and Pastoral History in East Africa', in T. Falola and C. Jennings (eds), *Spoken, Written, Unearthed Sources and Methods in African Historical Research* (Rochester: University of Rochester Press, forthcoming); for the Turkana, see J. Lamphear, 'The People of the Grey Bull', *JAH*, 1988, 29, 1; also my 'Brothers in Arms: Military Aspects of East African Age-Class Systems in Historical Perspective', in E. Kurimoto and S. Simonse (eds), *Conflict, Age and Power in North East Africa* (Oxford: James Currey, 1998).

15 A. Gold, 'The Nandi in Transition', *Kenya Historical Review*, 1981, 8; J. Lamphear, ' "The Rage of Ancestors who Died in Ancient Wars": The Military Background to the Maji Maji Rebellion', paper presented at the Maji Maji Workshop Conference, Carleton College, Northfield, MN, 2001b; L. Thompson, *Survival in Two Worlds: Moshoeshoe of Lesotho* (Oxford: Clarendon, 1975).

16 The basic aspects of the debate can be gleaned from Smith, op. cit.; J. Smaldone, 'Firearms in the Central Sudan: A Revaluation', *JAH*, 1972, 13, 2; Kea, op. cit.; W. Richards, 'The Import of Firearms into West Africa in the Eighteenth Century', *JAH*, 1980, 21, 2; R. Low, 'Horses, Firearms and Political Power in Pre-Colonial West Africa', *Past and Present*, 1976, 72. Also see J.E. Inikori, 'The Import of Firearms into West Africa 1750–1807', *JAH*, 1977, 28, 2.

17 Little work on the impact of firearms in regions other than West Africa has been carried out. For East Africa see R. Beachey, 'The Arms Trade in East Africa in the Late Nineteenth Century', *JAH*, 1962, 3, 3; and J. Lamphear, 'The Arrival and Use of Firearms in East Africa Before 1865', paper presented at the British Institute in Eastern Africa and French Institute for Research in Africa Joint Seminar, Nairobi, Kenya, 2001a. For Madagascar, see A. Thompson, 'The Role of Firearms in the Development of Military Techniques in Merina Warfare', *Revue française d'histoire d'outre-mer*, 1974, 61, 224. For Ethiopia, see Caulk, op. cit. For an overview of sub-Saharan Africa as a whole, see G. White, 'Firearms in Africa: An Introduction', *JAH*, 1971, 12, 2. Useful information for other parts of Africa can be found in the special issue of *JAH*, 1971, 12, 2 and 4, comprising entirely articles on firearms; and C. Spring, op. cit.

18 I. Wilks, *Asante in the Nineteenth Century* (London: Cambridge University Press, 1975); A. Shorter, 'Nyungu-ya-Mawe and the Empire of the Ruga Ruga', *JAH*, 1968, 9, 2; N. Bennett, *Mirambo of Tanzania* (New York: Oxford University Press, 1971); A. Sheriff, *Slaves, Spices and Ivory in Zanzibar* (London: James Currey, 1987).

19 J. Miller, 'Chokwe Trade and Conquest in the Nineteenth Century', in R. Gray and D. Birmingham (eds), *Pre-Colonial African Trade* (London: Oxford University Press, 1966); E. Alpers, *Ivory and Slaves in Central Africa* (London: Heinemann, 1975).

20 R. Reid, 1998a, op. cit.; R. Edgerton, *Warrior Women* (Boulder: Westview Press, 2000); A. Kanya-Forstner, 'Mali-Tukolor', in M. Crowder (ed.), *West African Resistance* (London: Hutchinson & Co., 1971).

21 R. Caulk, 'Armies as Predators', *IJAHS*, 1978, 11, 3; D. Crummey, 'Tewodros as Reformer and Modernizer', *JAH*, 1969, 10, 1; Thompson, op. cit.; M. Legassick, 'Firearms, Horses and Samorian Army Organization', *JAH*, 1966, 71,1.

22 A. Sheriff, op. cit.; T. Falola and G. Oguntomisin, *Yoruba Warlords in the Nineteenth Century* (Trenton: Africa World Press, 2001); R. Low, op. cit.

23 One of the few documented examples of innovative evolution in raiding war of which I am aware is from my own fieldwork with the Jie, among whom the remarkable commander Loriang made fundamental changes to military structures at the turn of the twentieth century. See J. Lamphear, *The Traditional History of the Jie of Uganda* (Oxford: Clarendon, 1976), pp. 227–48.

24 For a broader discussion of the alteration of military psyche, see J. Lamphear 2001b, op. cit.; for 'force' and 'power', see E. Luttwak, *The Grand Strategy of the Roman Army* (Baltimore and London: Johns Hopkins University Press, 1976), pp. 195–200; also see L. Keeley, op. cit., pp. 149–50.

25 For the non-specialist, B. Vandervort, *Wars of Imperial Conquest in Africa 1830–1914* (Bloomington and Indianapolis: Indiana University Press, 1998), provides the best one-volume overview and contains a useful bibliography to locate sources on many specific conflicts; M. Crowder (ed.), *West African Resistance* (London: Hutchinson & Co., 1971), is useful for that region; D. Porch, 'Imperial Wars', in C. Townshend (ed.), *The Oxford History of Modern War* (Oxford: Oxford University Press, 2000), establishes the global context.

26 B. Vandervort, op. cit.; for readable accounts of the Asante and Zulu Wars, see F. Myatt, *The Golden Stool* (London: William Kimber, 1966) and D. Morris, *The Washing of the Spears* (New York: Simon & Schuster, 1972), respectively.

27 B. Vandervort, op. cit.; J. Lamphear, *The Scattering Time: Turkana Responses to Colonial Rule* (Oxford: Clarendon, 1992); for fundamental reinterpretations of the Maji Maji rebellion as a continuation of African conflicts, see T. Sunseri, 'Statist Narratives and Maji Maji Ellipses', 2000, *IJAHS*, 33, 3; and J. Lamphear 2001b, op. cit.

28 J. Lamphear, 1992, op. cit.; Y. Person, 'Guinea-Samori', in M. Crowder, op. cit. The lone example of successful armed resistance was that of Ethiopia, gained through a

set-piece battle, Adowa, in 1898. Although the Ethiopian army was one of the most modernized in Africa, the victory stemmed more from Ethiopia's political and cultural solidarity – and Italian incompetence – than from military efficiency. For an intelligent appraisal see B. Vandervort, op. cit., pp. 156–66.

29 Fundamental sources on colonial armies include: H. Moyse-Bartlett, *The Kings African Rifles* (Aldershot: Gale & Polden, 1956); C. Balesi, *From Adversaries to Comrades-in-Arms* (Waltham: Crossroads Books, 1979); and A. Clayton and D. Killingray, *Khaki and Blue: Military and Police in British Colonial Africa* (Athens: Ohio University Center for International Studies, Africa Series No. 51). Important revisionist treatments include T. Parsons, *The African Rank and File* (Portsmouth: Heinemann, 1999); M. Echenberg, *Colonial Conscripts* (Portsmouth: Heinemann, 1991); N. Lawler, *Soldiers of Misfortune* (Athens: Ohio University Press, 1992). Parsons advances an especially persuasive analysis of the integration of African troops into the colonial political economy.

30 While such operations actually 'pacified' a great many African societies – especially decentralized ones – they have received little attention and badly need a systematic investigation.

31 There are many sources dealing with African participation in the World Wars, but one might best begin with the articles in the special issue of *JAH* (1978, 19, 1) which deals entirely with the First World War, and the special issue of the same journal (1985, 26, 4), which treats the Second World War.

32 Although in some ways flawed, the most useful single-volume treatment of African post-independence wars is A. Clayton, *Frontiersmen: Warfare in Africa since 1950* (London: UCL Press, 1999). It contains a useful chronology of specific conflicts and its bibliography provides a basic guide to works on some of the main wars. The global context of recent African conflicts is established by R. Harkavy and S. Neumann, *Warfare and the Third World* (New York: Palgrave, 2001).

33 See A. Clayton's bibliography for works on specific conflicts. Broader investigations of the military in early independent Africa include: C. Welch (ed.), *Soldier and State in Africa* (Evanston: Northwestern University Press, 1970); S. Decalo, *Coups and Army Rule in Africa* (New Haven: Yale University Press, 1976); R. Rotberg and A. Mazrui (eds), *Protest and Power in Black Africa* (New York: Oxford University Press, 1970).

34 A. Clayton, op. cit., touches on a great many of these LICs. Also see, among many others, G. Goodwin-Gill and J. Cohn, *Child Soldiers* (Oxford: Clarendon, 1994); G. Prunier, *The Rwanda Crisis* (New York: Columbia University Press, 1995); W. Reno, *Warlord Politics and African States* (Boulder and London: Lynne Rienner, 1999); T. Negash and K. Tronvoll, *Brothers at War: Making Sense of the Eritrean–Ethiopian War* (Oxford: James Currey, 2000); K. Fukui and J. Markakis (eds), *Ethnicity and Conflict in the Horn of Africa* (London: James Currey, 1994). For a technological overview, see Martin van Creveld, 'Technology II: Postmodern War?', in Townshend, op. cit. Many chronic African conflicts go virtually unnoticed. In the Spring of 2001, I visited northern Uganda; although not usually considered by outsiders as a significant area of LIC, skirmishes, raids and ambushes were daily occurrences, and I saw large numbers of small arms in private hands.

35 T. Shinichi, 'Understanding Conflict in Africa: Reflections on its recent characteristics', in E. Kurimoto (ed.), *Rewriting Africa: Toward Renaissance or Collapse?* (Osaka: National Museum of Ethnology, 2001); Marina Ottoway, 'An End to Africa's Wars: Rethinking International Intervention', *Harvard International Review*, Winter, 2001.

36 Two useful studies of the perpetuation of traditional warfare in recent conflicts are D. Lan, *Guns and Rain: Guerrillas and Spirit Mediums in Zimbabwe* (Los Angeles and Berkeley: University of California Press, 1983) and H. Behrens, *Alice Lakwena and the Holy Spirits* (Oxford: James Currey, 1999).

8

EUROPEAN WARFARE
1815–2000

Peter H. Wilson

The history of war in nineteenth- and twentieth-century Europe has been written from many different perspectives. The focus varies depending on national historical tradition and scholarly approach, creating different versions of the same story, inhibiting generalization, but telling us much about what war has meant for past generations of Europeans. Three phenomena emerge from this voluminous literature as major themes. Each identifies an aspect of the complex interrelationship between war and wider European history that has not only affected the impact of conflict on the continent's development, but has also shaped the way its inhabitants have perceived these changes. European attitudes to war, including both pacifism and militarism, are themselves worthy of consideration but will be largely omitted for reasons of space from this discussion, which seeks instead to place European warfare in its global context.

War as a political phenomenon

The first of these three aspects is political and involves war as a factor in European international relations and as a force behind the formation of European states. The prolonged conflict of the French Revolutionary and Napoleonic Wars 1792–1815 is generally seen as the great watershed of modern European history. The political history after Napoleon's defeat at Waterloo is characterized as an era of reaction as the restored monarchs attempted to fit a radically changing Europe into the shell of the old regime. This attempt to put 'new wine into old bottles' ignored the underlying structural changes, as well as the new problems associated with nationalism, liberalism and industrialization.[1] However, this metaphor obscures important continuities across the eighteenth and nineteenth centuries, as well as under-estimating the resilience and adaptability of European monarchies. Perhaps more significantly, it exaggerates the speed and extent of the changes following the French Revolution of 1789. Though significant, the transformations wrought in these years were part of a longer, gradual and uneven process of replacing a system structured around strong local particularlism and weak universalist ideals of a single Christian Europe by one based on the sovereign state and its associated demarcation between domestic and foreign policy. This transformation was endorsed by the Vienna Settlement of 1814–15, ending the Napoleonic Wars, which further eroded the complex hierarchy of European rulers with overlapping jurisdictions by sharpening the distinction between sovereign governments and their subjects.[2]

The political dimension of war in nineteenth- and twentieth-century Europe was determined by its relationship to this sovereign-states system. The European idea of a state was increasingly defined as a monopoly of legitimate powers within a given territory. This public authority was also distinguished more clearly from the 'private' lives of its subject population. Society was largely demilitarized and disarmed, with 'private' war-making and acts of violence becoming criminal offences. In contrast to the early modern era, this state monopoly of violence was no longer in dispute by 1815 and war was regarded as exclusively the responsibility of the sovereign state. Politics now centred on disputes over which social groups should control war-making and the rest of the state apparatus, as well as what form their control should take and how far they and their supporters could benefit personally from it. In the early nineteenth century, these disputes took the form of liberal challenges to still fairly exclusive and limited forms of constitutional monarchy. A century later, the arguments were between proponents of various forms of totalitarianism and mass-participatory democracy. These disputes also shaped the debates over how war should be legitimized, as the competing political ideologies entailed different arguments for and against the use of war in certain circumstances. Though the control and use of the monopoly of violence has remained central to European politics, the scope of debates has widened considerably since the early nineteenth century as other areas of public activity became more important. Discussions over which areas legitimately belong to the public sphere have now reached the point where the continued existence of the sovereign state itself is being called into question, at least in most of western and central Europe where the traditional state ideal is not only being eroded through political co-operation within the European Union, but also by new forms of economic activity and mass communication.

The sovereign state ideal relegated these disputes to the sphere of domestic politics that were supposed to be settled without violence. War was regarded as a force for external relations, to be used to define the position of the state in the wider European system by defending and extending its territory and influence as required. Regardless of their specific content, all political ideologies saw conflict as a matter of last resort, to be used by recognized sovereign governments when attempts to find a peaceful solution had failed. Conduct of operations had to adhere to certain norms and be waged by identifiable military personnel. These norms were articulated in international agreements and political theories, and became what we might describe as the modern European model of war. Curbs on mercenary service had long been part of European state legislation as early modern governments sought to retain an exclusive call on their subject populations. Laws prohibiting other states from recruiting within national frontiers were an important expression of sovereignty and essential to preserving neutrality during international conflict. It remained difficult to prevent subjects voluntarily enlisting in foreign armies, despite this being declared illegal in France (1804), Britain (1819), Switzerland (1853), and most other European countries by the 1880s. However, private military activity was effectively eliminated as the state assumed sole control over all organized forces. This norm was embodied in the Treaty of Paris of 1856, which in addition to ending the Crimean War, included a declaration banning privateering and establishing the principle of the neutral flag to protect maritime trade. Thirty-five European and eight Latin American countries joined this agreement within a year, though the US delayed until 1898. This norm served European interests since it was principally intended to prevent weaker countries from harassing the shipping of the major imperial powers. Its enforcement began long before its formal promulgation and was part of the wider process of the imposition of European ideas on other parts of the world. The French occupation of Algeria ended attacks by the Barbary corsairs in 1830 and, elsewhere, British and later American gunboats stamped out piracy and other armed actions by people not recognized as sovereign governments.[3]

In contrast to earlier peace settlements, that of Vienna in 1814–15 proved remarkably successful in curbing international conflict and there was no immediate resumption of war between the European great powers. Though the Napoleonic empire was dismantled, France was still larger and more compact than it had been before 1792. The Habsburg monarchy recovered much of its former territory and enhanced its position in Italy. Prussia was enlarged and shifted westwards through the acquisition of parts of northern Germany. Rivalry between these two German powers was contained for the moment by the federal framework of the German Confederation, which bound them together with the other, smaller, sovereign German states. This relative balance was supplemented on Europe's periphery by the continent's other two great powers, Britain and Russia. Both had enlarged their extra-European empires while maintaining an active role in the continent's affairs. Even during the height of its global power in the age of 'Pax Britannica' 1815–80, Britain was very much part of Europe and its period of 'splendid isolation' remained a short interlude in the late nineteenth century, which came to a swift end when it became obvious that the country could not sustain its strategic position from its own imperial resources.[4]

Contrary to the formal European model, the greatest danger of war after 1815 came not from a new clash between these powers, but from the internal problems facing most governments. The overthrow of the French monarchy in 1789 left a potent legacy of domestic revolutionary violence that was fed by the frustration and disappointment felt by many in the era of political restoration and reaction after 1815. Impatience for change grew as the existing governments struggled with the profound social and economic changes taking place since the sustained rise in Europe's population began in the mid-eighteenth century. These internal problems led to further international conflict chiefly because of the ambiguous and unsatisfactory nature of the European state. Though not a product of the French Revolution, the ideal of national sovereignty had received a considerable boost from the events after 1789. In its utopian form, this ideal envisaged the division of Europe into a family of nation–states, based primarily on the cultural and linguistic characteristics of the European peoples. This, it was felt, was a more rational and acceptable way of delineating power than the dynastic and hereditary rights of individual monarchs to rule particular lands. In reality, nationality was always contested, creating not only claims to land held by others but also calls for self-determination by peoples claiming oppression by alien rule. These problems were not confined to the multi-national central and eastern European Prussian, Habsburg and Russian empires. Western countries like Britain and Spain also contained minorities and regions that felt they should govern themselves.

These problems were exacerbated by the way many Europeans conceptualized the nation–state as powerful, rationalized, efficient, and centralized. Though often portrayed as part of wider, beneficial and peaceful progress, this ideal was inherently belligerent. The nationalists' goal was always to unite those they identified as their countrymen within a single, contiguous territory, ruled by a government supposedly embodying a 'national will'. The Napoleonic Wars had appeared to demonstrate the potency of nationality and numbers as the basis of great power, through the French example of a united, motivated and large population under arms. The process of national unification challenged the international balance by creating new, more efficient states capable of mobilizing such forces. It was this that made the 'unification' of Germany so disturbing. Austria was excluded from the relatively decentralized German Confederation, which passed in 1866 to the control of the more efficient and dynamic Prussian monarchy. Prussia swiftly launched a war against France in 1870 to consolidate its new position.[5] Similar fears accompanied Italian unification between 1859 and 1870 and indicated that the achievement of nationalist goals aroused the suspicion of neighbours, who might decide to intervene militarily or who might have to be defeated, as in the case of France and Austria, for the process of unification to be completed. The discrepancy between nationalist rhetoric and its practical implementation led to disappointment and frustration, fuelling further conflict. Regions or peoples previously associated with 'historic' homelands were usually still excluded, while even united nations felt threatened and insecure, particularly as their new governments failed to resolve other social or economic problems. In this atmosphere, new wars might appear justified, either to realize a national 'destiny' or to escape from domestic crisis.

These tensions produced the wars punctuating nineteenth- and twentieth-century European history. The waves of violent internal disorder in 1820–1, 1830–1 and 1848–9 were essentially struggles to control the apparatus of the continent's states. These armed insurrections were often led or supported by regular soldiers and had the character of civil wars. Though the European model assigned the military the primary role of external defence, the political climate of the early nineteenth century encouraged a belief in a small, reliable professional army as a bulwark against popular revolution. This did not prevent some officers from acting as the self-proclaimed spokesmen of the national will, as in Spain in 1821 and 1836, Sardinia in 1821 and Russia in 1825. In 1843 a Greek military coup forced King Otto to grant a constitution. Another military revolt deposed him in 1862, while a third forced a further change of government in 1909. Spain was particularly affected by this form of violent resolution of domestic politics, suffering further civil wars 1833–7, 1870–6, as well as the better-known conflict of 1936–9. However, though the French Army also intervened in domestic politics in 1958 and 1962, ending the Fourth Republic, European armed forces have played a less overt role since 1945. Whereas approximately 40 per cent of the world's states are currently under some form of military rule, this has been rare in Europe with the exception of Greece 1967–74, and Poland and Turkey briefly in the 1980s. There were 312 successful or attempted *coup d'états* worldwide in the four decades after the Second World War, but only fifteen of these took place in Europe, one-third of which occurred in Turkey.[6]

In the nineteenth century such domestic conflicts were interwoven with the struggle for national self-determination in the Low Countries, Italy, Germany, Poland, and the Balkans. Each case had international repercussions, as the creation of new states inevitably affected the wider European balance. Foreign intervention helped secure the independence of Greece from Turkey in 1829 and Belgium from the Netherlands in 1831. The question of German nationality underlay two wars formally waged by the German Confederation against Denmark in 1848 and 1864.[7] Domestic issues also contributed to the Crimean War of 1853–6, which was the first European great-power war after 1815.[8] Sardinian involvement, for instance, was largely motivated by the desire of its leadership to win international backing for Italian unification under the house of Savoy. This mixture of power politics and national desires was particularly creative in the Balkans where Bulgaria, Romania and Serbia all emerged as new, sovereign states after the Russo-Turkish War of 1877–8. Disappointments and frustrated national claims following this conflict contributed to two further Balkan Wars 1912–13, which witnessed the creation of Albania after further international intervention. Though national myths present Europe's main 'wars of unification' as straightforward international struggles, Italian and German unification also included an element of internal conflict. Though completed respectively by Sardinian and Prussian victories over 'alien' Habsburg rule, both wars involved the destruction of other

Italian and German states, including the end to the territorial power of the papacy in Italy. The return to peace after the convulsions of 1853–71 was deceptive, because the untidy process of nation-building left a sense of anxiety that contributed to the outbreak of renewed great power war in 1914.[9]

The absence of large-scale war in Europe after 1871 coincided with the peak of European global influence. The proportion of the world's surface under European control rose from 67 per cent in 1878 to 84 per cent by 1914, and the British empire alone encompassed 13.5 million square miles, or three and a half times the size of Europe itself.[10] However, European world power was already being undermined before the continent imploded in 1914. The long lines of battleships assembled to celebrate Queen Victoria's Diamond Jubilee 1897 masked the fact that Britain's military might was sustained by a shrinking share of world resources. The immediate challenger was the newly united Germany, which also began building a battlefleet and pursuing a colonial *Weltpolitik*, and by 1914 the strength of the Royal Navy had been diverted from the empire to defending the North Sea.[11] The difficulty in defeating Germany during the First World War (1914–18) encouraged the first significant challenge to the European ideal of the sovereign state. The victorious Allied powers denied the defeated German government full control of its monopoly of violence by trying to limit the size of its armed forces in the Peace of Versailles in 1919. Traditional sovereignty was further challenged by the Russian Revolution of 1917, as Soviet communism was inherently opposed to the established state system that it was dedicated to overthrowing.

The changes in Russia raise two important interpretative questions. There is the issue of continuity in Russian history between the Tsarist and Soviet eras, as well as the wider problem of the country's place in European and world history. As far as these issues concern the theme of war, they extend beyond determining when Russian military influence began to raise the question whether it can be discussed alongside that of the other European powers, or should be seen as a separate phenomenon. It is not simply a matter of assessing the significance of the peculiarities of Russian military power. The history of all European states and their military systems exhibit certain distinctive national traits, as well as some broad similarities. Russia certainly shared some of these common characteristics, such as the use of certain types of weaponry and the general reliance on a state-controlled, uniformed regular army as the principal organized force in modern times. However, these phenomena can be identified in other countries outside Europe, such as the US and Latin American republics, at roughly the same time. Yet Russia has remained distinct from the other great powers associated with Europe, in many ways more akin to the Ottoman empire in that it has straddled several continents and cultures for around half a millennium.

Russia was clearly a major European power by the time of its victory over Sweden in 1721. This position was consolidated by involvement in further mid eighteenth century struggles that saw Russian troops serving on the Rhine as early as 1735. However, Russian imperial power already predated this European influence by at least two hundred years through its expansion into Siberia and Central Asia, and Moscow controlled a large land mass well before the western European kingdoms established their maritime colonial empires. Soviet Russia retained this characteristic till the end of the twentieth century, long after the demise of western European formal imperialism. Russia's global influence thus predated the era of its full involvement in European politics, which had become established by the beginning of the nineteenth century. Together with Napoleonic France, Russia took the lead in redrawing the map of central Europe in 1801–6. Its particular status was confirmed by the fact that, apart from Britain, it was the only major state to escape total defeat during the Napoleonic Wars, and it retained its position as one of the five great powers despite the subsequent set-backs of the Crimean War and Russo–Japanese War.

Germany's growing military potential after 1871 changed Russia's strategic relationship with the rest of Europe, because it now faced possible invasion from the West for the first time since Napoleon's attack in 1812. This fundamental shift compounded the existing problems of economic and technological under-development, despite rapid industrialization in the late nineteenth century. Russian power was largely misunderstood by its potential enemies, since it was never as strong as it seemed in moments of victory nor as weak as it appeared in defeat. Its strength rested on the resilience of its social, political and military institutions, and serious reverses occurred only when none of these functioned adequately.[12]

Geography ensured that the USSR inherited many of the Tsarist regime's strategic concerns in 1917, but it did so under fundamentally different circumstances. The First World War accelerated the underlying changes in the world economy and global balance of power, promoting the rise of the US and, more immediately, Japan, as Russian concerns. These developments made a material difference, but the accompanying shift in attitudes was probably even more significant. The USSR was a novel state in a new world. Its ideological basis was fundamentally European, but the practical adaptation of nineteenth-century socialism to the realities of early twentieth-century Russia imparted distinctive, largely unforeseen characteristics, changing the way that the new regime conducted itself in the international arena as well as how it was perceived by its neighbours. Together with its great size and formidable potential, this set the USSR apart from the other European powers. This distinctiveness persisted into the 1980s and was heightened by the new regime's formal objectives of global liberation and the defeat of capitalism. The growth in Soviet economic and military power during the Second World War convinced its enemies that it had the capacity to achieve these goals, particularly as the regime moved over from the largely rhetorical support of the 1920s and 1930s, to providing substantial material assistance to revolutionary and liberation movements in Africa, Asia and Latin America.

While such support played a significant role in hastening the end of the old colonial empires after 1945, the outbreak of war six years earlier had already made formal European global dominance untenable.[13] However, it would be wrong to conclude that European history 'ended within a single week in December 1941' when the first counter-attacks of the Red Army revealed the might of the USSR and when the Japanese attack on Pearl Harbor brought the US into the conflict.[14] American and Japanese power was already growing at a faster rate than that of the major European states prior to 1914. The pace quickened during the First World War, during which the US merchant marine grew from 2 million to 12.5 million tons, or more than two-thirds of that of Britain. Whereas Britain's share of new capital warships brought into service had remained steady at about one-third of the entire world's navies between 1860 and 1919, the US proportion doubled after 1890 to reach 12 per cent by 1910. Thereafter, about half of the world's major warship construction has been for the US Navy.[15] Europe's military decline has been relative and linked to its decreasing share of an expanding world economy. Though European countries continued to spend more on defence throughout the twentieth century, they have been unable to sustain their global position. For example, British spending on the Royal Navy adjusted for inflation in 1982 was three and half times that in 1914, yet the country was no longer in the first rank of world sea powers. In fact, British military power remained roughly equivalent to that of the US until the middle of 1943; a factor which sustained British strategic influence despite the US entry into the war. However, Britain was by then operating at maximum capacity with 46 per cent of its labour force in the armed forces, civil defence and war industries, whereas the American economy was still largely civilian-orientated. As it geared for war, the US soon outstripped Europe; from being equalled in munitions output by Britain in 1942, the US was already producing six times as much two years later. Though the British economy continued to grow, the rate of its expansion lagged behind that of the US and Japan. Britain lost its lead in world trade by 1910 and by 1952 its GNP was only equivalent to 12.6 per cent of that of the US. Though its economy was still over two and half times the size of the Japanese in 1952, this margin had shrunk to 40 per cent within twenty years.[16]

This underlying decline was reinforced by the advent of the nuclear age in 1945. Prior to the advent of nuclear weapons, naval power had been the mainstay of empire and global influence. Thereafter it was marginalized though not entirely replaced by the ability to launch a nuclear strike, initially by air, and later by missiles fired from land or sea. Europe's relative position thus received a double set-back in that the US emerged as both the dominant sea and nuclear power after 1945. This has not been off-set by the acquisition of nuclear capability by Britain (1952) or France (1960), since the USSR (1949), China (1964) and India (1974) have also deployed such weapons. Though France maintained a more independent position, British nuclear capability soon became heavily dependent on the US, which provided the Polaris system after

1962. Serious problems emerged in the 1980s as replacement became necessary, and it became obvious that no European country could keep pace with the escalating cost of nuclear weaponry, particularly after the launch of President Reagan's SDI programme in 1983, which extended the scope of national defence beyond the Earth's atmosphere.[17]

The Cold War division of Europe after 1945 further reduced the scope for independent action by individual states. Both the US and USSR deployed significant forces in Europe within the frameworks of their respective alliance systems, NATO and the Warsaw Pact. These arrangements in turn bound their members to sustain preparations for future war in Europe at a time when the global position of individual European countries was crumbling. Britain was bound by the Brussels Pact of 1948 to station troops in western Germany to confront a potential Soviet invasion; maintenance of this British Army on the Rhine was the single largest item of defence spending, amounting to over 39 per cent of expenditure in 1989. The failure of Anglo–French intervention in Egypt during the Suez crisis of 1956 demonstrated the limited potential of combined European action outside the superpower alliance blocs. Defence of European colonial empires was largely the effort of individual imperial powers and resulted in a series of major failures: France lost its struggle to retain Indo-China 1945–54 and Algeria 1954–62, while Portugal abandoned its African possessions by 1974–5. British decolonialization was generally less violent after the 1950s. Its ability to defeat the Argentine invasion of the Falkland Islands in 1982 rested in a large part on the timing of the attack which occurred before the implementation of Defence Secretary John Nott's cuts, 57 per cent of which were intended for the Royal Navy.[18] The end of the Cold War has not reversed the underlying relative decline in Europe's global military position, since there has been widespread retrenchment in defence spending after 1991 as all European governments sought to divert the 'peace dividend' into other areas of expenditure. The number employed in the German arms industries, for instance, has fallen from 280,000 to 100,000 between 1990 and 1998.[19] The dissolution of the USSR also removed the one superpower with a European base, fragmenting its economic and military infrastructure and creating a range of new medium and lesser powers, Russia included. Kazakhstan, for instance, has inherited the main space facilities, while the Ukraine acquired the Nikolaiev shipyards, the only dock capable of servicing Russia's remaining large warships. Chronic economic and social problems have prevented the replacement or upgrading of this underfunded, crumbling and increasingly obsolete infrastructure, the problems of which were graphically demonstrated by the loss of Russia's *Kursk* nuclear submarine in August 2000.

At the close of the twentieth century there were signs that the European model of war was increasingly open to question, as the ideal of the sovereign nation state on which it depended was also under threat. The nineteenth-century ideal of harmonizing national identity and state organization had proved an illusion. Difficulties in defining national identity contributed to two world wars in Europe, in turn encouraging the development of an alternative supra-national organization in the European Union, which evolved from the Treaty of Rome in 1956. Though currently contested, this form of European federalism is a further symptom of the continent's declining global military influence, as it is both an experiment in conflict resolution through greater economic and political co-operation, and a limited attempt to address the spiralling cost of defence through collective security and the pooling of resources. Whether within the EU framework or that of the Cold War alliance systems, European international co-operation has dampened traditional inter-state conflict and the Turkish invasion of Cyprus in 1974 has remained an isolated occurrence. However, the violent collapse of Yugoslavia after 1991 suggests that the traditional European model is no longer appropriate and that current conflict is not so much about sustaining or extending sovereign states as about the violent resolution of the discrepancy between formal political institutions and a sense of community. In such circumstances, it becomes impossible to identify a formal sovereign monopoly of armed force as the competing groups themselves contest the existence of the state.[20] Simultaneously, the 'information revolution' of the 1980s and 1990s has transformed wealth creation by greatly increasing productivity, at least in highly industrialized societies, offering a more peaceful path to prosperity than the conquest of foreign lands and resources.

War as a technological and military phenomenon

The nineteenth century witnessed the birth of modern European military history, much of it sponsored by official organizations like army general staffs. This approach is characterized by its concentration on armed forces as military institutions, and by its concern for questions of organization, tactics, uniforms, and other technical matters. The focus has narrowed in some respects during the twentieth century as weaponry appeared to become more decisive than human skill or even sheer numbers. Many accounts have become heavily technologically determinist, creating a false 'progress of destruction' that implies that the wider historical impact and significance of war has grown with the greater potency and sophistication of modern weaponry.[21] Change in European warfare was not driven exclusively by technological advance, but filtered through shifting cultural perceptions of how armies should be organized and how war should be fought.

The mixed legacy of the Revolutionary and Napoleonic Wars was fundamental in shaping nineteenth-century attitudes to European military practice. One tradition continued the ideal of the revolutionary peoples' war as a new way of fighting, associated with the spirit of French popular resistance to invasion in 1792 as well as the practical experience of guerrilla warfare in Spain, Russia, Prussia, and elsewhere during the Napoleonic Wars. Liberal nationalists, like Guiseppe Mazzini and Thaddeus Kosciuszko, argued that alien oppression could be overthrown by mass popular insurrection. The limited attempts to put this into practice are chiefly associated with Guiseppe Garibaldi, though his involvement in the revolutionary struggles of Brazil and Uruguay 1835–48 were arguably more significant than his military role in Italian unification which, like that in Germany, was largely achieved by conventional forces. The revolutionary tradition received a severe set-back when popular risings across Europe were crushed by regular forces in 1848–9. The Polish insurrection of 1863 also failed and the Paris Commune of 1871 was the last, bloody finale.

The growing pace of military technology and organization only partly explains this outcome. Government regular forces were better armed by the mid-century, but improved communications were probably more significant than weaponry, as the telegraph and railways enabled a more flexible and rapid response to domestic strife. It is significant that the first occasion that troops travelled by rail in the Habsburg monarchy was when they were sent to crush a rebellion in Cracow in 1846.[22] However, the advantages were not always with the government. Despite the concern for counter-revolution, soldiers were poorly trained to deal with popular protest and the relative effectiveness of their firearms proved a liability in 1848 when heavy civilian casualties simply enraged the opposition. Despite being better equipped, French republican forces only retook Paris after heavy street fighting during the suppression of the Commune. Though soldiers continued to be deployed against civil opposition, particularly in France where they assisted in strike-breaking into the twentieth century, most governments developed more sophisticated measures to manage domestic protest. These included the continued demilitarization and disarming of society, the creation of civilian police forces and the widening of the franchise to accommodate broader sections of the population. Violent protest declined, but remained difficult to control as indicated by the development of late nineteenth-century anarchism and twentieth-century terrorism.

Governments rejected revolutionary warfare as a viable means of waging their conflicts and instead sought to harness the potential of popular mobilization within the conservative framework of the regular army, as exemplified by Prussia after 1813.[23] Opinion was divided as to how best to achieve this, as illustrated by the contrast between its two leading exponents. Baron Antoine Henri de Jomini (1779–1869) deduced from numerous studies of Napoleon and Frederick the Great that war was a science of concentrating numerical superiority for a decisive battle.[24] This rationalist approach largely ignored the friction of guerrilla activity, logistical failure and general lack of reliable information. However, it conveyed a comforting sense of professional competence and political reliability. The other great interpreter of Napoleon was the Prussian officer, Carl von Clausewitz (1780–1831). Though better known now, Clausewitz was relatively obscure before the later nineteenth century, largely because his emphasis on the 'fog and friction' of war was at odds with orthodox thinking.[25]

These arguments are indicative of the general difficulty in reconciling lessons from the past with technological change, especially as the rate of innovation in weaponry was itself uneven and often misunderstood. The timing of new technical advances did not always coincide with the duration of European conflicts and there was often a considerable gap before the implications of new weaponry became clear. Technological change in land warfare before 1914 was dominated by the evolution of firearms.[26] All armies began the nineteenth century primarily armed with muzzle-loading, smooth-bore flintlock muskets with an effective range of no more than 200 metres. First, muzzle-loading percussion rifles were gradually introduced between the 1830s and 1850s, improving range and performance, followed by breach–loading bolt-action rifles by 1870, which could be fired from a prone position, making it easier for soldiers to use cover. The latter was first invented by Johann Nicolaus Dreyse in 1830, but it was not adopted by the Prussian army for ten years and took a further 25 before all soldiers received one.

Since these innovations largely took place in peacetime, it proved difficult to assess their implications and European armies entered the great conflicts of the mid nineteenth century with very different sets of tactical doctrine and equipment. Lessons were often falsely diagnosed. The Austrians believed they had been defeated by French shock tactics in 1859 and re-emphasized bayonet attacks in their 1862 regulations with disastrous results in the wars of 1864 and 1866.[27] Prussia's success in the latter conflict and that of 1870–1 against France also led to a muddled reaction. Though the French had a better rifle in 1870, they were defeated by Prussia's superior mobilization and concentration of resources, particularly the deployment of significant numbers of trained reservists who collectively outnumbered the French professional army.[28] These events were interpreted through the lens of Jomini's scientific approach to war and led to the belief that careful planning and the effective mobilization of superior numbers were the keys to success. Ironically, it was Clausewitz's home, the Prussian General Staff, which excelled in these areas and became a widely emulated model, adopted not only in Austria-Hungary (1874), Italy (1882) and Britain (1904), but also outside Europe in Japan (1878) and the US (1903).[29] The contemporary description of the general staff as the 'brain of the army' reveals the prevailing faith in scientific method to solve all problems. In practice, it led to an obsession with planning based on qualitative and quanti-tative assessments of likely opponents, which contributed to the arms race before the First World War. The defeat of the smaller French professional army in 1870 implied an advantage in quantity over quality that also appeared to be necessary to absorb the heavy losses inherent in assaulting well-armed opponents. The growth of mass conscript armies, which were introduced by the major and most of the minor continental powers after 1871, coincided with further improvements in weaponry, including metallic cartridges, smokeless powder and magazine rifles.[30] By 1914 all major European armies were equipped with rifles accurate up to 4,000 metres, or twenty times the range of the muskets used at Waterloo. Artillery made similar exponential advances, particularly with the introduction of recoil mechanisms and TNT (trinitro-toluene) ammunition in the 1890s, which improved the rate of fire and destructive impact of shells.

These developments were posing serious technical problems by 1914. Discipline dictated that the mass conscript armies operate in tight groups that were easier for officers to control, yet the destructiveness of modern weaponry necessitated looser, more open formations. Armies now required several hundred square miles to deploy, greatly complicating the problems of command and logistics. It seemed to some that war was becoming technically unfeasible. In his famous work *The Future of War* (1897), the Polish banker Ivan S. Bloch provided six volumes of statistics indicating that it was impossible for attacking troops to cross the 'fire zone' of their opponents' guns without being annihilated. Bloch's conclusion that war had become futile was rejected by most professionals, who continued to hope that their national *élan* and superior numbers would prevail. Bloch appears prophetic in hindsight, yet the terrible casualties during the First World War were not caused simply by incompetent generalship, but rather the result of a discrepancy between weapon's effective-ness and the relatively low level of training in most armies. This problem has persisted throughout the twentieth century and the recent conflicts in the Balkans have proved again that modern small arms can be very lethal, even in the hands of poorly trained paramilitary forces. Attacking forces required skill and flexibility to avoid heavy losses, but this in turn depended on devolving initiative to unit commanders and their subordinates. Such attacks were first successful in the Balkan Wars of 1912–13 and were repeated again in the Russian Brusilov offensive (1916) and the German Ludendorff offensive (1918) during the First World War. They involved attacks by small groups, supported by mobile forces, including motorized infantry, and succeeded not by crushing the enemy but by disrupting his coherence, throwing him into confusion.

These tactics provided the origins of the German *Blitzkrieg* of the Second World War, which is more usually associated with mechanized, tank assaults. In fact, a shortage of petrol in the Third Reich meant that only six out of 54 active German divisions were armoured by 1939 and much of the army's transport was still horse-drawn. The German success against Poland and France in 1939–40 was due not so much to better weaponry as to its more effective use. In particular, the Germans learnt from the experience of the Spanish Civil War and made more effective use of air support for ground attacks. Air power was first demonstrated by the Bulgarian bombing of Turkish-held Edirne in 1913 and became a major preoccupation by the 1930s, when European governments and their populations became acutely concerned at the possibility of the long-range bombing of civilian targets. This became a major element of strategic planning on both sides during the Second World War, though its efficacy remains a matter of some controversy.

Whereas air power developed at a time when Europe was losing its world lead in military technology, the rise of the armoured, powered warship occurred at the height of European imperialism. European sea powers entered the nineteenth century with fleets of wooden, broadside battery sailing ships that had been developed since the sixteenth century. Naval architecture underwent a fundamental transformation from the 1830s, when auxiliary steam propulsion was first introduced. Sails were completely abandoned by the 1880s and the transition from coal to oil-burning ships was made during the First World War.[31] The launch of the French *Gloire* (1859) and the British *Warrior* (1860) ushered in the era of the armoured warship, introduced to counter the impact of rifled, shell-firing guns that had been carried since the 1840s. Steel replaced iron construction in the 1880s and new, lighter forms of tougher armour were introduced by the end of the century.[32] European warship design reached its peak with the launch of the British *Dreadnought* in 1905, the first all-big-gun, turbine-driven battleship, which was copied by Germany (1907), Russia and Japan (1909), France (1910), and other powers by 1914.[33]

These changes proved as confusing as those in land warfare. The great European powers were involved in few large-scale naval engagements prior to the First World War and often found it difficult to assess the significance of changes in warship design. The one battle between European ironclad fleets was fought by the Austrians against the Italians at Lissa in 1866 and led to the false conclusion that ramming rather than gunfire was a major weapon. The rapidity of the mid-century technological innovations had serious consequences for British naval supremacy, which rested till 1860 on maintaining a largely conventional navy.[34] The USN Chief Engineer J.W. King noted in 1876 that the vast majority of the Royal Navy's 530 ships were useless despite the fact that 84 obsolete vessels had already been scrapped. The fact that the US failed to build new warships after 1865 enabled it to learn from Britain's experimental failures and spared it from investing in an ironclad fleet that was already obsolete by the 1880s.[35] By the 1890s the average life-span of a major warship was only ten to twelve years, compelling naval powers to dispense with reserve fleets and invest heavily in current, front-line units. This 'cost escalation' is inherent in the development of all military technology since the nineteenth century, but has been particularly pronounced in naval and air power. As one British civil servant noted, 'military competition differs from normal economic competition in that normal performance standards are self-referring and self-reinforcing', compelling each power to continually up-grade its equipment to 'keep up with the Joneses'.[36] HMS *Warrior* cost £379,154, or nearly six times that of an eighteenth-century ship of the line. HMS *Nile*, a first-rate battleship launched in 1888, cost twice as much as the *Warrior*, and the *Dreadnought* was twice as much again. The *Queen Elizabeth* class dreadnoughts launched in 1912–16, were already double the price of their prototype.

Britain's naval supremacy was only sustained after 1860 through the comparative weakness of its main European rivals. This changed in the 1880s with the rapid expansion of the French, German, Russian, Italian, and even Austro-Hungarian navies, as well as the advent of the US 'steel navy' and the emergence of Japan as a major sea power. The British Naval Defence Act of 1889 formally endorsed the 'two-power standard', requiring the Royal Navy to be equivalent to its two nearest rivals. Annual naval expenditure jumped from £7 million in the mid nineteenth century to £40.4 million by 1910, while the programme of 48 dreadnoughts and battlecruisers constructed between 1905 and 1920 cost £151 million.[37] This could not be sustained indefinitely and the 1902 naval alliance with Japan was already a sign of Britain's underlying weakness. Though the world cruise of the American 'Great White Fleet' 1907–9 exposed its technical deficiencies, the trend was clear and US naval expenditure already exceeded that of Britain's main continental rival, Germany, between 1904 and 1913.[38] The Washington Naval Limitation Treaty of 1922 merely postponed US predominance by fixing the size of the major fleets and it is significant that Germany, Europe's second naval power in the battleship era, never completed an aircraft carrier, the capital warship of the mid twentieth century.

Such details are instructive as they force us to reconsider the place of military technology in Europe's global influence. Much traditional military history is Eurocentric and sees the colonial victories of the imperial powers as the result of their superior technology since the arrival of the conquistadors in Central America.[39] Though clearly significant, the impact of such weaponry was far from decisive. There were obvious, if rather infrequent, European defeats such as Isandlwana (1879) or Adowa (1896). Perhaps more significantly, European forces were forced to modify their tactics and approach to suit local conditions.[40] Cutting-edge technology of the great powers was not always suited to confronting non-European opponents, and Belgium managed to acquire its huge colonial empire without ever possessing a warship larger than a river gunboat.[41]

Possession of European technology also did not guarantee the success of other countries. The Chilean Krupp artillery did out-range the Peruvians' home-made cannon and contribute to the victory in the War of the Pacific (1879–84), yet the Chinese were defeated by France (1884) and Japan (1894–5) despite having most of their warships built in Europe. Brazil, Argentina and Uruguay all employed modern European weapons in their six-year struggle against Paraguay (1864–70), but failed to achieve a swift victory.[42] Surplus American equipment made an appearance in the later stages of this conflict, signalling the intrusion of the US onto the world's arms market and it was not long before American firms were supplying European forces: the Turks held off the Russians at Plevna in 1877 using American-made Peabody rifles.

European arms sales were linked to a wider process of the adoption of foreign norms and methods by non-Europeans.[43] European technicians and advisers were already prominent in the nineteenth century. English mechanics serviced the Paraguayan fleet and ran its arsenal, while German and Austrian advisers helped establish the telegraph system during the War of the Triple Alliance.[44] In some cases, these men took a more active role, such as the Russian gunners who operated the Ethiopian artillery at Adowa. The transfer of military technology and practice is one area where theories of the 'development of underdevelopment' are perhaps most apt, since European assistance was often part of a wider strategy to foster the continued dependence of non-European countries. For example, British banks provided loans to China to pay its war indemnity to Japan in 1895, on the condition that it re-equipped its fleet with warships built in England.[45] Such influence has persisted after colonial withdrawal. For instance, British officers and specialists continued to serve in Gulf Arab armies long after Britain abandoned its political and military role in the region in 1971. Importing European models often brought other unintended consequences. Reformers frequently changed more than they originally planned, because European military organization required permanent armies and modern weaponry that were more expensive than traditional forces. They were also based on different ideas of discipline and professionalism, which disrupted existing social and political institutions and could arouse profound opposition.

In addition to Turkey, Russia is the one country associated with Europe most affected by these difficulties. Russian military development is often discussed in terms of progressive 'Europeanization', whereby the adoption of Western ideas and technology is associated with political, economic and social 'moderniz-ation'. However, attempts to assess the relative merits of 'Western' or 'Russian' systems often minimize the extent to which these were not mutually exclusive but evolved together, albeit unevenly and with considerable human cost. This was already apparent during the reign of Tsar Peter the Great (1689–1725) which saw the establishment of a military system integrating conscription and economic production based on formal servitude.[46] This system served Russia remarkably well, not least because it was never completely closed to change, including further indigenous technological development, such as improvements in artillery made during the later eighteenth century. Its resilience was proved during the victory over Napoleon in 1812–14, while administrative reforms in the 1830s considerably enhanced its efficiency.[47] However, it ultimately placed quantity above quality; a deficiency that proved a liability along with the country's underdeveloped transportation system during the Crimean War. Wide social and military reforms dismantled the Petrine service state between 1861 and 1874.[48] Further modifications followed the defeat in the Russo-Japanese war and coincided with the intensification of industrialization and the acceleration of social and political change. Like the earlier reforms, the rapid rearmament after 1905 combined adaptation and indigenous innovation rather than a wholesale importation of foreign models. Both the scale and the rate of Russian military development remained impressive until the last decade of the Soviet era, but the results were often mixed.[49]

PETER H. WILSON

War as a social and economic phenomenon

The Revolutionary and Napoleonic Wars are also often regarded as a turning point in the broader social and economic context of European warfare, signalling the end to the supposedly limited conflicts of the old regime, and the start of mass mobilization of motivated citizens-in-arms. This view is related to the assumption that armies always reflect the societies they serve and since the French Revolution transformed European society and politics, it must have similarly affected military organization.[50] As with other such interrelationships, the connections are far from straightforward.

The social and political rise of the bourgeoisie was reflected in their growing place in the officer corps, which had traditionally been a bastion of the European aristocracy. From having been largely excluded in 1815, middle-class officers rose from 35 per cent of the total in Prussia in 1860 to 70 per cent by 1913, including 48 per cent of the senior positions.[51] Similar statistics can be mustered for other countries, but are deceptive. Aristocrats still dominated the guards and other élite units, while many bourgeois officers willingly or otherwise adopted entrenched attitudes. This is regarded as having been pronounced in Prussia, where acceptance of conservative values was essential to assimilation and where the status of reserve officer was part of a wider bourgeois emulation of aristocratic lifestyle.[52] The expansion of the Prussian officer corps to over 51,000 by 1914 necessitated casting the net beyond a narrow social élite. However, aristocratic officers were not always opposed to change. Acceptance of commoners was also possible in Prussia because of the growing appreciation of technical expertise and education.

Similarly, the introduction of universal service was not necessarily democratic or 'progressive' but inherently ambiguous, at once implying that the duty to serve should be related to rights of citizenship, yet also signifying a considerable extension of the state's power to tap the human resources of its population. This ambiguity was already present in the mass levies of revolutionary France after 1793 and contributed to the rejection of such methods after 1815.[53] Arming the people also seemed politically unwise and a military liability, according to the Jominian interpretation of the Napoleonic legacy. It was especially problematic for the multi-national empires of central and eastern Europe, as it implied a homogenous national composition that was impossible to achieve: German-speakers accounted for only 26 per cent of Habsburg personnel in 1865, yet the army still provided the cement of the empire and loyally resisted revolution in 1848.[54] Elsewhere, national homogeneity was diluted by the continued use of foreign mercenaries, despite the efforts to prohibit this. Though France disbanded its last Swiss regiment in 1830, it established the Foreign Legion the following year, a formation that still numbered over 8,000 in the 1980s. Britain also hired 16,500 foreigners during the Crimean War, but thereafter the number of Europeans serving other countries declined and the idea of mercenary service was replaced by that of the ideologically motivated volunteer, most notably in the International Brigades during the Spanish Civil War of 1936–9.[55] Foreign soldiers were increasingly drawn from subject colonial populations rather than other European countries after the mid nineteenth century. This was prominent in France, which raised its first Zouave unit in Algeria in 1830 and was the only European power to introduce universal service into its colonies (1912–60). North African troops were first deployed to defend France in 1870 and were used in greater numbers in the First World War.[56]

The deployment of mass conscript armies in that conflict has been linked to the concept of total war, which embraces several elements. The first is a qualitative as well as quantitative change in the scale of mobilization, indicating that not only a larger proportion of the male population was now under arms but also that significant numbers of women were mobilized as well, particularly in war industries. The second is that total war implies a new, more ruthless conduct of war, widening its scope and objectives. It is certainly possible to observe elements of these changes in Europe during the two World Wars. Whereas the German mobilization of 1.2 million soldiers represented 3 per cent of the population in 1870, the proportion increased to 5.7 per cent with the 3.82 million assembled in 1914. By 1918, no less than 13.25 million were under arms, representing 19.7 per cent of the German population. Industrialization both necessitated and facilitated this increase. More men were required to achieve numerical superiority in an age of mass armies and modern weaponry, yet more men were also available thanks to the mechanization of the labour process, something which contrasted sharply with the wars of the mid nineteenth century, which occurred at a time when most countries' economies were still primarily agrarian and labour-intensive.

Industrialization also changed the conduct of war by helping to shift the ratio of men, money and materials. Whereas the first two had been the dominant factors in Europe before the late nineteenth century, the outcome of the First World War was greatly influenced by industrial output and economic efficiency. The full impact of mass armies and modern weaponry were felt for the first time. Already by 1904 a brigade of 3,000 men could fire more artillery and rifle rounds in a single minute than Wellington's entire army of 60,000 at Waterloo.[57] Armies could no longer survive on the traditional mix of supply dumps and requisitioning from the civilian population, but now required an industrial base and a sophisticated transport system. This only became more acute as mechanization progressed in the twentieth century, since vehicles required fuel that itself had to be transported, whereas earlier armies could rely on grazing for transport and cavalry horses.

The concept of total war is more problematic when its social and economic consequences are considered. In very general terms, more Europeans have died in twentieth-century conflicts than all previous wars combined (see Table 1). Growing numbers of civilians have also been affected, not only as casualties, where they accounted for over half the losses in the Second World War, but also

Table 1 Total military and civilian casualties in European conflicts

Time Period	Casualties (millions)
17th century	3.3
18th century	3.9
1792–1815	4.9
1815–1914	2.2
1914–18	10.0
1919–38	1.3
1939–45	56.5

Sources
B.Z. Urlanis, *Bilanz der Kriege. Die Menschenverluste Europas vom 17. Jahrhundert bis zur Gegenwart* (Berlin, 1965); R.A.C. Parker, *Struggle for Survival. The History of the Second World War* (Oxford, 1990), pp. 281–5.

as displaced persons, such as the 14 million Germans expelled from Eastern Europe in 1945. Terrible though these figures are, it is questionable whether the two World Wars necessarily had a greater impact than some past European conflicts. Europe's population of 200 million in 1800 more than doubled over the nineteenth century, and grew by another 360 million in the next. Comparative figures reveal that the proportion of the population mobilized in 1792–1815 was equivalent to that in the First World War. The mortality rate of the French generation of 1790–5 was 38 per cent, or 14 per cent higher than that suffered by the generation of 1890–5.[58] The economic impact is also relative. Britain's peacetime defence spending has remained constant at 2–5 per cent of GNP between 1698 and 1983. Its annual growth in military spending is also in line with the general expansion of European industrial economies which has averaged 1.5 to 4 per cent each year of the twentieth century, except for the Depression.[59] Though British military expenditure soared to 51 per cent of GNP in 1914–18 and 60 per cent in 1939–45, its questionable whether these bursts of activity have been more instrumental in affecting qualitative change, such as improved rights for women, than the long-term underlying transformation of the economy through the changing pattern of industrialization.[60]

The question of greater ruthlessness is also problematic. Total war implies the use of all available means to destroy the enemy and has been seen as characteristic of twentieth-century Europe, particularly Nazi Germany. Its origins are generally traced to the wars of 1864–71 and specifically the Prussian bombardment of civilian districts in Strasbourg and Paris as a terror weapon to break French morale.[61] In fact, such bombardments were scarcely novel in European conflicts and were even a feature of the supposedly limited wars of the eighteenth century. The French Revolution did introduce a new ruthlessness at strategic level, particularly through its more flexible political use of force and its mobilization of national sentiment. Incidents like Napoleon's execution of 4,400 Turkish prisoners at Jaffa in 1799, or the bitter resistance of the civilian population of Saragossa 1808–9 also seem to point to future brutality.[62] Yet, the period after 1815 witnessed a return to more 'limited' war, as exemplified by the establishment of the humanitarian Red Cross (1864), and a series of international declarations and conferences establishing laws regulating the conduct of war (1856, 1864, 1874, 1899, 1906, 1907). These articulated the norms inherent in the European model by defining forms of war in relation to the state monopoly of violence; for example by exempting civilians from the list of legitimate targets. The absence of large-scale conflict in Europe apart from 1853–71 helped sustain the belief that war had been civilized, despite the growing destructiveness of modern weaponry. However, the willingness of Europeans to use the full potential of military technology was demonstrated in nineteenth-century colonial conflicts, such as the British bombardment of Alexandria in 1882 and perhaps most cruelly by the systematic and ruthless suppression by Germany of the revolt in South West Africa 1904–7, in which three-quarters of the Herero and half the Nama peoples were slaughtered or starved to death.[63]

Though there has been a reaction against such ruthlessness after 1945, this is difficult to measure with precision. Open glorification of war is now relatively rare, at least in western Europe, outside the ideological 'armed struggles' of terrorist groups. The military strength of European states, which was a matter of national pride to be celebrated openly, is now generally concealed from the eyes of an often critical electorate. The contemporary presentation of war in the media and political debate describes a battlefield that is simultaneously expanding and contracting. Long-range weaponry has partly depersonalized killing, since it is possible to strike unseen opponents – potentially in another continent in the case of nuclear war. Yet, the battlefield has also shrunk with the growing focus on the experience of individual combatants. This partly stems from concern for military efficiency, which led armies to pay more serious attention to the psychological aspects of warfare after 1914. Humanitarian concerns may also play a part, but the dramatic expansion of forms of communication are probably more important. Europeans now have access to an unprecedented range of documentation about personal experiences in word, sound and image, which, for contemporary conflict, can be brought almost instantaneously via satellite into most homes. The commemoration of the two World Wars has strengthened this, fixing attention on the experience of 'ordinary' individuals surviving traumatic events.[64] This is reflected in official policy, as anxiety over casualties has influenced a preference for 'smart bombs' and other forms of 'clean killing' that avoid the need to expose personnel to retaliatory fire.[65] Armed forces have also been repackaged to make them more acceptable to a critical public. Current British recruiting advertisements emphasize the role of soldiers as humanitarian aid workers and depict sailors combating drug smuggling. This has not dampened public interest in conflict, and the passing of the generations who experienced the two World Wars brought a boom in publications and films in the 1970s and 1990s. Memories of unsuccessful or controversial conflicts are still partially repressed. For example, there are few public monuments to the Algerian War in France, and this conflict has yet to enter mainstream cinema and literature in the way that Vietnam has done in the US.[66] However, the highest-grossing film on both sides of the Atlantic in 2001 was the $135 million *Pearl Harbor*, while camouflage and combat trousers were the fashion accessories of that summer.[67]

Notes

1   D. Thomson, *Europe since Napoleon* (Harmondsworth, 1966).
2   J. Burkhardt, 'Die Friedlosigkeit der Frühen Neuzeit. Grundlegung einer Theorie der Bellizität Europas', *Zeitschrift für Historische Forschung*, 24 (1997), 509–74; M.S. Anderson, *The Rise of Modern Diplomacy 1450–1919* (Harlow, 1993).
3   J.E. Thomson, *Mercenaries, Pirates and Sovereigns. State-building and Extra-territorial Violence in Early Modern Europe* (Princeton, 1994).
4   D. French, *The British Way in Warfare 1688–2000* (London, 1990).
5   On the problems of the decentralized defence structure see E. Wienhöfer, *Das Militärwesen des Deutschen Bundes und das Ringen zwischen Österreich und Preussen um die Vorherrschaft in Deutschland 1815–1866* (Osnabrück, 1973); J. Angelow, *Von Wien nach Königgrätz. Die Sicherheitspolitik des Deutschen Bundes im europäischen Gleichgewicht 1815–1866* (Munich, 1996).
6   P. Mansel, *Pillars of Monarchy. An Outline of the Political and Social History of Royal Guards 1400–1984* (London, 1984); A. Horne, *The French Army in Politics 1870–1970* (New York, 1984); A. Perlmutter, *Political Roles and Military Rulers* (London, 1981); C. Tilly, *Coercion, Capital and European States, AD 990–1992* (Oxford, 1992), pp. 209–24; G. Ferguson, *Coup d'état. A Practical Manual* (Poole, 1987), pp. 197–202. The countries affected by coups are: Turkey (five times), Greece (three), Portugal (two), France (two), Spain (one), Cyprus (one), and Czechoslovakia (one).
7   G. Stolz, *Die schleswig-holsteinische Erhebung. Die nationale Auseinandersetzung in und um Schleswig-Holstein von 1848/51* (Husum, 1996); W. Vogel, *Entscheidung 1864* (Bonn, 1996).
8   W. Baumgart, *The Crimean War 1853–1856* (London, 1999).
9   R. Hall, *The Balkan Wars 1912–1913. Prelude to the First World War* (London, 2000); J.W. Langdon, *July 1914. The Long Debate 1918–1990* (New York/Oxford, 1991); S.R. Williamson Jr., *Austria-Hungary and the Origins of the First World War* (Basingstoke, 1991).
10 D.K. Fieldhouse, *Economics and Empire 1830–1914* (Ithaca, 1973). The European share in 1800 had been 35 per cent.
11 P.M. Kennedy, *The Rise of the Anglo–German Antagonism 1869–1914* (London, 1980).
12 F.W. Kagan, 'Russia's geopolitical dilemma and the question of backwardness', in F.W. Kagan and R. Higham (eds), *The Military History of Tsarist Russia* (Basingstoke, 2002), pp. 249–57.
13 P.M.H. Bell, *The Origins of the Second World War* (2nd edn, Harlow, 1999).
14 M. Howard, *War in European History* (Oxford, 1976).
15 P. Padfield, *Rule Britannia. The Victorian and Edwardian Navy* (London, 1981), p. 248; P. Pugh, *The Cost of Sea Power. The Influence on Naval Affairs from 1815 to the Present Day* (London, 1986), pp. 160–1.

16 French, *British Way*, pp. 203–4. Further examples in P. Kennedy, *The Rise and Fall of the Great Powers* (London, 1988).

17 A. Corvisier (general ed.), *Histoire militaire de la France* (4 vols, Paris, 1994), IV 349–54; R.A. Doughty *et al.*, *American Military History and the Evolution of Warfare in the Western World* (Lexington, 1996), pp. 578–602.

18 M.E. Chamberlain, *Decolonialisation and the Fall of the European Empires* (Oxford, 1999).

19 *Frankfurter Allgemeine Zeitung*, 7 October 1999, p. 8.

20 For a theoretical discussion see K.J. Holsti, *The State, War and the State of War* (Cambridge, 1996). The collapse of Yugoslavia is analysed by V. Meier, *Yugoslavia. A History of its Demise* (London, 1999); N.M. Naimark, *Fires of Hatred. Ethnic Cleansing in Twentieth-century Europe* (Cambridge, Mass., 2000). For the place of the Bosnian War in European military development, see W. Chin, 'The transformation of war in Europe 1945–2000', in J. Black (ed.), *European Warfare 1815–2000* (Basingstoke, 2002), pp. 192–217.

21 R. Higham (ed.), *Official Histories* (Manhattan, Kansas, 1970); M. Raschke, *Der politisierende Generalstab. Die friderizianischen Kriege in der amtlichen deutschen Militärgeschichtsschreibung 1890–1914* (Freiburg, 1993). For an example of techno-logical determinism see M. van Creveld, *Technology and War from 2000 BC to the Present* (New York, 1989). A contrasting view is offered by R.L. O'Connell, *Of Arms and Men. A History of War, Weapons and Aggression* (New York/Oxford, 1989).

22 J. Niemeyer, *Das österreichische Militärwesen im Umbruch. Untersuchungen zum Kriegsbild zwischen 1830 und 1866* (Osnabrück, 1979), p. 162.

23 M. Rink, *Vom 'Partheygänger' zum Partisanen. Die Konzeption des kleinen krieges in Preußen 1740–1813* (Frankfurt/M., 1999).

24 Examples include A.H. de Jomini, *Précis de l'art de la guerre* (Paris, 1838), and his *Treatise on Grand Military Operations* (2 vols, New York, 1865). For the debate, see also A. Gat, *The Origins of Military Thought from the Enlightenment to Clausewitz* (Oxford, 1989).

25 C. v. Clausewitz, *On War* (ed. and trans. M. Howard and P. Paret, Princeton, 1976); P. Paret, *Clausewitz and the State* (Oxford, 1976), and his *Understanding War. Essays on Clausewitz and the History of Military Power* (Princeton, 1992).

26 For the evolutionary nature of these changes, see H. Strachan, *From Waterloo to Balaclava. Tactics, Technology and the British Army 1815–1854* (Cambridge, 1985); J.J. Sweetman, *War and Administration. The Significance of the Crimean War for the British Army* (Edinburgh, 1984). For the technical details see the two works by G. Ortenburg: *Waffe und Waffengebrauch im Zeitalter der Einigungskriege* (Koblenz, 1990), and *Waffe und Waffengebrauch im Zeitalter der Millionenheere* (Koblenz, 1992).

27 G.E. Rothenburg, *The Army of Francis Joseph* (West Lafayette, 1998), pp. 63–6; W. Wagner, *Von Austerlitz bis Königgrätz. Österreichische Kampftaktik im Spiegel der Reglements 1805–1864* (Osnabrück, 1978); G. Wawro, *The Austro–Prussian War. Austria's War with Prussia and Italy in 1866* (Cambridge, 1996).

28 T.J. Adriance, *The Last Gaiter Button. A Study of the Mobilisation and Concentration of the French Army in the War of 1870* (New York, 1987); G.P. Cox, *The Halt in the Mud. French Strategic Planning from Waterloo to Sedan* (Boulder, 1994); M. Howard, *The Franco–Prussian War* (New York, 1969).

29 J.D. Hittle, *The Military Staff. Its History and Development* (2nd edn, Harrisburg, Pa., 1949); S.W. Lackey, *The Rebirth of the Habsburg Army. Friedrich Beck and the Rise of the General Staff* (Westport, Conn., 1995).

30 European conscription systems are compared in G. Papke and W. Petter (general eds), *Handbuch zur deutschen Militärgeschichte 1648–1939* (11 vols, Frankfurt/M., 1964–81), V 41–9.

31   R. Armstrong, *Powered Ships: the Beginnings* (London, 1975); D.K. Brown, *Paddle Warships. The Earliest Powered Fighting Ships 1815–1850* (London, 1993).

32   A. Lambert, *Warrior* (London, 1987); W. Hovgaard, *Modern History of Warships* (London, 1978); P. Hodges, *The Big Gun: Battleship Main Armament 1860–1945* (London, 1989).

33   For a reinterpretation of the design and introduction of the *Dreadnought* see J.T. Sumida, *In Defence of Naval Supremacy. Finance, Technology and British Naval Policy 1889–1914* (London, 1993).

34   G.A. Ballard, *The Black Battlefleet* (London, 1980); B. Greenhill and A. Gifford, *Steam, Politics and Patronage. The Transformation of the Royal Navy 1815–1854* (London, 1994); A. Lambert, *Battleships in Transition. The Creation of the Steam Battlefleet 1815–60* (London, 1984).

35   J.W. King, *The Warships of Europe* (Portsmouth, 1878), pp. 1–6, 313–15.

36   P. Pugh, *Cost of Sea Power*, pp. 139–40, 151.

37   P.M. Kennedy, *The Rise and Fall of British Naval Mastery* (Basingstoke, 1983). For the development of other navies see H.H. Herwig, *Luxury Fleet. The Imperial German Navy 1888–1918* (London, 1987); T. Ropp, *The Development of a Modern Navy. French Naval Policy 1871–1904* (Annapolis, 1987); E.H. Jenkins, *A History of the French Navy* (London, 1973); A.F. Sokol, *The Imperial and Royal Austro-Hungarian Navy* (Annapolis, 1968); M.N. Vego, *Austro-Hungarian Naval Policy 1904–1914* (London, 1996); J.C. Reilly and R.L. Scheina, *American Battleships 1886–1923* (London, 1980); H. Jentsura and D.M. Jung, *Warships of the Imperial Japanese Navy 1869–1945* (London, 1977).

38   Viscount Hythe (ed.), *The Naval Annual 1913* (Portsmouth, 1913), p. 96.

39   G. Parker, *The Military Revolution. Military Innovation and the Rise of the West, 1500–1800* (Cambridge, 1988).

40   B. Vandervort, *Wars of Imperial Conquest in Africa 1830–1914* (London, 1998).

41   *Conway's All the World's Fighting Ships 1860–1905* (London, 1979), p. 415.

42   H.W. Wilson, *Ironclads in Action. A Sketch of Naval Warfare 1855–1895* (2 vols, 4th edn, London, 1896), II 4–15, 51–135; C.J. Kolinski, *Independence or Death! The Story of the Paraguayan War* (Gainesville, 1965); B.W. Farcau, *The Ten Cents War. Chile, Peru and Bolivia in the War of the Pacific 1879–1884* (Westport, 2000).

43   D.B. Ralston, *Importing the European Army. The Introduction of European Military Techniques and Institutions into the Extra-European World, 1600–1914* (Chicago, 1990); W.F. Sater and H.H. Herwig, *The Grand Illusion. The Prussianization of the Chilean Army* (Lincoln/London, 1999); F.M. Nunn, 'Emil Körner and the Prussianization of the Chilean army: origins, process and consequences 1885–1920', *Hispanic American Historical Review*, 50 (1970), 300–22.

44   For European technicians, see J.H. Williams, 'Foreign technicos and the modern-isation of Paraguay, 1840–1870', *Journal of Interamerican Studies and World Affairs*, 19 (1977), 233–57; T.L. Whigham, 'The iron works at Ybycui. Paraguayan industrial development in the mid-nineteenth century', *The Americas*, 35 (1978), 201–18; H.G. Warren, 'The Paraguayan Central Railway, 1856–1889', *Inter American Economic Affairs*, 20 (1967), 3–22.

45   Ropp, *Development of a Modern Navy*, p. 71. However, the argument that such efforts extended to European pressure on developing countries to fight wars on their behalf has come under sustained scholarly criticism. For a useful example with reference to the further literature, see the discussions of the origins of the War of the Triple Alliance by L. Bethell, *The Paraguayan War (1864–70)* (London, 1996), and E.N. Tate, 'Britain and Latin America in the nineteenth century. The case of Paraguay 1811–1870', *Ibero-Amerikanisches Archiv*, n.s. 5 (1979), 39–70.

46   C. Duffy, *Russia's Military Way to the West. Origins and Nature of Russian Military Power 1700–1800* (London, 1981); L. Hughes, *Russia in the Age of Peter the Great* (New Haven, 2000), pp. 63–91.

47   F.W. Kagan, *The Military Reforms of Nicolas I. The Origins of the Modern Russian Army* (Basingstoke, 1999); J.H.L. Keep, *Soldiers of the Tsar. Army and Society in Russia 1492–1874* (Oxford, 1985).

48   B.W. Menning, *Bayonets before Bullets. The Imperial Russian Army, 1861–1914* (Bloomington, 1992).

49   J.N. Westwood, *Russian Naval Construction 1905–45* (Basingstoke, 1994); R.R. Reese, *The Soviet Military Experience. A History of the Soviet Army 1917–1991* (London, 2000).

50   J.A. Lynn, 'The evolution of army style in the modern west 800–2000', *International History Review*, 18 (1996), 505–45.

51   S.E. Clemente, *For King and Kaiser! The Making of the Prussian Army Officer, 1860–1914* (New York, 1992), p. 205. See generally P.M. Pilbeam, *The Middle Classes in Europe 1789–1914* (Basingstoke, 1990), pp. 144–72; D. Lieven, *The Aristocracy in Europe 1815–1914* (Basingstoke, 1992), pp. 181–202.

52   H.H. Herwig, *The German Naval Officer Corps. A Social and Political History* (Oxford, 1973); K. Demeter, *The German Officer Corps in Society and State 1650–1945* (New York, 1965); M. Kitchen, *The German Officer Corps, 1890–1914* (Oxford, 1968).

53   A. Forrest, *Conscripts and Deserters. The Army and French Society during the Revolution and Empire* (Oxford, 1989); R.G. Foerster (ed.), *Die Wehrpflicht. Entstehung, Erscheinungsformen und politisch-militärisch Wirkung* (Munich, 1994).

54   Rothenburg, *Army of Francis Joseph*, p. 61; A. Sked, *The Survival of the Habsburg Empire. Radetzky, the Imperial Army and the Class War, 1848* (London, 1979); I. Deák, *Beyond Nationalism. A Social and Political History of the Habsburg Officer Corps 1848–1918* (Oxford, 1990).

55   C.C. Bayley, *Mercenaries for the Crimea. The German, Swiss and Italian Legions in British Service 1854–1856* (Montreal, 1977).

56   E. Detaille, *L'armée française. An Illustrated History of the French Army 1790–1885* (New York, 1992; 1st 1889), pp. 189–232 describes the l'armée d'Afrique. M. Echenberg, *Colonial conscripts. The Tirailleurs Sénégalais in French West Africa, 1857–1960* (Portsmouth, NH, 1991).

57   G. Wawro, *Warfare and Society in Europe 1792–1914* (London, 2000), p. 156. See also M. van Creveld, *Supplying War. Logistics from Wallenstein to Patton* (Cambridge, 1977).

58   D. Gates, *The Napoleonic Wars 1803–1815* (London, 1997), p. 272. Further examples in C.J. Esdaile, *The Wars of Napoleon* (Harlow, 1995), pp. 298–301.

59   P. Pugh, *Cost of Sea Power*, pp. 9–11, 23.

60   A. Marwick (ed.), *Total War and Social Change* (Basingstoke, 1988). Further discussion in G. Kolko, *Century of War. Politics, Conflict and Society since 1914* (New York, 1994).

61   B. Bond, *War and Society in Europe, 1870–1970* (Leicester, 1984).

62   D. Chandler, *The Campaigns of Napoleon* (London, 1966), p. 236; R. Rudorff, *War to the Death. The Sieges of Saragossa 1808–1809* (London, 1974).

63   T. Dedering, ' "A certain rigorous treatment of all parts of the population". The annihilation of the Herero in German South West Africa, 1904', in M. Levene and P. Roberts (eds), *The Massacre in History* (New York, 1999), pp. 205–22.

64   G.L. Mosse, *Fallen Soldiers. Reshaping the Memory of the World Wars* (Oxford, 1990); C. Reanick, *The French in Love and War. Popular Culture in the Era of the World Wars* (New Haven/London, 1997).

65 J. Black, *War in the World. Military Power and the Fate of Continents 1450–2000* (New Haven/London, 1998), pp. 274–6; J. Bourke, *An Intimate History of Killing. Face to Face Killing in Twentieth-century Warfare* (London, 1999).
66 P. Dines, *Images of the Algerian War. French Fiction and Film 1954–1992* (Oxford, 1994).
67 *The Times Magazine*, 17 March 2001.

9

NAVAL POWER AND WARFARE
1815–2000

Jan Glete

Navies and modern warfare

Navies have traditionally been organized by states for warfare at sea. Such warfare is essentially a contest about the sea lines of communication. During wars, these lines are used for transport of essential resources, power projection against foreign coasts and territories, or as an area for active defence against invasions. However, in the nineteenth and twentieth centuries, warfare became difficult to divide into warfare on land and at sea. It is not only the introduction of air power which made this division less useful. Grand strategy has always been about what to do with both land and sea forces during wars. Operations may often involve two or three armed services and the rapid development of new technology has meant that these services often also have to co-operate on the tactical level, that is, in combat with the enemy.

The sea is international and it can be used to the advantage of those who are able to control it and develop technology for economic and political purposes. During the nineteenth and twentieth centuries, several European powers, the United States and Japan used the sea for extending their power to most parts of the world, by opening markets, conquering territories and enforcing a European-style control of violence on the rest of the world. Creation and defence of informal and formal empires was a main task for many navies. It often involved them in warfare, although seldom against other navies. This was a part of the development of an integrated world economy that is dependent on the ability of ships to move natural resources, food and industrial products from one part of the world to another. The sea connects major markets with widely different resources, and industrialization reduced the ability of societies to survive and fight wars if they are isolated. This made control of the sea of decisive importance in major wars. Human ingenuity also made it possible to create mobile and floating military societies, warships and fleets, which permanently or temporarily could be deployed to any part of the world in order to change the balance of power. This was used to project power across the sea, either with offensive strike forces during wars or with peace-time deployments of naval forces that were used to protect communications and merchant ships, and to influence political, social and economic events on land.

Technology and naval warfare

This chapter concentrates on the interaction between technology and doctrines that have shaped the navies and the strategic, operational and tactical experiences of wars on technology and doctrines. Early modern technology had made naval operations and combined operations with armies and navies fairly predictable as the gun was the dominating weapon at sea, in coast defence and for naval support of army forces. The force that could dominate the sea and coastal areas with firepower from guns had the freedom to determine the operation. There was no other weapon that could seriously harm warships. The limits of sea power were primarily geography, climate, human endurance, and the range of naval guns. The supremacy of gunnery remained a centre-piece of most naval doctrines until World War II. Most navies up to then were dominated by senior officers who were gunnery specialists.

A few decades after 1815 this technological stability began to disappear. By 1850 the change gained momentum and before 1870 all navies had radically changed. The stability never returned and naval power has remained highly dependent on technology. Navies have met greater technical challenges and opportunities than any other established organization in the nineteenth and twentieth centuries. Naval architecture, metallurgy, mechanics, chemistry, steam engineering, internal combustion engines, electricity, optical technology, electronics, nuclear power, computers, hydro-acoustic technology, food preservation technology, and medical science have created a broad spectrum of weapons, sensors, weapon carriers, and command, communication and control systems, as well as better possibilities for seamen to stay at sea in good health for long periods. Nineteenth-century progress in medical science and food preservation was particularly important in making life at sea less dangerous than in the early modern world. Epidemics were brought under control, scurvy disappeared and the wounded gained a better chance to survive and recover.

The technical developments that challenged navies were often initiated by civilian inventors and companies as well as by other armed services, armies and air forces. Opportunities have often been created by the navies themselves, when they began to develop new technology in order to change their own organization. In the mid nineteenth century, the challenges posed by iron, steam and even new types of artillery (shell guns, wrought iron and steel guns, rifled gun-barrels, breech-loading) were mainly developed outside the navies. The sailing navies were not the reactionary institutions they are often presented as. Sails, for example, were retained until the late nineteenth century because early steam engines gave too short a radius of action for warships for long-distance service. Nevertheless, the navies did not have the initiative in the great upheaval of naval technology from about 1840 to 1870. They adapted to it, rather than created it.

In the following decades, active demands for new technology from the navies became much more important. Naval officers and engineers became experts in many branches of the new technology and developed networks of contacts with the most advanced manufacturers. Steel for hulls, improved armour, heavy guns with armour-piercing shells, quick-firing guns, torpedoes, mines, new types of boilers and steam engines, steam turbines, high-speed torpedo craft and submarines were developed with much support and co-operation from the navies. The private manufacturers of many of these products and of complete warships grew to become some of the largest industrial companies of the age: Armstrong, Krupp, Vickers, Skoda, Bethlehem Steel. Navies became parts of large military–industrial networks dominated by steel, armour, shipbuilding, steam engineering, guns, and explosives that reached their apogee before and during World War I.

These networks declined in importance after 1918. From 1922 battleship construction almost totally ceased for more than a decade due to the international treaties on naval arms limitation. Instead, dynamic innovations in naval warfare during most of the twentieth century came from interaction between navies and manufacturers of aircraft and helicopters, submarine technology (electricity, diesel engines, nuclear reactors), systems for fire control, sensors, command and communication (mechanical and electronic computers, radar, sonar, integrated systems for combat information), and increasingly sophisticated self-propelled missiles (torpedoes, guided missiles, strategic ballistic missiles). The most serious technical challenge to traditional sea power after World War I came from air forces and manufacturers of aircraft and aircraft engines. Air power became a serious threat to both navies and armies, but for the navies they were also a threat to their prestigious position as the most technologically advanced armed force.

On the other hand, technical change allowed dynamic naval organizations to develop new doctrines and know-how that gave them a large role in the total defence organization of a state. A few of the major navies, primarily those of the United States, Britain and Japan integrated carrier-borne air power with their organizations, in the British case after an inter-service struggle with the Royal Air Force. Anti-submarine warfare might involve land and ship-based aircraft and helicopters, surface warships and submarines, and these could use the same weapons, for example homing torpedoes. In World War II, the Allied air forces seem to have underestimated the role they might have played in the anti-submarine campaigns, as pre-war air doctrine had been focused on the bombing of cities and battleships rather than on protection of sea lines of communication from the air. After World War II nuclear bombs were originally exclusively an air force weapon, but rapid development of nuclear-powered submarines and ballistic missiles, which could be fired from submarines hidden in the oceans, had by 1960 made it possible for navies to become a major part of the strategic deterrence forces. As a result of technical development, naval organizations are no longer primarily created for decisive battles at sea or with the competence to handle highly specialized naval weapons. Rather, they are organized around operational doctrines and competences connected with control of the sea for power projection or transportation of goods and with ships as cost-efficient weapon platforms with a wide range of offensive and defensive capabilities.

From the advent of the revolution in naval technology around 1850, advanced naval technology became concentrated in the industrially most-developed countries. Initially, Britain and France were the leaders, later joined by Germany, Austria, Italy, and the United States. Russia and later the Soviet Union manufactured ships and weapons of good quality but was, up to the mid twentieth century, frequently dependent on foreign supply of the most recent technology. Japan, on the other hand, rapidly changed from total dependence on foreign technology as late as 1905 to being an innovative manufacturer of warships, weapons and naval aircraft from the 1920s. Medium-sized and minor navies were normally dependent on foreign technology although a few, notably the Netherlands and Sweden, remained to a considerable extent able to procure their own ships and weapon systems.

Domestic supply of the most advanced and innovative technology has been important, and navies that actively search for and develop such technology may gain advantages in actual warfare. Not even the advanced naval powers have always been able to lead in everything. Britain was generally the leader in naval technology before 1914, but, during the 1880s, France may have gained a temporary lead in naval gunnery. World War I showed that the British navy had problems with the reliability of mines and armour-piercing shells. German capital ships had better underwater protection than British ships, while Britain gained a lead in steam turbines. The Russian navy proved inferior in gunnery in the war against Japan in 1904–5, but in World War I it was frequently very good in accurate long-range gunfire.

Naval doctrine and the use of naval power

Technical factors explain much of what happened during wars, but the doctrines on how men, weapons and warships are used in wartime may be at least as important. Navies may be used as concentrated battle forces, as dispersed sea control or sea denial forces, as the naval part of amphibious forces, or as coastal defence forces. A wide range of ships and weapons may be used for these varied types of warfare. However, specialization of warships for different purposes are often cost-efficient or even necessary. Ships and weaponry are long-term investments, however, and specialization requires a firm doctrine on the role of the navy. The doctrine must define the strategic purpose of the navy, the most probable operations it should expect to undertake in order to achieve that purpose, and the best tactics to use when these operations lead to encounters with enemy forces. If these operational parameters are successfully determined, warships and weapons may be designed to suit them. Many navies have been prepared for more than one type of operation at the same time, typically battle fleet actions and sea control (protection of trade), or sea denial (attacks against enemy trade) combined with coastal defence.

Battle fleets are formed to create mobile strategic positions in areas with important lines of communication or as assault forces against vital enemy interests. Major amphibious operations are normally supposed to be protected by a battle fleet. The very existence of a battle fleet with the ability to move to another area creates a threat that must be contained or eliminated even if the fleet stays in its base. Battle fleets were traditionally composed of well-protected warships armed with large guns; these were called ships of the line in the last century of sail and battleships after the introduction of steam and armour. The strategic role of these capital ships did not change fundamentally during the nineteenth century, but the technological revolution brought about a race between gunnery and armour that forced the size of battleships upwards. The size was also increased because battleships had to be protected against under-water weapons (rams, mines and torpedoes) and finally bombs from aircraft. Battle fleets used cruisers for reconnaissance, and the threat from torpedo boats and later submarines made it necessary to develop the destroyer as an escort vessel, a sign that battleships were no longer supreme at sea.

After World War I, even great powers could afford only a small number of the by now gigantic battleships. Their main task was to fight enemy armoured warships, and battleships remained important as long as they were the best means of destroying ships of their own kind. In theory, heavy guns with advanced fire-control systems could do that quickly at long range. However, battleships often had difficulties in gaining and maintaining contact with enemies who wished to avoid battle, especially as their movements were restricted by threats from destroyers, submarines, mines, and aircraft. Carrier-borne aircraft and light naval forces were supposed to attack enemy ships and reduce their speed in order to give the battleships opportunities to sink them. When submarines and aircraft became increasingly cost-efficient as destroyers of major warships, gun-armed battleships became uneconomical. Carriers could also attack enemies in their bases, thus eliminating an advantage for the inferior fleet.

The major navies had since the end of World War I developed aircraft carriers as a new capital ship. From 1942 carriers rather than battleships dominated battle-fleet strategy. Carriers could fulfil the role of capital ships because their aircraft had the range, speed and weapons to damage enemy forces in a wide area more effectively than gun- and torpedo-armed surface warships. They could also carry fighters and anti-submarine aircraft for the protection of the same area. Air-warning radar and improved fighter-direction systems made carrier-borne fighters into powerful defensive forces. Carriers with their surface escort ships could in day-time dominate the surface of the sea, the air and littoral areas, and even contain the threat from submarines. Radar-equipped gun- and torpedo-armed warships remained important for combat during night-time and bad weather, and for the bombardment of shores during amphibious operations. After World War II, the development of safer landing systems on carriers and all-weather aircraft with advanced radar have made carriers even more powerful, although such aircraft (and carriers) have also grown extremely expensive.

Up to World War I, sea control and sea denial forces comprised gun-armed cruisers (earlier called frigates, corvettes and sloops) and gunboats that could attack and protect merchantmen. Cruisers were gun-armed warships that were smaller and less heavily armed than battleships but usually faster and with a greater radius of action. From the 1880s they were at least lightly armoured. In peace-time, cruising warships often protected national and economic interests in distant waters, typically in areas where there were no sufficiently strong states that could control violence. Gunboat diplomacy became a common term for such operations. The role of sea-control and sea-denial forces changed little with the introduction of steam but the importance of convoys for trade protection was forgotten.

World War I showed that sea control in a modern war required a large number of vessels for anti-submarine warfare and minesweeping, while submarines rather than surface raiders became the main threat to trade. This experience was repeated during World War II to such an extent that escort ships with anti-submarine and anti-aircraft weapons became the main surface forces in most post-war navies. Both wars also showed that convoys were superior to other forms of trade protection. Since 1945 escort vessels together with submarines have fulfilled most of the old roles of the gun-armed cruiser. From the 1970s, escort ships were normally also armed with surface-to-surface missiles, which have given such ships a considerable potential against surface warships. Mine-countermeasure vessels, which originally were hired trawlers or vessels of a simple design, have become sophisticated warships. They are needed to contain the threat from mines, which have become increasingly 'intelligent' and lethal sea-denial weapons, easy to hide and difficult to detect.

Amphibious forces were present in early modern navies. Major sailing navies, especially the British, had developed efficient systems for power projection with warships or merchantmen serving as transports and oared vessels as assault landing craft. Oared warships were always inherently amphibious and well suited for littoral warfare, and in the eighteenth century the Baltic states had developed amphibious oared warfare to a high level of sophistication. These competences largely disappeared during the technological revolution in the mid nineteenth century. Amphibious operations were supposed to be possible to improvise, as indeed they were during some of the wars around 1900. The problem of how an assault landing against an enemy coast, defended by mines and well-entrenched infantry and artillery, should be carried out was not given much attention. The failure of the Allied forces at the Dardanelles in 1915 illustrated these problems. The solution came in World War II, when the British and the Americans developed specialized amphibious ships and landing craft and procedures for combined operations. Soldiers and weapons, even heavy tanks, could be speedily landed on beaches under the cover of gunfire from ships and land- or carrier-based aircraft. In the 1950s, the helicopter was introduced as a versatile component in amphibious warfare.

Coastal defence fleets were the product of the technological revolution that created new opportunities for the defender. Their task was to make it difficult or impossible for a superior fleet to invade, bombard or blockade the coast and ports of an inferior power. Even major powers like Russia and the United States had coastal defence navies in the late nineteenth century, and in France coastal defence was regarded as an alternative to a battle fleet. The British developed gunboats and small armoured ships for coastal warfare from the 1850s to the 1870s, but primarily with the aim of attacking enemy bases. Initially, coastal defence forces mainly consisted of relatively small armoured ships armed with a few heavy guns. Such ships, which could be built much more cheaply than battleships, were a serious threat against enemy cruisers and transport ships in an invading fleet and they could operate in shallower waters than battleships. Their existence might force an enemy continuously to expose his battleships close to an enemy coast in order to contain them. Gradually, mines, surface torpedo forces, submarines, and aircraft supplemented and replaced gun-armed coast defence ships, just as they replaced the battleships. In some states, the coastal artillery was integrated with the navy in order to provide a coherent coastal defence system. Late twentieth-century coastal defence fleets primarily used submarines, missile-armed vessels and mines.

Navies and warfare 1815–1905

Up to the mid nineteenth century warfare at sea had been fairly predictable and was based on technology shared by all naval powers. Strategic, operational and tactical doctrines never changed radically, but technical development tended to increase the operational freedom of the superior sea power. The theoretical possibility of projecting power and defending maritime interests world-wide with naval power that existed in 1500 had by 1815 become a reality that changed the world. Britain built a maritime empire and protected its mercantile marine and economic and political interests in European waters, the Atlantic, the Indian Ocean, and the China Seas with early modern technology. In the nineteenth century, Britain was the world's leading economy and the only power that might be called a world power. Naval power had been decisive in establishing this enviable position and it remained the key factor in its defence.

Britain's naval power was embodied in both battleships, built for the formation of battle fleets in strategically decisive areas, and in a large number of cruising warships, which exercised control of the global sea lines of communication. Powers that tried to challenge British mastery at sea up to the 1940s oscillated between attempts to create battle fleets and attempts to gain a lead by radically new weapons and weapon systems. Up to the early years of the twentieth century, France was the leading challenger to British naval power. Napoleon I had bequeathed a battle fleet. The restored Bourbon monarchy started a programme of building large cruisers (frigates), while the Orleans monarchy (1830–48) was interested in steam and shell guns as equalizers. Napoleon III continued these lines of development but he also expanded the battle fleet and introduced iron armour to naval warfare. These changes culminated in the introduction of armoured capital ships around 1860 and a shipbuilding race with Britain.

The post-1871 French navy was divided by a conflict between adherents to a battle fleet strategy and a 'New school' (*Jeune école*) that believed torpedo boats for coastal defence and modern, fast cruisers for attacks against enemy trade and coastal cities were better weapon systems to use against the traditional enemy. By 1900, battleships had again established their supremacy in French naval doctrine. The peace-time use of the post-1815 French fleet was similar to the British, with cruisers and squadrons of battleships deployed to various parts of the world to protect and promote French commercial and political interests. The French navy was very important in the creation of a new French empire in Africa, Asia and the Pacific, and it was adequate for its protection against all other European powers except Britain.

Another challenger to British post-1815 supremacy was Russia. This challenge was primarily continental as Russia wished to move its positions to the south from the Balkans to Korea, but British responses were based on the possibilities offered by sea power. Russian positions in the Baltic and the Black Sea were vulnerable to attacks from the sea. Russia initially continued its traditional battle fleet policy, which however was a failure when Britain and France united their forces in 1854–6 and supported the Ottoman Empire against Russia. Russia then tried new technology and built coastal defence armoured ships and cruisers for trade warfare, developed mines and introduced torpedoes. From the 1880s, a new Russian battle fleet was created. It was increasingly used for an expansionistic policy in Eastern Asia. This policy and the battle fleet met its fate in the Russo–Japanese War of 1904–5.

The United States was also a potential enemy of Britain: the two powers had fought a war as late as 1812–15. For the United States, operations with large frigates were one of the few successes of that war. Such frigates remained important, but post-war American naval policy also emphasized the importance of battleships as blockade breakers. Most nineteenth-century American naval activities were however rather similar to the British and French use of naval power to promote trade and political influence in those parts of the world that increasingly became regarded as less-developed and in need of better relations with the modern world. The 'opening' of Japan by American naval expeditions in 1853–4 is the best-known example of that policy.

The American Civil War (1861–5) took place during the naval technological revolution and that determined much of the naval side of this conflict. The South used steam- and sail-powered cruisers for trade warfare and showed the great potential of even a few such ships against a large mercantile marine. In home waters, the South used primitive armoured ships for coast defence together with early underwater weapons: mines, spar-torpedoes and semi-submerged boats. The North responded with blockades enforced by steam cruisers, attacks on fortifications and armoured ships by turret ironclads (monitors), and offensive operations along the great rivers with armoured and unarmoured shallow-draught ships. The post-1865 American naval policy was moulded by the experience that the South with small resources had been able to resist a much superior fleet for an extended period. Up to the 1890s, the United States Navy consisted of coastal defence armoured ships and cruisers for trade warfare, with the potential to fight the British as the South had fought the North.

The technological revolution from 1850 to 1870 radically transformed several navies and also saw the birth of some new navies. Traditional battle fleets such as those of the Netherlands, Denmark and Sweden were transformed into coastal defence forces with small armoured ships, gunboats and a growing interest in underwater weapons (mines, later torpedo craft). This did not primarily reflect diminished ambitions. It was rather an attempt to use the new technology for purposes that were tailor-made for the defensive strategies these countries already had adopted. Austria-Hungary and Prussia (from 1871 Imperial Germany), on the other hand, created battle fleets almost without a naval tradition and rapidly developed professionalism connected to modern technology. Italy (unified in 1860), Spain and the Ottoman Empire transformed their navies into steam-powered armoured battle fleets but only Italy remained as a battle fleet power by the late nineteenth century. From the 1860s, China and Japan began to build warships with modern technology.

Except for the American Civil War, wars in this period were rather short. The Crimean War, which for the navies was a major war both in the Baltic Sea and the Black Sea, saw a naval battle between the Russians and the Turks at Sinope in 1853, a large-scale amphibious operation against Crimea in 1854, and several naval bombardments of coastal fortifications. Shell guns, steam power and armour were tested and found to be efficient. The brief war of Prussia and Italy against Austria in 1866 led to the naval battle of Lissa, where the inferior Austrian fleet defeated the Italians with an attack in three wedge-formed lines of ships against a conventional single battle-line. This was the only major fleet action for several decades and its tactical lessons were much discussed. In particular, the use of the ram, an ancient weapon revived with the armoured steam battleships, was fascinating for many sea officers, who saw it as a weapon that favoured skilled ship-handlers.

In the next major naval war, between China and Japan in 1894–5, the inferior Japanese fleet inflicted a defeat on the Chinese at the battle of Yalu in 1894. This time the victorious fleet had fought in the traditional line-ahead formation while the defeated fleet had tried to form a wedge-formed line-abreast. Superior speed and better training was decisive but the line-ahead formation was from now on regarded as the tactical formation that made it possible to combine much gunfire with simplicity and flexibility, at least if the line was not too long. At Yalu, the Japanese divided their battle-line into fast and slow divisions that acted independently, a tactical idea that reappeared in various forms as long as guns were the main weapon at sea. In 1898, the US and Spain fought a brief but decisive war, where the naval battles of Manila and Santiago were victories for the much larger American fleet. Finally, the war between Japan and Russia in 1904–5 saw an amphibious expedition to Korea, a blockade of the Russian naval base at Port Arthur, and two encounters between battle fleets formed in battle lines. Both were Japanese victories and the battle of Tsushima in 1905 was an annihilation, dominated by a decisive long-range gun duel during the day, followed by some successful Japanese night attacks with torpedo craft against major Russian warships. The heavy guns seemed to be the dominant weapon in warfare at sea and if they were used at long range the effects of torpedoes could be minimized. These lessons were incorporated in the new large 'all-big-gun' battleships, called dreadnoughts after their British prototype, which was completed in 1906.

Navies and warfare 1906–45

Around 1900, navies were generally regarded as very important. Navalism, the idea that naval power based on a great high-technology battle fleet was the way to national greatness, was a political force of importance in an epoch when nationalism and protectionism had considerable popular support. Most states with battle fleets had also acquired colonial empires that were dependent on sea lines of communication. Important foreign markets like China were penetrated with the support of naval power. To nationalists and geostrategists, naval power meant world power through control of communication between continents or at least command of the sea in regions of national importance. Britain and Germany, the established world power and the rising political and industrial giant on the European continent, became involved in a naval armaments race that dominated the political relations between these two countries. It also determined much of the political realignment in Europe before 1914. Broad groups in both countries sincerely believed that the number of dreadnoughts in their navies was a question of national survival.

The three wars from 1894 to 1905, especially the Russo–Japanese War, confirmed the increasingly stable and homogeneous shipbuilding programmes that had emerged by the 1890s with battleships, large, medium and small cruisers, and flotillas of torpedo craft formed into 'balanced' fleets. Such fleets were able to act as battle fleet, as sea-control and sea-denial forces, or as powerful coastal defence forces, depending on the relative strength and strategic aims of the contending powers. Britain, France, Germany, Italy, Russia, the United States, Japan, and Austria systematically developed such fleets with increasingly large battleships as the most expensive component. The growing consensus on naval doctrines interacted with the rise of navalism, as the quantitative strength of the navies became easy to compare and demands for increased naval funds could be supported with reference to well-defined threats from potential enemies and supposed combinations of enemies. For most officers, policy-makers and naval enthusiasts, naval power was equated with battleships and the number of heavy guns they carried.

By 1914 most navies had developed rather similar ideas about strategies. Wars were supposed to be short and at sea they should be decided by battles between concentrated battle fleets. Offensive operations were preferred to defence and convoys for merchantmen were regarded as impractical. Trade warfare was not supposed to be important except as a form of economic pressure, amphibious warfare was supposed to be possible to improvise and coastal warfare was important only for much inferior navies. These were the lessons of the four latest naval wars and the battles of Lissa, Yalu, Santiago, and Tsushima. However, much of the theory behind the navalism around 1900 was based on supposed lessons from the great maritime wars fought with sailing fleets up to 1815. The American sea officer Alfred Th. Mahan was not the only, though the most important, strategic thinker and ideologist behind such ideas. He was a careful and analytically sophisticated naval historian, but much of what he wrote was determined by his ambition to convince his compatriots of the importance of a battle fleet in opposition to the traditional American naval doctrine of attack against trade and coastal defence. Mahan's emphasis on the importance of the destruction of the enemy battle fleet was logical in theory, but as a strategic lesson it worked both ways. Policy-makers became even more convinced that their battle fleets must be carefully preserved.

World War I turned out to be a long war of attrition. The superior British, French and Italian battle fleets did not attack or blockade their German and Austrian adversaries within the North Sea and the Adriatic, as that might expose them to mines, submarines and night attacks by surface torpedo forces. The latter avoided exposing themselves far from harbour as the enemy was clearly superior in a battle with heavy guns. The Russian Baltic fleet was in a similar position in the Gulf of Finland, but there it was at least useful as a shield for the Russian capital, Petrograd. The German fleet controlled the Baltic Sea, but was as unwilling as the German army to use this for a combined operation in the rear of the Russian army. At the same time, the inactivity of the battle fleets was depressing. Most fleet commanders attempted to bait some ingenious trap for the enemy that might lure his battle fleet to fight, but only under conditions that made victory certain for the side that planned the deceptive operation. Typically, they planned a bombardment raid against an enemy coast or a feinted landing operation in order to provoke the enemy to do something ill-considered. Practically all such plans were void of substantial operational meaning. The only goal was to bring about a decisive fight between battle fleets.

Naval wars fought up to 1815 had indeed something to teach policymakers and admirals of World War I. They had been long wars, combat between battle fleets had seldom been decisive and trade protection through a well-organized convoy system had been economical for the superior naval power, while amphibious operations were successful only when carefully prepared. Battle fleets had often acted as defensive instruments for creating operational freedom for the armies and for the free passage of convoys or, conversely, for reducing the operational freedom of the enemy and his ability to use sea lines of communication. Sometimes this had led to battle fleet contests but inferior battle fleets normally – for obvious reasons – avoided fighting decisive battles. Such battles usually occurred when impatient, desperate or ignorant political decision-makers urged their admirals to 'do something'. This was also the origin of at least three of the 'decisive' naval battles in the four major naval wars between 1866 and 1905. The battle of Yalu in 1894 was the result of the strategically motivated transport of an army from China to northern Korea ordered by the Chinese government, while the operations that led to Lissa, Santiago and Tsushima are difficult to describe as anything other than political demonstrations from the sides that lost the battles.

The conditions of these wars did not repeat themselves in the war of 1914–18. The only battle fleet contest took place in the North Sea on 31 May 1916, when the German High Sea Fleet had set a trap for the British, which almost closed around the Germans themselves when the British Grand Fleet came out in full strength. Just as in the pre-1815 wars, battle fleets were primarily of defensive value. The two Central Powers defended their coasts and the Baltic Sea and the British and French their control of the oceans by distant blockades by battle fleets, strategies which undoubtedly reduced the operational freedom of the adversary's fleet. The same lack of success for offensive warfare dominated the Western Front during almost the whole war. Defence was the strong form of war in the early twentieth century, a fact that political leaders and commanders who strongly believed in offensives found difficult to accept.

When the war lasted much longer than expected, the sea lines of communication became increasingly important to economies dominated by the war efforts. German submarine attacks against vital Allied trade routes turned out to be cost-effective and possibly even a war-winning strategy until a reluctant British navy in the Spring of 1917 re-introduced convoys which worked well. Large-scale amphibious warfare was improvised once, by the Allies in the Dardanelles in 1915, and turned out to be disastrous. Coastal warfare, such as minelaying, minesweeping and bombardment of enemy positions on land, turned out to be important but unspectacular routine operations. Large mine barrages were set up by the Allies in the Channel, the North Sea and the mouth of the Adriatic, in an attempt to blockade submarines. In addition to the existing fleets, navies had to mass-produce submarines, anti-submarine escorts, mines, and minesweepers for unexpected forms of warfare. Gradually, the active war efforts were concentrated on the sea lines of communication. In early 1918, the British decided that the primary task of the Grand Fleet was to maintain a blockade of the German battle fleet, rather than to take risks in pursuing the possibility of defeating it. Other battle fleets saw their combat readiness decline when younger officers and skilled seamen were sent to the growing light forces in order to fight the 'real' war: submarine and mine warfare.

The two decades between the World Wars saw little radical change in naval technology and doctrine. One factor behind this was that the potential threat to established doctrines, air power, for a long time remained mainly potential. Up to the mid-1930s air forces were small and aircraft technology still rather primitive. High-level bombers, the main contenders for air supremacy, were – correctly – not seen as a major threat to warships, while torpedo-planes, a serious threat, were not favoured by air forces. The high-performance dive bombers and fighters that turned out to be very effective in the early years of World War II appeared so suddenly that navies had little time to react. When naval shipbuilding started on a large scale in several navies in the mid-1930s, very large and fast battleships and numerous cruisers still dominated the great powers' navies. Aircraft carriers were primarily built by Britain, the United States and Japan, but they were still regarded as supplements to the battle fleets. Submarines and aircraft carriers had been added to the late nineteenth-century 'balanced fleet' doctrine without fundamentally changing the belief in the supremacy of the gun, upon which that doctrine was founded.

The obsession with the decisive battle, however, had diminished in European navies. In the Mediterranean, France and Italy developed navies with many submarines, high-speed destroyers and cruisers. This reflected a doctrine based on World War I experience, whereby light forces were supposed to fight active and offensive wars, with battleships as a last resort that should be used cautiously. In the Pacific, the Japanese and to a considerable extent the Americans were still planning for a single battle fleet encounter that could decide the war. These two powers, especially the Japanese, had not experienced the frustrations of World War I as the Europeans had; had a naval war broken out in the Pacific, concentrated fleets were more likely to meet. From the 1920s, Britain prepared for a war against Japan in the China Seas and the Pacific, in which cruisers would attack Japanese trade and submarines would fight a war of attrition until the British battle fleet from Europe arrived at the new base at Singapore.

Such British ambitions to continue as a world naval power were realistic as long as other European navies remained at the level to which they had declined after 1918. Germany had been forced to disarm, the Russian navy had collapsed after the Revolution, Austria-Hungary had disappeared, and Italy and France seemed to balance each other. When from the mid-1930s Italy, Germany and the Soviet Union began to recreate big battle fleets and Italy showed imperialistic ambitions in Africa and the Mediterranean, the British faced a situation where they might have to choose whether they would take a firm stand in Europe or in Asia, where they had a huge empire. In practice, the British became engaged with the most impatient aggressor. In 1939, Adolf Hitler first decided to build a large 'world power' battle fleet that should be ready to fight the British by 1944, then started a war the German navy had to fight with available resources. These were small but modern.

World War II developed into a strategic situation in which the British navy, for a time helped by the French, had to fight Germany and Italy in a struggle around the coasts of Europe in order to contain the victorious Axis armies, and frequently also to evacuate Allied armies. This type of operation went on from Norway to the Eastern Mediterranean from 1940 to 1942. It was also a war between Axis air forces and the British navy. Both sides showed greater willingness to take risks with their major surface forces than in World War I. Surface operations were no longer feints to bring the enemy into traps but real operations, aiming at gaining control of a territory or an essential sea route. Germany invaded Norway to gain bases and sent out battleships and heavy cruisers on raids into the Atlantic. In the Mediterranean, the British navy fought the Italian navy and Axis air forces for control of the sea and logistical support of the armies. Convoys to Russia and Malta became major fleet operations. From the autumn of 1942, the British and American navies were part of the Allied counter-offensive and landed army forces in North Africa (1942), Italy (1943) and France (1944) with the help of new mass-produced amphibious fleets.

When Japan launched her great offensive towards South East Asia in late 1941, Allied naval power was overwhelmed by the size and ruthless efficiency of the Japanese navy. The United States was able to stem Japanese offensives in mid 1942 and start a counter-offensive. During 1943 a great fleet of new American aircraft carriers was commissioned and, with that fleet, a rapid offensive was launched during 1944. In this ocean, concentrated battle fleets met in decisive battles, but these were mainly fought with carrier-borne aircraft.

Strategically, World War II became a global war in which the Allies had superiority in men, raw material and industrial production. However, these resources were spread around the world and had to be transported across the sea if they were to be concentrated for decisive action. The Axis powers had to occupy quickly as much territory as possible in order to gain resources and deny the Allies the freedom to use the oceans. The Germans, helped in the Mediterranean by the Italians, understood the general character of the problem from their experience in World War I. In the Atlantic, a large struggle along the sea lines went on from the first day of the war to the last, with convoy battles and mass production of submarines, escort ships and merchantmen as the main elements of the conflict. The Japanese, who had initiated the Pacific war to gain resources, especially oil, were remarkably uninterested both in attacking the long American supply lines and in protecting their own lines of supply of essential resources from the conquered territories. This appears to be a legacy of their experience from earlier wars, in which long-distance transportation had been unimportant. The Allies gained command of the oceans during 1943 when the German submarine threat in the Atlantic was mastered, the Mediterranean brought under Allied control, and the American submarine war against Japan began rapidly to erode Japanese transport capacity.

World War II at sea was a high-technology war in which timing was all-important. This war was fought in laboratories and industries by scientists and engineers. The advanced British aircraft carriers had to wait for American aircraft for their potential to be fully exploited. Britain and the United States were unable to develop efficient automatic anti-aircraft guns between the wars and the British navy was also deficient in anti-aircraft fire control until helped by the Americans, who also developed the very important proximity fuse for anti-aircraft ammunition. The British suffered much more than the Americans from these deficiencies, as they had to fight a desperate war around the coasts of Europe for years until they got high-performance fighters on their carriers and effective anti-aircraft weapons on all warships. The British and Americans, on the other hand, had a lead in radar technology, especially compared to Italy and Japan, which proved important in surface night-fighting, anti-submarine warfare and air defence.

The United States Navy and American industry had developed reliable high-pressure steam propulsion systems with low oil consumption in the 1930s, which gave American warships an advantage in range in the Pacific War. The German navy attempted to develop both advanced steam turbines and diesels for surface warships, but had reliability problems with both. The nominally backward British marine turbines seem to have been fairly reliable. The Japanese went to war in 1941 with combat-ready torpedoes with very long range, while for more than a year after the outbreak of the Pacific War the United States Navy had major problems with its new and advanced submarine torpedoes. In the Atlantic, German submarine technology initially had success with World War I-style submarines, which used new group tactics (wolf packs) and were helped by long-range reconnaissance aircraft. The submarines were temporarily defeated by Allied aircraft, new types of radars and new anti-submarine weapons in 1943 and only partially saved by the innovative (Dutch) snorkel. New German submarines with high submerged speed that might have defeated these technologies were designed and in production, but they began to enter service only in the last months of the war.

Naval power after 1945: the oceans as arsenals

There has been no major naval war since 1945 but there have been intense preparations to fight such wars. Until about 1990, the Cold War was a long arms race during which the Soviet Union, the United States and the NATO coalition attempted to gain advantages by both quantitative increases in their strength and by technological break-throughs. In the North Atlantic and European hemisphere, where the main contest would have been fought, the navies prepared for a modernized version of World War II. Control of the sea lines across the Atlantic was absolutely essential for the survival of NATO, and consequently these lines were a primary target for the Soviet navy. The Soviet Union built the largest submarine fleet the world had ever seen to fight a war of sea denial and created a large base system in the Arctic to give the navy free access to the Atlantic. This was met by major NATO efforts to build anti-submarine forces.

Western battle fleets, centred on aircraft carriers, were supposed to make major efforts on the flanks of the central European front: in the North Atlantic/Norwegian Sea and the Mediterranean, possibly also against Soviet and Chinese forces in the Far East. The importance and aim of such operations was disputed and, by 1970, United States naval strategy no longer regarded such operations as realistic. Instead, all resources were concentrated on protection of the Atlantic bridge. A radical break with this thinking came with the Reagan administration, which in 1981 introduced the 'Maritime Strategy', actually a new battle fleet doctrine. According to this, the United States Navy should concentrate as much carrier air power as possible in an attack against the Soviet bases in the Arctic. Massive Soviet counter-attacks using aircraft armed with long-range missiles, submarines and surface forces were expected and indeed invited by this American strategy. The idea was to fight a battle in which these offensive Soviet forces would be defeated by superior technology, thus decisively weakening Soviet ability to fight an offensive war.

The idea that a battle fleet should fight a decisive battle with an air force was not entirely new, as repeated air–sea battles had occurred during World War II. It did however highlight a development that had been very important for the major navies after 1945. They have increasingly been using the oceans as arsenals for weapons and combat-ready forces that in themselves are not strictly naval. By the end of the twentieth century, the major nuclear powers had submarines armed with ballistic missiles with nuclear warheads as their ultimate strategic weapons. Such submarines, the most lethal warships ever built, are not expected to take part in naval battles. In addition, tactical weapons carried on ships can reach far into land and influence warfare and political events in most parts of the world. Aircraft carriers are the most powerful carriers of weapon systems that can attack and protect objects on land, but increasingly, cruise missiles have become important weapons for strikes against static targets on land. Such missiles can easily be carried by all surface warships and submarines as well as by aircraft, although they require satellites, air reconnaissance or observers on land to acquire target information. Military forces permanently based on amphibious ships can be sent ashore quickly and be supported in their combat missions by guns and missiles on ships, as well as by aircraft and helicopters from ships. On the other hand, weapons and weapon carriers –

aircraft, missiles and small warships – based on land can reach far out to sea and destroy or damage even the largest ships.

By the end of the twentieth century, only the United States could afford to have a fleet of large carriers with advanced aircraft. Britain reduced its ambitions to small sea-control carriers in the 1970s, France has built carriers with only limited abilities and the Soviet attempt to create a carrier fleet in the 1970s and 1980s overstrained the capabilities of that power. Carrier-based aircraft were important in the Korean War (1950–3), in the two Vietnam Wars (French carriers up to 1954, United States carriers 1964–72), in the Anglo–French intervention in Egypt in 1956, in the Falklands War in 1982, and in the Desert Storm campaign against Iraq in 1991. Their main role was to attack enemy positions on land and support military operations; they only rarely attacked ships. In international politics since 1945, the presence of a carrier force in a sensitive area has been a visible demonstration of power and the determination to use it. Aircraft carriers are however not supreme or invulnerable. Modern high-speed submarines, especially with nuclear power, are so powerful and invulnerable that they may dominate the surface of the sea in a future naval war. They are, however, unable to control the air above the sea. After World War II the old dominating role of the battleship in a concentrated battle fleet has been divided between the aircraft carrier, its aircraft and escort ships, and the submarine. Warfare at sea has become three-dimensional, as it is fought above, on and under the surface of the sea.

The leading naval power since World War II has been the United States, which by geography is a continental rather than a maritime power. Britain, the dominating naval power from the eighteenth century to the 1940s, was an island power, dependent on the navy for territorial defence and vital trade. It turned this into an advantage by developing a superior navy that effectively ruled the seas around the globe. Since the late eighteenth century the US has had need for a naval anti-invasion force against British, German and Japanese naval power, but it has not been dependent on maritime trade or imported resources for its survival. The role and size of the United States Navy have not been uncontroversial, and the historical and cultural heritage from Britain and its naval and maritime tradition should not be underestimated in explanations of why the United States rather willingly created a great navy. This navy has developed sea power as a means to exercise global power and contain crises in the interest of a still rather young nation, which has oscillated between isolationism and an intense willingness to take part in global power politics across the oceans.

The great contrast to the United States and to Euro-American thinking about the role of navies is provided by China. Europe and America stand for the tradition that the sea is something to be used for defensive and offensive actions, as well as trade on a global scale. China, with potentially enormous resources as a world power, has consistently followed a tradition in which the ambitions of the state at sea is limited to coastal defence. If that changes with growing

Chinese economic strength, the twenty-first century may experience dramatic events at sea.

Further reading

This is a selective list of recent works in English, but with a certain emphasis on other navies than the well-known Royal Navy of Britain and the United States Navy.

Historiography with bibliographies

J.B. Hattendorf (ed.), *Ubi sumus? The State of Naval and Maritime History*, Newport: NWCP 1994.

General

G. Modelski and W.R. Thompson, *Seapower in Global Politics, 1494–1993*, Seattle: University of Washington Press, 1988; J. Glete, *Navies and Nations*, 2 vols, Stockholm: AWI, 1993; M.S. Lindberg, *Geographical Impact on Coastal Navies*, London: Macmillan. 1998; G. Rystad *et al.* (eds), *In Quest of Trade and Security: The Baltic in Power Politics, 1500–1990*, 2 vols, Lund: Lund UP, 1994–5; R.L. Scheina, *Latin America: A Naval History, 1810–1987*, Annapolis: USNIP, 1987.

Warfare at sea

C.G. Reynolds, *Command of the Sea*, Malabar: Krieger, 1983; L. Sondhaus, *Naval Warfare, 1815–1914*, London: Routledge, 2001; A.D. Lambert, *The Crimean War*, Manchester: Manchester UP, 1990; P.G. Halpern, *A Naval History of World War I*, London: UCL Press, 1994; J. Terraine, *Business in Great Waters: The U-boat War 1914–1945*, London: Leo Cooper, 1989.

Warships and technology

Conway's All the World's Fighting Ships, 1860–1995, 4 vols, London: Conway, 1979–95; R. Gardiner (ed.), *Conway's History of the Ship* (several volumes), London: Conway, 1992–93; N. Friedman, *Seapower and Space*, London: Chatham, 2000.

Navies

Great Britain

J.R. Hill (ed.), *The Oxford Illustrated History of the Royal Navy*, Oxford: Oxford UP, 1995; D.K. Brown has published three volumes about British warship design and development 1860–1945, London: Chatham 1997–2000.

United States

K.J. Hagan (ed.), *In Peace and War*, Westport: Greenwood, 1984; K.J. Hagan, *This People's Navy*, New York: Free Press, 1991; W.N. Still, Jr. (ed.), *The Confederate Navy*, London: Conway, 1997; Modern studies of US warships have been written by D.L. Canney and N. Friedman.

France

M. Battesti, *La marine de Napoléon III*, 2 vols, Vincennes: Service Historique de la marine, 1997; T. Ropp, *The Development of a Modern Navy: French Naval Policy, 1871–1904* (ed. by S.S. Roberts), Annapolis: USNIP, 1987; R. Walser, *France's Search for a Battle Fleet: Naval Policy and Naval Power, 1898–1914*, New York: Garland, 1992; P. Masson, *La marine française et la guerre 1939–1945*, Paris: Tallandier, 1991.

Germany

I.N. Lambi, *The Navy and German Power, 1862–1914*, Boston: Allen & Unwin 1984; C.-A. Gemzell, *Organization, Conflict and Innovation: A Study of German Naval Strategic Planning, 1888–1940*, Lund: Esselte, 1973; G. E. Weir, *Building the Kaiser's Navy: The Imperial Naval Office and German Industry in the von Tirpitz Era, 1890–1919*, Annapolis: USNIP, 1992; J. Dülffer, *Weimar, Hitler und die Marine: Reichspolitik und Flottenbau 1920 bis 1939*, Düsseldorf: Droste, 1973.

Austria

L. Sondhaus, *The Habsburg Empire and the Sea* and *The Naval Policy of Austria-Hungary*, West Lafayette: Purdue UP, 1989 and 1994.

Italy

R. Mallett, *The Italian Navy and Fascist Expansionism, 1935–1940*, London: Frank Cass, 2000; J.J. Sadkovich, *The Italian Navy in World War II*, Westport: Greenwood, 1994.

Russia/Soviet Union

J.C. Daly, *Russian Seapower and the 'Eastern Question', 1827–41*, London: Macmillan, 1991; R.W. Herrick, *Soviet Naval Theory and Policy*, Newport: NWCP, 1988; B. Ranft and G. Till, *The Sea in Soviet Strategy*, London: Macmillan, 1989.

Japan

D.C. Evans and M.R. Peattie, *Kaigun: Strategy, Tactics and Technology in the Imperial Japanese Navy, 1887–1941*, Annapolis: USNIP, 1997.

China

B. Swanson, *Eighth Voyage of the Dragon: A History of China's Quest for Seapower*, Annapolis: USNIP 1982.

Sweden

A. Berge, 'The Swedish navy in the inter-war period: Strategic thinking at the cross-roads', *Militärhistorisk Tidskrift*, 1983; J. Glete, 'Coastal defence and technological change', G. Rystad (ed.), *The Swedish Armed Forces and Foreign Influences, 1870–1945*, Militärhistoriska förlaget, Stockholm, 1992.

10

AIR POWER AND THE MODERN WORLD

John Buckley

> As the twentieth century draws to a close, air power dominates
> warfare. Those who have air power overwhelm those who don't;
> those who don't have it spend their energies trying to get it,
> thwart it or escape it.
>
> Colonel John Warden, USAF[1]

There can be little doubt that air power has been the most important
innovation in warfare during the modern era. Only nuclear weaponry can be
said to have had anything like the same impact on the nature of war, but
ultimately even this force requires three-dimensional projection to be effective.
The aeroplane has shaped, revolutionized and driven warfare in wholly new
directions, and at the turn of the millennium, its arch-proponents were making
increasingly optimistic claims for the capability of air power, both actual
and potential. Indeed, it has been a relatively short, though painful, journey
from the first faltering leaps into the air by the Wright brothers in 1903,
through the devastation of cities in World War Two, to the apparent domination
of conflict by air power in the years since the collapse of the Soviet
Union.

Moreover, the aircraft has radically altered the relationship between society
and war, demanding ever-increasing investment of productive and technological resources, while simultaneously and dramatically increasing the divide
between states with significant air power capability and those without. Few
powers could ever hope to compete in the air with the major players of the
Western world, and the gap between the military capability of the industrialized
and non-industrialized world has been increased markedly and decisively by
the advent of air power. But a divide has also developed in the capabilities of
industrial military powers, a divide most obviously exposed by the requirements
of maintaining first-rate air power status. In the age of total war (*c.* 1914–45) the
nations able to compete meaningfully in the conduct of air war against all likely
opposition could be measured at considerably less than ten. By the height of the

Cold War it was reduced to two, and by the end of the twentieth century only the United States could be regarded as a first-rate air power.

However, although military operations are now considered air power dependent to the extent that intervention or force projection is dictated by the degree of air assets that can be mustered and applied, the status of air power is still a matter of debate in early twenty-first century armed forces and governments. There can be no doubt that conventional or traditional war is now dictated by the application of air power, and that aircraft carry massive destructive potential. But concomitant with this success have come serious developments. By the end of the century only one power, the United States, commands true aerial global reach, and as such is viewed with some reserve by a wider world not entirely at ease with the foreign policy employed by the American government. States and, perhaps more importantly, mass movements, political, economic or religious, appreciate the military potential of the United States, particularly the immediacy of its global air assets, and have sought to adapt accordingly. The events of 11 September 2001 indicated all too vividly the lengths to which anti-American groups would go in order to evade the conventional military strength of the most predominant military superpower of modern times. It has yet to be seen whether the response of the United States and its allies has been effective or appropriate in countering these measures. The multiplicity and diversity of threats and natures of opposition, often non-conventional, presents a direct challenge to the force structure, based on technological superiority and global aerial reach, held by the West and most obviously by the United States.

Air power supremacy has also precipitated a further problem for the West, one of casualty squeamishness. The degree to which the West now depends on technological supremacy and the ability of air power to project force with minimal and hopefully eventually zero casualties, has created a change, perhaps a weakness, in the West's understanding of war. Tainted by the mass destruction and bloodletting of two world wars, Western governments believe that their populations will support military intervention only if it is both rapidly decisive and cheap in human life, friendly casualties in particular. The concept of clean and quick war, such as the Gulf War of 1991, is now an illusion deployed by Western governments to garner support for military intervention, and it is an illusion founded on the effectiveness of air power. Notably, over 90 per cent of the ordnance dropped in the Gulf War was 'dumb', not 'smart' weaponry, but the media impact of guided armaments delivering low-casualty military successes sparked great political interest in the benefits of such technology.[2] The increasing use of smart weapons delivered from aerial platforms in the last decade of the century has been utilized effectively in a political sense to boost support for Western military activity as, because of air power, it is perceived to be both more humane and effective. Reared on a diet of low-casualty conflict and airborne strike capability, which generally eschews commitment of ground forces, it remains to be seen what might happen should neither of these cases pertain to a future conflict. Both are dependent on an enemy vulnerable to air power and on a scenario that presupposes technological supremacy.

The realization of air power

Indeed, the history of air power has been one of disappointment in the realization of the claims of its proponents and prophets. Despite the images painted by the earliest speculative air power literature, the actual capabilities of the aeroplane in war have lagged some way behind realistic strategic effectiveness, and too often the mismatch between vision and reality has resulted in frustration and perceived failure. The first views on air power were rooted in predictive fiction of the late nineteenth and early twentieth centuries, from the period before powered controlled flight was an actuality.[3] Writers such as Jules Verne and more importantly H.G. Wells, described a future in which aircraft dominated the world, in the case of Wells' famous *The War in the Air* (1908), to such an extent they provided the means by which civilization was destroyed. Prior to the First World War, growth in air-mindedness can be detected, a phenomenon whereby excitement over the arrival of true aeroplanes in Europe caused a rapid surge in interest in the strategic and military applications of aircraft. In Britain, for example, Lord Northcliffe, the newspaper tycoon, declared that because of the aeroplane Britain was 'no longer an island' and pressed for increasing expenditure on air forces.[4] Such media interest helped push the British government into increasing its air power budget by a factor of 55 in just four years leading up to the Great War.[5] Across the industrialized world air leagues and development programmes flourished, but it was in the theoretical and independent application of air forces that most interest burgeoned.

Even as the Great War was beginning, plans were in place to use air forces in a strategic sense, to by-pass ground and naval units and attack enemy states direct. The Holy Grail of air power, to force an enemy nation to capitulate by aerial attack alone, dates back as early as this. Indeed, although such aspirations were never realistic in the Great War, lessons were drawn and inferences taken that in the future, air power would be able to deliver savage knockout blows to an enemy, attacks against which there could be no defence and which would be so devastating that long, attritional conflict would be a feature of the past. During the interwar era, air forces began examining the practicalities of massed aerial bombardment, though few in government were converts to this new and apparently savage method of waging war.[6] The most famous advocate of direct air attack on an enemy's cities and population was Giulio Douhet, an Italian writer of the 1920s.[7] He argued that there was no realistic defence against air attack, and that by delivering highly destructive rapid knockout blows to an enemy, a war could be won in a very short space of time. Moreover, he claimed that the more brutal and stunning the initial attacks were, the more likely would be the enemy's rapid defeat, with a consequent reduction in the long-term damage caused by indecisive and attritional ground wars. To this end he openly advocated the deployment of poison gas. Too often labelled as an amoral and bloodthirsty warmonger, Douhet believed that his vision of war, dictated by air power, would actually be cheaper in human and material costs.[8] However, the great problem for the advocates of Douhet's concept in the years that followed was putting his ideas into practice.

Although it was a tempting idea to end wars quickly and decisively rather than suffer the agony of another conflict such as the Great War, it proved an inordinately more difficult proposition to transform theory into practice. The vision often blinded airmen to the harsh realities, and they allowed themselves to found doctrine on faith rather than hard evidence. The airship and heavy bomber raids conducted against Britain in the Great War were interpreted as proof that civilian morale could not withstand heavy aerial bombardment, when this was clearly far from being evident. Moreover, political and service pressures also distorted findings, and Allied bombing of German towns in 1918 caused such pitiful amounts of physical damage that post-war investigators, seeking to justify the bombing campaign, spuriously emphasized the damage inflicted on German morale instead.[9] In the interwar years, the British bombing advocates delved little into the practicalities of targeting, bomb aiming and navigation, and failed to react to the emergence of radar and high-speed interceptor aircraft, both pioneered by the RAF.[10] Similarly, the USAAC (United States Army Air Corps) shaped its doctrine without regard to the latest developments, relying on the concept of the self-defending bomber group to ward off enemy fighters.[11] One might argue that at the very least the American doctrine for strategic bombardment had some credibility and deserved to be disproved by war, but it took until late 1943 for the USAAF to come to terms with the problems underlying their bombing strategy. In both cases, the Allies overestimated the impact of, and underestimated the difficulties inherent in, mounting their strategic bombing campaigns, certainly until the final year of the war. Moreover, the *matériel* and human investment in making the campaign work was enormous and only sustainable because of the overwhelming advantage in resources enjoyed by the Allies. Greater faith in the realistic thinking of other air-power planners and strategists of the interwar period may seem to be due, as they seemed to see through the chimera of the airborne knockout blow. However, Soviet, French and German air forces all devoted time and effort to strategic bombing to greater and lesser degrees, and were lured away from such thinking only by more immediate pressures, technological shortcomings and economic deficiencies.[12]

Nevertheless, the Allies persevered and ultimately realized part of the potential of strategic bombing in World War Two. The air campaigns against Germany and Japan should be measured as failures only by the standards set by the arch advocates of air power, such as Alexander De Seversky, the RAF's Arthur 'Bomber' Harris or the USAAF's Carl Spaatz. In terms of Allied victory in the war, bombing contributed enormously, though not necessarily in the manner imagined or planned. Clearly air power alone did not bring about the defeat of the Axis powers, but it had significant effects on the ability of Germany in particular and, to a lesser degree, Japan to wage war.[13] That it took until 1944 for the campaigns to bite, and that it is difficult to disaggregate the impact of bombing from the effects of the other armed services on the Axis nations, should not distract us from the importance of strategic bombing in hindering production, absorbing resources and crippling enemy air assets. In the Far East, the effects of the bombing campaign against Japan were probably less marked. The Japanese economy was brought to a standstill by blockade, not air bombardment, and although air power contributed to the strangulation of Japan's maritime trade routes, the 'torching' of Japanese cities from March 1945 onwards did little to bring about the collapse of the Japanese military's will to fight on. It is also by no means proven that the atomic bombings of Hiroshima and Nagasaki were the decisive factors in precipitating Japanese surrender.[14]

By the post-1945 world, nevertheless, air power appeared to have fulfilled the criteria laid down for it by Douhet. With the linking of nuclear weaponry to long-range bombers, the age of Douhet seemed to have been visited upon the world. The reservations about strategic bombing in World War Two, largely political and driven by concern over the mass slaughter of civilians, could be put into perspective as now the means of delivering the knockout blow was available. However, the determination to prove Douhet correct and to apply his vision to the strategic situation of the Cold War led air power up a doctrinal cul-de-sac. From the beginnings of nuclear strategy until the 1980s, air power was employed at the politico–strategic level to enforce a growing deterrent of mass destruction, which by the 1960s was almost apocalyptic and total in its lethality. As both superpowers, and a number of medium powers, developed nuclear weaponry, strategic nuclear air power proved to be of limited tangible value. Little, other than preventing the other side from utilizing nuclear blackmail, could be derived from the possession of nuclear weaponry. In many ways, strategic air power had become too successful by offering the means with which to level whole cities and societies in the space of a few minutes, and the likelihood of this being inflicted simultaneously on both sides rendered its employment self-defeating.

Nevertheless, the impact of the predominance of nuclear air forces was the diminution of other forms of air power. Air force structure was constructed to fight hot or high-intensity war, most probably in Europe, and consequently there was little focus on tactical or conventional air forces. The impact of this was most markedly illustrated by the inconclusiveness of the application of air assets to the United States' intervention in Vietnam and the Soviet invasion of Afghanistan. Both air forces, created to support direct superpower confrontation and designed for nuclear warfare, proved inadequate in the face of differing kinds of opposition. Indeed, so ill-prepared to fight the campaign thrust upon them were they that USAF and USN aircraft suffered embarrassing defeats at the hands of enemy fighters. Victory to loss ratios fell from 8 to 1 in the Second World War to 2.4 to 1 over Vietnam, and at times it was considerably worse than this.[15]

Attempts by the Americans to rediscover the role of air power in war, the realities of prosecution rather than simple deterrence, developed as a consequence of the shifting political situation of the 1980s, the development of new technologies and the experience of Vietnam. By the time of the Second Cold War in the early Eighties, United States air power thinking had moved on from the simplistic and redundant days of Douhetism. The concept of the Air–Land Battle represented a new examination of the means by which air power, this time as part of an integrated strategy, could play a politico-strategic role by delivering the ability to defeat the larger conventional Warsaw Pact forces in Europe. NATO had accepted their inferior conventional capabilities since the late 1950s and had relied on the threatened use of tactical nuclear weapons to deter a Soviet-backed invasion of Western Europe. Soviet aero-technology had also delivered to the Warsaw Pact a series of combat advantages, particularly in the field of air superiority fighters, as demonstrated by the American loss rates in South East Asia. To make matters worse, Moscow had increased the size of the VVS (Voyenno Voznushnyye Sily – Soviet Air Forces) by 50 per cent between 1967 and 1977.[16] To combat this, the Air–Land Battle planned to utilize emerging technology in communications, control, targeting, and delivery systems, principally spearheaded from the air, to break up more numerous, but technologically weaker Warsaw Pact forces. The concept was not fully realized during the Cold War, but the potential was a factor in increasing the pressure on the Soviet leadership at a critical moment.[17]

Nevertheless, the reorientation of air-power theory during the 1980s away from the mass destruction of Douhetism resulted in a re-evaluation of what air forces could achieve, especially if linked with cutting-edge technology. Where mass bombing had proved useful but indecisive in World War Two, new degrees of accuracy and capability, if properly focused, might be appropriate in a pivotal sense in late twentieth century conflict. This was certainly the view of Colonel John Warden, the doyen of air power advocates in the 1990s. His impact, and that of his associates, in shaping air power policy during Operation Desert Storm, in the Gulf War of 1990–1, represented a shift in the role of air power from army support to leading the offensive against Iraq in a strategic sense. In some ways, the use of air power to cripple the resistance of Saddam Hussein's military harked back to the intent, if not the methods, of the earliest air power writers, who foresaw a time when air power would be the truly decisive factor in war. In Desert Storm, Warden and his team argued that by the use of precision, stealth and appropriate targeting, the defeat of Iraq, principally from the air, could be achieved, and this mirrored the notions of the USAAF air war plans division thinking prior to the Second World War. The prosecution of the campaigns may well have differed and the levels of opposition may have been radically different, but the intent was similar. Whereas the 1942–5 campaign suffered from a variety of doctrinal difficulties and poorly focused and variable targeting policies, in contrast, that of 1991 seemed to have realized the dream of air power.

However, this view requires closer scrutiny. Although air power was remarkably successful against Iraq, it proved unable to provide an answer in more complex political situations and difficult operating circumstances as pertained in the Balkans and the Horn of Africa. The United States and Soviet air assets may have been inappropriately employed and structured for Vietnam and Afghanistan, but they were also engaged in campaigns that required a sophisticated, integrated and subtle approach. Even in Kosovo there is great uncertainty over the actual impact of air power. The campaign against the Serbian military forces proved indecisive, and the political and economic pressure applied to Serbia itself inconclusive. The extent to which the Milosović regime's decision to withdraw was dictated by air power alone, or was forced by the threat of NATO ground force intervention and an already fomenting domestic political situation, is unclear. Moreover, the response to the events of 11 September 2001, although much more effective in the rapidity with which the Taliban government in Kabul was dislodged, has yet to underpin the claims of the air power advocates. Ground forces in some strength were required to defeat the enemy, and the broader political aims of the 'War against Terrorism' have yet to be achieved. It could still be argued that modern air power is highly effective in dealing with conventional campaigns, but only so long as technological superiority is obvious and emphatic and if employed in a largely coalition framework. In scenarios where air power has not been so employed, during the Iran–Iraq conflict of the 1980s for example, it has still proved indecisive. Moreover, it remains to be seen whether air power of the type developed by Western nations, when deployed against formidable opponents, perhaps a resurgent Russia or belligerent China, would be able to realize fully the aims set down for it a century ago.

Air power and the conduct of war

The grand vision of air power has to a significant extent dominated the history of the aeroplane's impact on the conduct of war. The strategic level of air power was, and is, viewed as the truly revolutionary aspect of the weapon, contrasting with the operational or tactical employment of air forces. Indeed, some arch-advocates of air power argued in the interwar era that the non-strategic use of aircraft, particularly bombers, was a waste of their potential.[18] In the nuclear age, emphasis was placed squarely on the long-range bombing capabilities of aircraft, and the tactical dimension, particularly air-to-air combat, was pushed to the periphery.

Yet, air power has in fact shaped and altered the conduct of war more obviously and most decisively away from the strategic level, notwithstanding the success enjoyed in the latter stages of World War Two by the Allied strategic air forces and by the NATO forces over the Balkans in 1999. Aircraft became crucial to the success of land and maritime operations by the mid-point of the twentieth century to such a degree that prosecuting Operation Overlord, the Allied invasion of Europe in 1944, was unthinkable without at the very least air superiority. In fact the RAF and the USAAF had achieved a higher degree of dominance, air supremacy, which offered even greater opportunities for air power to intervene decisively in the campaign.[19]

In many ways, although greatly exaggerated, the coming of age of air power in influencing ground warfare coincided with the great successes of the Axis powers in World War Two. First the Germans and then the Japanese swept all before them with a dynamic mode of warfare founded on air power and operational proficiency. As the *Blitzkrieg* eliminated enemies previously unbowed by four years of attritional struggle in the Great War, it seemed as though the aeroplane had instilled high tempo and decisiveness back into warfare. German and Japanese air power was fundamental to their early victories and paradoxically a cause of their ultimate defeat, as they failed to expand their air forces rapidly enough and soon surrendered control over the battlefields to their enemies. By 1944 Allied air power dominated to such an extent that German ground forces were forced to operate under the constant threat of air attack, while the Luftwaffe was conspicuous by its absence. Over Normandy on 6 June 1944 the western Allied forces could call upon the support of in excess of 12,000 aircraft, whereas the Wehrmacht could muster only 300.[20]

Yet, in spite of the critical nature of air support to the success of ground operations in World War Two and the clear evidence that without control of the air, tactical acumen of ground forces alone could not prevail, the Cold War witnessed the eclipse of operational and tactical air power. Strategic air power predominated and the skills and doctrine of battlefield air support withered away to the extent that by Vietnam and arguably Afghanistan the superpowers had to relearn the lessons of World War Two. The United States' air forces were unable to establish true air superiority and proved incapable of delivering decisive battlefield advantages to the ground forces. Such lessons caused a major rethink and by the time of the Gulf War heavy investment in an integrated approach to air-to-ground capability yielded great benefits. It has now become a basic and unassailable principle of battlefield air support that air superiority at least, but preferably total air supremacy, be established prior to the use of air assets to support ground offensives, a lesson first learned in the First and Second World Wars.

Maritime war has been influenced and shaped by air power to an even greater degree than land warfare. In the First World War the role of aircraft in providing cover to convoys was crucial, and by the Second World War it was essential. Indeed, more than anything else, *Ultra* intelligence included, it was the establishment of continuous air cover across the Atlantic that ended the Battle of the Atlantic in favour of the Allies in 1943.[21] Reconnaissance and gunnery-direction aircraft were developed during the First World War, but it was the ability of land-based and aircraft carrier-borne aeroplanes to intervene in naval warfare that caused an even greater shift in the balance of maritime power. Throughout the interwar period the world's navies fought a bitter and protracted rearguard action against the increasing shadow cast by the aeroplane over their much-vaunted and expensive surface battleships. Although many navies claimed that modern battleships were safe from air attack, during the Second World War it became apparent that they could only rarely operate without air cover. The *Bismarck* was crippled and doomed by air attacks, the *Prince of Wales* and the *Repulse* were helpless in the face of concerted bombing, and the two largest battleships ever built, the Japanese *Yamato* and *Musashi,* were sunk by single-engine United States naval bombers in the last months of the war. Carrier based aviation also came of age, dominating the Pacific war throughout.[22] The Royal Navy had illustrated what could be achieved with its successful air attack on the Italian fleet at Taranto in 1940, but it was the Japanese and the Americans who fully exploited the aircraft carrier's potential between 1941 and 1945. Offensive operations were dominated by air power, and amphibious action, the cornerstone to success in the Pacific, was only viable when air superiority was assured.

Indeed, by the post-war era, maritime operations existed only so long as air power allowed. The great expensive carrier fleets themselves became highly vulnerable to nuclear missile attack and for much of the Cold War, with strategic emphasis placed squarely on the requirements of superpower confrontation, navies desperately endeavoured to justify themselves. In the post Cold War environment, however, the self-supporting conventional carrier task force has perhaps re-established itself as a means of aerial power projection and as a political tool or symbol of intent. Undoubtedly, carriers can now deliver a tremendous punch and, spared the spectre of annihilation at the hands of a tactical nuclear missile, have proved highly effective in a variety of scenarios.

Global air power

The ability of industrial powers to project air power across the globe, from aircraft carriers or more recently from highly sophisticated long-range strike aeroplanes, has emphatically illustrated a trend in the relationship between advanced air powers and those of a lesser status or with no discernible air assets at all. Since the latter half of the nineteenth century modern industrial states have developed an increasing technological supremacy over non-industrial societies, and the advent of the aeroplane has accelerated that trend.

The Italians were the first to employ air power against enemies unused to such technology; it was they who carried out the first bombing raids in actions against the Turks in 1912.[23] In the post 1918 era the imperial powers saw great benefit in deploying aircraft against indigenous forces that could not retaliate in any way. The British deployed the RAF against rebels in the Third Afghan War in 1919 and with considerable success against an uprising in Iraq from 1922 onwards. In Middle Eastern conditions air power proved to be more effective and indeed cheaper than ground forces in policing the empire, cutting costs in Iraq from £23.36m in 1922 to £7.81m the following year.[24] The Spanish and French mirrored the British in their employment of air power against uprisings in Morocco during the Riff War 1921–6, and the United States utilized Marine Corps aircraft against rebels in Central America between 1927 and 1933, all with significant success. The apogee of colonial air power came with the Italian invasion of Ethiopian in 1935, where aircraft, using poison gas, were widely employed, notably with a much greater level of effectiveness than other Western technological enhancements, such as the tank.

However, air power was also an effective tool in drawing together the sprawling European empires and building closer links with disparate outposts across the globe. Civil aviation routes rapidly sprang up in the post-1918 era and by 1930 many of the famous European air lines had been established: KLM was flying to the Dutch East Indies; Air France to Indochina and Africa; and Britain's Imperial Airways throughout the Empire.[25] The British also used long-range flying boats in the interwar period to tour the Far East, visiting Hong Kong, Singapore and Australia, while aircraft flew across vast tracts of Africa, on one occasion from Cairo to Capetown.[26] Such endeavours were statements of British commitment to the Empire, and the psychological effectiveness of aircraft was duly recorded, it being an intimidating expression of Western technological and military superiority.[27]

However, the effectiveness of military air power was by no means assured. In the post 1945 era, in an age where the world was used to air power, aircraft were of less value, unless fully integrated into a considered and coordinated strategy. The disaster that befell the French at Dien Bien Phu in 1953–4 demonstrated that air power was of limited tactical value in certain situations and when utilized without effective ground support. The US and Soviets came to similar conclusions in Vietnam and Afghanistan, and although global reach has now been attained, with United States bombers able to range over the entire planet should it be deemed necessary, the value of air strikes alone, despite the over-whelming technological advantages held by Western powers, is by no means certain. It is still the case, despite the claims of the air power gurus, that ground forces have to be available to enforce the advantages gained by air power. The campaign over Kosovo and Serbia in 1999 came closest to proving air power's case, but the fighting on the ground in Afghanistan and Iraq in the wake of the destruction of the World Trade Centre has underscored the argument that air power alone cannot be enough to meet the challenges likely to confront the west.

Air power and technology

The increasing fascination of the world's populations with the technological achievements of air power, particularly in the years since the end of the

Cold War, illustrates a key facet of the complex relationship between aero-technology and the conduct of war. In its crudest sense, technological supremacy, particularly in the field of air power, has increasingly been viewed as the determining factor in attaining success. Indeed, military writing and thinking has long been dominated by a particularly masculine perspective and interpretation, precipitating a view perhaps too often shaped by a techno-logically oriented slant. It is straightforward and understandably simplistic to explain the outcome of campaigns by means of clearly defined technical capabilities, and aeroplanes, so obviously determined by factors such as speed, manoeuvrability and firepower, fall very neatly into this category. Consequently, a degree of technological determinism is apparent in the development of air power, and continues to plague analysis. Explanations of victory or defeat in air campaigns since the First World War have been repeatedly based upon the perceived consequences of technical inferiority or superiority. The success of the British in the Battle of Britain is explained by the edge provided by the Spitfire; the destruction of the Luftwaffe in 1944 a result of the P-51's hold over contemporary German interceptors; and the root cause of failure over Vietnam was supposedly the inadequacy of USAAF and USN air superiority combat planes. Indeed, in 1994 one air power analyst claimed that the USAAF had 'long worshipped at the altar of technology' and that policy, doctrine and operational art were too often driven by technological determinism.[28]

However, all these explanations are inadequate. Technology has naturally played a key role in determining the effectiveness of air power, but only fleetingly has it been the linchpin of victory. Perhaps the first and most obvious such case was the short-term superiority created by the German employed Fokker Eindekker in 1915 and 1916. This aircraft was the first to marry a forward-firing machine gun, fitted with an interrupter device to allow it to fire through the propeller blades, in a nimble single-seat fighter aircraft. The Eindekker provided a critical advantage, but its success was short lived as the Allies rapidly responded.[29] For the rest of the Great War, increasingly sophisticated aircraft were introduced, but at no time did the performance advantage conferred by specific designs impact dramatically enough on the campaign to warrant the epithet decisive.

There were significant innovations in aircraft capabilities and design between 1939 and 1945, but despite claims to the contrary again it did not decide the outcome of air campaigns. In 1940 the Messerschmitt Bf 109 was a fair match for the Spitfire, and was clearly not the cause of Germany's failure in the Battle of Britain. Moreover, the Luftwaffe lost control over Germany in 1944 principally because of the decline in the quality of its pilots and its dwindling fuel reserves.[30] The concern expressed by some Allied air strategists in 1944 that the new Messerschmitt Me 262 jet fighter could redress the balance because of its superior performance misread the situation completely. The Me 262 could not make up for a lack of experienced pilots any more than it could the over-whelming resources of the Allies. In studying the Second World War, however, air power analysts put aside such considerations and focused more on the supposed technologically driven decisiveness of the B-29 Superfortress or the F6F Hellcat over the Pacific and the P-51 in Europe. The post-war period again saw technological determinism distorting explanations of success and failure. Vietnam conclusively proved that technological superiority does not confer victory, as United States forces held all the technological trump cards but singularly failed between 1965 and 1973.

The advantages created by technology can also sometimes be illusory. Missile technology, especially that designed for employment beyond visual range, has not had the success imagined. Despite the capabilities of the weaponry, air-crew have demonstrated reluctance to use the armaments at the full potential range because of concerns over hitting friendly aircraft: crews preferred the reassurance of visual identity before using their long-range missiles, defeating the object of having them. Moreover, in the contemporary post Cold War age, although technological capabilities are often the barometer by which success can be tested, it is still the case that the bad weather over Europe which all too often thwarted air forces in World War Two, continued to plague the aircraft operating over the Balkans in 1999.

Indeed, there are other factors that have contributed more crucially to success or failure in air combat, most notably situation awareness developed by combat experience and appropriate training. Manfred von Richthofen claimed many of his kills by downing slow-moving reconnaissance aircraft unable to react to his assault as he used the tactical situation to attack from blind spots, often out of the sun. Evidence from the Second World War and South East Asia supported the view that when the vast majority of aircraft were shot down, perhaps in some 80 per cent of cases, the pilots never saw the attack coming.[31] Tests carried out in the late 1970s on the disadvantages faced by similarly trained United States aircrew operating with inferior aircraft or armaments against the latest and most sophisticated equipment underpinned this interpretation. Although the pilots flying the inferior aircraft had to work harder, technological shortcomings could be compensated for and had negligible impact on combat outcomes.[32]

Nevertheless, although superior technology did not guarantee victory, it could fuse with minor advantages in training, experience and support to bring victory in the skies. The difficulty for Western air forces in particular has been overcoming this tendency to technological interpretation as a first and most convincing explanation of how and why success has occurred.

Air power and total war

Managing the input of technology into war was a fundamental facet of air power. In combination with the industrial management and economic organization of air power, aero-technology has been a critical measure of a state's ability to wage modern war successfully, especially that defined as total war. There is little doubt that the military aeroplane was the embodiment of total war, for it was more dependent on economic and technological support than any other weapon, required vast investment in an effort to stave off obsolescence, and frittered away a nation's assets and resources in the most profligate manner. As the twentieth century progressed it became clear that only a dwindling number of powers could meet this challenge of maintaining first-rate air power status.

Competition between mass air powers grew from the Great War onwards and culminated in the Second World War. Indeed, Richard Overy has argued that the era from 1935 to 1950 was peculiar in air power history and witnessed an age of mass air power. Prior to the late 1930s air power was important but not decisive enough in the prosecution of war to be fundamental to success, most obviously because aircraft capabilities were too limited to provide huge battlefield and strategic advantages. By the 1950s, however, aircraft technology and capabilities had increased exponentially and success in war was now inextricably linked with air power. Paradoxically, the major problem confronting states by the time of the Cold War was the escalating cost of building and maintaining large air forces, and ultimately it no longer proved viable to do so. Consequently, the Second World War was a period in which modern aircraft were not expensive enough to prevent the creation of mass air forces, but at the same time were still sufficiently potent to determine markedly the outcome of the conflict.[33]

The demands made on states by air forces were great both in terms of output and technological investment. The pressures to meet the demands of air power were intense throughout the period, and unlike those placed upon armies and navies, the consequences of failure could be immediate and potentially catastrophic. Unfortunately, the nature of air power was such that not only were there problems of mass-production of equipment to arm the air force, but crucial issues also arose concerning training and the input of science. Because air power had thrown up so many new problems of navigation, accuracy, aerial firepower, targeting, and so forth, problems quite different to those of the past, so the drive to solve them had to rely heavily on scientific investigation and reasoning. Trial and error by the military was no longer enough and the more successful air powers were those that linked science and technology effectively with the requirements of the military.

Overcoming the problems of rapidly developing military air power was no easy task. Great War pilots and aircrew initially shot at each other with small arms, but by the end of the war, heavy bombers flew long-range missions that interceptors sought to prevent with forward firing machine guns. By the Second World War, science was crucial to facilitating success in air war, with the development of radar and radio-assisted bombing and interception measures. Radar, or RDF (radio direction-finding as it was known in Britain) conferred great advantages on the RAF in 1940, and the lack of it was a key factor in the destruction of Japan's carrier fleet at Midway in 1942. In a similar vein, technological aspects of the strategic bombing offensives against Germany and Japan were crucial elements in these campaigns' successes. Increasingly more sophisticated aircraft were introduced in an attempt to win operational advantages. Innovations could yield significant short-term coups, for example, the introduction of *x-verhafen* radio beams that resulted in the heavy damage inflicted upon Coventry in 1940, the deployment of 'window' by the British in 1943 that precipitated the destruction of Hamburg, and the atomic bombings in 1945 that heralded the nuclear age. Since 1945, even without large-scale wars, the industrial powers have worked slavishly to maintain parity in aero-technology, for not to do so might have unhinged the delicate balancing act that the superpowers imposed upon themselves in the late 1940s. Moreover, it is considered that the American F-22 development programme will top $100bn, demonstrating the demands still made on states by air power.

Although the resulting advantages conferred by technological innovation were rarely decisive in themselves, they did indicate the relative position of the belligerents and the manner in which they were coping with the stresses and exigencies of total war. For the most part it was the Allies in the Second World War who were best able to marry science, technology and air power into a formidable combination, in a way that the more rigid and martially oriented Axis powers could not. Initially the German and Japanese air forces held both qualitative and often quantitative advantages over their adversaries, particularly the smaller powers confronting them, such as Poland, Belgium, the Netherlands, Yugoslavia, and Greece. Nevertheless, despite the early successes, the Luftwaffe and Imperial Japanese naval and army air forces began to stagnate and fall behind their Allied counterparts in the implementation of new technology and personnel investment. Innovative design did not defeat them, as the jet programmes initiated in Germany and the later Japanese airframes indicated, but the ability to build enough high-quality aircraft efficiently and quickly proved beyond them.[34] Moreover, the Axis air powers were crippled still further by an inability to train enough pilots to fly their new aircraft, and it was the lack of aircrew as much as anything that defeated the Luftwaffe in the final year of the war.

The popular view, therefore, that the Allies' mediocre many defeated the Axis powers' superior few is wholly inaccurate. By the end of the war, Allied air power, Soviet as well as Western, not only greatly outnumbered that of its enemies, but also largely outclassed it. This was not so much in the field of design and theory as in what was readily available and had trained, experienced aircrew to fly it. The ability to mass-produce effective equipment and train sufficient personnel was the cornerstone of Allied success in World War Two, and a clear indication of the demands of air war on modern states. It was a challenge that the more sophisticated capitalist economies, or the centrally organized command economy of the Soviet Union, met more effectively than their disorganized and disparate Axis counterparts. The failure of Germany and Japan to respond to the heavy and specific demands made on them by the requirements of mass air war proved to be the most profound manifestation of the root cause of the defeat of the Axis powers in World War Two.

In addition to the economic and scientific demands of total air war, air power was a driving force in the totality of the experience of war. Aircraft provided the means by which war could be taken directly to the home front – to the civilian populations of the belligerent powers. Non-combatants had felt the effects of war since human civilization had first emerged, through siege, blockade and acts of genocide, but the aeroplane added a completely new dimension to this interaction. For many states, especially those in Europe that existed in close proximity to each other, the threat of direct attack upon their cities from the air was very real. Europe in the 1930s was living in the shadow of the bomber, while by the Cold War the possibility of nuclear holocaust hung over the world like the sword of Damocles.[35] Even in the United States, far removed from the most of this process until the development of inter-continental ballistic missiles in the 1960s, the fear of air attack grew to ridiculous proportions even in the interwar era. The likelihood of Japanese carrier-borne air strikes on the west coast, or German air assault from bases in South America, however far-fetched or remote, was taken very seriously by Washington.[36]

Air power was beginning to globalize war for the first time, a process from which few, or indeed no one, would be immune by the close of the twentieth century. Whole societies came to fear Armageddon from the air, long before it became a reality. The novels and fiction of the late nineteenth and early twentieth centuries did much to create this, but from the 1930s onwards new and graphic versions began to appear at the cinema, such as the H.G. Wells-inspired *Things to Come* (1936), *On the Beach* (1959), *Dr Strangelove* (1964), and *Threads* (1984). In the interwar era, fear of the bomber first became acute, especially when linked with poison gas. Stanley Baldwin's infamous statement that 'the bomber will always get through' encapsulated the mood of the period all too vividly, and indeed, it was the British, for so long shielded from the physical realities of war by the English Channel, who developed a tremendous fear of air assault. Moreover, the major concern of 1930s governments was the level of support they would continue to enjoy from populations under aerial bombardment. Why should the masses suffer to sustain a war fought for public élites and private wealth? In an effort to ease the potential burden, significant measures were put in place to protect society from collapse under air attack – gas masks were distributed, air raid shelters built, children evacuated, blackout procedures instigated, and so on.

However, far from undermining political support for governments as many argued it would, air raids actually forced the many strata of society, even within the most divided of communities, to pull together in the interests of mutual survival. Indeed, air bombardment almost certainly helped to consolidate opinion against enemies during war and some historians have even argued that bombing may have been counterproductive to the perpetrators in that it hardened the resolve of populations and convinced them to go on fighting. Far from wanting to overthrow their political leadership, populations insisted on 'giving as good as they got'. There is in fact no evidence that civilian morale collapsed to the extent that the outcome of any war was dictated by such concerns. Populations, even when subjected to the most sustained heavy bombing, grudgingly carried on regardless. German and Japanese civilians suffered tremendously in the closing stages of the Second World War, with 100,000 deaths in Tokyo in one night in March 1945 and some 80,000 killed in Dresden in the previous month. Yet neither nation capitulated because of the impact of such raids on public morale. Air power may have asked many questions of societies' resolve in the face of heavy aerial bombardment, but populations were able to endure in a manner not imagined.

Ethics and air war

Nevertheless, although societies under intense air attack proved resilient, the methods that were employed to prosecute so-called total war came under close scrutiny. The levels of destruction in the closing stages of World War Two, highlighted by the appalling destruction of German and Japanese cities, raised crucial issues of morality and the ethical justification of such strategies. Prior to the Second World War, although concern was expressed in many quarters over what unfettered air attack might inflict on civilians, there was little tangible evidence upon which to pronounce, with only Guernica and Japanese bombing of Chinese cities indicating what may be about to come. The excesses of the 1939–45 conflict, and the potential of nuclear-armed air power in the Cold War world pushed the rights and wrongs of air attack, whatever the strategic justification, onto the political agenda. Yet, the conduct of war throughout history has been influenced less by morality and more by military capability, qualified by political acceptability and by the objectives for which a society was fighting. In wars such as that fought against the Axis powers, the consequences of defeat were so unpalatable that all measures considered necessary and effective were deemed acceptable.[37]

Nevertheless, bombing urban centres, on whatever pretext, resulted in the deaths of civilians, and to many this was an unwelcome and immoral escalation of the already brutal activity of war. Efforts to distinguish between combatants and non-combatants in war had been ongoing prior to the emergence of the aeroplane, but the development of air power complicated matters no end and resulted in many odd discrepancies. At the 1899 and 1907 Hague Conferences, set up to delineate and moderate the conduct of war, ambiguities emerged. Attacks on undefended urban centres, by whatever means, aircraft included, were not allowed, but naval bombardment of a military target was, even if in the vicinity of the civilian population.[38] Moreover, history is replete with examples of civilians being deliberately targeted in war, especially in sieges and times of blockade. Indeed, more German civilians died as a result of the Allied maritime blockade in World War One than were killed by bombing in World War Two. Was indiscriminate starvation any better than indiscriminate aerial bombardment?

However, accepting a level of civilian death as a result of military action was one thing, but deliberately targeting non-combatants was another. During the First World War bombing strategy, although directed against military targets, was predicated upon the notion that inaccurate bombing would probably kill civilians and this would still be useful in undermining enemy morale. However, by the interwar era, although the essence of Douhetism remained in targeting the enemy's civilian morale, other methods of employing aerial bombardment were planned, not because of squeamishness over civilian casualties but because damaging the enemy's military and economic centres was viewed as a more effective use of resources. In a future war the RAF and the USAAC both intended to cripple enemy states by attacking key elements in their infrastructure. Emphasis was placed squarely upon precision bombing. However, the experience of war for the RAF implied that accurate bombing and acceptable loss rates were incompatible, and in 1942 the British switched to a policy of area bombing of German cities as an alternative. Although it was never openly admitted, the RAF, under the cover of the 'dehousing' euphemism, was endeavouring to kill German workers. In effect this was a policy of deliberately destroying urban centres and their populations in an effort to cause disruption and chaos and thereby undermine the enemy state. Moreover, while the Americans persisted with precision bombing over Europe, when this proved ineffective against Japan they too switched to area bombing of Japanese cities as an alternative.[39]

Such tactics could be defended, it was reasoned, if they could be demonstrated to be strategically effective. Despite continuing claims to the contrary, bombing in World War Two – area bombing included – did make a major contribution to the defeat of the Axis powers. Yet, lingering uncertainty over the moral justification implies a high degree of unease surrounding the employment of such tactics. Acceptable behaviour in war is governed more by prevailing attitudes in belligerent and neutral societies, often loosely termed 'world opinion', than legalistic clauses. The fact that controversy still surrounds the firebombing of Dresden and Tokyo, to say nothing of the atomic bombings of Hiroshima and Nagasaki, implies that Western civilization was, and is, uncomfortable with such actions. The continuing desire to perfect 'clean' air war, in which smart bombs deliver ordnance with pinpoint accuracy and minimal civilian casualties, is driven as much by the concerns over the inadequacies of the World War Two campaigns as by the pressure imposed by a scrutinizing and often sceptical world-wide media.

However, in large-scale industrial war, of which the Second World War is the most obvious example, distinctions between civilians and combatants become very blurred. Why should those organizing and supporting the war effort in Germany be less of a legitimate target than soldiers fighting at the front, especially in an age when most troops are conscripts and may have been indifferent supporters of or even hostile to the Nazi regime? Moreover, are those who build and manufacture the weapons of war any less culpable than those who use them? The argument that such workers are undefended surely collapses with the development of anti-aircraft guns, high-performance interceptors, night-fighters, and radar defences.

It could be argued that ethical problems surrounding strategic bombing vary in proportion to perceptions of effectiveness. If it contributed significantly to the defeat of the Axis powers, it becomes more acceptable; if it caused immense suffering with little discernible strategic benefit as in Vietnam, then it becomes less so. Those states that have employed such methods, and continue to do so, realized that they were and are travelling a dangerous and perilous moral path. The fact that in the past they sought to conceal the scale and nature of their actions, and in the present seek to limit civilian casualties and media images thereof, reveals much about their self-doubt and how much stomach they imagine their own populations have for such tactics. As one veteran of the bombing of Germany confessed, if television images of the death and destruction meted out during the intense bombing of Hamburg in 1943 had been beamed all over the world, there would have been no repetition.[40]

Conclusion

The first hundred years or so of air power has radically altered the nature of war in a variety of ways. Most obviously, it has precipitated a major escalation in the level of destruction that could be brought to bear on an enemy, ultimately to the point that the potential use of such power has become counterproductive, both militarily and politically. Moreover, the immediacy of attack from the air has reduced the diplomatic and political manoeuvring space available to regimes in times of negotiation and bargaining. Indeed, by the late 1930s, erroneous interpretation of intent or actions could lead, theoretically within hours, to dreadful repercussions and by the 1950s to nuclear devastation. Additionally, air power also deepened the experience of war in two critical ways. First, the maintenance of high-quality, first-rate air forces required states to invest heavily in production, design and organizational resources, thus precipitating populations being drawn into the war effort to ever-increasing levels. Consequently, and second, as a result of the demands made by air power on economies and national infrastructure, society was drawn fully into the military arena as a legitimate target during war. Thus, air power deepened and broadened the nature of conflict by creating both a cause and the method of bringing war to the home front.

Air power has also accelerated the growing divide between the technologically driven industrial powers and the wider world. Initially, when few states had military aircraft, the aeroplane provided an effective and potent method for imperial powers to exert control over their possessions. Here was a weapon that non-industrial societies were not only unable to combat without great difficulty or good fortune, but also a force that could not be copied. The military power of the United States and Europe grew to such levels, principally driven by air power, that smaller states or groups could no longer even contemplate competing on the same terms. By the end of the twentieth century, the United States had the ability to project air strikes across the globe in virtually undetectable stealth aircraft using smart weapons that in theory could pick out very precise targets and destroy them without any ground support whatsoever. This is the vision that arch air power advocates continue to peddle in the early twenty-first century.

But it can be challenged in many ways. First and foremost, only the United States, spending more on its armed forces than Britain, France, Russia, Germany, India, Japan, and China combined, and five times more than the whole of Europe on military research and development, is capable or willing to attain such a level of aerial supremacy. For the secondary powers, such as Russia, China or the Western Europeans, air power plays a more integrated and less messianic role. More apparent, however, is the reality that hugely powerful though air power has been and will continue to be, it suffers from practical and political shortcomings. It cannot deal with many of the threats likely to confront the industrial world in the next decades, threats often born precisely because of the overwhelming military and economic strength enjoyed by such nations. Indeed, it could be argued that the latest technological innovations in air power have and continue to prepare the United States to confront a type of conventional enemy that has been consigned to history. Thus, air power may well have permanently altered the relationship between the strong industrial–military powers and the supposed pygmies by making the gap in capability so vast that entirely new methods of war have been and will continue to be sought.

Further reading

M.J. Armitage and Tony Mason, *Air Power in the Nuclear Age 1945–1982* (Basingstoke: Macmillan, 1985).

John Buckley, *Air Power in the Age of Total War* (London: UCL Press, 1999).

Mark Clodfelter, *The Limits of Air Power: The American Bombing of North Vietnam* (London: Collier Macmillan, 1989).

Robin Higham, *A Concise History of Air Power* (New York: St Martin's Press, 1972).

Richard Hallion (ed.), *Air Power Confronts an Unstable World* (London: Brassey's, 1997).

Richard Hallion, *Storm Over Iraq: Air Power and the Gulf War* (Washington: Smithsonian Institution Press, 1992).

Lee Kennett, *The First Air War 1914–1918* (New York: Free Press, 1991).

Tony Mason, *Air Power: A Centennial Appraisal* (London: Brassey's, 1995).

Lon O. Nordeen, *Air Warfare in the Missile Age* (Washington: Smithsonian Institution Press, 1985).

Richard Overy, *The Air War 1939–1945* (London: Macmillan, 1990).
Robert Pape, *Bombing to Win: Air Power and Coercion in War* (London: Cornell University Press, 1996).

Notes

1 John Warden, 'Afterword: Challenges and Opportunities', in Richard Hallion (ed.), *Air Power Confronts an Unstable World* (London: Brassey's, 1997), p. 227.
2 Richard Hallion, *Storm over Iraq: Air Power and the Gulf War* (Washington: Smithsonian Institution Press, 1992), pp. 303–7.
3 See Michael Paris, *Winged Warfare: The Literature and Theory of Aerial Warfare in Britain 1859–1917* (Manchester: Manchester University Press, 1991).
4 Alfred Gollin, *No Longer an Island* (London: Heinemann, 1984), pp. 26–9.
5 John H. Morrow, *The Great War in the Air – Military Aviation from 1909–1921* (Washington: Smithsonian Institution Press, 1993), p. 22.
6 Malcolm Smith, *British Air Strategy between the Wars* (Oxford: Oxford University Press) demonstrates this very effectively.
7 Giulio Douhet, *The Command of the Air* (London: Faber & Faber, 1942). Douhet was little read in the Anglophone world until the 1940s and his importance to the development of strategic air power is attributed retrospectively. Nevertheless, Douhet's name has entered the convoluted lexicography of air power.
8 Claudio Segre, 'Giulio Douhet: Strategist, Theorist, Prophet?', *Journal of Strategic Studies,* vol. 15, no. 3, 1992; see also Azar Gat, *Fascist and Liberal Vision of War: Fuller, Liddell Hart, Douhet et al.* (Oxford: Oxford University Press, 1998).
9 For a full discussion see Tami Davis Biddle, *Rhetoric and Reality in Air Warfare: The Evolution of British and American Ideas About Strategic Bombing 1914–1945* (Princeton University Press, 2002).
10 Tami Davis Biddle, 'British and American Approaches to Strategic Bombing: Their Origins and Implementation in the World War II Combined Bomber Offensive', in *Airpower: Theory and Practice*, edited by John Gooch.
11 Irving B. Holley, Jr., 'The Development of Defensive Armament for US Army Bombers 1918–41: A Study Doctrinal Failure and Production Success', in *The Conduct of the Air War in the Second World War: An International Comparison*, ed. Horst Boog.
12 On the Soviets see R. Higham and J.T. Greenwood, *Russian Aviation and Air Power* (London: Frank Cass, 1998); on the French see C. Christienne and P. Lissarrague, *Histoire de l'Aviation Militaire Française* (Paris: Limoges, 1980); on the Germans see W. Murray, *Luftwaffe 1933–45: Strategy for Defeat* (Washington: Allen & Unwin), 1985.
13 Compare Robert Pape, *Bombing to Win – Air Power and Coercion in War* (New York: Cornell University Press, 1996) with Richard Overy's works, particularly *Why the Allies Won* (London: Jonathan Cape, 1995).
14 There is an ongoing debate centred on this subject. As a starting point see Gar Alperovitz, *The Decision to Use the Atomic Bomb and the Architecture of an American Myth* (New York: Knopf, 1995).
15 Bruce K. Holloway, 'Air Superiority in Tactical Air Warfare', *Air University Review*, vol. 19, no. 3 (March–April 1968), pp. 8–9.
16 J.H. Hanson, 'Development of Soviet aviation support', *International Defence Review*, vol. 5, 1980.
17 B. Rogers, 'Greater flexibility for NATO's flexible response', *Strategic Review*, Spring 1983; D.A. Starry, 'Extending the battlefield', *Military Review*, March, 1981; T.A. Mason, *Air Power: A Centennial Appraisal* (London: Brassey's, 1995), pp. 97–104.

18 AIR 41/45, D.V. Peyton-Ward, *The RAF in the Maritime War – volume I*, pp. 146–7. Public Record Office (PRO), Kew, London.
19 For a discussion of levels of air power domination, see R.P. Hallion, 'Air Power Past, Present and Future', in *Air Power Confronts an Unstable World*, ed. Hallion, pp. 3–5.
20 H.H. Arnold, *Second Report of the Commanding General of the USAAF* (Washington: Government Printing Office, 1945), p. 36.
21 John Buckley, *The RAF and Trade Defence 1919–1945: Constant Endeavour* (Keele: Keele University Press, 1995), pp. 132–7; Correlli Barnett, *Engage the Enemy More Closely* (London: W.W. Norton, 1991), see the chapter 'The Battle of the Air'.
22 Clark Reynolds, *The Fast Carriers: The Forging of an Air Navy* (New York: McGraw-Hill, 1968).
23 Michael Paris, 'The First Air Wars – North Africa and the Balkans', *Journal of Contemporary History*, vol. 26, 1991, pp. 97–109.
24 David Omissi, *Air Power and Colonial Control: The RAF 1919–1939* (Manchester: Manchester University Press, 1990), p. 37.
25 Robin Higham, *A Concise History of Air Power* (London: St Martin's, 1972), pp. 75–7.
26 AIR 9/15, notes on 1926–7 Far Eastern flying boat cruise; AIR 9/15, report on flying-boat cruises to investigate monsoon conditions, 16 June to 22 October 1929; AIR 15/67, cruise of Iris flying boat to Iceland, June–July 1930; W.S. Douglas, 'A Floatplane Tour in the South Sudan', *RAF Quarterly*, vol. II, 1931.
27 AIR 2/249 S.23084, Admiralty/Air Ministry correspondence with regard to proposed world cruise by the First Light Cruiser Squadron, 20 October 1923; P.B. Joubert de la Ferté, *Birds and Fishes* (London: Hutchinson, 1960), p. 76.
28 C.H. Builder, *The Icarus Syndrome: The Role of Air Power Theory in the Evolution and Fate of the US Air Force* (London: Transaction, 1994), p. 155.
29 Lee Kennett, *The First Air War 1914–1918* (New York: Free Press, 1991), p. 70; F. von Bülow, *Geschicte der Luftwaffe* (Frankfurt: Moritz Diensterweg, 1937), pp. 65–71.
30 W. Murray, *Luftwaffe*, pp. 209–56.
31 R.F. Toliver and T.J. Constable, *The Blond Knight of Germany* (New York: Doubleday, 1970), p. 173; M.E. Hubbard in W.E. Kepner, 'The Long Reach: Deep Fighter Escort Tactics', Eighth Fighter Command, 29 May 1944, p. 10; B.D. Watts, 'Doctrine, Technology and Air Warfare', in R. Hallion (ed.), *Air Power Confronts an Unstable World*, pp. 24–5.
32 C.A. Robinson, 'Fighter, Missile Gains Pressed', *Aviation Week and Space Technology*, 4 April 1977 and 'Aerial Combat Test to Advance', *Aviation Week and Space Technology*, 25 April 1977, pp. 28–30.
33 Richard Overy, 'Air Power and the Second World War: Historical Themes and Theories', in H. Boog (ed.), *Conduct of the Air War*.
34 R.J. Overy, *The Air War 1939–1945* (London: Macmillan, 1980), chapters 6, 7 and 8.
35 See Uri Bialer, *The Shadow of the Bomber: The Fear of Air Attack and British Politics 1932–1939* (London: Royal Historical Society, 1981).
36 T.L. Kraus, 'Planning the defense of the Atlantic 1939–41: Securing Brazil', in *To Die Gallantly: The Battle of the Atlantic*, ed. T. Runyan and J.M. Copes (Oxford: Westview, 1994).
37 S.A. Garrett, *Ethics and Air Power in World War Two* (New York: St Martin's, 1993).
38 Geoffrey Best, *Humanity in Warfare* (London: Weidenfeld & Nicolson, 1980), pp. 262–3.
39 C. Crane, *Bombs, Cities and Civilians: American Airpower Strategy in World War Two* (Kansas: University Press, 1993).
40 Film: *Death by Moonlight (The Valour and the Horror)* National Film Board of Canada, (1992).

INDEX

Abyssinia *see* Ethiopia
Adowa, battle of 180, 191, fn. 28
Adriatic 227, 229
Afghan, Third War 1919 245
Afghanistan 2, 4–5, 12, 43, 241, 246–8,
    254, 343–4; Soviet air power 241, 243,
    246
Africa 224, 230
Africa, Sub-Saharan: age-regiments in
    173, 177, 180; 'asset-stripping' in 186;
    cavalry in 172, 176; child soldiers in
    185–8; Cold War in 183, 184, 185,
    187; colonial troops in 177, 179,
    180–2, 188; conflict resolution in 184,
    186–8; contemporary warfare,
    similarities to traditional warfare in
    187–8; 'conventional' recent wars in
    184; European Imperial conquest of
    178–81; European trade with 174,
    175; firearms in 174, 175, 176, 177,
    179, 180, 181; 'force' vs. 'power' applied
    in 178, 188; fortifications in 174, 180;
    geography of 170–1; guerrilla war in
    181–8, 191, fn. 30; historical
    reconstruction in 170–1; infantry in
    172; *jihads* in 172, 176; liberation
    struggles in 183; LICs in 183, 185–8;
    logistics in 171, 175, 177–80, 185, 186;
    military coups in 183; navies in 172;
    prophet/diviners, military leadership in
    174, 181, 188; 'ragged wars' in 182–8;
    'raiding war' vs. 'campaigning war' in
    171–2, 190, fn. 23; raids in 171–2, 175,
    176, 178–81; recent arms trade to 184,
    185–6; refugees in 186; secession wars
    in 184; slave trade in 175, 176; standing
    armies in 173, 176, 177, 183–8;

traditional social and military
    organization in 170–1, 172, 178;
    warlord armies in 176, 177, 185, 186,
    188; World Wars and 182
Ahmadu Lobo, Seka 172
Aiguebelle, Paul d' 27
air defence 231
air force, air power 217, 229
air power, American 125, 127, 130–1,
    134–9, 238, 241–8, 250, 252–5
air power, Japanese 91–2
aircraft 219, 221, 223, 229–33
aircraft carrier 221, 229–33
Air–Land Battle 242
Albania 196
Albanians 14
Aleutian Islands 86
Alexandria 211
Algeria 4, 182, 194, 200, 109, 212
Al-Hajj Umar 172, 176
Al-Kanemi 174
American Civil War 119–21, 145, 224–5
American Expeditionary Forces (AEF),
    126
Amin, Idi 14, 184, 186
amphibious operations, amphibious
    warfare 220–2, 225, 228, 230
amphibious ship 223, 232
Amritsar 60, 66
anarchism 202
Angola 157, 176, 183–4, 186–7; Cuban
    intervention 157
anti-aircraft gun 231
anti-submarine aircraft 221, 222
anti-submarine warfare 219, 223, 227,
    231
Arctic 232

258